DOODEM AND COUNCIL FIRE

Anishinaabe Governance through Alliance

Combining socio-legal and ethnohistorical studies, this book presents the history of doodem, or clan identification markings, used by Anishinaabe on treaties and other legal documents from the seventeenth through the nineteenth centuries. These doodem images reflected fundamental principles behind Anishinaabe governance that were often ignored by Europeans, who referred to Indigenous polities in terms of tribe, nation, band, or village – classifications that failed to fully encompass long-standing cultural traditions of political authority and alliances within Anishinaabe society.

Making creative use of natural history, treaty pictographs, and the Anishinaabe language as analytical tools, *Doodem and Council Fire* delivers groundbreaking insights into Anishinaabe law. The book also outlines the continuities, changes, and innovations in Anishinaabe governance through the concept of council fires and the alliances between them. Offering a fresh approach to Indigenous history, *Doodem and Council Fire* presents a new interpretation grounded in a deep understanding of the nuances and distinctiveness of Anishinaabe culture and Indigenous traditions.

(Osgoode Society for Canadian Legal History)

HEIDI BOHAKER is an associate professor in the Department of History at the University of Toronto.

DOODEM AND COUNCIL FIRE

Anishinaabe Governance through Alliance

HEIDI BOHAKER

Published for The Osgoode Society for Canadian Legal History by
University of Toronto Press
Toronto Buffalo London

© University of Toronto Press 2020
Toronto Buffalo London
utorontopress.com
osgoodesociety.ca
Printed in the U.S.A

Reprinted in paperback 2021

ISBN 978-1-4426-4731-2 (cloth)   ISBN 978-1-4426-6786-0 (PDF)
ISBN 978-1-4426-1543-4 (paper)   ISBN 978-1-4426-6787-7 (EPUB)

Library and Archives Canada Cataloguing in Publication

Title: Doodem and council fire : Anishinaabe governance through alliance
/ Heidi Bohaker.
Names: Bohaker, Heidi, 1968– author.
Series: Osgoode Society for Canadian Legal History series.
Description: Series statement: The Osgoode Society for Canadian
Legal History | Includes bibliographical references and index.
Identifiers: Canadiana (print) 2020028861X | Canadiana (print)
20210232129 | Canadiana (ebook) 20200288814 | ISBN 9781442647312
(hardcover) | ISBN 9781442615434 (softcover) |
ISBN 9781442667860 (PDF) | ISBN 9781442667877 (EPUB)
Subjects: LCSH: Indigenous peoples – Canada – Politics and government. |
LCSH: Indigenous peoples – Canada – Social life and customs. |
LCSH: Indigenous peoples – Canada – History. | CSH: Indigenous peoples
– Legal status, laws, etc. – Canada.
Classification: LCC E99.C6 B64 2021 | DDC 305.897/333071 – dc23

University of Toronto Press acknowledges the financial assistance to its
publishing program of the Canada Council for the Arts and the Ontario
Arts Council, an agency of the Government of Ontario.

Canada Council   Conseil des Arts
for the Arts   du Canada

ONTARIO ARTS COUNCIL
CONSEIL DES ARTS DE L'ONTARIO
an Ontario government agency
un organisme du gouvernement de l'Ontario

Funded by the   Financé par le
Government   gouvernement
of Canada   du Canada

Canadä

For Naakwegiishigookwe

Contents

MAP ix

PREFACE xiii

ACKNOWLEDGMENTS xxix

Introduction 3

1 The Doodem Tradition 41

2 Family in All Four Directions 70

3 Anishinaabe Constitutionalism 103

4 Governance in Action 135

5 Doodem in the Era of Settler Colonialism 170

Conclusion 199

BIBLIOGRAPHY 207

ILLUSTRATION CREDITS 225

INDEX 231

Colour photos follow page 112

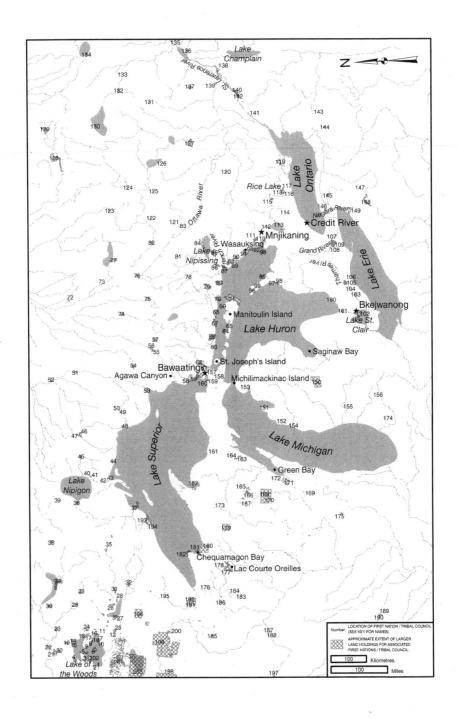

N

Lake Champlain

St. Lawrence River

Ottawa River

Rice Lake

Lake Ontario

Credit River

Mnjikaning

Wasauksing

Lake Nipissing

Lake Nosbonsing

Grand River

Niagara River

Lake Erie

Thames River

Bkejwanong

Lake St. Clair

Manitoulin Island

Lake Huron

Saginaw Bay

St. Joseph's Island

Bawaating

Agawa Canyon

Michilimackinac Island

Lake Superior

Lake Michigan

Green Bay

Lake Nipigon

Chequamagon Bay

Lac Courte Oreilles

Lake of the Woods

LOCATION OF FIRST NATION / TRIBAL COUNCIL (SEE KEY FOR NAMES)

Number

APPROXIMATE EXTENT OF LARGER LAND HOLDINGS FOR ASSOCIATED FIRST NATIONS / TRIBAL COUNCIL

100 Kilometres

100 Miles

Map of the Great Lakes region featuring place names discussed in *Doodem and Council Fire*, along with present-day First Nations (Canada)/Tribal Councils (United States), associated trust lands, hunting territories, and jointly managed lands

Language key: Anishinaabemowin-speaking   *Siouan-speaking*

Related Algonquian-language family   **Iroquoian-speaking**

Note: Some First Nations/Tribal Councils have multiple entries to reflect multiple reserves or reservation lands. Many First Nations/Tribal Councils manage multiple distinct tracts of land but where the lands are close together for the scale of the map only one number was used.

1	Buffalo Point First Nation	26	Nigigoonsiminikaaning (Red Gut) First Nation
2	Buffalo Point First Nation Reed River Reserve	27	Couchiching First Nation
3	Northwest Angle #33	28	Seine River First Nation
4	Shoal Lake #40 First Nation	29	Eagle Lake First Nation
5	Animikee Wa Zhing 37 First Nation	30	Wabauskang First Nation
6	Anishinaabe of Naongashiing First Nation (Big Island Reserve)	31	Seine River First Nation
7	Mishkosiminiziibiing (Big Grassy River) First Nation	32	Lac La Croix First Nation (Neguaguon Lake)
8	Anishinaabe of Naongashiing First Nation	33	Wabigoon Lake First Nation
9	Agency Reserve No 30 & No. 1 (shared territory)	34	Lac Seul First Nation
10	Assabaka (shared territory: Onigaming & Mishkosiminiziibiing)	35	Lac Des Mille Lacs First Nation
11	Rainy River First Nation	36	Ojibway Nation Of Saugeen
12	Rainy River First Nation	37	Fort William First Nation
13	Naotkamegwanning First Nation	38	Kiashke Zaaging Anishinaabek (Gull Bay First Nation)
14	Wauzhushk Onigum First Nation	39	Whitesand First Nation
15	Obashkaandagaang Bay First Nation	40	Bingwi Neyaashi Anishinaabek First Nation
16	Ojibways of Onigaming First Nation	41	Biinjitiwaabik Zaaging Anishinaabek
17	Obabikong Reserve (Big Grassy First Nation)	42	Red Rock Indian Band
18	Anishinaabeg of Naongashiing	43	Red Rock Indian Band
19	Niisaachewan Anishinaabe Nation	44	Pays Plat First Nation
20	Swan Lake First Nation	45	Animbiigoo Zaagi'igan Anishinaabek (Lake Nipigon)
21	Wabaseemoong Independent Nation	46	Ginoogaming First Nation
22	Wabaseemoong Independent Nation	47	Long Lake #58 First Nation
23	Asubpeeschoseewagong First Nation (Grassy Narrows)	48	Biigtigong Nishnaabeg (Pic River First Nation)
24	Naotkamegwanning First Nation	49	Netimizaagamig Nishnaabeg (Pic Mobert First Nation-South)
25	Rainy River First Nation (Manitou Rapids Indian Reserve No. 11)	50	Netimizaagamig Nishnaabeg (Pic Mobert First Nation-North)

51	Constance Lake First Nation	85	Dokis First Nation
52	Constance Lake First Nation (English River 66)	86	Henvey Inlet First Nation (Reserve No. 13)
53	Michipicoten First Nation (2 parcels)	87	Henvey Inlet First Nation (Reserve No. 2)
54	Missanabie Cree First Nation	88	Magnetawan First Nation
55	Chapleau Ojibway First Nation & Chapleau Cree First Nation (5 parcels)	89	Shawanaga First Nation (Naiscoutaing)
56	Brunswick House First Nation	90	Shawanaga First Nation (Reserve No. 17)
57	Brunswick House First Nation	91	Wasauksing First Nation
58	Batchewana First Nation of Ojibways (Obadjiwan)	92	Moose Deer Point First Nation
59	Batchewana First Nation of Ojibways (Goulais Bay)	93	Beausoleil First Nation (Christian Island)
60	Batchewana First Nation of Ojibways (Whitefish Island)	94	Chippewas of Georgina Island First Nation (Chippewa Island)
61	Batchewana First Nation of Ojibways (Rankin)	95	Neyaashiinigmiing First Nation
62	Ketegaunseebee (Garden River First Nation)	96	Neyaashiinigmiing Hunting Grounds
		97	Saugeen First Nation (Chief's Point)
63	Ojibways of Thessalon First Nation	98	Saugeen First Nation
64	Zhiibaahaasing First Nation (2 parcels)	99	Saugeen First Nation Hunting Grounds
65	Sheshegwaning First Nation	100	Kettle and Stoney Point First Nation
66	Mississaga First Nation	101	Aamjiwnaang First Nation (Chippewas of Sarnia First Nation)
67	Serpent River First Nation	102	Bkejwanong Territory, Walpole Island First Nation
68	Sagamok Anishnawbek		
69	Aundeck Omni Kaning First Nation	103	Delaware Nation at Moraviantown
70	Whitefish River First Nation	104	Chippewa Of The Thames First Nation
71	Wikwemikong Unceded Territory	105	Munsee-Delaware Nation
72	Taykwa Tagamou Nation	106	Oneida Nation of the Thames
73	Taykwa Tagamou Nation (New Post)	107	Six Nations of the Grand River
74	Flying Post First Nation	108	Woodland Cultural Centre & Mohawk Institute Residential School (Glebe Farm Reserve)
75	Mattagami First Nation		
76	Matachewan First Nation	109	Mississaugas of the Credit First Nation
77	Wahgoshig First Nation	110	Wahta Mohawk Territory
78	Wahnapitae First Nation	111	Indian River Reserve (Chippewas of Rama First Nation and the Wahta Mohawk)
79	Atikameksheng Anishnawbek		
80	Point Grondine Park (Wikwemikong Unceded Territory)	112	Chippewas Of Rama First Nation
81	Temagami First Nation	113	Chippewas Of Georgina Island First Nation (2 parcels)
82	Timiskaming First Nation	114	Mississaugas Of Scugog Island First Nation
83	Kebaowek (Eagle Village First Nation)	115	Curve Lake First Nation
84	Nipissing First Nation	116	Mississaugi of Hiawatha First Nation
		117	Alderville First Nation

118 Alderville (Sugar Island)

119 Mohawks of the Bay of Quinte - Tyendinaga Mohawk Territory

120 Algonquins of Pikwakanagan

121 Wolf Lake First Nation (Hunters Point)

122 Long Point First Nation Anishnabe Aki

123 Algonquian Anishinabeg Nation (Pikogan)

124 Algonquian Anishinabeg Nation (Lac Simon)

125 Anicinape De Kitcisakik Community (Grand Lac)

126 Algonquins of Barrière Lake (Rapid Lake)

127 Algonquian Anishinabeg Nation (Kitigan Zibi)

128 Cree Nation of Waswanipi

129 Ouge Bougomou Cree Nation

130 Atikamekw of Opitciwan Obedjiwan Indian Reserve No. 28

131 Communauté Atikamekw De Manawan (Atikamekw First Nation)

132 Communauté de Wemotaci (Atikamekw First Nation)

133 Coucoucache (Atikamekw First Nation) Indian Reserve No. 24A

134 Pekuakamiulnuatsh Takuhikan (Innu) First Nation

135 Wôlinak Abenaki First Nations Indian Reserve No. 11

136 Odonak Abenaki First Nations Odanak Reserve No. 12

137 Kahnawake Mohawk Territory (Doncaster Indian Reserve No. 17)

138 Kahnawake Mohawk Territory

139 Mohawk Council of Kanesatake Lands

140 Mohawk Nation at Akwesasne (No. 15)

141 Mohawk Nation at Akwesasne (No. 59)

142 St. Regis Mohawk Tribe Reservation (Akwesasne)

143 Oneida Indian Nation Reservation

144 Onondaga Nation (People of the Hills) Reservation

145 Tonawanda Seneca Nation Reservation

146 Tuscarora Nation Reservation

147 Seneca Nation of Indians Oil Springs Reservation

148 Seneca Nation of IndiansAllegany Reservation

149 Seneca Nation of Indians Cattaraugus Reservation

150 Saginaw Chippewa Indian Tribe Isabella Reservation (5 parcels)

151 Grand Traverse Band of Ottawa & Chippewa Indians Reservation (8 parcels)

152 Grand Traverse Band of Ottawa & Chippewa Indians Trust Land (4 parcels)

153 Little Traverse Bay Bands Reservation (2 parcels)

154 Little River Band of Ottawa Indians of Michigan (2 parcels)

155 Match-E-Be-Nash-She-Wish Band of Pottawatomi Indians of Michigan (Gun Lake Tribe)

156 Nottawaseppi Huron Band of the Potawatomi Reservation

157 Sault Ste. Marie Tribe of Chippewa Indians Reservation (6 parcels)

158 Sault Ste. Marie Tribe of Chippewa Indians Trust Land (9 parcels)

159 Gnoozhekaaning: Bay Mills Indian Community Reservation (3 parcels)

160 Gnoozhekaaning: Bay Mills Indian Community Trust Land (3 parcels)

161 Keweenaw Bay Indian Community L'Anse Trust Land (2 parcels)

162 Keweenaw Bay Indian Community L'Anse (Ontonagon) Reservation (2 parcels)

163 Hannahville Community Band of Potawatomi (11 parcels)

164 Hannahville Community Band of Potawatomi Trust Land (2 parcels)

165 Forest County Potawatomi Reservation (39 parcels)

166 Forest County Potawatomi Trust Land (2 parcels)

167 Sokaogon Chippewa Community (Mole Lake Band of Lake Superior Chippewa) Reservation

168 Menominee Indian Tribe of Wisconsin Reservation

169 Menominee Indian Tribe of Wisconsin Trust Land

170 Stockbridge-Munsee Mohican Tribe Reservation

171 Oneida Nation of Wisconsin Reservation

172 Oneida Nation of Wisconsin Trust Land (2 parcels)

173 Lac Vieux Desert Band of Lake Superior Chippewa Reservation (3 parcels)

174 Pokégnek Bodéwadmik (Pokagon Band of Potawatomi Indians)

175 Ho-Chunk Nation (57 parcels)

176 Ho-Chunk Trust Land (23 parcels)

177 Lac Courte Oreilles Band of Lake Superior Chippewa Indians Reservation (4 parcels)

178 Lac Courte Oreilles Band of Lake Superior Chippewa Indians Trust Land (23 parcels)

179 Lac du Flambeau Band of Lake Superior Chippewa Reservation

180 Mashkiiziibii: Bad River Band of the Lake Superior Tribe of Chippewa Reservation (2 parcels)

181 Mashkiiziibii: Bad River Band of the Lake Superior Tribe of Chippewa Trust Land (3 parcels)

182 Miskwaabekong: Red Cliff Band of Lake Superior Chippewa Reservation

183 St. Croix Chippewa Indians of Wisconsin Reservation (11 parcels)

184 St. Croix Chippewa Indians of Wisconsin Trust Land (7 parcels)

185 Mille Lacs Band of Ojibwe (of the Minnesota Chippewa Tribe) Reservation (23 parcels)

186 Mille Lacs Band of Ojibwe (of the Minnesota Chippewa Tribe) Trust Land (18 parcels)

187 Shakopee Mdewakanton Sioux Community (4 parcels)

188 Shakopee Mdewakanton Sioux Community Trust Land (6 parcels)

189 Meskwaki Nation (Sac and Fox Tribe of the Mississippi in Iowa) Reservation (2 parcels)

190 Meskwaki Nation (Sac and Fox Tribe of the Mississippi in Iowa) Trust Land (5 parcels)

191 Fond du Lac Band of Lake Superior Chippewa (of the Minnesota Chippewa Tribe) Reservation

192 Fond du Lac Band of Lake Superior Chippewa (of the Minnesota Chippewa Tribe) Land

193 Grand Portage Band of Chippewa (of the Minnesota Chippewa Tribe) Reservation (18 parcels)

194 Grand Portage Band of Chippewa (of the Minnesota Chippewa Tribe)Trust Land

195 Minnesota Chippewa Tribe Homestead Trust Lands (7 parcels)

196 Bois Forte Band of Chippewa (of the Minnesota Chippewa Tribe) Reservation

197 Lower Sioux (Mdewakanton Band of Dakota) Indian Community Reservation

198 Gaa-waabaabiganikaag: White Earth Nation of Ojibwe (of the Minnesota Chippewa Tribe) Reservation

199 Leech Lake Band of Ojibwe (of the Minnesota Chippewa Tribe) Reservation, (3 parcels)

200 Leech Lake Band of Ojibwe (of the Minnesota Chippewa Tribe)Trust Land (4 parcels)

201 Miskwaagamiiwi-zaaga'igan: Red Lake Nation (Red Lake Band of Chippewa) Ceded Lands (432 parcels)

202 Miskwaagamiiwi-zaaga'igan: Red Lake Nation (Red Lake Band of Chippewa) Trust Land (25 parcels)

203 Miskwaagamiiwi-zaaga'igan: Red Lake Nation (Red Lake Band of Chippewa) Reservation

Map created by Nicky Recollet, Geospatial/GIS Specialist, Crane's Atlas (https://www.cranesatlas.ca/) and Robinson Huron Waawiindaamaagewin (http://rhw1850treaty.com/).

Preface

During the eighteenth and nineteenth centuries, Anishinaabe leaders inscribed the images shown here and thousands of others like them in place of signatures on treaties, petitions, and letters. The images are outline sketches and sometimes the track marks of the ensouled beings who call North America's Great Lakes region home. Western-trained readers might categorize these images differently, seeing instead images of plants, animals, and mythical creatures. How we read these images depends upon our worldview or our cultural perspective. These different approaches to categorization reflect significant diversities between Anishinaabe and Western thought worlds. Such differences matter.[1] They inform respective understandings of time, space, history, law, philosophy, ethics, and, most significantly, the foundational relationship between human beings and the world in which humans live. Anishinaabe leaders wrote these images on documents pertaining to their lands, at councils held on those lands, reflecting the decisions of those councils. These images are expressions of Anishinaabe law.

The images also represent a uniquely Anishinaabe category of kinship: the *doodem* identity of the signatory – doh-DEM, or doh-DE-mahg (*doodemag*) in the plural form – in which members of the same doodem

---

1 Vine Deloria Jr. eloquently described the fundamental differences between Native North American spiritualtiy and Christianity. See Deloria, *God is Red*. But Deloria's crucial observations about different understandings of space, time, and history apply well beyond Christianity to the secular West as well, a secular world nonetheless deeply and profoundly shaped by Christianity and Christian values.

consider each other closely related, as close as siblings are constructed within Western kinship systems.[2] Anishinaabe use of doodem as a category of kinship is also an articulation of Anishinaabe philosophy and law – one that places humans in interdependent relationships with other-than-human beings, who are considered persons with a soul and also relatives to whom one owes a duty of care.[3] Doodem is an old category; images of this identity appear on rock art, and one can also find doodem stories in origin narratives. Both expressions of doodem long pre-date the appearance of these images on eighteenth- and nineteenth-century treaty documents signed by Anishinaabe leaders, such as the examples at the start of this preface.[4]

The word *Anishinabek* is also old; it is a collective noun that describes people who developed a distinct civilization in the Great Lakes Region of North America.[5] Anishinabek cultural and political traditions, and

---

2 In Anishinaabemowin the word *doodem* belongs to a special class of nouns known as dependent nouns. As these nouns never appear without a possessive adjective, it is awkward to write them in English, where there is an expectation that a noun should be able to stand apart from the person or people who possesses it. In previous publications, I used *nindoodem,* retaining the first person pronoun as a prefix and in so doing following established linguistic conventions. But as this makes for awkward reading and as, increasingly, other Anishinaabemowin vocabulary is being used in English, I have decided to drop the first-person prefix in favour of the easier to read and pronounce *doodem*. But the reader should continue to keep in mind that when Anishinaabe peoples spoke of *doodemag* they would always have indicated, through the use of the possessive form, to whose *doodem* they were referring. See Valentine, *Nishnaabemwin Reference Grammar*, 106–7. Previous works of mine that use *nindoodem* are Bohaker, "*Nindoodemag*: Anishinaabe Identities in the Eastern Great Lakes Region" and "*Nindoodemag*: The Significance of Algonquian Kinship Networks."

3 This concept of an "other-than-human" being as distinct from a human being was used by Irving Hallowell in his attempt to explain Anishinaabe cosmology to outsiders. See Hallowell, "Ojibwa Ontology." As Michael Angel has pointed out, this concept expressing difference between humans and other-than-humans is an act of interpretation, not one "intrinsic to the Ojibwe world view." It is, as Angel points out, more accurate to collapse the distinction between humans and non/other-than-humans in Anishinaabe worldview and to think instead of ensouled beings. Angel, *Preserving the Sacred*, 41.

4 I first made the case for the antiquity of the doodem tradition in Bohaker, "*Nindoodemag*: The Significance of Algonquian Kinship Networks."

5 Anishinaabe people speak Anishinaabemowin. "Anishinaabe" can be translated as "original men" or "original people." Anishinaabe people would not use "Anishinaabe" to describe other Indigenous peoples, such as the Haudenosaunee Confederacy (the Six Nations speak different languages. In Kanien'kéha [Mohawk], the Confederacy's name is the Rotinonhson:ni – in colonial documents called the Iroquois Confederacy). Anishinaabe is for a person in the singular, a male person,

therefore their legal traditions, were, and continue to be, derived from the *aadizookaanag*, or sacred stories. In these narratives, the land and waters are simultaneously spiritual and physical spaces. People who call themselves Anishinaabe today include people who may also identify or be described in archival documents as Ojibwe or Ojibwa, Chippewa, Ottawa or Odawa, Mississauga, Potawatomi, and Algonquin.[6] Doodem was, and remains for many Anishinaabe people today, an essential part of what it means to be an Anishinaabe person. By consciously representing themselves as their doodem beings on treaty documents and petitions, Anishinaabe leaders were clearly articulating the centrality of doodem to their system of government and were tying that identity to the lands described within the treaty texts. As this book will show, the principles of Anishinaabe governance are based on the concept of alliance between different doodemag, a lived expression of the interdependence of all life in the region.

The word *doodem* often appears as "totem" in both archival documents and in academic publications (in Anishinaabemowin, the letters "d" and "t" represent the same sound and do not indicate a difference in meaning), and *totem* itself has come to have a range of meanings

---

or can be used as an adjective, as in the Anishinaabe language. Anishinabek (or Anishinaabek) is the plural. Some speakers shorten it to Nishnaabek. Algon**quin** refers to Anishinabek living in what is now eastern Ontario/western Quebec about the Ottawa River area. Algon**quian** (or Algon**kian**) is the term for the language family (really Central Algonquian, a subfamily of Algic) to which linguists have classified Anishinaabemowin, along with Cree, Kickapoo, Menominee, and others. See the dictionary entries for Anishinaabe in Baraga, *Dictionary of the Otchipwe Language*, 38–9; Rhodes, *Eastern Ojibwa/Chippewa-Ottawa Dictionary*, 20.

6 These identifiers are in contemporary use and have specific political meanings and great significance for those who use them. In using "Anishinaabe" here, I do not mean to suggest that it should replace these other forms, unless communities themselves desire it. In the past two centuries of settler colonialism these names have come to evoke nations, in the sense defined by Benedict Anderson as imagined communities, shaped by reading publics and the rise of print, and defined in no small way by nineteenth-century Anishinaabe authors including William Warren, Peter Jones, Andrew Blackbird, George Copway and Francis Assiginack, who all made cases in print and in speeches for the independence and sovereignty of their people. For a description of this process, see Konkle, *Writing Indian Nations*; Anderson, *Imagined Communities*. For the writings of leading nineteenth-century Anishinaabe intellectuals, see Assiginack, "Legends and Traditions of the Odahwah Indians"; Blackbird, *History of the Ottawa and Chippewa Indians*, 45; Copway, *Traditional History and Characteristic Sketches*; *Indian Life and Indian History*; Jones, *History*; Warren and Neill, *History*.

and uses in English.[7] This book focuses on the Anishinaabe meaning of the word, using doodem as a category of analysis. I study doodem images on treaty and other political and legal documents such as petitions and receipts for annual annuity payments to explore fundamental principles of Anishinaabe governance that both European colonizers and subsequent generations of historians, until recently, have ignored.[8] Doodem images on treaty and other documents are a key into the political and legal history of the Anishinabek. There are only a few documents signed with these images before the outbreak of the Seven Years' War in 1756 but such documents number in the thousands following the American Revolution and into the mid-nineteenth century, as colonial officials and settler governments increasingly engaged with different communities of Anishinabek in efforts to secure title to more and more of their land. The doodem-bearing treaty and other documents analyzed for this work have in common the fact that they were the products of Anishinaabe council fires – specific and long-standing

---

7   *Totem* appears to have entered general English use in the 1790s. Early British anthropologists in the 1850s then applied it to other peoples and practices globally, to refer to kinship networks that were identified by an animal "or less commonly a plant or other natural object," and also to guardian spirits "who may be applied to or worshipped." See "totem, n.," OED Online, http://www.oed.com, accessed 24 March 2016. The word was made famous by Viennese psychiatrist Sigmund Freud in his classic book *Totem and Taboo* (1913), in which he brought these ideas of kinship networks and guardian spirits together. He then used this construction as a foil to compare those he thought had "primitive minds" with the mentally ill (the "neurotics") he was treating. Anthropologists, including the noted French anthropologist Claude Lévi-Strauss, critiqued Freud's generalizations and misapplications, but the confusion has persisted, along with the uninformed and inaccurate pejorative of primitivism. In compound form, the word totem has also been applied to the monumental art of Northwest Coast civilizations as "totem poles" (beginning in the 1880s) and in that context is also used figuratively in English, as in "he's the low man on the totem." Historian Theresa Schenck has nicely sorted out all this semantic confusion and discovered that the error crept into English usage when colonial visitors to the Great Lakes region confused doodem with the guardian being that Anishinaabe children acquired during puberty fasts. Schenck, "Algonquian Totem and Totemism."

8   There was some limited antiquarian interest initially. See Mallery, "Picture Writing," and Schoolcraft's multi-volume *American Indians*. Anthropologists and ethnohistorians picked up the subject of doodem again beginning in the 1960s. See Hickerson, *Chippewa and Their Neighbours*; Bishop, "Question of Ojibwa Clans"; Peers, *Ojibwa of Western Canada*; Vastokas, "History without Writing"; Brown and Peers, "'There Is No End to Relationship.'"

deliberative bodies that were constituted and recognized through and by other Anishinaabe councils to have responsibility for the lands, waters, and peoples of a particular territory. As the treaty in Figure 1 illustrates, the images identify that council fire's civil leadership: sometimes simply the *ogimaa* (or chief in English), sometimes the ogimaa and *aanikeogimaa* (second chief, deputy), and in many cases, especially on land sale/purchase agreements, also the *gichi-Anishinabek* (councillors).[9] The gichi-Anishinabek, aanikeogimaa, and ogimaa were also historically leaders of their own *indinaakonigewin* (those whom one overwintered with, a group of usually twenty to forty people).[10] Doodem images in these contexts nearly always reflect only the council of gichi-Anishinabek together with the ogimaa and aanikeogimaa.

But there were two other equally important councils that advised and significantly influenced decisions – the council of women and the council of young men (warriors); mention of the existence of these councils shows up occasionally in treaty documents, too. While council fires could each make decisions independent of the others, doodem kin ties created and sustained lateral connections between different council fires, ties that spread over the region. Kinship ties reinforced the political principle of interdependence through alliance. Since there was a widespread taboo against marrying anyone with the same doodem, a marriage was by definition an alliance that brought two doodemag together. Council fires were comprised of people living in alliance relationships with one another.[11] So doodem images on treaty and other documents tell a much larger story about the decentralized, interconnected, and interdependent alliance networks that formed the governments of the Anishinaabe peoples. These images therefore have much to say about Anishinaabe law. They are the tangible expression of the connection between Anishinaabe law as expressed in oral traditions and decisions taken by councils in accordance with that law.[12]

---

9 Cary Miller, *Ogimaag*, 76–7.
10 Ibid., 77–8.
11 Recent work that acknowledges the importance of doodem to the Anishinabek includes Cary Miller, *Ogimaag*; Treuer, *Assassination of Hole in the Day*; Witgen, *Infinity of Nations*; McDonnell, *Masters of Empire*; Willmott, "Anishinaabe Doodem Pictographs."
12 John Borrows makes the case for Anishinaabe law embedded in oral tradition. See his *Drawing Out Law* and *Canada's Indigenous Constitution*. For a broader discussion of Indigenous law, see Napoleon, *Thinking about Indigenous Legal Orders*.

This book is an interdisciplinary socio-legal and ethnohistorical study that aims to historicize doodemag as a living tradition central to Anishinaabe governance. I trace continuities, changes, and innovations in Anishinaabe governance through the concept of council fires and the alliances between them, from the seventeenth through the nineteenth centuries. In short, this work is a study of Anishinaabe law. By situating doodem as a foundational principle within a framework of Indigenous legal traditions writ large, the Anishinaabe tradition shares with its common and civil law counterparts "considerable pluralism."[13] That is, there were regional and local variations in custom and practice but all under the umbrella of a shared ontology that was particularly notable for extending the legal concept of personhood to other-than-human beings. In the Great Lakes region, humans were accountable not only to other humans for their actions but also to the animals and plants, to all ensouled life. This is a much broader ethical and legal space than either European common or civil law traditions. Anishinaabe law also borrowed from its Siouan- and Iroquoian-speaking neighbours, as well as later from colonial law. The evidence of such exchanges is visible in the archival record at the time of the earliest European arrivals in the region, indicating that the practices had begun before. Great Lakes Indigenous legal traditions maintained their autonomy and distinctiveness even as these diverse peoples developed a common set of regional practices, a body of international law, and sets of diplomatic protocols useful for promoting peace and social relationships between their societies.[14] In the Great Lakes region, people spoke languages from three distinct language families: Algonquian, Iroquoian, and Siouan. Anishinaabemowin is as distinct from the languages of the Wendat (whom the French called "Hurons") and Haudenosaunee Confederacies as English is from Arabic.

As a settler and descendant of settlers growing up on Anishinaabe land I knew very little of this history, despite the fact that I was born

---

13 Girard, Phillips, and Brown, *History of Law in Canada*, 1.

14 Girard, Phillips, and Brown stated, "It is not known whether Indigenous legal traditions borrowed from each other prior to European contact, but they did begin to draw inspiration from colonial law afterwards" (*History of Law in Canada*, 6). There was earlier borrowing between Indigenous nations, especially in the development of intercultural diplomatic protocols, such as the use of wampum and calumet ceremonies, in place when Europeans arrived.

on Michi Saagig Anishinaabe territory and in a province (Ontario) and a country (Canada) whose names are derived from Onkwehon:we languages.[15] These lands, as I later came to learn, were governed by existing treaty and alliance relations, including alliances between Onkwehon:we and Anishinaabe council fires that long pre-dated the legislated beginnings of Canadian Confederation in 1867. Although there is more public awareness today of Indigenous histories in both Canada and the United States, settler colonial tropes continue to dominate the histories of both countries, including erroneous and frankly quite racist and unexamined statements about the supposedly limited historic capacities and effectiveness of Indigenous governments. Recent scholarship, however, demonstrates quite the opposite.[16] Anishinaabe oral traditions structured Anishinaabe society, in which law was "integrated with all other aspects of life, as opposed to confined to a separate realm."[17]

My hope is that this work, despite its inevitable limitations, will also contribute to contemporary conversations about Indigenous–settler treaty relations and to renewed research into Canada's treaty history. As Indigenous leaders have long pointed out, the treaties entered into in the past need to be understood as compacts between two cohesive and complex, yet culturally and philosophically distinct worldviews. Settler states in both Canada and the United States have treated this difference as an existential threat and created policies and laws intended to force the assimilation of Indigenous peoples and the breakup of their distinct societies. In Canada, the release of the 2015 report of the Truth and Reconciliation Commission (TRC) on residential schools provides extensive and irrefutable evidence of the harm such policies caused to

---

15 For an Anishinaabe history of this region see Gidigaa Migizi, *Michi Saagiig*.

16 See, for example, in the Great Lakes region: Cary Miller, *Ogimaag*; Witgen, *Infinity of Nations*; Hill, *Clay We Are Made Of*; Child, *Holding Our World Together*. Chapter 2 of Girard, Phillips, and Brown, *History of Law in Canada* (26–41) has an excellent recent summary of scholarship pertaining to Indigenous legal traditions, including governance, across what is now Canada. The socio-legal/historical work of John Borrows, Darlene Johnston, Heidi Kiiwetinepinesiik Stark, Mark Walters, and Aaron Mills on Anishinaabe law is also supported by a broader flowering of interest in Anishinaabe studies, with new insights coming, it seems, every day. My work has also been influenced by new scholarship in the productive and innovative academic discipline of Indigenous Studies, and as well by new work in colonial and imperial histories, anthropology, art history, and linguistics.

17 Girard, Phillips, and Brown, *History of Law in Canada*, 4.

so many people.[18] The TRC report calls for the recognition and honouring of historic treaty relationships as part of the work of (re)conciliation.[19] To do so meaningfully will require coming to terms with both our shared histories and the separate ontologies that have have informed our respective legal traditions and structures of governance.

Anishinaabe leaders have been teaching (or trying to teach) their laws and philosophy to European newcomers in the Great Lakes region for more than four hundred years. While seventeenth- and eighteenth-century colonial officials eventually mastered the art of *performing* governance through alliance, it is evident that these representatives of first France and later Britian did not entirely embrace the spirit and intent of what these alliance relationships were intended to be. Following the War of 1812, the settler populations in the Great Lakes region on both sides of the border rapidly increased and soon outnumbered the Anishinabek and other Great Lakes Indigenous nations. By the mid-nineteenth century, what Patrick Wolfe calls settler colonialism's "logic of elimination," which "destroys to replace," was fully operational.[20] Reports prepared for colonial and dominion legislatures dismissed Indigenous governments as primitive and backwards and their people as being in need of assimilation; residential schools in both Canada and the United States were ultimately one part of that program.[21] By the 1860s, the governments of both the United States and the new Dominion of Canada no longer saw in the treaties anything other than a means by which to acquire title to land as cheaply as possible in order to make it available to (white) settlement. Despite this, Indigenous leaders, including Anishinaabe ogimaawag, continued to assert treaty rights and to peacefully protest against violations of the treaty agreements.[22] In so doing,

---

18 Truth and Reconciliation Canada, *Honouring the Truth*. The summary and the full report along with primary sources related to the establishment of the schools in Canada are permanently archived and available for download at the National Centre for Truth and Reconciliation at the University of Manitoba: https://nctr.ca.

19 Truth and Reconciliation Canada, *Honouring the Truth*, 183–5.

20 Wolfe, "Settler Colonialism."

21 See for example Province of Canada: Bagot Commission Report of 1844; Report on the Affairs of the Indians in Canada; Pennefather Commission of 1858; and Davin, *Report on Industrial Schools*.

22 See here evidence of protest and resistance in Donald Smith, *Sacred Feathers*; Chute, *Legacy of Shingwaukonse*; Blair, *Lament for a First Nation*; and in contemporary court rulings or negotiated settlements concerning pre-Confederation treaties such as Restoule v. Canada; the Williams Treaty Claim Settlement of 2018; and the 2010 final

they "exist, resist, and persist," while continuing to confront a structure (settler colonialism) that, as Hawaiian scholar J. Kēhaulani Kauanui has shown, in turn resists their resistance.[23]

By bringing forward evidence of Anishinaabe governance in earlier colonial sources, I show how Anishinaabe leaders explained their law to newcomers, before the advent of settler colonialism. One can thus see how and where colonial officials were respecting and trying to understand Anishinaabe law or, later, in the nineteenth and twentieth centuries, where they ignored it. What is clear, though, is that earlier generations of officials were willing to play the part of ally as the Anishinabek understood it when it suited colonial purposes, first to survive in a new land, then to secure military allies against imperial enemies, and later to acquire land for settlements.[24] Anishinaabe councils had a different understanding of alliance that affected how they viewed these treaties. The work here has significant implications for the interpretation of pre-Confederation era treaties. Land sale agreements that comprise the contemporary set of recognized "treaties" are not standalone agreements concerned solely with a specific property transaction. Rather these treaties must be understood as a modification of the larger alliance relationships between interdependent council fires in accordance with the laws of Great Lakes Indigenous nations. As I will demonstrate, Anishinaabe councils treated colonial governments as if they too were council fires, and colonial governments in turn performed as if that is what they were in their relationships with Anishinaabe peoples.

This book has been a long time coming. In 2006, I published an article on the importance of the doodem tradition to the survival of the Anishinaabe peoples and civilization in the wake of mid-seventeenth-century epidemics of diseases brought by Europeans and the resulting wars between Great Lakes nations that were sparked by the high mortality rate, as nations looked to outsiders as potential causes of these waves of death.[25] Doodem images provided evidence that that the Anishinabek

---

settlement of the Mississaugas of the New Credit First Nation's Brant Tract and Toronto Purchase Specific Claims.

23 Kauanui, "A Structure, Not an Event."

24 This model of treaty as an agreement to fulfil a specific purpose (either for commerce, military support, or land) structures the classic survey of treaties in Canada. See James Miller, *Compact, Contract, Covenant*.

25 Bohaker, "*Nindoodemag*: The Significance of Algonquian Kinship Networks."

drew from the resources of their own cultural and political tradition to reconstitute themselves and their society after 1650. But despite the fact that I was staring at hundreds of documents all signed with doodem images, I failed at the time to see the common element – that all were produced *in council*. Signed land purchase agreements, products of the common law tradition, were also infused with evidence of Anishinaabe legal tradition. The treaty documents articulated the crucial relationship between doodem images and how Anishinaabe governments were historically organized; it just took me a very long time to see it, as I too worked with and through my own assumptions and biases of how Anishinaabe governance functioned and how their governance practices changed over time.

By 2006, I was also engaged in another research project that eventually did open my eyes and unstop my ears to other important sources of Anishinaabe governance and law: the Great Lakes Research Alliance for the Study of Aboriginal Arts and Cultures, or GRASAC (https:// grasac.org). I am one of its co-founders. GRASAC, as we explain on our website, is an organization where "researchers from Indigenous communities, universities, museums and archives work together to locate, study, and create deeper understandings of Great Lakes arts, languages, identities, territoriality and governance."[26] GRASAC's origins go back to the beginning of this century. In the early 2000s Anishinaabe legal historian Darlene Johnston (*Waabizheshi* [Marten] doodem), Alan Ojig Corbiere (*Bne* [Ruffed Grouse] doodem), and I were planning to build a database for treaty-related documents. As anyone working in this field or attempting to research a land claim knows, there is no one archive containing the relevant material. Treaties themselves and their associated council minutes are scattered over a great many repositories and fonds. We were also all interested in the doodem images we observed on many of these documents.

Around the same time, the noted Great Lakes art historian Ruth B. Phillips thought about digitizing the database of the slides she had accumulated over her long career of studying Great Lakes material culture in museums both on Turtle Island and overseas. The anthropologist Cory Willmott, who knew of my previous work with databases in an earlier career, connected Ruth and me at a Rupertsland Society meeting in Kenora in 2004. We agreed to work together to produce a

---

26 "About GRASAC," https://grasac.org/about.

database that would include both material culture and archival documents. Alan Corbiere was already researching his community's history and was interested in further investigation into medals, wampum belts, and other diplomatic gifts related to treaties. Ruth then sought grant funding to bring a large group of Anishinaabe and Haudenosaunee scholars and community researchers to Carleton University to meet with museum curators and archivists. Together we discussed what such a collaboration might look like. What came out of the meeting was a plan to do more than digitize a slide collection. We recognized the need to take interdisciplinary and cross-cultural teams into repositories, examine those items as a group in situ, and take much more detailed, high-resolution images and video so that communities could continue to research the items after we returned home. At that meeting, GRASAC was created and with it, our governance and ethical protocols and our commitment to develop a reciprocal and collaborative research methodology.[27]

Although I was still working to complete my dissertation, I began working with Ruth to design the first database, and we planned our first trip, to the National Museums of Scotland in December of 2006. GRASAC members have now researched collections in more than eighty institutions and have made detailed records of nearly six thousand items of Great Lakes cultural heritage. We have also held multiple research gatherings and developed an extensive network of contributors. I originally thought GRASAC was something extra I was doing, almost separate from my work as a historian, but the past fifteen years have shown me how wrong that thinking was. As we worked in museum storage areas documenting medals, wampum belts, pipes, suits of clothing, and other gifts given in council as part of Great Lakes Indigenous diplomacy with imperial powers, it became clear that here really was an enormously significant Indigenous archive of governance and law, an archive that has increasingly been recognized as such by those working in the fields of Indigenous philosophy and law.[28] Moreover, the beauty and artistry of the items we study are a powerful corrective to persistent settler colonial discourses of primitivism and to the excessive focus on Indigenous participation in colonial wars in

---

27 This history is discussed in Bohaker, Corbiere, and Phillips, "Wampum Unites Us."
28 Bohaker, "Indigenous Histories and Archival Media in the Early Modern Great
    Lakes"; Morito, *Ethic of Mutual Respect*; John Borrows, "Wampum at Niagara."

the archival and historical record.[29] The material evidence, when one includes archeologically recovered items (which we do in GRASAC), speaks volumes about cultural continuities and dynamic, self-directed changes within the distinct societies of Great Lakes Indigenous peoples. This research has been a crucial source of my own understanding of how Anishinaabe leaders used gifts given in council to create and renew alliance relationships. By integrating the study of these items with archival descriptions of how they were exchanged in formal alliance-making and renewal contexts, we are better able to appreciate how such gifts form part of Anishinaabe law. These items are tangible evidence of how the terms of the alliance or treaty can be embodied in physical forms. Furthermore, some Anishinaabe material culture also contains or has been inscribed with doodem images, connecting the item into a broader world of kinship and politics. I have woven evidence from these material culture sources into the narrative of this book.

The work with GRASAC has afforded me the great privilege of studying this rich material heritage in museums and travelling to Great Lakes communities as part of our collaborative methodology. Our teams have been graciously welcomed and hosted by the communities we have visited. It is clear to me that the cultural practices of gifting, alliance-making, and consensus-based decision-making described by Jesuit missionaries and colonial officials in the seventeenth century are very much alive in Anishinaabe community life today. Listening to the histories told by Elders and Knowledge Holders has also helped me to describe what earlier generations of settlers and visitors were writing about when they too visited Anishinaabe communities. Specifically, conversations with Lewis Debassige, Darlene Johnston, and Alan Corbiere have been especially important in sparking me to look at colonial-authored sources with fresh eyes. Johnston contributed enormously to my understanding of doodem as both anchored in deep time and connected to place. She was an early and crucial partner in this research, and our many long conversations about how to read doodem images and what they meant are essential to the findings in this work.[30] Her continuing research in seventeenth-century missionary dictionaries

---

29 Indigenous scholars are confronting these discourses and old tropes head-on, through deep dives into studies of language, oral history, and traditional teachings. See for example, Geniuz, *Our Knowledge is Not Primitive*.

30 Darlene Johnston, "Litigating Identity"; *Connecting People to Place*.

for vocabulary relating to doodem and governance will fundamentally change the way we write about Anishinaabe history in the first century of French–Anishinaabe relationships. Alan Corbiere has significantly enriched my understanding of Anishinaabe leadership and governance, Anishinaabe use of wampum, the symbolic importance of medals, and the ways in which leaders communicated meaning through dress and gesture.[31] His own research on doodem genealogies of Manitoulin Island and Georgian Bay Anishinaabe communities has confirmed my own findings.[32] And his recently completed doctoral thesis marks a major contribution to the field of Anishinaabe studies, presenting Anishinaabe history, specifically treaty history, from an Anishinaabe perspective, using sources written in Anishinaabeowin and "by incorporating stories of Anishinaabe Manidoog (spirits) back" into this history."[33] M'Chigeeng Elder Lewis Debassige (*Adik* [Caribou] doodem) has been a source of tremendous insight and knowledge of Anishinaabe oral histories. Mr. Debassige, who passed away on 13 May 2019, is a lineal descendant of Ogaa, who signed the 1798 treaty for St. Joseph Island with an image of representing the Caribou doodem. As co-founder of the Ojibwe Cultural Foundation and a long-time activist and strategist for Indigenous control of education and for economic development on Manitoulin Island, Mr. Debassige drew on his deep knowledge of Anishinaabe history, culture, and language to create opportunities for subsequent generations.

I am also greatly indebted to conversations with anthropologist Cory Willmott at the State University of Illinois (Edwardsville) and her scholarship on doodemag. She used the term "lateral alliance" to explain how Anishinaabe families had access to resources from more than one doodem through marriage alliances, as people kept their birth doodem when they married. Her work on the communication of doodem identity through dress also taught me to think "outside the archive" and to look to material culture to understand how Anishinaabe leaders used clothing to communicate their political responsibilities and doodemag. Most recently, she has contributed a marvellous essay that explores later nineteenth- and twentieth-century innovations in how Anishinaabe

---

31 Alan Corbiere, "Anishinaabe Headgear"; "Dbaad'dang Wiigwaaskeng"; Bohaker, Corbiere, and Phillips, "Wampum Unites Us."
32 See for example the permanent exhibit on Anishinaabe doodem curated by Mr. Corbiere at the Ojibwe Cultural Foundation, M'Chigeeng First Nation.
33 Alan Corbiere, "Anishinaabe Treaty-Making," 19–20.

people receive their doodem.[34] Willmott and Johnston both stressed the continuing political significance of doodem, an idea expressed by nineteenth-century Anishinaabe writers Peter Jones and William Warren and again in the more recent publications of Anishinaabe writers Eddie Benton Banai, Basil Johnston, and Gidigaa Migizi (Doug Williams).[35]

If doodem describes the *who* of Anishinaabe governance, then councils (or council fires) describe the *where* – the seats of decision-making and the lands for which the councils were responsible. My thinking about this aspect of Anishinaabe governance was influenced by multiple people and their work. Jones and Warren, described above, both described the important roles of councils and their different responsibilities in their respective works. The significance of fire as an Anishinaabe political metaphor is beautifully expressed in Heidi Kiiwetinepinesiik Stark's research on the political use of allegory in Anishinaabe oral histories.[36] Conversations about governance with long-time GRASAC members have helped tremendously as well. John Borrows, one of Canada's leading Indigenous legal scholars, unpacks Anishinaabe legal principles and governance practices in action from those same narratives in *Drawing Out Law* and *Canada's Indigenous Constitution*.[37] Jeffrey Hewitt, legal counsel for the Chippewas of Rama and Assistant Professor of Law at Osgoode Hall Law School, talked to me about wampum belts as constitutions and got me thinking about Anishinaabe constitutionalism as a practice within Anishinaabe law. Collections work in the company of Ruth B. Phillips, Cory Willmott, Alan Corbiere, Laura Peers, Sherry Farrell Racette, Darlene Johnston, John Borrows, Mikinaak Migwans, Marge Bruchac, and other GRASAC colleagues has been one master class after another, where critical conversations around different epistemological ways of engaging with the multiple meanings of items in museum collections have greatly enriched my understanding of why material history matters.[38] Sherry Farrell Racette has remarked that when she opens museum drawers she is "often overwhelmed by

---

34 Willmott, "Clothed Encounters"; Willmott and Brownlee, "Dressing for the Homeward Journey"; Willmott, "Anishinaabe Doodem Pictographs."
35 Jones, *History*; Warren and Neill, *History*; Benton-Banai, *Mishomis Book*; Basil Johnston, *Ojibway Heritage*; Gidigaa Migizi, *Michi Saagiig*.
36 Stark, "Marked by Fire."
37 John Borrows, *Drawing Out Law*; *Canada's Indigenous Constitution*.
38 See especially Farrell Racette, "Pieces Left along the Trail." For what the material study of dress and clothing can reveal, see Willmott, "Beavers and Sheep."

the loss of knowledge that collections represent. It is why I am there."
Alan Corbiere explains his research as a broader project of recovery,
reclamation, and revitalization: "I am looking for pieces of our past, our
identity, pieces of our foundations so we can build it up again."[39] His
work on headdresses, wampum, and medals has helped me to visualize
historic council meetings and better recognize the important meanings
communicated through gifts exchanged in councils.[40] Tuscarora artist and art historian Jolene Rickard's theoretical framings of the deep
connection between Indigenous arts and articulations of philosophy,
law, and governance are powerful tools for re-reading and reinterpreting old colonial records of treaties and council meetings, for moving
beyond the colonizing text and the colonial gaze.[41]

In *Doodem and Council Fire*, I stress the importance of using Anishinaabe political categories and terms in Anishinaabemowin rather
than reaching for analogies from other political and cultural traditions. Imported concepts such as band, tribe, village, and nation do not
adequately describe Anishinaabe polities and law. Further, such terms
render invisible the presence and power of Anishinaabe alliances and
governance through alliance. I do this despite my own limited skills in
Anishinaabemowin, although I will continue to learn this metaphorically rich language. I am therefore beyond grateful for the insights
into Anishinaabemowin and its metaphors from the work of and conversations with Alan Corbiere, Mary Ann Naokwegijig-Corbiere (no
relation), Lewis Debassige, Rand Valentine, Alex McKay, Maya Chabacy, and Darlene Johnston, who have opened up the deeply layered
thought worlds of Anishinaabe people as expressed in and through
Anishinaabemowin, as the language too has changed over time.[42] I look

39 Farrell Racette, "Pieces Left along the Trail," 225.
40 Jeffrey Hewitt, personal communications, 2008 and 2009. Ruth Phillips is one of the
   leading art historians in Great Lakes material culture – see, for example, her *Patterns
   of Power*; "Dreams and Designs"; and *Trading Identities*; see also Alan Corbiere,
   "Anishinaabe Headgear."
41 Jolene Rickard calls for use of sovereignty as a concept that "could serve as an
   overarching concept for interpreting the interconnected space of the colonial
   gaze, deconstruction of the colonizing image or text, and Indigeneity." Rickard,
   "Visualizing Sovereignty in the Time of Biometric Sensors," 471.
42 As all languages do. For an overview of the discipline of historical linguistics see
   Campbell, *Historical Linguistics*. Alan Corbiere's deep and beautifully researched
   studies have been especially informative. Corbiere has also explored how
   Anishinaabe leaders from Manitoulin Island adopted writing Anishinaabemowin

forward to the day when the field of North American Indigenous histories will be researched and written with and in Indigenous languages.

I accumulated many more scholarly and personal debts in writing this book that are described in the Acknowledgments, including to Elders and Knowledge Holders from eastern Great Lakes communities who took the time to share their knowledge with me and through many wonderful conversations and collaborations with other GRASAC colleagues and with students over the past fifteen years. I felt it important in this preface, though, to draw the reader's attention to the interdisciplinary scholarship and many conversations upon which the findings of this book depend. *Doodem and Council Fire* is a study fundamentally about the centrality of alliances to Anishinaabe governance and treaty law. Significantly, my research was also a product of alliance and collaboration. I can only hope that the history I present here is a sufficient *bagijigan* in return for the many gifts I am so grateful to have received from people who shared their insights and understandings with me. But all faults and errors in this work are mine, and mine alone.[43]

---

in alphabetic script as a political strategy in the mid-nineteenth century. See Alan Corbiere, "Exploring Historical Literacy"; Valentine, *Nishnaabemwin Reference Grammar*; Mary Ann Corbiere, "Flying Blind over Strange Terrain"; Corbiere and Valentine, *Dictionary of Nishnabewin Database.*

43 Bagijige – the act of making a gift or offering – is the central framing of an important collection of essays on Anishinaaabe philosophy, ethics, law, and spirituality, on Anishinaabewin or Anishinaabe ways of being. See Doerfler, Sinclair, and Stark, *Centering Anishinaabeg Studies.*

Acknowledgments

A book project that takes as long as this one did accumulates a stagger-ing pile of debts, both scholarly and personal. I am profoundly grateful for the kindness of so many people who have – in both large and small ways – helped me through to completion. In addition to those men-tioned in the preface, I would like to acknowledge others here and hope that I have not forgotten anyone.

I would first like to say a resounding *chi-miigwetch* to the Anishi-naabe communities whose history this is and to express my profound gratitude for the tremendous kindness and patience you have shown this outsider/settler. You have so kindly welcomed me over the years, shared research and teachings, and taught me much, although I still have so much to learn. I would like to say a special thank you to the Mississaugas of the Credit First Nation, Mississauga First Nation, Wiik-wemkoong Unceded Territory, M'Chigeeng First Nation, Chippewas of Rama First Nation, Chippewas of Nawash Unceded First Nation, Curve Lake First Nation, and Sagamok Anishnawbek First Nation. I also have been very fortunate to be invited regularly to speak at the Mississaugas of the Credit First Nation's annual multi-day historical gathering, now in its tenth year, which has grown to attract hundreds of attendees.

I am also honoured that Osgoode Society for Canadian Legal History selected *Doodem and Council Fire* as the members' book for 2020. Jim Phillips and Philip Gerard are a talented team of editors; they made the final version of this manuscript that much stronger. I thank Jim for encouraging me to see my work as legal history and for inviting me to move into the field of legal history from the sidelines.

Since I signed my first contract with the University of Toronto Press many years ago, Len Husband has been strongly supportive of this project, unflagging in his enthusiasm, patient and kind. Thank you, Len! The entire University of Toronto Press team has been a delight to work with, even during a global pandemic and under work-from-home rules. Thank you especially to Managing Editor Lisa Jemison who shepherded this book through the final stages, while like so many of us juggling child care and working odd hours. Thanks also to Beth McAuley of The Editing Company and Jonathan Adjemian for copy editing and indexing.

I am also so grateful to the thoughtful comments from anonymous reviewers for the University of Toronto Press. One in particular deeply engaged with a previous version of the manuscript, providing a lengthy report on the strengths and deficits of the book's research and organization. This reviewer still recommended publication, but raised such important questions it was clear that the structure and overall argument would be much better if rethought. My colleague and faculty mentor Adrienne Hood generously read the manuscript through in light of feedback and helped me formulate a plan for both reorganization and restructuring. Chi-miigwetch to Adrienne and to all of the anonymous reviewers. I hope the revisions were worth the wait.

In 2016 I was asked to be an expert witness in Restoule v. Canada, 2018 ONSC 7701. Preparing my expert report and participating in the trial contributed significantly to my analysis in this book. I am grateful for the many excellent questions posed by the plaintiff's legal team of Nahwegahbow Corbiere especially David Nahwegahbow, Dianne Corbiere, Scott Robertson, and Chris Albinati, as well as Joe Arvay and Catherine Boies Parker of Arvay Finlay. I acknowledge the Elders who testified and shared so much of their knowledge: Rita Corbiere of Wiikwemkoong, Irene Stevens of Batchawana First Nation, Irene Makadebin of Sagamok Anishnawbek, and Fred Kelly from Treaty #3, as well as the Fire Keepers who ensured that a central symbol of Anishinaabek law was present on the land, adjacent to the court building, burning twenty-four hours a day, for the duration of the trial. Counsel for Ontario and Canada played their part too. While being cross-examined is never a pleasant experience, it certainly helps to hone one's argument.

My brother Scott Bohaker read multiple versions of draft chapters and has a talent for asking just the right questions. He also taught me to stop burying the lead. I am also grateful for feedback on earlier drafts from Michael Saver, Kristen Chew, and Chandra Murdoch, and on the penultimate draft by Jeffrey Hewitt, Darlene Johnston, and Grace Lau.

Darlene Johnston, Alan Corbiere, Donald Smith, Reg Good, and the truly exceptional now-retired archivist of Library and Archives Canada, Patricia Kennedy, generously pointed me to doodem-bearing documents they had encountered in their own work, some in places I never would have thought to look on my own.

In addition to those named in the preface, thanks also to colleagues and friends for great conversations on the subject of doodemag (you might not remember, but I do!), email queries answered, thoughtful comments offered, encouragement and support for this work over these many years: Laurie Bertram, Anne Bigwind, James Bird, Jennifer S.H. Brown, Carol Chin, Paul Cohen, Natalie Zemon Davis, Allan Greer, Sean Hawkins, Susan Hill, Heather Howard, Carolyn King, Cara Krmpotich, Stacey Laforme, Daniel Laxer, Nicholas May, Michael A. McDonnell, Mia McKie, Ken Mills, Sean Mills, Joan Morningstar, Melanie Newton, Reg Niganobe, Alison Norman, Christopher Parsons, Tom Peace, Laura Peers, Steve Penfold, Carolyn Podruchny, Naomi Recollet, Audrey Rochette, Margaret Sault, Alison Smith, Katrina Srigley, Alan Taylor, Anne Taylor, Nick Terpstra, Sylvia Van Kirk, Germaine Warkentin, my many wonderful colleagues in The Great Lakes Research Alliance for the Study of Aboriginal Arts and Cultures (GRASAC), my incredible students in HIS366/69: Aboriginal Peoples of the Great Lakes and HIS418: Canada by Treaty, and my talented graduate students.

The research for this book was supported by parts of multiple SSHRC grants, including a SSHRC doctoral fellowship, post-doctoral fellowship, and an Insight Development Grant. SSHRC has also supported GRASAC through multiple grants, and I am very grateful for their support. My university and department have been generous too, supporting GRASAC as an alliance and this work. My book benefited from the Connaught New Researcher Award and several SSHRC Institutional Grants. This funding along with SSHRC support funded graduate and undergraduate student research assistants including Kata Bohus, June Allison, Jennifer Hayter, Zachary Smith, Chandra Murdoch, Stephanie Davis, and John Stewart. Thank you for all of your hard work!

The manuscript was delivered to the press at the end of February, just as the COVID-19 epidemic was ravaging Italy and truly becoming a global health emergency. Many museums, libraries, art galleries, and archives, as less essential workplaces, shuttered, and some remain closed to visitors as of August 2020. In some cases, due to COVID-restrictions, I was unable to obtain a publication-quality colour images, and in other cases, COVID forced the substitution of originally planned images as staff were unable to access collections for photography. That there are images in this book at all is due to the kindness of archivists, librarians, and museum staff working remotely, granting permission to use GRASAC research images in lieu of in-house photography and in some cases making special trips into closed buildings to take the pictures themselves. I would especially like to acknowledge Roma Kail (Head, Reader Services at E.J. Pratt Library, Victoria University at the University of Toronto), John Shoesmith (Outreach Librarian, Thomas Fisher Rare Book Library), and Jonathan Barker (Archives Collection Officer, Kent History and Library Centre) for capturing high-resolution images on my behalf when their reproduction services were closed. Caleesha Murray at the Archives of Ontario remotely arranged for special manuscript retrieval and photography despite the AO's closure. Emanuela Rossi, Professore Associato at the Università degli Studi di Firenze, helped me connect with the Museo civico di Scienze naturali di Bergamo during the shutdown. Thanks also to Jacqueline Vincent (Brechin Group), Monika Zessnik (Ethnologisches Museum Berlin), Tricia Walker (Royal Ontario Museum), and Erin Wilson (Canadian Museum of History) for speedy help acquiring images and permissions while working from home. Ingmars Lindbergs (Bonhams) arranged for high-resolution photos of the 1836 Treaty Pipe. Nicky Recollet of Crane's Atlas was an incredible collaborator on the map. Thanks to you all!

Friends and family have cheered on this project for many years, offered welcome breaks when needed, and/or provided space to write: thanks especially to Dora Alveszo, Jim Barnsley, Sophie Bender Johnston and Grace Lau, Greg and Maxine Bohaker, Scott Bohaker, Julie Michels and Joey Morin, Bruno Morin, Sandra Morin, Melanie Phillip, Tracy and Warren Synnott, and Julie K. Wong.

Last, but most certainly not least, my husband and son have provided unflagging support and encouragement despite the length of time it has taken me to complete this project. Claude Morin has believed in me and this work from the beginning; he's talked me through the challenges that have come up and helped me to find solutions. He also lent his professional IT skills to support the development of GRASAC's database in its early days. Our son, Alexander, arrived in 2010 when I thought this book was almost done, and then it wasn't. He has grown up with it. Rather than asking "are we there yet?" the question in our house was "is the book done yet, Mama?" Chi-miigwetch for your patience, Aniksaanten.

And yes, finally, it is.

DOODEM AND COUNCIL FIRE

Anishinaabe Governance through Alliance

Introduction

As the summer days of 1642 grew shorter and the annual meteor show-ers began to light the night skies, Anishinaabe families from council fires around the north shore of Lake Huron, Georgian Bay, and Lake Nipissing packed their canoes with gifts and food. They paddled towards a large island on the eastern side of the Bay, about ninety to one hundred kilometres north of Wendake.[1] In total, about two thou-sand people made the trip during this *Manoominike-giizis* (the Ricing Moon) month.[2] Others remained behind to help finish the harvest of wild rice, of berries, and of cultivated crops planted near Anishinaabe

---

1 The author of the eyewitness report discussed here noted the following with respect to the location: "The spot selected for this purpose was at a Bay of the great Lake, distant about twenty leagues from the country of the Hurons." Possible sites would be Parry Island or Ojibway Island. A land league is an obsolete measurement of the amount of time a person could walk in an hour – roughly three miles or five kilometers. Jérôme Lalemant, "Of the Mission of the Holy Ghost Among the Algonquins, the Nearest to the Hurons," from "Relation of 1642–1643," in Thwaites, *Jesuit Relations*, 23:205–33.

2 The Anishinaabe calendar historically divided the year into thirteen moons, each with a name connected to important ceremonies and sometimes also to particular collective activities such as the maple sugar harvest or sucker fishery. There are teachings and aadizookaanag associated with each moon. There are some regional differences in the calendars across the Great Lakes. The Ricing Moon was the time of year for the wild rice harvest.

council sites, or because age or infirmity made the prospect of a journey difficult to contemplate. Those who journeyed came together for a regional gathering and a general council.[3] This year it was the Nipissing council fire's turn as host.[4]

As was the practice for these types of gatherings, the Nipissing council had sent runners early in the spring to invite the other council fires. These young people, who would rival today's ultra-marathoners and elite athletes with the speed and distance they could travel on foot or by canoe, carried the news of the Nipissing's intention to host as well as the location for the gathering and the agenda for the political business to be discussed. This gave time for the other councils to deliberate at home on the questions and to prepare the many gifts they would bring with them to renew their alliances with one another. At this event, the Nipissing specifically sought ratification of their new leaders from their allies. The gathering had a sombre purpose too, for each council brought to the gathering the bones of their dead who had been born on another council's territory so that those remains could be sent home to the place of their birth. The Nipissing had invited other guests as well – particularly three Jesuit priests and the Wendat, with whom the Nipissing also

---

3 This 1642 gathering was first analyzed by anthropologist Harold Hickerson in 1960, who analyzed it and other accounts of similar gatherings in the Jesuit Relations and the writings of Nicolas Perrot. Hickerson was reacting against ideas in circulation in the twentieth century scholarship that the Anishinabek were historically without real governments – that their culture was individualistic and their political life simplistic. In his examination of seventeenth-century sources, Hickerson concluded that such a picture was not historically accurate, and that he had found in seventeenth-century sources significant evidence of a much greater level of social and political cohesion than had been previously thought. However, he drew some erroneous conclusions, too. He assumed, because Lalemant referred to this event as a "Feast of the Dead," that it was a cultural phenomenon imported from the Wendat, with whom they were allied; and that, because descriptions of only a handful of ceremonies labelled "Feast of the Dead" exist in seventeenth-century colonial-authored sources, the practice stopped or had petered out by the eighteenth century. However, it was Lalemant himself who applied the label "Feast of the Dead" to this event, and when he did, he noted that it differed "much from those of our Hurons." The Anishinabek did not borrow the idea for these ceremonies from the Wendat because the Wendat practiced a secondary burial in a communal ossuary. The redistribution of bones back to the lands of one's birth was a distinctive Anishinaabe practice. See Hickerson, "Feast of the Dead." For Wendat mortuary practices, see Seeman, *Huron-Wendat Feast of the Dead*.

4 The French fur trader Nicolas Perrot described these as annual events for which common councils took turns hosting. See Perrot, "Mémoire," in Blair, *Indian Tribes*, 1:86.

intended to renew a long-standing alliance.[5] The Jesuits' record of what occurred is the only surviving written source describing this event, and it is particularly noteworthy for the richness of the description. Since gatherings such as these were intra-Indigenous councils, it is not surprising that written accounts of only a handful of these gatherings appear in colonial archives or the memoirs of missionaries. Merchants, missionaries, and imperial governments typically prioritized their own interests in the documentary records that they created, privileging the fur trade, military conflicts, and efforts to proselytize.[6] Such a source bias has distorted the writing of Great Lakes histories, making this 1642 recounting of Anishinaabe peoples' gathering together of particular historical significance, as it is a window into seventeenth-century Anishinaabe law, governance, and community life.

As the canoes carrying the families from the various councils arrived at the gathering site, each party waited off shore until there were hosts on shore to receive them. This was a regular part of regional diplomatic protocol. The guests waited to be formally welcomed into the territory of their hosts. This act was a public recognition of the host's responsibility for the lands, analogous to the idea of jurisdiction. Once the reception party arrived, each ogimaa in turn stood in his canoe and spoke to those on shore, to explain why they had come and what business had brought them there. They brought gifts for their hosts in gratitude and appreciation for being welcomed to their territory. Some items intended as general gifts for the host community were thrown overboard, creating a flurry of activity as young people swam out to collect items floating on the surface or to dive down for them if they sank. The items varied, as the Jesuits described: "a mat, wrought as tapestries are in France, another a Beaver skin; others got a hatchet, or a dish, or some Porcelaine beads [wampum]." Figures 2 to 5 show some examples of these types of gifts. As the paddlers pulled their canoes ashore,

5 Lalemant, "Of the Mission of the Holy Ghost," in Thwaites, *Jesuit Relations*, 23:205–33. Lalemant was the Superior of the Huron Mission from 1638–45. See Pouliot, "Lalemant, Jérome."

6 As scholars of imperial archives and archival formation have long noted, colonial and imperial archives are far from neutral repositories of data. In summarizing this critical scholarship, Antoinette Burton notes that archives "all have dynamic relationships, not just to the past and the present, but to the fate of regimes, the physical environment, the serendipity of bureaucrats, and the care and neglect of archivists as well." Burton, "Introduction," 6.

people greeted each other with tremendous excitement – for many it would have been months or a year since they last met. As one missionary in attendance recorded: "there was nothing but joy, cries, and public acclamations, to which the Rocks surrounding the great Lake return an Echo that drowns all their voices."[7] They may have shouted "*shataahaa*" to one another – an Anishinaabemowin greeting reserved for occasions when people reconnected with one another after a long absence.[8] Women found spots to set up their family's *wiigiwaam*, each infant snuggled in a *tikinaagan* (cradleboard), safe while their mothers worked.[9] Older children played as grandparents kept a watchful eye on their activities and caught up on the news with each other. As night fell, the light from the many fires would have sparkled upon the water, reflecting the brilliant display of the stars overhead.

Once all the guest council fires had arrived, the renewal of alliances and work of council could begin. The host nation was responsible for maintaining the fire that would remain lit throughout the gathering. All the people (including children) came together in a circle at the grounds prepared for the council meeting. Lalemant observed: "When the Nations are assembled and divided, each in their own seats, Beaver Robes, skins of Otter, of Caribou, of wild Cats, and of Moose; Hatchets, Kettles, Porcelain Beads, and all things that are precious in this country are exhibited. Each Chief of a Nation presents his own gift to those who hold the Feast, giving to each present some name that seems best suited to it."[10]

The name given to each gift was significant. While Lalemant is not specific about what was said on this occasion, at other such gatherings the name given to the gift described a specific treaty term, a pipe given to commemorate the peace, for example, or a kettle so that people could feast together.[11] As the Jesuit Barthélemy Vimont would remark three

---

7 Lalemant, "Relation of 1642–1643," in Thwaites, *Jesuit Relations*, 23:211.

8 Farrell Racette, "Shaataahaa: Indigenous Methodologies."

9 Nahwegahbow, "Springtime in n'Daki Menan" describes the historic and contemporary practices of tikinaagan use by *Anishinabekwe*.

10 Lalemant, "Relation of 1642–1643," in Thwaites, *Jesuit Relations*, 23:211.

11 In 1645, the Jesuit Vimont recorded the details of each present exchanged in a formal peace agreement made between eastern Anishinaabe council fires, the Wendat, the French, and the Mohawk. The Mohawk orator, Kiosaeton, brought seventeen "collars" of wampum with him to the initial peace talks in July of that year. As he spoke, he explained the purpose of each. The first wampum on which he spoke thanked the French governor for saving the life of Tokhrahenehiaron, another

years later in his observations of a 1645 peace treaty, "It is needless for me to repeat so often that words of importance in this country are presents."[12] Because these gifts were given in formal council, they became more than gifts: they expressed the thoughts and intention of each ogimaa on behalf of the council or nation presenting the gift. Each gift expressed a term of the treaty relationship that constituted the alliance and the duty of care owed the other.[13] Gifts were, as Vimont observed, a fundamental communication tool – not only between humans but between humans, spirits, and other-than-human beings.[14] The giving and receiving of the present transformed the gift into both physical proof and a memory aid of the specific terms of alliance. If the gift was rejected, so too was the specific term or the larger alliance itself.[15]

Here in this opening event, speakers gave gifts for a different purpose – to ease the sorrow of those who had lost loved ones. When their turn came, the Jesuits also gave a gift. But in the Jesuits' account it is clear that their words breached protocol and likely offended their hosts. Father Lalemant, who was the superior of the mission at Sainte Marie, and the two priests who accompanied him, Fathers Pijart and Raymbaut, refused to offer their gift with the intention that people expected. Instead they gave presents in memory of those who

---

Mohawk man. The fourth was a present intended "to assure us [the French] that the thought of their people killed in war no longer affected them; that they cast their weapons under their feet." While Kiosaeton used wampum as a present to embody a present or proposal, the Anishinabek brought a mix of wampum and other gifts. See Vimont, "Relation of 1644–45," in Thwaites, *Jesuit Relations*, 27:246–304. The French fur trader Pierre Radisson also described using this diplomatic form and speaking on presents during a council with western Lake Superior Anishinabek at Lac Courte Oreilles, in present-day Sawyer County, Wisconsin. See Radisson, *Collected Writings*, 1:265–7. Gilles Havard also observed the substitution of specific gifts for wampum, and wampum for specific gifts (where wampum was used to symbolize a particular gift) at the negotiations around the 1701 Peace of Montreal. See Havard, *Great Peace of Montreal*, 23–5.

12 Vimont, "Relation of 1644–45," in Thwaites, *Jesuit Relations*, 27:281.
13 On the responsibilities that gifts conferred on those who received them, see Bruce White, "Give Us a Little Milk"; Cary Miller, "Gifts as Treaties."
14 Sims, "Algonkian-British Relations," 36. See also the concept of gift discussed in Simpson, "Looking after Gdoo-naaganinaa."
15 As Cary Miller noted with respect to Anishinaabe treaties negotiated in the early nineteenth century: "The presence of the items in a person's lodge served as a reminder of the terms agreed to, and the holder accorded them the same respect that he felt for the agreement." Miller, "Gifts as Treaties," 225.

had died "that we might wish to the living the same happiness that we hope to enjoy in Heaven when they shall have acknowledged the same GOD whom we serve on Earth."[16] Lalemant reported that he told those assembled that "only the hope that we had of seeing them become Christians led us to desire their friendship."[17] In other words, the Jesuits' gift was conditional. He then mentioned that those assembled were "astonish[ed]" by their remarks. But to offer a conditional gift was antithetical to Anishinaabe understanding of governance through alliance. The Anishinaabe had built a civilization through braiding together difference – different doodemag, different people, and different ideas – where the parts remained intact but contributed to a stronger whole.[18] To be in an alliance relationship carried with it the responsibility to care for the other. The idea of a conditional gift or partial relationship was an astonishing concept indeed.

Following the condolence ceremony, it was the Jesuits' turn to be astonished as they witnessed the grace, beauty, and athleticism in the dances that followed.[19] The first dancers to come into the middle of the circle were from Bawaating, a council fire located on the river where the waters of Lake Superior flow into Lake Huron. They performed three dances, the Jesuits observed, "to the sounds of voices and of a sort of drum, in such harmonious accord that they rendered all the tones that are most agreeable in Music." Historically, dancing was an integral part of Anishinaabe gatherings, and it remains so today. The first was a war dance, and like every war or hunt dance, it had stories to tell. The Jesuits recognized this fact – they called this performance a ballet. This dance figured hand-to-hand combat between single fighters. Each dancer was armed differently, one with a hatchet, another a spear, another a bow and arrows, the fourth with a shield and *bgamaagan* or war club. The Jesuits observed that this dance was highly choreographed and complex; each

---

16 Lalemant, "Relation of 1642–1643," in Thwaites, *Jesuit Relations*, 23:213.
17 Ibid.
18 I am consciously using the metaphor of "braiding" as one would for braiding sweetgrass. My colleague Alan Corbiere proposed the name "Braiding Knowledges" for our 2006 SSHRC Aboriginal Research Grant application to capture the ways in which GRASAC sought to bring understandings from different ontologies together. Braiding as a metaphor is also used this way in Kimmerer, *Braiding Sweetgrass*.
19 On the importance of dance, see DesJarlait, "Contest Powwow Versus the Traditional Powwow." Basil Johnston also discusses the cultural and spiritual significance of dance in *Ojibway Ceremonies*, especially 1–4, 67–9, and 125.

gesture, glance, and step was different, and yet as Lalemant reported, it appeared coordinated by "one mind." As soon as dance ended, the next began. Lalemant called this one a "dance on a large scale" and noted that eight male dancers started the performance, "then by twelve, then by sixteen, ever increasing in proportion," adding four dancers each time. Finally the women danced in a style in a style that Lalemant only describes as follows: "as agreeable as the others and in no wise offensive to modesty."[20]

The weapons carried by the war dancers were themselves works of art, carefully made, beautifully balanced and sometimes indicating the doodem identity of the owner. The portraits in Figures 6 and 7 show a spear and a hatchet. While most such weapons in museums today date from the eighteenth century or later, the bgamaagan in Figure 8 is clearly older. It came into the French Royal Collection before the capture of New France in 1760. The weapon was carved from hardwood and is a well-balanced piece. Viewed from the side, one can see that the artist carved the weapon to portray an otter holding a ball in its open mouth. But view the ball head-on and one comes face to face with another otter. There are two round indentations for eyes and the iron point becomes the nose; otter whiskers radiate out the sides. In other pieces, such indentations hold glass beads for eyes and these may have as well. The upper jaws of the otter on each side of the club also form otters, carved in the round, and it is these otters that form the "ears" on the ball. This weapon likely proclaims the otter doodem identity of its owner, and it does so with wit and style.[21] On another such weapon in the British Museum, the artist carved an eagle wearing wampum as the regalia of an ogimaa into the handle.[22] I have observed other sculptural forms or inscriptions on such weapons, including a catfish and a marten.[23] Not all weapons

---

20 Lalemant, "Relation of 1642–1643," in Thwaites, *Jesuit Relations*, 23:213–15.

21 Unknown Anishinaabe artist, Great Lakes Region. Ball-headed war club with iron spike. Weapon weight (balanced, made of hardwood). Currently in the Musée du quai Branly, Paris, France, 71.1917.3.10 D. Item photographed and described as part of a GRASAC research trip in May 2013 in which I took part; GRASAC item id 26253. Analysis: A. Corbiere, M. Migwans, R. Phillips, C. Willmott.

22 Unknown Anishinaabe artist, Great Lakes, "Gunstock club" with iron spike. Currently in the British Museum, Am.5408. Item photographed and described as part of a GRASAC research trip December 2007 in which I took part; GRASAC item id 26228.

23 See, for example, Unknown Anishinaabe artist, Great Lakes, Club with marten motif. Currently in the British Museum, Am.4976 Item photographed and described as part of a GRASAC research trip December 2007 in which I took part; GRASAC item id

necessarily evoked doodem identity. Some recorded events through pictographs or evoked images of *manidoog*. But others did. Regardless of the imagery, as part of the regalia of the dancers, all of these weapons would have displayed their makers' artistry and skill.

As the dancers left the circle, set up for the next event began. The host nation put two prizes, a deer hide and a kettle, on the top of what Father Lalemant described as a "pole of considerable height." Not only had the bark been stripped from the trunk but the Nipissing man who tied the prizes then greased the pole on his way back to the ground. Many attempted to climb it, some making a greater height than others, but all fell to the bottom, to the amusement and delight of those watching. Finally, a Wendat man who had joined the gathering on his way to Quebec tried to climb it and made it about half-way up before he realized he was going to have the same result as the others. He then used his knife to cut notches in the tree and, taking some cord, fashioned a stirrup to take himself higher. The audience hooted and shouted their disapproval of what they regarded as a cheat but he repeated this technique until he reached the top and claimed the prizes as his own. He then continued on his travels. The Anishinaaabe ogimaawag complained to the Wendat about this action, and the Wendat leadership "taxed themselves for a present of Porcelain beads [a string of wampum]," thereby acknowledging the wrong and resolving the conflict.[24]

After the dancing and games that were part of the ceremonies of renewing alliances, the new leadership of the Nipissing council fire was ratified by all assembled. The Jesuits recognized the political significance of this event. At the beginning of his account, Lalemant had called this gathering one of "Confederated Nations" (*"les Nations confederées"*), which in seventeenth-century French meant allied nations or allied peoples.[25] Lalemant called the ratification ceremony an election, but it was more likely that the Nipissing council had already nominated their leaders. What the Nipissing community needed was the

---

25396. Catfish doodem images appear on a presentation pipe carved as a war club dating from the first half of the nineteenth-century, in the collections of the McCord Museum, M15889.

24 Lalemant, "Relation of 1642–1643," in Thwaites, *Jesuit Relations*, 23:215–17.

25 See entries for "allier" in Jean Nicot, *Thresor de la langue françoyse tant ancienne que moderne*, vol. 1 (Paris: Douceur, 1606) and "confederé, confederée" in *Le Dictionnaire de l'Académie française 1694*, vol. 1 (Paris: Coignard, 1694), both available through the ARTFL Project (https://artfl-project.uchicago.edu).

larger regional alliances to recognize and acknowledge the choices of the Nipissing people. Lalemant says that "votes were taken" – the voices of approval ratifying the new Nipissing leaders. Public recognition of their leaders by their allies was a crucial part of Anishinaabe governance, as it was these new leaders who would bring the Nipissing council's perspective forward at regional gatherings.[26] Alliances, as consensual relationships, required mutual approval of changes. This was a central principle of Anishinaabe law with respect to alliance relationships. Unilateral changes could potentially harm the alliance. This practice of seeking consent from each other allowed allies to identify possible problems and to ensure that the alliance relationship remained strong. The Nipissing women who had married out into other council fires would also therefore be involved in confirming the leadership of their natal community. Doodem kin of those on the Nipissing council fire would also participate in ratifying the Nipissing leadership. No council fire was thus isolated from its neighbours; each instead was an integral part of the others in the alliance, and the practice of intermarriage ensured these connections were strong.

This particular ceremony confirmed the new leadership roles of multiple people – at the very least, for the recognition of a new ogimaa and aanikeogimaa for the Nipissing council. Once their appointments were ratified, the Jesuits observed how the *gichi-ogimaa* (whom Lalemant called their "chief Captain"), the ogimaa of the regional alliance, called each new leader forward. As evidence of the public importance of this event, the new leaders, Lalemant observed, were dressed "in their finest robes" when they came forward to receive what Lalemant called "their Commissions" – some tangible evidence of their new office.[27] These robes would have been tanned and smoked hide garments, meticulously adorned with porcupine quillwork featuring geometric and symbolic designs in brilliant shades of red, blue, yellow, white, and black.[28] In 1615, Samuel de Champlain described the quillwork he observed during his travels through Georgian Bay and the eastern Great Lakes as follows: "For they put on their robes strips of porcupine-quill which they dye a very beautiful scarlet colour; they value these strips very

---

26 Lalemant, "Relation of 1642–1643," in Thwaites, *Jesuit Relations*, 23:217.
27 Ibid.
28 These are the colours that appear on the many examples of early Anishinaabe quillwork that I have personally studied in museums in France and the United Kingdom.

highly and take them off to make them serve for other robes when they wish to make a change."[29]

Porcupine quillwork is evident on many items of Anishinaabe manufacture, including clothing and footwear. Figure 3 shows quillwork trim on a basket; Figure 5 shows quillwork on moccasins given to Jasper Grant, an Anglo-Irish officer serving in Upper Canada, 1795–1808. Figures 6 and 7 and Figure 9 are portraits of leaders from the Amikwa, Nipissing, and Bawaating council fires in the late seventeenth century, the earliest known such portraits, which show them wearing clothing that is both painted and decorated with quillwork as Champlain described.

The commissions that Lalemant mentioned were likely the neck ornaments and headdresses which ogimaawag wore. Leaders received and wore headdresses (such as those in Figure 9), as gifts of the community, to remind them of their responsibilities.[30] French and subsequently British colonial officers later joined in this process of ratification by offering medals to ogimaawag on their appointments, and the recipients also wore these medals around the neck. To demonstrate their capacity to take care of their people, the newly recognized leaders then gave gifts of beaver and moose hides to those in attendance. Following these gift exchanges, the council bestowed the names of prominent leaders who had died on their successors. Lalemant said this was so as "to perpetuate their memory," but this action was so much more – the name change also served to acknowledge the new leaders' position and to remind them of their responsibilities to those they served.[31]

The next day was one of remembrance, a memorial ceremony for those who had died since the last gathering of these allied council fires. The women first constructed a large longhouse "with an arched roof, about a hundred paces long, the width and height of which were in proportion." Inside this building, the same women brought in caskets of birch bark, containing the bones of those who had died in previous years outside the land of their birth. Each casket was covered with a robe of beaver skin and laid atop were belts and strings of wampum. The women sat inside the cabin, next to the caskets, in two long lines facing each other, while the men brought in food as a feast for them and to feed the souls of the departed. Lalemant explained that "this Feast is for the

---

29 Champlain, *Works*, 3:134.
30 Alan Corbiere, "Anishinaabe Headgear."
31 Lalemant, "Relation of 1642–43," in Thwaites, *Jesuit Relations*, 23:217.

women only, because they evince a deeper feeling of mourning."[32] That deeper feeling of mourning, or more immediate grief, makes sense in the context of Anishinaabe practices around marriage and beliefs about souls, discussed in detail in Chapter 1. Since Anishinaabe women in this period generally married men from another council fire and relocated to live with them after their first child was born, it would have been more likely that these were women's bodies whose bones were being sent home for final burial. And it would be other women from those home communities who might be first hearing of a sister, mother, grandmother, or auntie's death at one of these gatherings; certainly it would be the first time that they would confront their remains. And so, indeed, their grief would have been raw and deep.

Following this feast, Lalemant described how twelve men entered the cabin and sang a mourning song, together with the women. They kept a vigil over the bones for the entire night, with only a fire lit at each end of the cabin for illumination. When the dawn broke, the women who mourned then distributed gifts to those in attendance: "corn, moccasins, and other small articles." The small articles may have included, in addition to the quillwork-decorated moccasins, intricately made birch bark containers bound with sweetgrass (*wiingashk*), or beautifully woven bags of nettlestock, bulrush, or other plant fibres, of the types used to hold medicines. Such gifts were also tangible connections to the places their materials came from. As Madeline Whetung points out, such places were "unmoveable sites of much of women's labour."[33] These gifts also carried spiritual and secular meanings. Sweetgrass, used to bind containers, is one of the four Anishinaabe sacred medicines. Bulrushes, used to weave the mats upon which people sat in council, evoke principles of Anishinaabe governance.[34] After they distributed their presents, the women mourners continued to sing and chant, waving branches they held in their hands to speed the souls of the dead on their journey home. The ceremony ended when a party of warriors came to the cabin and chased the souls away. At that point, the women left, and the warriors in turn took their place for more dancing and feasting.[35] These ceremonies of mourning showed the support and care given to

---

32 Ibid., 23:217–19.
33 Whetung, "(En)Gendering Shoreline Law," 28.
34 Kimmerer, *Braiding Sweetgrass*; Migwans, "Naaknashk miinawaa Naaknigewin."
35 Lalemant, "Relation of 1642–43," in Thwaites, *Jesuit Relations*, 23:219–21.

those who had lost a loved one and in turn the reciprocal acknowledgement of that care returned through gifts given to those who attended
the ceremony.

The next events were the renewal of the alliance between the Nipissing and the other "Confederated Nations" of Lake Huron and Georgian
Bay and the formal return of remains to their communities of origin.
These activities were closely connected. Caskets of bones were returned
to their families of origin "borne between the presents given to the most
intimate of friends, and were accompanied by the most precious robes
and by collars of porcelain beads, which are the gold, the pearls and
the diamonds of this Country."[36] Families gave presents "according
to the extent of the Alliance that existed between the Nipissirieniens
and them." It is through the giving of these gifts that the family among
whom the deceased had lived acknowledged to the birth family of the
deceased how important and valued the deceased had been to them.
Each person who left their birth family to marry into another council
fire strengthened the alliances that sustained the Anishinaabe peoples.
Returning the remains of the person to their family of origin surrounded
by all of these gifts was an expression of deep gratitude for the gift of
that person's life. It was a tangible gift symbolizing respect for the work
they had done, not only for the community that the person had married
into but also for the work required to maintain the alliance between the
two council fires.

Following this poignant return of remains between families was a
separate ceremony renewing the alliance between the Nipissing council fire, the other Anishinaabe councils in attendance, and the Wendat
Confederacy. To reaffirm this alliance, the Nipissing gave new gifts to
all the leaders in attendance. As Kathryn Labelle persuasively argues,
this long-standing alliance was central to the quality of life all enjoyed
in the eastern Great Lakes.[37] The alliance ensured that all parties could
maintain their distinctive ways of life and their political autonomy,
while creating a climate of peaceful co-existence. Eastern Anishinaabe
families gained access to the extensive crops grown by the Wendat;
in return the eastern Anishinabek exchanged with them the furs they
traded with their more northern neighbours, the Omushkego peoples
of what is now called James Bay. But this alliance was far more than a

---

36 Ibid., 23:221.
37 Labelle, *Dispersed But Not Destroyed*.

trading pact. Such gift exchanges, as Cary Miller has noted in her study of later Anishinaabe treaty ceremonies, were ultimately about maintaining and expanding interdependent social relations that ensured the well-being of all allied members. The Jesuits reported that they were singled out at this ceremony, given "the Highest seat, the first titles of honour and marks of affection above all of their Confederates."[38] The Nipissing were not placing the Jesuits on a pedestal here in some sort of social hierarchy. Rather, they were inviting the Jesuits into a system of interdependent social relationships that were intended to be mutually beneficial over the long term, if they were not always perfectly equal in their exchanges. When the needs of one party were greater, the neediest would receive the most. In their acceptance of the gifts bestowed upon them, the Jesuits would have been communicating that they understood, as Miller explains, the "ideas, commitments, or political agreements that accompanied them."[39] Such gift-giving also placed the Wendat, and the allied Anishinabek too, under an obligation when the Jesuits accepted the gifts – to meet the needs of their new allies. If those needs involved making the time to listen to what their new allies the Jesuits were preaching, the Wendat and Anishinaabe allies would undertake that task as well.

The exchange of presents and the distribution of gifts awed the Jesuits, but it was an integral part of the Anishinaabe economy at work. There were the gifts given when the guest nations arrived, those tossed into the water for the young people to retrieve during the grand entry, the formal presentations of gifts to the hosts to condole them for their losses, prizes given to the winners of games of skill and agility, giveaways by the newly elected Nipissing leaders to all those in attendance, gifts given by women mourning lost relatives to those who came to feast their dead together, and gifts given to reaffirm alliances. In addition to this, regional gatherings were places where people would trade for medicines and other goods with each other. People took home as much as they brought, strengthened and with their alliances renewed. The gifts pictured in Figures 2 to 5 demonstrate the beauty of these items, reflecting many hours of work and significant artistic skill.

Indeed, Lalemant tried to put a monetary value on what he had seen, and he concluded that "although the riches of this Country are not

---

38 Lalemant, "Relation of 1642–43," in Thwaites, *Jesuit Relations*, 23: 221.
39 Cary Miller, "Gifts as Treaties," 224.

sought for in the bowels of the Earth, and although most of them consist only in the spoils of animals – nevertheless, if they were transported to Europe, they would have their value. The presents that the Nipissirieniens gave to the other Nations alone would have cost in France forty or even fifty thousand francs."[40] This was an impressive amount of wealth, which quickly became concerning to French officials who struggled to understand why people would give away so much of their wealth. Nicolas Perrot noted that the hosts of these gatherings "reduce themselves to such an extreme of poverty that they do not even reserve for themselves a single hatchet or knife." Perrot said the practice was declining because "the Frenchmen who have gone among them have made them realize that these useless extravagances of theirs were ruining their families, and reducing them to a lack of even the necessities of life."[41] But of course such poverty wasn't poverty at all. In the first place, being "impoverished" through giving away of gifts was only a temporary state, since being impoverished obligated the allied nations and relations to help out the former hosts in return. For example, after a gathering later held in 1670 near Manitoulin Island, the host community, the Amikwa (the council fire led by the Beaver doodem), was depleted as Perrot described. But in a later section of his memoir, Perrot notes that during that same winter people from the council fire at Bawaating (led by the Crane doodem) came to help them hunt on Manitoulin Island, and together they took 2,400 moose.[42] This is an example of the interdependent alliances that the Anishinabek created. One didn't simply give all one's possessions away; communities also received, and in receiving, their wealth and prosperity was restored.[43]

---

40 Lalemant, "Relation of 1642–43," in Thwaites, *Jesuit Relations*, 23:217.

41 Perrot, "Mémoire," in Blair, ed., *Indian Tribes*, 1:88.

42 Perrot, "Mémoire," in Blair, ed., *Indian Tribes*, 1:221. Communual hunting is also described in Hickerson, "Feast of the Dead," 97. While this may seem like a large number of moose, I suspect that the hunt occurred not only on Manitoulin Island but on the many smaller islands around Manitoulin as well. Depending on the quality of habitat, the moose carrying capacity of land can be anywhere from 0.2 to 3 moose or more per square kilometre, based on contemporary scholarship. See Gingras, et al., "Adjacent Moose Populations."

43 Elder Lewis Debassige of M'Chigeeng First Nation described this wealth redistribution practice as a circle to me on numerous occasions, a circle where each community placed a small part of their wealth in a common feast bowl and gave the rest of their wealth away. Of course, as the gifts travelled in the circle, each community received back all that it needed, with the added benefit of strengthened social and political ties.

Once this work of formal alliance renewal and governance ended at the gathering, those assembled turned to more games and contests of "physical strength, for bodily skill and for agility" in which both men and women participated for the prizes that were given away. As the gathering concluded, the people from Bawaating, who had travelled from the farthest distance, then invited the Jesuits to come visit them. Two Jesuits, Pijart and Isaac Jogues, accepted the invitation and travelled to the Bawaating council site in mid-October with several members of the Wendat Confederacy. There they found another two thousand people assembled for yet another gathering, met some Anishinaabemowin-speaking Potawatomi who the Jesuits reported were taking refuge among their relatives, and learned about the many other people living along Lake Superior and far into the interior.[44] The gifts that the people from Bawaating had received at their council with the Nipissing thus became part of the redistribution network at this next council, while the news they had acquired was also shared with those who gathered at Bawaating. Those who received would give, and those who gave would receive. The council fire at Bawaating maintained alliances with many other fires throughout the Great Lakes. Through regular meetings of formal councils, Anishinaabe peoples were able to govern themselves and maintain their way of life over a very large region even as individual council fires or alliances of council fires pursued their own autonomous policies with respect to relationships with outsiders.

More than two hundred years after this 1642 gathering, Anishinaabe missionary and author Kakewaquonaby Peter Jones explained (in his *History of the Ojibwe*) the basic structure of Anishinaabe governance as consisting of two types of councils. Jones dedicated one chapter of his manuscript to this topic, in which he explained the centrality of the council fire as both an Anishinaabe metaphor for governance and the physical location where decisions were ratified.[45] He demonstrated to his readers how a highly decentralized system of government could exercise effective responsibility over the vast lands and waters through two functionally different types of formal councils, each with their own areas of jurisdiction and competency, who yet remained interdependent. Common councils, Jones noted, concerned themselves with matters *within* a territory, including the resolution of disputes, the decision

---

44 Lalemant, "Relation of 1642–1643," in Thwaites, *Jesuit Relations*, 23: 225–7.
45 Jones, *History*.

to adopt outsiders, and matters relating to land. General councils, he explained, comprised meetings of Anishinaabe people from a regional set of common councils. At general councils, those assembled recognized new leaders of common councils, as common councils made or renewed alliances with each other and as boundaries between territories of common councils were established or adjusted as need be.[46] As Jones wrote, it was at common councils (those led by an ogimaa), that "their local affairs are settled, such as sale and division of their lands, settling disputes, adopting other Indians into their own body, and the transaction of business with the British government." All people could access the common councils as Jones noted: "each person is at liberty to give his opinion on all matters before the council." At general councils, which involved people attending from a much larger area, the assembled Anishinabek discussed issues of a wider, or regional, concern. As Jones explained: "At these councils federal unions are formed, war or peace is declared, treaties are made or renewed, and boundaries of territories established."[47] The "nations" that Lalemant described as part of the "Confederated Nations" who attended the 1642 gathering were the common councils that Jones described. The alliance renewal and ratification ceremony hosted by the common council of the Nipissing in 1642 was just one example of a general council held at a regional gathering.

People who attended regional gatherings would stay together anywhere from one to three weeks before heading back home to their respective territories. For gatherings held in the late summer, those returning home would be preparing for the fall and winter hunts. Decisions about who would hunt where and on what land were then made at common councils, before the extended families who comprised those councils headed off to their respective winter hunting territories. Such gatherings as the one in 1642 were part of the Anishinaabe annual round. As Lalemant observed two years before of the Nipissing:

> They seem to have as many abodes as the year has seasons – the Spring a part of them remain for fishing, where they consider it the best; a part go away with the tribes which gather on the shore of the North or icy sea [James Bay], upon which they voyage ten days, after having spent

---

46 Ibid., 106–9.
47 Ibid., 105–9.
48 Lalemant, "Relation of 1640–41," in Thwaites, *Jesuit Relations*, 21:239–41.

thirty days upon the rivers, in order to reach it. In summer they all gather together, on the road of the Hurons to the French [the Ottawa River], on the border of a large lake which bears their name ... About the middle of Autumn, they begin to approach our Hurons, upon whose lands they generally spend the winter.[48]

What Lalemant described was no more nomadic than the annual relocations of today's wealthy city dwellers who spend summers at a cottage and winters at a ski chalet or in Florida. The community of each Anishinaabe common council was responsible for the lands within its territories. People moved regularly in widespread but seasonally expected, politically negotiated movements on these lands and exercised their laws through decisions made in common and general councils.

While common and general councils were responsible for different types of decisions, neither was subordinate to the other. Writing in the mid-nineteenth century, Peter Jones compared common councils to "independent states" – as each was effectively able to pursue its own policies with respect to alliances and citizenship based upon the collective wishes of their people, since the authority of leaders, as he noted, "extends no further their own body."[49] But Jones in writing "independent states" was using an analogy to help his mid-nineteenth-century settler readers understand the Anishinaabe principle of political autonomy, in a mid-nineteenth-century context of state formation in both Europe and North America.[50] But of course, common councils – the nations that Lalemant described in 1642 – were not truly independent states. Rather, in keeping with Anishinaabe philosophy, they were *interdependent* ones. The ceremonies that opened and closed councils, the protocols of smoking the pipe, gift-giving, and ceremonies of condolence described by Jones in his chapter on governance all embodied and were performances of Anishinaabe law and moral philosophy – performances that Lalemant and other French visitors had witnessed more than two centuries before. These ceremonies grounded political power in the entire community, to whom leaders owed their positions. But

---

49 Jones, *History*, 106–9.
50 The mid-nineteenth century was a period of political maturation in the British North American colonies and an age of revolution and state formation in Europe. For a discussion of the political changes within the mid-nineteenth-century colony of Canada, see the introduction and essays in Greer and Radforth, *Colonial Leviathan*.

because of the way in which doodem and marriage alliances created kin ties between the common councils, and across the broader region, Anishinaabe peoples were always interconnected beyond the boundaries of their own common council's territory.[51] These practices created the continuity and consistency in Anishinaabe social life and political practice and in Anishinaabe law over the lands and waters around the Great Lakes.[52]

It was these laws and practices that helped the Anishinaabe weather the initial storms brought by colonial intrusions on their land. Most significantly, the newcomers brought disease. As early as 1615, the Lake Nipissing Anishinabek had been affected by at least one smallpox epidemic.[53] Beginning in the late 1630s, a particularly virulent smallpox strain devastated many communities in northeastern North America, especially those living in the densely populated year-round settlements of the Wendat, the Haudenosaunee, and other Iroquoian-speaking horticulturists in the region.[54] The 1642 Nipissing-hosted gathering was held just two years after the worst of these terrible epidemics began. After that, the mortality rate increased. Within ten short years – between 1639 and 1649 – approximately two-thirds of the Wendat had died. The Haudenosaunee and other Iroquoian-speaking peoples, including the Wenro, Erie, and the Neutral living along the Niagara peninsula, experienced similar mortality rates.[55] The Anishinabek were also affected, but their practice of living in smaller population concentrations may have limited disease transmission among them. Furthermore, the survivors of the 1615 epidemic among the Lake Nipissing Anishinabek would have had some immunity against this new outbreak.[56] These factors meant that the smallpox, influenza, and measles outbreaks that

---

51 This concept is discussed in Bauerkemper and Stark, "Trans/National Terrain."

52 Readers who have attended contemporary Anishinaabe community councils will recognize similarities with the smudging and thanksgiving addresses that open such gatherings today.

53 A document describes a Nipissing man as being pock-marked. Bibliothèque nationale de France, departement des manuscrits, Cinq-Cents de Colbert, Lettre du père Denis Jamay au cardinal de Joyeuse, 15 July 1615; Microfilm at the LAC, MG7-IA7, Microfilm of the transcript, reel no. C-12868.

54 Tanner, *Atlas of Great Lakes Indian History*, Map 32.

55 Trigger, *Children of Aataentsic*, 601–2; Richter, *Ordeal of the Longhouse*, 58–9.

56 For a critical re-evaluation of the impact of sixteenth- and seventeenth-century epidemics, see Jones, "Virgin Soils Revisited."

tore through Indigenous populations at the time, while locally disruptive, likely did not have the same impact on the Anishinabek during the 1640s as they did on Iroquoian-speaking peoples. Nevertheless, the epidemics still brought devastating losses that shook the region and caused widespread grief.

These major waves of epidemic disease sparked increased violence that is well documented in the historical record. In the late 1640s, fighting broke out between the Haudenosaunee and other Iroquoian-speaking peoples in what is now central and southern Ontario – the Wendat, the Neutral, the Erie, and the Wenro – as people reacted to horrible new illnesses with high mortality rates that devastated entire communities. These internal deaths spurred communities to war on outsiders as they sought to replace those who had died and to avenge their deaths. The resulting conflicts culminated in the well-documented breakup of the Wendat and Neutral Confederacies. The Haudenosaunee absorbed so many survivors into their longhouses that, by the 1660s, almost two-thirds of the Haudenosaunee were adoptees.[57] This catastrophe affected the eastern Anishinabek too, especially those whose councils were in alliance with the Wendat and who had historically wintered among them, such as the Nipissing and the Kinouchespiriri from eastern Ontario, forcing the survivors to relocate from their lands temporarily. They covered their council fires but did not extinguish them. Those who did go moved west to the Sault and beyond up to Lake Superior, to live among their relations and allies in places that were already familiar to them. Some women knew these places as the lands of their childhoods, other community members from regular travels and gatherings. During the years that followed, the Haudenosaunee Confederacy established communities on the north side of Lake Ontario.[58]

But these relocations were relatively short-lived. Gatherings like the one in 1642 described above continued. The Anishinabek also pushed back against the Haudenosaunee attacks and the allied council fires of Lake Huron remained strong. In the 1650s, allied Anishinabek led a coordinated effort against the Haudenosaunee war parties. The war chiefs were from the Crane and Thunderbird doodemag from the Bawaating and the Mississagi council fires, and Mahiingan of the Beaver doodem from the council fire of the Amikwa. Their collective accomplishments

---

57 Richter, *Ordeal of the Longhouse*, 58–9.
58 Konrad, "Iroquois Frontier."

were recorded in rock art painted at Agawa Canyon. Mahiingan was especially noted for leading the party that killed all but one of a 120-man strong Haudenosaunee raiding party.[59] Mahiingan died in 1667, and in 1670 it was the turn of the Amikwa to host a regional gathering – this time to see Mahiingan's eldest son become ogimaa. Although Father Louys André, who attended this gathering, provided fewer details about the event than Lalemant had twenty-eight years earlier, it is clear from André's description that this 1670 event had the same structure and purpose. André estimated that about 1,500 to 1,600 people, including the "chiefs of many Nations," had gathered on Ouiebitchiouan, an island north of Manitoulin. As in 1642 and at other general councils held before or since, the occasion of families and friends reuniting was one of joy and celebration; there were "games and spectacles" in addition to the return of remains. Figure 10, a painting of a canoe race at Bawaating made nearly two centuries later in 1836, illustrates one type of popular entertainment that was enjoyed by young and old alike for generations. At the 1670 gathering decribed by Father Andre, the infants in tikinaagan and the children who played in 1642 were now the adults, parents, and leaders at this 1670 gathering; the adults of 1642 were now the elders. One can almost feel sorry for poor Father André, who tried to preach to those assembled, as he reported that he "had difficulty in making himself heard – although I spoke in a very loud tone – on account of the noise and din caused by the promiscuous intermingling of so many families."[60] Clearly these men, women, and children had better things to do than to listen to the missionary's homily. André's account, despite its brevity, conveys a sense of vitality and happiness and of the continuity of Anishinaabe law and society, as those assembled once again confirmed new leaders.

Ten short months later in June of 1671, there was yet another general council – this one at Bawaating, the place of the rapids, where Sault Ste. Marie is today. Bawaating has been an important meeting place for centuries, and because of the abundant fishery it could support very large gatherings. The council site itself was on a tall hilltop overlooking

---

59 Elder Fred Pine Sr. of Bawaating told the story to the archaeologist Thor Conway. See Conway, *Spirits On Stone*, 28. For a discussion of other pictographs related to Mahiingan's spiritual powers and accomplishments as a leader, see Alan Corbiere, "Anishinaabe Treaty-Making," 4–6.

60 Louys, "Relation of 1670," in Thwaites, *Jesuit Relations*, 55:135–9.

the river. On this occasion some additional guests were present: a small party of men, emissaries of the French king, sent by the Intendant of New France, Jean Talon, and ogimaawag of other councils from throughout the Great Lakes. The French visitors came with the intention of claiming the Great Lakes region for the King of France through a European legal ritual known as a *prise-de-possession*[61] and making the Anishinabek there subjects of the French king. Had such an idea been successfully translated, it would have been thoroughly rejected. What happened instead was that the French, who brought gifts with them obstensibly intended to purchase the region, received gifts as well from the Anishinabek at the council; and in so doing, they performed from an Anishinaabe perspective the protocols for making or renewing an alliance. But when the Intendant of New France later wrote to the king about what had transpired, he reported to His Majesty the happy news that the copper mines of Lake Superior and the whole of the Great Lakes region had cost the king nothing, since the Anishinabek at the ceremony had given bundles of beaver furs in equal value to the goods that the Sieur de St. Lusson, the leader of the expedition, had brought for the purchase of the Great Lakes.[62]

These radically different understandings – the creation of a binding, ongoing alliance relationship on the one hand, or the purchase and sale of land on the other – are at the root of contemporary debates about the meanings of treaties signed between Indigenous peoples and imperial governments and their descendant settler states. Such differences are evident in the earliest recorded treaties between Crown representatives and Indigenous peoples and much more recent agreements, including those signed in the twentieth century. These different understandings occurred because multiple legal traditions were present at the site of treaty signings, and each legal tradition was itself a product of a different ontology.[63] Each party's respective understanding of what had transpired was informed by their own separate worldviews. However, it is hard to imagine that, at the very least, the Sieur de St. Lusson and his interpreter Nicolas Perrot did not have some understanding of the

---

61 For descriptions and the history of these ceremonies, see Seed, *Ceremonies of Possession*.

62 Talon to the King, 2 November 1671, Fonds des Colonies. Série C11A. Correspondance générale, Canada, vol. 3, fol.159–171v, ANOM, France.

63 For an excellent discussion of the significance and challenges of these ontological differences for historical research, see Doxtator, "Inclusive and Exclusive Perceptions."

significance of the alliance ceremony they performed, even as the intendant reported the substantial savings to the king.

One must also wonder about the Anishinaabe reaction to the legal ceremony of prise-de-possession that the French performed during the council proceedings. The Sieur de St. Lusson, with Perrot as his interpreter, gestured to his men to first raise a cross and then a cedar pole, to which he nailed an iron shield displaying the coat of arms of the King of France. Next, he grabbed a handful of soil and, holding it aloft, gave an impassioned speech. Then to conclude his performance, he produced a piece of paper (a statement of the ceremony) and invited the ogimaawag to sign. What must they have thought about this? Nevertheless, these leaders, seventeen in all, responded by inscribing pictographs that represented their doodem identities. According to one eyewitness, they inscribed "the insignia of their families; some of them drew a beaver, others an otter, a sturgeon, a deer or an elk."[64] Although writing or inscribing signatures to agreements on paper was not a conventional Anishinaabe diplomatic practice in this period, these leaders still knew how to respond – with their doodem images – as such images appeared on the Agawa canyon pictograph. And in so doing they began a convention that would continue through two more centuries of treaty-making. Leaders in council signed documents intended for colonial audiences with their doodem images. Unfortunately, the document they signed became separated from the official report sometime after its submission, and its current location is not known. Only Perrot's description of the signing ceremony remains. But another document signed thirty years later has pictographs that compare favourably to those described (see Figure 11). In 1701, at the Peace of Montreal, Anishinaabe leaders from the Great Lakes region were invited to sign the text of the treaty, and again they responded with doodem images of the ogimaawag attending and the council fires they represented – this

---

64 Le Roy, Claude Charles, Sieur de Bacqueville de la Potherie, "Histoire de l'Amérique septentrionale", in Blair, ed., *Indian Tribes*, 1:347. La Potherie was not an eyewitness and relied on the interpreter Nicolas Perrot (who was there) for his information about this event. The manuscript original of this prise-de-possession has not yet been found. The Intendant of New France, Jean Talon, indicated in his letter to the king that he would bring the document to Paris himself when he next came, but the document is not in the colonial archives with Talon's other correspondence. See Talon to the King, 2 November 1671, Fonds des Colonies. Série C11A. Correspondence générale, Canada, vol. 3, fol.159–171v, ANOM, France.

time with beaver, cranes, thunderbirds, bears, and catfish. As signing in this way became an Anishinaabe treaty convention, Anishinaabe leaders inserted evidence of their governance practices and legal traditions into the imperial archival record.

Despite the presence of doodem identities, French officials remained uncertain about exactly what the images represented, and so they attempted to insert the Anishinabek into French political categories. In Talon's November 1671 report to Louis XIV, he described the leaders who signed as representing seventeen *nations* and the leaders as having the authority to bind their people to the French king as the king's new subjects. By asserting that Anishinaabe leaders represented what they thought of as nations, St. Lusson, Talon, and others were reasoning by analogy with their own French practices and from within their own political categories. "Nation," as defined in the various dialects of French spoken in this period, did not mean state, and it certainly did not mean council fire. Seventeenth-century visitors to the region, including Samuel de Champlain, Gabriel Sagard, and Jesuit missionaries, all used the French word nation, or the Latin word *natio*, to label Indigenous polities. Sometimes they said *gens* – simply "people." In the early seventeenth-century French dictionary, *Thresor de la Langue Française*, the French word "nation" is defined by both the Latin words natio and gens. In Latin, gens and natio can be synonyms. Natio specifically connotes birth, or being born – by association "a breed, stock, kind, species or race." The Latin gens (whose root is *gen*, "that which belongs together by birth or descent") meant "a race or clan, embracing several families united together by a common name and by certain religious rites."[65] And in the broad European heraldic tradition of the same period, the idea of the nation could also connote the collective body of people who were the monarch's subjects, represented symbolically by the coat of arms of the monarch's family line.[66]

In defining Anishinaabe polities as "nations," and in describing leaders signing with coats of arms or the insignia of their families, seventeenth-century French writers were grappling with how to make sense of the Indigenous polities they were encountering. They struggled to

---

65 See Aimar de Ranconnet, *Thresor de la Langue Francoyse, tant Ancienne que Moderne*, ed. Jean Niçot (1606), s.v. "nation" and s.v. "gens,"; *Dictionarie de l'Academie française* [1764], 2:197, both available via ARTFL, https://artfl-project.uchicago.edu/; Charlton T. Lewis and Charles Short, *A Latin Dictionary* (Oxford, 1879).
66 Bedos-Rezak, "Medieval Identity."

describe a decentralized interdependent system of governance while they were themselves increasingly part of a centralizing imperial world, structured by hierarchies of social rank and gender. The French King Louis XIV was a chief architect of this model. He ascended the throne in 1643 at the age of five and assumed control of government in 1661. At that point he began to implement his vision of absolutism. A decade later, in 1671, he was in complete command, exercising his own political philosophy in which he, as the "Sun King," was at the apex of a pyramid of political power, with nobility, gentry, clergy, and the vast French peasantry arranged below him in descending layers of social rank. Louis XIV consolidated his power in France at his palace at Versailles as he and his ministers worked to extend French territorial holdings throughout the world, in competition with other European empires. This, in essence, was the purpose of St. Lusson's prise-de-possession ceremony: to make a claim for part of North America that would be recognized by other European powers, especially England.[67]

By attempting to claim the Great Lakes region on behalf of the King of France, St. Lusson was enacting a performance intended to define a cartographic zone of exclusivity. But the political world of the Anishinabek was utterly different from that of the French. As historian Michael Witgen has persuasively shown in his *An Infinity of Nations*, the Anishinabek made a fundamental distinction between *inawemaagen* (relatives) and *eyaagizid* (foreigners). Relatives were people that Anishinaabe individuals had responsibility for. They were also people with whom one could trade. The Anishinabek did not deploy a separate semantic category for ally, trading partner, or friend.[68] You were either inawemaagen or you were not. If you were not doodem kin, you became inawemaagen through ceremony. Such alliances were the basis for all political relationships.

Historian Michael McDonnell has cautioned against the tendency to "exoticize these kinship relations" on the grounds that of course both European officials and Euro-American settlers were also connected into their own networks of relations: "networks of allegiances, obligations, and resource sharing that was often tied to the relations among nuclear

---

67 See Seed, *Ceremonies of Possession*, especially Chapter 2, "Ceremonies: The Theatrical Rituals of French Political Possession," 41–68, and Michel Witgen's analysis that this ceremony in particular represented nothing more than imperial rhetoric, in Witgen, "Rituals of Possession."

68 Witgen, *Infinity of Nations*, 33.

and extended families."[69] While I agree that such kinship relations should not be exoticized, as they are perfectly comprehensible, I do feel that we scholars have not respected their difference from Western categories enough. In other words, both colonial-era newcomers and contemporary historians have reached for analogies to explain these differences and to make Indigenous worldviews comprehensible to themselves. In so doing, however, crucial distinctions have been lost. Of course Europeans had their own informal family networks that were as, or perhaps even more, important than "formal structures of government" in explaining how decisions were made or actions taken in the histories of those countries. But how Europeans and Euro-Americans made distinctions between kin and non-kin differed quite significantly from the Anishinabek and other Indigenous peoples, as, perhaps even more importantly, did the type of obligations owed to those kin. Furthermore, the extension of kinship to other-than-human beings is a radical departure from European thought worlds, which sharply divide humans from non-humans in a way that Anishinaabe philosophy does not. Both of these differences have tremendous significance for the legal traditions of their respective cultures.

The *ethic* of kinship is also quite distinct in the Great Lakes region from Western European historic and present norms; the Anishinabek have responsibility for and kin obligations towards beings that in Western thought are animals or inanimate property. A birch tree in Anishinaabe worldview is an animate, ensouled being and can have human kin who are in relationship to it and who have responsibilities for it.[70] In Anishinaabe law, personhood is a greatly expanded concept that includes all ensouled beings. Anishinaabe law therefore treats as persons those beings (animals, plants) who in Canadian common law – and indeed in international legal orders today – are regarded as property.[71]

---

69 McDonnell, *Masters of Empire*, 12fn18.

70 This principle is well-documented in Anishinabek studies, scholarship, and Elders' teachings. One excellent explanation of this principle in practice can be found in Pitawanakwat and Paper, "Communicating the Intangible." For a discussion of this principle in operation during the late eighteenth and early nineteenth centuries, see Bruce White, "Woman Who Married a Beaver."

71 In 2017, however, New Zealand granted legal personhood to a river, by the Whanganui Iwi Deed of Settlement. The river has its own guardians and will be able to exercise its legal rights against other legal persons (like corporations or individuals) who pollute it. Debates about the extension of personhood to other beings including animals and ecosystem are ongoing. See Hutchison, "Whanganui River as a Legal Person."

As colonizers arrived with different theologies and philosophies, they struggled to make sense of a worldview so at odds with their own. Nor did many, except those most closely connected to Anishinaabe peoples, appreciate the political significance or the centrality of this worldview in shaping the alliance relationships they were making with the Anishinabek and what it *really* meant to live as allies and with whom – that, in fact, it meant to live in relationship.[72] All of these differences matter when it comes to interpreting what treaties mean.

Lacking any deep understanding of Anishinaabe political structures, the French and later the British misunderstood the crucial distinction between *authority over* and *responsibility for* as the defining characteristics of political leaders from their different cultural traditions. In their speeches at the 1671 prise-de-possession ceremony, the Jesuits referred to the King of France as a "captain" in order to equate his political position to that of an Anishinaabe ogimaa – whom they also called a captain – but also to a level of French leadership of which with the Anishinabek already had first-hand experience. However, both French kings and French captains had authority over the people under them. Anishinaabe ogimaawag, in contrast, could not compel the behaviour of others. Instead, ogimaawag had responsibility (and lots of it) for the people under their care and the lands and resources they were entrusted to manage. When Anishinabek heard the word ogimaa applied to a French monarch, or later to an English one, they applied their own understandings of what that role meant. When colonial officials gave presents to Anishinaabe peoples in the name of the monarch, that monarch was being, from an Anishinaabe perspective, a good ogimaa. In making a formal exchange of gifts of equal value, Anishinaabe leaders symbolically enacted with their allies the mutual promise of responsibility for the other, the same sort of responsibility that leaders, that ogimaawag, had for their own people. Talon, when he wrote to the king, knew or chose to communicate nothing of this. He reported instead a successful territorial acquisition for France and how the people of seventeen Indigenous nations were now subject to the authority of the French king. As Michael Witgen has demonstrated, Talon's claims were not based in fact.[73]

Anishinaabe polities consisted of networks of alliances – some very large, others much smaller. Alliance was and is a foundational

---

72 Mills, "What Is a Treaty?," 211.
73 Witgen, *Infinity of Nations*, 69–77.

Anishinaabe cultural practice and legal principle. Marriage, for example, brought together people of different doodemag. When couples married, they continued to keep their own doodem identity. Each marriage therefore constituted a micro-alliance between two individuals, each with a distinct doodem. Therefore, any group of Anishinaabe peoples for councils such as the one held in 1642 or at Bawaating in 1671 included people of more than one doodem. Large gatherings brought individuals of many doodemag together. Any mixed-gendered group of Anishinaabe peoples that included spouses would by definition have included people with multiple doodem identities who understood their relationship to one another through the concept of alliance. Common councils and regional councils were also sites of alliances, the first between people with different doodemag, and the second between different doodemag and different council fires.

Historians have for some time now suggested that Indigenous societies used the alliance relationships they constructed with Europeans through kinship metaphors for strategic and tactical purposes, in order to play competing imperial powers off against each other, and to maintain control and autonomy in their own homelands. Such interpretations of how Indigenous peoples used alliance relationships, however, are inevitably grounded in a European normative political framework. They contain the underlying assumption that Indigenous peoples used alliance in roughly the same way that Europeans did, for roughly the same political purposes. Within this framework, in which contemporary eyewitnesses who produced the sources were also situated, scholars have described alliances as being made between different nations to achieve specific outcomes such as peace, trade, or combining military forces against a common foe.[74]

But Anishinaabe understandings of alliance are far different, and they are in fact central to a distinct Anishinaabe theory of government through treaty relationships.[75] The regional gatherings described in this introduction were sites of significant ontological difference between

---

74 For example, James Miller's discussion of treaty history in Canada in *Compact, Contract, Covenant* organizes treaties into these categories and also includes treaties for land sales.

75 Aspects of Anishinaabe theory of government through alliance is expressed in the work of Anishinaabe scholars previously cited in the Preface, especially by Borrows, Mills, Stark, and Miller.

the Anishinabek who gathered there and the French who came to visit. The impact of such divergent worldviews has continued to the present, affecting contemporary interpretations of treaties and alliances, because subsequent generations of political actors from Western European countries struggled to comprehend Indigenous thought worlds or chose to dismiss them as irrelevant. Because these same individuals produced the primary sources upon which historians have to date almost exclusively relied, our interpretations have been necessarily limited. This is not to say that, over time, local colonial officials on the ground did not come to some basic understanding about the importance of doodemag. They certainly learned the diplomatic protocols of Anishinaabe councils and the locations of regionally significant council fires. Later, following the end of the Seven Years' War in 1763, British colonial officials recognized the doodem images that Anishinaabe leaders signed as equivalent to their signatures. They were not, but colonial officials acted as if they were. Regardless of what officials thought at the time, the Anishinabek knew what their doodem images meant and consistently wrote them on documents that pertained to the work of governance, to reflect the alliances between doodemag that comprised their councils, their legal traditions, and, indeed, their political world.

Doodemag in the Archive

Doodem and Council Fire uses the evidence of doodem images on treaty and other documents as a key to recover the political history of the Anishinabek in North America's Great Lakes region. The doodem images cited here come from a range of documents dating from 1671 to circa 1915.[76] The treaty documents on which many of these images appear were produced by colonial officials and then presented to Anishinaabe delegates to sign in the context of a formal council to negotiate the treaty. In many cases, the clerk who wrote out the manuscript document was also the individual who inscribed the names of the Anishinaabe chiefs in roman orthography beside each pictograph. The ordering of colonial signatories on treaties reflects Euro-American social rank, with the most important or senior person signing first and subsequent officials and witnesses signing below in descending order

---

76 For an excellent discussion of the challenges of working with manuscript treaty documents, see Kennedy, "Treaty Texts."

of rank. This ordering pattern appears to be consistent throughout the treaty-signing period. Interpreters, who were sometimes barely literate or illiterate fur traders, typically signed last, sometimes with an X-mark.

Significantly, while colonial clerks prepared these treaty documents and wrote out Anishinaabe names, the patterns of doodem images on treaties respects and reflects Indigenous protocols concerning political roles and the local importance of particular doodem identities.[77] On treaties negotiated with American officials after their Revolution, for example, Indigenous signatories were grouped together by council fire and, within that grouping, by political role, with the most senior ogimaa or gitchi-ogimaa topping the list. There are six treaties negotiated between the Anishinabek and the American government that contain doodem images, from the 1785 Treaty of Fort McIntosh up to the 1817 Treaty at the Rapids of the Miami. The 1785 Treaty of Fort McIntosh was widely regarded at the time of its signing as invalid because it was only negotiated with minor chiefs and headmen. It had too few signatories to be a legitimate peace (only twelve minor chiefs, none of whom had the authority to either make peace or to cede land). Twenty-eight chiefs signed the replacement – the Treaty of Fort Harmar in 1789 – and these were the civil leaders. The newly constituted United States government had been forced to toss out the Treaty of Fort McIntosh in the wake of a public outcry on the part of those regional leaders who knew the agreement was not legitimate.[78] Subsequent US agreements were regional in scope and specifically identified the discrete "nations" to which the signatories were associated: the Ottawas, the Chippewas, or the Potawatomis, for example. Under each bracketed grouping, though, leaders signed with their doodem images. On the last treaty, only the most senior leaders signed with doodem images; all others were shown with an X. American treaties with the Anishinabek signed after 1817 have X-marks in lieu of doodem images.

Treaties signed north of the new border in British North America followed a similar pattern in cases where multiple council fires were involved. In the case of land purchases from a single council fire, the

---

77 I discuss these relationships and patterns in Bohaker, "Anishinaabe 'toodaims.'"
78 National Archives and Records Administration at College Park, MD (NACP), General Records of the United States Government, RG 11, Indian Treaties, 1722–1869, and available on National Archives Microfilm Publication M668, roll 1. See also Prucha, *American Indian Treaties*, Chapter 1.

listing of signatories also reflects local political contexts. Clearly, local local colonial officials had a reasonable understanding of Anishinaabe politics. Anishinaabe protocols also influenced the treaty process. On treaty documents for the eastern Great Lakes, the first image in any column of Anishinaabe pictographsis that of the ogimaa belonging to the doodem identity acknowledged to be the keepers of the council fire. As will be discussed in greater detail in Chapter 4, crane doodem images appear first in the column of doodem images for treaties negotiated around Sault Ste. Marie and around Rice Lake in eastern Ontario; Caribou doodem images around the Lake Simcoe, Mnjikaning area; and Eagle images on treaties related to the Mississauga-Anishinabek from the north shore of Lake Ontario.

An examination of doodem images produced on treaty and other documents over more than three centuries reveals that there was a significant change in what – or more precisely, who – each doodem image could represent. On seventeenth- and eighteenth-century documents, a single image could represent an entire family under the leadership of a gichi-Anishinaabe or ogimaa or be the doodem of the ogimaa, representing an entire council fire. After the 1671 prise-de-possession ceremony, interpreter Nicolas Perrot told the Sieur de Bacqueville de la Potherie that each leader drew just one image as the "mark" of their families. On the Peace of Montreal of 1701, while specific leaders were sometimes identified by name, there was only one doodem image on the document for each council fire in attendance.[79]

Over the eighteenth century, the practice changed and each ogimaa or gichi-Anishinaabe of an entire council signed. Some marginalia on treaty documents are suggestive of changing practices. On a 1774 private land deed for lands around Detroit, the author of the document penned "father and sons" beside the doodem of a wolf. On another private deed for lands around Detroit signed in 1788, the author or clerk who prepared the document wrote two and sometimes three names beside each doodem image, clearly suggesting that the doodem images represented multiple people.[80] In his 1795 letter to General Anthony

79 Claude Charles Le Roy, Sieur de Bacqueville de la Potherie, "Histoire de l'Amérique septentrionale," in Blair, ed. *Indian Tribes*, 1:343–8; "Ratification de la paix," 4 August 1701, Fonds des Colonies. Série C11A. Correspondence générale, Canada, vol. 19, fol.41–44, ANOM.
80 Deed of land on the Detroit River from the Chiefs of the Ottawa Indians at Detroit, 7 June 1774, Archives of Ontario, Toronto, Hiram Walker Historical Museum

Wayne, Benjamin Henfrey enclosed a signed copy of council proceedings from 18 September 1795. On it, one ogimaa signed a Bear doodem, but a note in the margin indicates that it was both for himself and on behalf of three others. Similarly, on the same document, the names of Chechogwas and Nathanena are recorded using one thunderbird image, as the one image stood for the both of them. One signatory named Nawac signed, as the marginalia attested, for both himself and his brother Asimettic, while the notation beside Sinade's Beaver doodem reads "for the Beaver," suggesting that Sinade's image also represented more than one person who shared that identity.[81]

Doodem images are not equivalents to personal signatures, as the Anishinabek did not consistently draw their own images on the document. In some cases, it is clear that the same hand drew all of the images, while in others the variations in style, line thickness, and evident familiarity (or lack thereof) with a quill pen suggest that more than one person was involved. Occasionally documents identify the person who drew the images. On the signed council proceedings Benjamin Henfrey included in his 1795 letter to General Wayne, there are ten doodemag where Henfrey noted "the above characters was [sic] drawn by the Chief Kee Sap at the request of all present." By this, it seems that Kee Sap drew all of the images; they certainly appear to have all been drawn by one hand. It is possible that Kee Sap was chosen because he was familiar with using a quill pen, but he may simply have been Henfrey's choice and not that of the council attendees. A margin notation by Kee Sap's image displays Henfrey's assessment of him: "a good man and I will answer for him will be found a true Friend to the United States."[82] But sometimes there are explicit notes that each person signed their own doodem. In 1800, an Anishinaabe council at the Delaware mission village run by the Moravians on the Thames River had a document produced and the notation added to explain "we have caused this speech to written [sic] for us to sign that you [Joseph Brant] may

Collection F378, James Sterling Papers (20–217); 20 September 1788, Proclamation concerning the free and voluntary granting of land on the north side of the Thames River to Jonathan Scieffelin of Detroit, merchant, by the Chippeway [sic] Nation of Indians at Detroit, Archives of Ontario, Toronto, Miscellaneous Collection F775, MU2099.

81   Letter of Benjamin Henfrey, 2 October 1795, The Historical Society of Pennsylvania (HSP), Anthony Wayne Papers, Collection #699 (Volume XXXIX, page 9).

82   Ibid.

show them [the Indian Department] that these are our wishes." The corresponding doodem images each appear to be by distinct hands.[83] Explanatory marginalia on late-eighteenth-century treaty documents reveal an uncertainty on the part of the British and Americans with regard to Anishinaabe practices. On the 1781 sale and purchase of Michilimackinac Island, for example, the clerk wrote next to the two Loon doodem images that the second one, although representing the same bird as the first, in fact represented a different person. Such a notation was most likely for the benefit of British officials who were less familiar with Anishinaabe political tradition. The shared doodem identities of these two Anishinaabe leaders concerned this clerk – would his counterparts understand that two or more Anishinaabe men could be represented by two images of the same animal, or in other cases, where several names were written beside a single doodem?

During the first half of the nineteenth century, writers of doodem images began more frequently to sign documents as individuals, and this was particularly the case in British North America, where signing documents with doodem images was a regular occurrence. Anishinaabe leaders entering into any formal business with Crown officials signed land sale agreements, receipts, petitions and other documents, all with doodem images. Typically each name was written by a colonial official (usually a clerk) and the doodem image was either inscribed by each person beside their own name or the images were drawn by a common hand. During this period, there appears to be a shift from earlier practices of having only leaders sign to having all adult males in a community (or at the very least, heads of households) sign the documents. But by the mid-nineteenth century not only were there typically more doodem images or X-marks on documents, but each mark or image was clearly associated with one individual.

The British concern with authorship and authority on treaty documents can be traced back to before the Proclamation of 1763, but in the wake of Pontiac's War colonial officials and landowners were concerned about the need to regularize the securing of title to Indigenous land in the Great Lakes region. Sir William Johnson,

---

83 Speech from the Chipewas, to Joseph Brant, 21 May 1800, Wisconsin Historical Society, Madison (WHS), Lyman Copeland Draper Manuscripts, Joseph Brant papers, 1710–1879, Series F, Volume 21, Document 3, consulted on microfilm at the University of Western Ontario.

then the British Superintendent of Indian Affairs for the Northern District, established the practices following the Proclamation to ensure that documents, duly signed and sealed, were obtained for all land transactions. However, despite Johnson's efforts, other military and colonial authorities continued to be anxious about the appropriateness of using doodemag as signatures, particularly when more than one person was represented by the same image. Despite this, there seems to have been no significant move in British North America to force the replacement of doodem images with X-marks.[84] Americans also continued with the practice of permitting doodem images to be signed on treaty documents until after the end of the War of 1812. After 1817, doodemag no longer appear on American treaty documents with the Anishinabek. The continuing use of doodem images and symbolic picture writing in America by the Anishinabek through the American Civil War on other types of documents and media, however, suggests that the decision to discontinue the practice came at the instigation of American officials.[85]

The British, by the 1820s, seemed less concerned about ending the practice than they were about insisting that all signatories be represented by their own distinct doodem image. Specifically, the British wanted to stop the practice of one image "standing" for an entire band or even for a family of father and sons. By the 1830s, Indian Department officials had become frustrated with the slow pace of cultural change among Indigenous peoples, many of whom were otherwise adapting to the new colonial reality by farming and participating in the settler economy. J.B. Clench, a superintendent of Indian Affairs from 1830 to 1854, received a pointed passage in a letter from one of his field agents about this problem:

I beg to take this occasion to observe that with respect to the Indians useing [sic] hieroglyphical marks for signatures, such a practice was common to all the uncivilized tribes in America with whom Treaties have been

---

84 Glover, *Paper Sovereigns;* "Plan for the Future Management of Indian Affairs, 1764," in O'Callaghan, *Documents Relative to the Colonial History of the State of New York,* 7:638–9.

85 Symbolic Petition of Chippewa Chiefs, presented at Washington, 28 January 1849, headed by Oshcabawis of Wisconsin. Pictograph A. Plate 60. Drawn by S. Eastman, USA, Printed in Color by P.S. Duval, Philadelphia, in Schoolcraft, *American Indians,* 416–17. See Figure 34.

held; but as they advance in knowledge they assume names, and as His Excellency's instructions have invariably directed my exertions to change their manners and reform their habits, and assimilate their mode of life to that of the whites, I have ever been influenced by those benevolent views. And request the Chiefs to lay aside their ancient customs and imitate those whose example we wish them to follow, but must they in future resume that mode? Although it operates much to my disadvantage.

You are well aware they are a cunning people and notice the least inconsistencies which might create a wavering in their minds, and cause a predilection in favour of old customs to which they are so strongly wedded: You will observe in their written request two signatures alike (Omicks) [amick, or Beaver doodem] and to show the correctness of signing by marks X I beg to state that the Head Chief is known by the name of John T[amicoo], his signature is the first "Omick" and there are five others in this village who bear the same Indian title and their signature (hieroglyphical) could not be distinguished.[86]

There are documents both in Canada and the United States, however, that contain a mix of X-marks and doodem images, suggesting that these practices co-existed for quite some time. X-marks were a recognized way in both British and American law for illiterate people to indicate their consent to the terms of a written contract. The shift to using X-marks was already evident on American treaties by 1817 but did.not predominate on treaties made on the British colonial side of the international boundary until the 1850s. The shift to using X-marks instead of doodem images purportedly occurred while the strength of traditional doodem governance practices, discussed in Chapter 5, was under pressure to change and conform to settler expectations, as the letter J.B. Clench received suggests. Anishinaabe leaders were also creatively adapting to these political pressures. They produced many petitions and letters signed in council with doodem images during this same period, some of which are cited in this book. This archival record of innovative responses to settler colonialism's world of print are also a critical archive of Anishinaabe doodem governance in action.

---

86 Rogers, "Algonquian Farmers"; Letter to J.B. Clench, of Indian Affairs, 19 January 1832, Chief Superintendent's Office, Upper Canada (Colonel J. Givins) – Correspondence, LAC RG10, Vol. 50: 55741–2.

Towards an Anishinaabe Political History

Doodem and Council Fire builds on scholarly interest in the intersection of Indigenous peoples and empires that has accelerated since the publication of Richard White's 1991 *The Middle Ground: Indians, Empires and Republics in the Great Lakes Region, 1615–1812.* Scholarship in this field includes my own 2006 article on the doodem tradition and 2010 article on doodem political metaphors and most recently includes Michel Witgen's 2013 *An Infinity of Nations* and Michael McDonnell's 2016 *Masters of Empire.*[87] While *Doodem and Council Fire* centres the Anishinaabe world on the Great Lakes proper and with a clear focus on the eastern Great Lakes, the narrative here follows Anishinaabe peoples as they moved through this region and out of it in all four directions. The web created by nodes of council fires and networks of doodem relations was thickest in the Great Lakes region proper but spread well beyond.[88]

This book shows how Anishinaabe governance and law was structured through alliances between doodemag, forged through marriage ties and between council fires across the region. In referring to alliance as a concept that structures governance and law, I am consciously evoking the contributions to anthropology by French anthropologist Claude Lévi-Strauss, and the school of structuralism more broadly, because it is a useful way to think about the way in which doodem created a framework for how the Anishinabek governed themselves.[89] However, I want very much to guard against ahistorical or rigidly prescriptive readings of doodemag – or what the doodem tradition meant or how people thought about the tradition – either through a social or a legal analysis. Anishinaabe governance with and through doodem was and is creative, innovative, and dynamic.

I have organized this book into five chapters. Chapter 1, "The Doodem Tradition," discusses doodem as a distinctly Anishinaabe category of kinship and situates its origins in the aadizookaanag (origin stories

---

87 In addition to Richard White, *Middle Ground*, see also Havard, *Great Peace of Montreal*; Taylor, *Divided Ground*; Witgen, *Infinity of Nations*; McDonnell, *Masters of Empire*; Havard, *Empire et Métissages*; DuVal, *Native Ground*; MacLeod, "Anishinabeg Point of View."

88 Doerfler, Sinclair, and Stark, "Bagijige: Making an Offering," in *Centering Anishinaabeg Studies*, xvii.

89 See especially his seminal *Elementary Structures of Kinship.*

or grandfather teachings). The aadizookaanag are the foundation of Anishinaabe law and principles of governance. The concept of doodem souls discussed here is critical for understanding the concept of being in relationship to particular territories and to other ensouled beings. Chapter 2, "Family in All Four Directions," explores doodem as a dynamic tradition within Anishinaabe worldview. The "Four Directions" is a reference to many things: the cardinal directions to which Anishinaabe peoples offer prayers of thanksgiving, the locations of winds, the stages of life. Here I use it to evoke the idea of each Anishinaabe individual at the centre of a cross of kin connections – future descendants (who come from the east, the dawn, through the eastern door), ancestors (whose souls have gone to the west, through the western door), and spouses and doodem kin. These two chapters together make the case for the centrality of doodem as defining what it means to be Anishinaabe and the importance of marriage as an alliance between doodemag, as the basis for the entire larger structures of Anishinaabe governance and law.

Chapter 3, "Anishinaabe Constitutionalism," explains the law through which the Anishinabek established sites of formal governance throughout the region. It is a study of how doodem beings functioned metaphorically as political allegory to explain why specific places in the Great Lakes region were the responsibility of those with particular doodem identities. These types of histories are constitutional in nature, as are histories of migration and more recent records of alliances. Each is a record of the founding (or kindling) of new council fires. Chapter 3 demonstrates how regional alliances created common council fires and how in turn regional councils were the place where people came together to negotiate and renew alliance relationships between common councils. Anishinaabe constitutionalism was fundamentally reciprocal, creating interdependent relationships through alliance.

Chapter 4, "Governance in Action," focuses on the period between the Treaty of Niagara in 1764 and the mid-nineteenth century. Drawing from treaties and council minutes, it takes a closer look at how Anishinaabe historic governance practices worked, how law was enacted in council, the differences and relationships between common and regional councils, and the political work that each did during the treaty-making era. Governance was widely distributed in Anishinaabe societies and was fundamentally non-hierarchical. Adult men and women shared leadership responsibilities in some areas and in others, particularly civil governance, gender and age determined political roles, as younger men participated on warriors' councils and women met as a separate advisory council to ogimaawag and gichi-Anishinabek. The set of land sale/purchase documents signed between 1781 and 1862 in British North America for what is now the Province of Ontario form a remarkable set of legal sources that reveal the changing composition of local and regional councils through the doodem images of those who signed treaty documents.

Chapter 5, "Doodem in the Era of Settler Colonialism," considers the implications of colonialism in the nineteenth century on Anishinaabe governance, law, and the doodem tradition. While the processes and structures of settler colonialism significantly disrupted Anishinaabe governance practices in this period, how, when, and where that change occurred varied over time and place. And while Canada and the United States both imposed elected band or tribal councils on Anishinaabe communities in the latter half of the nineteenth century, awareness of the doodem tradition itself persisted, even as core elements, such as the taboo against marrying someone with the same doodem, began to be disrupted. Christian missionization and residential schooling had most significant negative impacts, as Western kinship categories began to replace Anishinaabe historic ones and as alliances between council fires became harder to maintain during the reserve/reservation era. Indigenous people found themselves increasingly confined to reserves; when people travelled they experienced increasing racism and fears for their own safety. Some did travel, though, and there are multiple examples of grand and general councils from this period indicating that Anishinaabe governance practices continued. Despite the challenges faced, knowledge of traditional Anishinaabe governance practices, legal traditions, and the doodem tradition has survived, and these are undergoing revitalization as people reclaim their doodem identities and begin to explore ways that doodem can contribute to governance and law.

I use the term "Anishinabek" as a collective term in this book, fully aware that it describes a cultural tradition better than a political one, as Anishinaabe polities were instead the council fires themselves – both common *and* general. This is the crucial point: neither polity had jurisdiction over the other. Anishinaabe polities were mutually constitutive and embedded in reciprocal relationships with each other through alliances. Nevertheless, I use the term Anishinaabe (or Anishinabek, in the plural) because it is a meaningful category of belonging and does encompass people who spoke a common language and were part of the doodem tradition. I sometimes use a compound form, such as Ottawa-Anishinabek or Mississauga-Anishinabek where it is necessary to demonstrate a distinction, or where I feel such identification would be useful to the reader. However, the term "Anishinabek" itself is too general for writing political histories. We must focus instead on the histories of council fires and the multiple and differing alliances between them because this is how the Anishinabek exercised their jurisdiction. Such an exercise of jurisdiction was also a culturally distinctive practice. The Anishinabek did not exercise jurisdiction *over* lands and resources but rather *for* and *alongside* them, as lands and waters were also ensouled beings and legal persons within Anishinaabe worldview. This is why doodem images matter. What they offer is nothing less than Anishinaabe peoples' own articulation of a crucial political and legal category and the central role that category played in how Anishinaabe peoples governed themselves.

1

The Doodem Tradition

They derive their origin from a bear, others from a moose, and others similarly from various kinds of animals ... You will hear them say that their villages each bear the name of the animal which has given its people their being – as that of the crane, or the bear, or of other animals.

– Nicolas Perrot, circa 1715

Some are of the family of Michabous, – that is to say, of "the Great Hare" ... The second family of the Outaouacks maintain that they have sprung from Name-pich [*namebin*, white sucker].

– Sebastian Râle, 1723

Each grand family is known by a badge or symbol, taken from nature; being generally a quadruped, bird, fish or reptile ... the writer is disposed to consider, and therefore presents, the Totemic division as more important and more wor-thy of consideration than as generally been accorded to it by standard authors who have studied and written respecting the Indians.

– William Warren, circa 1852[1]

Anishinaabe aadizookaanag, or sacred stories, explain the origin of the doodem tradition. There is a large and rich body of Anishinaabe

---

1 These quotations in the epigraphs are from Perrot, "Mémoire," in Blair, *Indian Tribes*; Râle, "Lettre à Monsieur son Frére, October 12, 1723," in Thwaites, *Jesuit Relations*, 67:153–7; and Warren and Neill, *History*, 44.

aadizookaanag. George Copway said that he had "known some Indians who would commence to narrate legends and stories in the month of October and not end until quite late in the spring, sometimes quite late in the month of May, and on every evening of this long term tell a new story."[2] My discussion here is limited of necessity to excerpts in print that refer to the doodem tradition.[3] The epigraphs above were recorded by three men – two of whom (Perrot and Râle) learned Anishinaabemowin as adults. For Warren, Anishinaabemowin was his first language. Nicolas Perrot was a noted trader and interpreter who spent his entire adult career in the Great Lakes; during his retirement he recorded his observations on Anishinaabe social and political organization in a manuscript which contained aadizookaanag. Perrot was the interpreter attached to Sieur de St. Lusson's expedition in 1671. He gave a manuscript report of his career to the Intendant of New France in 1710, where presumably it helped to inform French colonial policy towards the Anishinabek, but the document did not appear in print until 1864.[4] Sebastian Râle, a Jesuit, began his missionary work among the Abenaki in 1689. The order sent him west to work with the Illinois at Kaskaskia in 1691. Interrupted in his travels due to bad weather, he spent the winter of 1691–2 at Michilimackinac where he learned these narratives that he later recorded.[5] The last quotation in the epigraph appeared in print for the first time in 1884. William Whipple Warren was a noted Anishinaabe politician, interpreter, and intellectual, and author of the *History of the Ojibway Peoples*. He was born in 1825 to an Anishinaabe mother and trader father. He died at the age of 29 from tuberculosis; his manuscript was published posthumously in 1885. Warren devoted an entire chapter of his book to the doodem tradition and its political importance as the basis for Anishinaabe civil governance. He summarized the narratives that he had been told by Elders in his community. These sources (Perrot, Râle, and Warren) all locate the origin of the doodem tradition in deep time. The Elders who told Warren the aadizookaanag he recorded were drawing from a corpus of very old

---

2 Copway, *Traditional History and Characteristic Sketches*, 98.
3 Scholars have studied Anishinaabe aadizookaanag as folklore, myth, and narrative within the academy. See Fisher, "Ojibwa Creation Myth." But aadizookaanag are becoming the centerpiece of Anishinaabe Studies as an academic discipline. See Doerfler, Sinclair, and Stark, *Centering Anishinaabe Studies*.
4 Perrault, "Perrot, Nicolas."
5 Charland, "Rale, Sébastien."

stories, not mythologizing a sixteenth- or seventeenth-century history. These narratives situated the origin of the doodem tradition together with the origin of the Anishinaabe as a distinct people in the distant past. Indeed, when the Jesuit Jérôme Lalemant described Anishinaabe society in his observations at the 1642 gathering discussed in the Introduction, he noted that they had a way of life "which has been led here for two, three even four thousand years."[6]

The question of time is an important one, especially when Western-trained historians approach the analysis and interpretation of Anishinaabe aadizookaanag that have been recorded in fragment or snippet form in colonial texts or in manuscripts like Warren's, those intended for a non-Indigenous audience.[7] However, these narratives still provide valuable evidence of the doodem tradition. Such narratives reveal doodem governance and law operating throughout the Great Lakes region. Because these early records are also snippets of aadizookaanag or origin narratives, they anchor this political tradition in deep time. The doodem tradition was a system that was well in place before the arrival of the first recording European in the region. Written versions of the narratives that record the origin of the doodem tradition also make it possible to assess the changes and continuities in those narratives since outsiders began recording them in translation in the late seventeenth century. Versions continued to be recorded through the nineteenth century and up to the present.

Beginning in the nineteenth century, as settlers pushed Anishinaabe peoples onto reserves (first in the south and east of the region and then, after mid-century, in the north and west) and as people increasingly converted to Christianity, they found it more difficult to talk about being related to or descended from animals, or having a shared doodem-soul. Such ideas were fundamentally at odds with Christianity. Some aspects of these narratives have changed over time (or at least those aspects shared with non-Anishinabek).[8] However, core elements,

---

6 Lalemant, "Relation of 1642–1643," in Thwaites, *Jesuit Relations*, 23:205.
7 Anishinaabe narratives include the aadizookaanag but also *dibaajimowin*, or everyday news. And of course, many Nanabozhoo stories recount incidents where the trickster gets himself into trouble, with generally hilarious results.
8 A clear example of this erasure of metamorphoses can be found in the oral history and archival research undertaken by Alan Corbiere concerning the story of "Gchi-Ogaa: 'The Great Pickerel.'" The oral history of Gchi-Ogaa's memorable escape from

including the connections between doodem, governance, and law, have remained. Such recorded narratives are also sources for change in the doodem tradition itself and include accounts of how new doodem identities were created or incorporated into Anishinaabe society. This chapter also discusses how to think about doodem as an analytical category for historical analysis. It matters that scholars speak of doodem and not reach to other kinship systems for analogies. Doodem is a particular and specifically Anishinaabe category of belonging.

The Origins of the Doodem Tradition

The earliest written account of the doodem tradition that I have been able to find is in the writings of the fur trader and interpreter Nicolas Perrot. This version was likely told to Perrot sometime in the third quarter of the seventeenth century, while he was working as a fur trader and interpreter in the Great Lakes region and overwintering with families.[9] Perrot's account provides evidence of two crucial points: first, that the Anishinabek constituted their governments as doodem beings who met in council, and second, that specific doodem beings took on responsibility for particular places in the Great Lakes region. Perrot's "Mémoire sur les moeurs" begins with an Anishinaabe *re*-creation story that followed a flood. The animals were gathered on a great wooden raft as it floated on a vast body of water, with no land in sight. This is the second flood event in Anishinaabe oral histories. An older flood describes the original creation of the world by Geezhigo-kwe, or Sky woman. She fell pregnant, landed on a turtle's back, and created the world from the soil brought up by a muskrat. Her descendants then, "millennia later ... dreamed Nanabush into being." After a second flood, it was Nanabush or Nanabozhoo's

---

an American naval vessel includes his transformation into a giant pickerel, which allows him to slip off the shackles he was bound with and to escape overboard. This story was told by Lewis Debassige, a lineal descendant of Ogaa. Corbiere found an 1877 petition by Chief Louis Debassige to the Indian Department concerning annuity payments for the Robinson-Huron treaty, which contains the same story and many of the same details of Ogaa's actions; however, in the version submitted to the Indian Department, Ogaa escapes over the side at night and does not turn into a fish.

9 Perrault, "Perrot, Nicolas."

turn to recreate "his world from a morsel of sand retrieved from the depths of the sea."[10]

In the version told to Perrot, which clearly picks up the plot thread from this second flood, Nanabozhoo is called the Great Hare. He is described as the leader of the animals.[11] It was he who asked a series of animals to dive for a grain of sand from the bottom of the sea. All failed until the muskrat tried, and it was the muskrat who finally succeeded.[12] Nanabozhoo took that sand and, as Perrot recalled, "let it fall upon the raft, when it began to increase; then he took a part of it, and scattered this about, which caused the mass of soil to grow larger and larger ... As soon as he thought it was large enough, he ordered the fox to go to inspect his work, with power to enlarge it still more; and the latter obeyed ... After the creation of the earth, all the other animals withdrew into the places which each kind found most suitable for obtaining therein their pasture or their prey."[13]

At this point there were no human beings in the world – the earth was inhabited by these "first ones," as Perrot described them. These first ones may not have been human, but they were *persons*. They had law and government. The Great Hare was their leader, and he called a council of all the beings to discuss what course of action should be taken to provide land for them and who should take on the responsibility of trying to acquire the sand. These beings all had souls, and they could pass their souls to subsequent generations of related beings. As Perrot then noted: "When the first ones died, the Great Hare caused the birth of men from their corpses, as also from those of the fishes which were found along the shores of the rivers which he had formed in creating the land."[14] Perrot goes on to explain that the Anishinabek therefore "derive their origin from a bear, others from a moose, and others similarly from various kinds of animals ... You will hear them say that their villages

---

10 Basil Johnston, "Is That All There Is?" 7–8.
11 Note that while Nicolas Perrot genders the Great Hare male, because there is no third-person masculine or feminine pronoun in Anishnaabemowin, the Great Hare/Nanabozhoo could be described as female by either the teller or the listener. Storytellers today do this as well. See for example the Mandaamin story as told by Lindsay Borrows, in which she changes genders of some of the characters. Lindsay Keegitah Borrows, *Otter's Journey*, 156–9.
12 Perrot, "Mémoire," in Blair, *Indian Tribes*, 1:32.
13 Perrot's words here are in translation from his original French by Emma Blair. Perrot, "Mémoire," in Blair, *Indian Tribes*, 1:31–7.
14 Ibid., 1:5–6.

each bear the name of the animal which has given its people their being – as that of the crane, or the bear, or of other animals."[15]

This narrative reveals some fundamental aspects of the Anishinaabe worldview, aspects that are distinct from Christianity.[16] In the Anishinaabe worldview, God or the Creator did not bring forth humans independent of animals; instead, humans came from the animals (a perspective, one might note, much more in alignment with contemporary science on evolution). Anishinaabe philosophy and worldview interprets this connection between humans and animals as one of interdependence or even simply dependence – where humans are dependent upon animals and other ensouled life. The human-animal relationship is similar to a sibling relationship – animals are the elder siblings, humans the younger. Humans have much to learn from their older siblings.[17] Perrot's story also demonstrates how doodemag define the Anishinabek as a distinct people. The version told by Perrot locates each doodem in a distinct territory, since each ancestor being "withdrew into the places where each kind found most suitable for obtaining therein their pasture or prey."[18] Only then did humans emerge from the bodies of the "first ones" and begin to take responsibility for the lands on which they were born. In the story told to Perrot, humans being are descended from, and therefore kin to, the other-than-human beings who are their doodem. Beaver people and beavers, for example, were related to one another. And as kin they had obligations to each other. In this version told to Perrot, the doodem tradition was created in the waters and on the lands of the Great Lakes region.

In a 1723 letter to his brother, the Jesuit Sebastian Râle recorded a flood origin story with elements similar to Perrot's version, which also situated the origins of the Anishinaabe people right in the Great Lakes. Râle had arrived in Quebec in the fall of 1689 and immediately began language studies. After a two-year sojourn among the Wabanaki (also known as the Algonquian-speaking Abenaki of what today are the northern New England states), Râle was recalled to Quebec and then sent out to a mission among the Illinois. With winter advancing, Râle was obliged to wait at Michilimackinac until spring with people

---

15 Ibid., 1:37–8.
16 Vine Deloria Jr. discusses these distinctions in *God is Red*.
17 Basil Johnston, *Ojibwe Heritage*, 46.
18 Perrot, "Mémoire," in Blair, *Indian Tribes*, 1:37.

he called the Outaouacks (the Ottawa-Anishinabek). Like Bawaating, Michilimackinac was a major historic council site. That winter, Râle heard their origin stories; he reproduced snippets in his letters to his brother about the origins of the principal doodemag comprising the council at Michilimackinac:

> They declare that they have come from three families, and each family is composed of five hundred persons.
>
> Some are of the family of Michabous, – that is to say, of "the Great Hare": They affirm that this Great Hare was a man of prodigious height; that he spread nets in water eighteen brasses deep, and that the water scarcely came to his armpits. They say one day, during the deluge, he sent out the Beaver to discover land; then, as that animal did not return, he despatched the Otter, which brought back a little soil covered with foam. He then proceeded to the place in the Lake where this soil was found, which made a little island; he walked all around it in the water, and this island became extraordinarily large. Therefore, they attribute to him the creation of the world. They add that, after having finished this work, he flew away to the Sky, which is his usual dwelling place; but before quitting the earth he directed that, when his descendants should die, their bodies should be burned, and their ashes scattered to the winds, so that they might be able to rise more easily to the Sky ...
>
> The second family of the Outaouacks maintain that they have sprung from Namepich [namebin, white sucker], – that is to say, from the Carp. They say that the carp having deposited its eggs upon the bank of a river, and the sun having shed rays upon them, there was formed a woman from whom they are descended; thus they are called, "the family of the Carp."
>
> The third family of the Outaouacks attributes its origin to the paw of a Machoua [makwa, bear] – that is to say, of a Bear; and they are called "the family of the Bear," but without explaining in what way they issued from it.[19]

Perrot and Râle independently provided accounts both of the creation of the Anishinaabe world and the foundation of the institution of doodemag, in which people are descended from and related to other-than-human beings. Michabous (the Great Hare) came from the sky world

---

19 Punctuation appears as in the original. Râle, "Lettre à Monsieur son Frére, October 12, 1723," in Thwaites, *Jesuit Relations*, 67:153–7. Râle reflects on his long career in this letter.

(his domain). Because of this fact, the souls of his descendants needed to be returned to the sky. The White Sucker doodem people are descended from a woman who emerged out of carp eggs deposited in a riverbank, and people who had this doodem would have known which river it was. The "family of the Bear" had the Bear's foot as their doodem – signifying their origin from "the paw of a Machoua [makwa, bear], connected to and part of the Bear doodem." The Bear doodem once had so many people, Warren later noted, that it was divided into families that were parts of the bear. The Mississauga-Anishinaabe leader Peter Jones also identified the Bear's foot as a separate Anishinaabe doodem in the mid-nineteenth century, and the anthropologist William Jones found people with this doodem in 1920s Minnesota.[20]

Returning to Râle's description, recall that spouses kept their doodem when they married. There the "family" which Râle described would have been the doodem of the ogimaa, gichi-Anishinabek, and their brothers, sons, and daughters. The wives of these men would have had different doodemag. European observers like Râle, recall, likened doodem to coats of arms or the "marks" of their families, and it is highly probable that French observers simply assumed that these identities would have been applied to women upon marriage. The fact that Râle reported that the family of the Carp described themselves as descended from a woman is also not necessarily an exception to the principle of patrilineal descent. Having been born from the eggs of a female sucker, the practice of patrilineal descent of the doodem was likely still followed by those who had this fish as their doodem. Together, these narratives are describe kinship of the soul between doodem beings and human beings.

The doodem origin narratives told in William Warren's *History of the Ojibway People* at first glance look quite different from Perrot's and Râle's and seem to be a history also of Anishinaabe migration. Yet on closer examination, Warren's version has much in common with these earlier versions. In Warren's account, the story opens with the Anishinaabe already alive, living on the "shores of a great salt water" at a time "when the earth was new." Six manidoog (ensouled spirit beings) emerged from the water and came into the homes of these Anishinaabe. One of the six cast his glance on an Anishinaabe and killed him with

---

20 See Warren and Neill, *History*, 49; William Jones, Ethnographic and linguistic field notes on the Ojibwa Indians, folder 1, APS.

Table 1. Doodem identities given in William Warren's *History of the Ojibwe People*

Original doodemag	A-wause (Channel Catfish)	Bus-in-as-see (Echo-maker, Crane)	Ah-ah-wauk (Loon)	Noka (Bear)	Moose-neeg (Moose)
Doodemag descended from original families	Merman Sturgeon Pike Whitefish Sucker	Crane Eagle	Goose Cormorant	Bear's Foot, Bear's Head, Bear's Rib, etc.	Marten Caribou

Including the original five described in the doodem origin story and additional new doodemag Warren described as descended from these original families.

Source: Warren, *History of the Ojibwe People*, 44–5.

that look; the other five beings decided that this sixth one was too powerful and sent him back into the water. The five remaining lived among the Anishinabek and bestowed upon their new allies their identities as gifts: Awause (Catfish), Businasee (Crane), Ahahwauk (Loon), Noka (Bear), and Mooseneeg (Moose). According to the oral histories told to Warren, all the many different doodemag he described were descended from one of these five original families.[21]

It is possible to draw the conclusion that Warren's creation story is a fundamentally different account than Perrot's. It seems to occur at an earlier point in the creation chronology. The migration story from a great salt water seems inconsistent with narratives that the Anishinaabe peoples have lived in the Great Lakes region since time immemorial or that their cultural and political traditions developed here. However, a careful reading of Warren's book reveals that he played with his readers.[22] Warren introduced puzzles and subverted the order of the narratives, while leaving verbal clues to indicate the intended order of the reading. For example, after discussing the origin of the doodem system in Chapter 2 (titled "Totemic Division of the O-Jib-Ways"), he waited until Chapter 3, "Origin of the O-Jib-Ways," to explain the Anishinaabe

---

21 Warren and Neill, *History*, 43–53.
22 I would like to acknowledge the importance of conversations with John Beishlag, a former fourth-year student of mine (HIS 472S, 2009) who wrote a fascinating term paper on the writings of William Warren. Beishlag found many examples where Warren was playing with the reader, proclaiming, for example, that he had never studied Hebrew, when in fact he had at the school he attended. Beishlag's work convinced me to take a fresh look at how Warren discussed the origins and importance of doodemag.

"Idea of Creation." One would think that, logically, creation would be discussed first. In Chapter 3, however, Warren told the story of the flood, which he clearly indicates occurred before the creation of the doodem tradition: "They fully believe, as it forms part of their religion, that the world has once been covered by a deluge, and that we are now living on what they term the 'new earth.'"[23] It was only after the flood, "through the medium of a powerful being, whom they denominated Man-ab-o-sho [Nanabozhoo], that they were allowed to exist, and means were given them whereby to subsist and support life."[24]

So here, as in Perrot and Râle's accounts collected two centuries earlier, there is a flood, and only following the flood does the doodem tradition emerge in the "new earth."[25] The clue to the correct ordering of the narrative is Warren's use of the phrase "new earth" in his mention of when the doodem tradition began – after the creation of the "new earth." Moreover, it is Man-ab-o-sho, or Nanabozhoo, the Great Hare, who restored the Anishinabek to life, although Warren did not reveal to his non-Anishinaabe audience exactly how the Great Hare brought the creation of the earth about.[26] In mid-nineteenth-century North America, claiming descent from other-than-human beings – or even according the category of personhood to other-than-human beings – would not have served Anishinaabe communities well, as they were already under intense pressure from colonial authorities to assimilate to the values of the now-dominant Christian society. This belief in other-than-human beings was still present in the early 1850s, when Warren wrote his manuscript. After all, none of the beings that emerged from the water to give the doodem tradition to the Anishinabek were human. It is these other-than-human beings who created the doodem tradition and, by extension, its founding the basis for Anishinaabe governance and law. The other-than-human actors remained key constitutional agents in Warren's narrative even if the tricky question of "how" the doodem beings bestowed their doodem identities on their descendants was left out of the story. As for the emergence of doodem beings from a great "salt water," it is important to keep in mind the dynamic hydrology of

---

23 Warren and Neill, *History*, 55.
24 Ibid. Warren also indicated that the Midewiwin medicine lodge appeared at the same time.
25 Ibid.
26 For a thorough discussion of Anishinaabe creation narratives, see Fisher, "Ojibwa Creation Myth."

North America following the last Ice Age. The Atlantic Ocean had an inlet as far as eastern Ontario around 12,000 to 10,000 years ago. The locations of the cities of Ottawa and Montreal were under as much as 100 metres of seawater at this time. Only as the continent rebounded from the weight of glaciation did the waters recede east slowly over time. Perhaps it is not that the ancestors of the Anishinabek migrated to the Great Lakes Region from what is now the east coast of North America but rather that the salt waters moved away from them.[27]

Other doodem origin narratives do not tie the idea of doodem to descent from another-than-human progenitor. However, they still connect doodem to place. One such story published in 1839 by Henry Rowe Schoolcraft, an Indian agent for the American government and an amateur anthropologist, linked the origin of the Crane doodem with Bawaating. In this version, human beings were already in existence. A particular family took the Crane as their family mark because a giant manidoo in the form of a crane ferried them safely across the rapids at Sault Ste. Marie, past another dangerous manidoo in the form of a woman's skull. The crane then took this skull and dashed it into the water, causing whitefish to be born from the maggots spilling out of the brain. In this story, those Anishinabek who took the Crane as their doodem now had a vital source of food as a gift from the First Crane.[28] This narrative still connects the doodem tradition to the realm of the sacred and is a powerful teaching about the importance of the First Crane. A manidoo is after all an ensouled being. In this story, there are two: one in the form of a crane and one in the form of a woman's skull. And regardless of physical form, the Crane manidoo was acting as a leader should, providing food for the people.

A third version collected in the early twentieth century by anthropologist Paul Radin places more evidence on the social function of doodemag. This version was also set in the days of Nanabozhoo, as he raised a family with his wife. As his children grew and left home, Nanabozhoo "thought he would have to do something in order that these people, as they multiplied, would know the relationship." He organized an enormous feast, to which he invited all his children and their families. As they were leaving, Nanabozhoo explained to them that, "your families are increasing very fast, and you will always be that

---

27 Gadd, *Late Quaternary Development of the Champlain Sea Basin.*
28 Schoolcraft, *Algic Researches*, 237–9. Citations refer to the Dover edition.

way. You will be scattered all over the country and will be far apart, so
I want each of you to take home one of these animals and one of the
fish, so that you, your children, your grandchildren, and their children
shall have them for totems. In this way you will know your relatives."[29]
In this version, there is no direct statement of descent from other-than-
human beings, although the story is ambiguous enough to suggest the
possibility that the animals and fish were also relatives. But the doodem
tradition was explained to Radin as if it were a badge of identity rather
than integrally connected to governance and spirituality. As I will discuss in detail in Chapter 5, the combined legislative, missionary and
regulatory assault on Indigenous polities was well underway by the last
quarter of the nineteenth century in both Canada and the United States.
Radin collected these narratives during his tour of southeastern Ontario
reserves from March to August 1912. These trips were funded by the
Geological Survey of Canada.[30] Those Radin interviewed included the
descendants of hereditary leaders, including Musquakie (Caribou doodem) at Rama and Robert Paudaush (Crane doodem) from Hiawatha.
It is hard to believe that these leaders and descendants of leaders were
not keenly aware the impact of Radin's research and of the dangers of
revealing any contemporary practice of "pagan" beliefs to outsiders.
While the narratives that Radin collected did contain stories of people
turning into animals, those narratives were set in mythic time. Furthermore, Radin's story of Nanabozhoo giving the doodem tradition to the
Anishinabek was not included in his published version.

The existence of different, and what appear at first to be competing,
versions of the origin of the doodem tradition can be understood when
the versions are themselves situated in larger narratives that provide
different explanations for how the Anishinabek came to be in the Great
Lakes. Narratives of in-situ emergence and narratives of migration
from the "shores of a great salt water" also record Anishinaabe historical experiences. The Great Lakes region has experienced major refor-
mations of its water and landscapes since the retreat of the last glaciers
11,0000 years ago that have had a correspondingly dramatic impact on
the ecosystem.[31] As discussed earlier in this chapter, only 10,000 years

---

29 Paul Radin, "Social and Religious Customs of the Ojibwa of Southeastern Ontario,"
    Canadian Museum of Civilization, Ethnological Records, Box 67 folder 1, 13–14.
30 Radin, *Some Myths and Tales*, v.
31 Clark, et al., "Model of Surface Water Hydrology."

ago the Atlantic Ocean had an inlet into North America that reached into southeastern Ontario. By 9,500 years ago, the lake levels were much lower than they are now. It was possible to walk from the Bruce Peninsula to Manitoulin Island. Over time, the lakes refilled, with occasions when water levels would have risen rapidly. Sometimes the rivers that drained into them experienced changes in the direction of their water flow due to isostatic rebound. These changes occurred while people were living in the region. Why would histories of such major environmental changes and dramatic events, such as rapidly changing water levels of lakes and rivers, not have survived? Stories of migration and movement also reflect lived historical experiences. As Chapter 3 will discuss in detail, the Anishinabek had developed protocols for establishing new sites of government and extending jurisdiction when required to deal with social and political change. While some Anishinaabe peoples maintained long-standing ties to particular lands, the Anishinaabe history of the Great Lakes also involves the movement of people and the relocation of council fires. Aadizookaanag that tell of floods, the emergence of the doodem tradition, and the migration of peoples are records of such experiences in deep time. These stories bundled Anishinaabe histories, environmental knowledge, and worldview into a form that passed down from generation to generation.

The Concept of Doodem Souls

The aadizookaanag that describe the origin of the doodem tradition also explain the close bond of kinship between the beings who share the same doodem. But in Anishinaabe worldview, kinship is expressed through the idea of shared souls, not shared blood. Understanding this distinction is critical for understanding the concept of personhood in Anishinaabe law. While both Anishinaabe and Christian beliefs include the concept of souls (an intangible animating essence, an animating life force), there are significant differences grounded in the worldviews of each tradition, each fundamentally concerned with humanity's place in the world in relationship to other life and to the spiritual world. Early and medieval Christians debated the character and the number of souls and engaged with the Greek philosopher Aristotle's idea of the soul as comprising three parts (of "nutrition, sensation and intellection") that effectively animate the body and manage its core functions. Other spiritual traditions also contributed to early Christian debates, including the Manichean idea from Late Antiquity Iran that humans had two souls, one good and one evil. Other early Christians argued against the idea of multiple souls (i.e., one of the body and one of the spirit), suggesting that these were but different aspects of one soul animating the body.[32] Medieval theologians including the noted scholar Thomas Aquinas concurred, contributing to a sense of the soul within the Catholic tradition as a single soul of three parts, united with the human body during life, divisible from the body at death, and reunited with the body at the Resurrection. The fate of the soul – whether it went on to eternal salvation or eternal damnation – depended on one's acceptance of Christianity, earthly behaviour, and divine judgment. Eternal salvation was something only the "rational" souls of human beings could achieve.[33] Debates about souls continued through the Renaissance period as part of the humanist movement, as scholars wrestled with the idea of what separates humans from animals and other forms of life.[34] When Jesuit missionaries arrived in the Great Lakes region in the early seventeenth century, they would have been well aware of these debates.

Anishinaabe sources expressed a radically different understanding of souls – one that considered humans as just one part of all life and not the most important part. In contrast with Christian theology, which understood human souls as something different from other life, Indigenous civilizations across Turtle Island shared a common belief that life was ensouled.[35] Furthermore, even something considered "not alive" in Western ontology could also have a spirit. As the example of the story of the Crane above shows, a manidoog could appear in the form of a woman's skull – something once part of a human but, in Western worldview, something considered not alive. Rock can also contain a soul. Life in Anishinaabe worldview is that which has a soul. If an entity has a soul, it is also a person in Anishinaabe law. An Anishinaabe soul is as an essence that can transcend physical forms and/or move between them.[36] In Anishinaabe worldview, the human body is home to at least two souls. One soul expresses the essence of the individual; it is this soul that can leave the

---

32 The scholarship in the fields of Christian theology and the study of religion on the question of souls from late Antiquity through the Early Modern period is large. The discussion here is from Bauerschmidt and Buckley, *Catholic Theology*; James Lee, "John Donne."

33 Bauerschmidt and Buckley, *Catholic Theology*, 86–7.

34 James Lee, "John Donne," 884–5.

35 Angel, *Preserving the Sacred*, 41.

36 Ibid., 35; Darlene Johnston, "Litigating Identity," 72.

body (even when the person is alive), and it is this soul that can travel to the afterlife.[37] The other soul is shared with the doodem, as the doodem itself also has a soul – an animating essence in common with all who have that doodem. Shared souls forge the relational link between doodem kin, both humans and other-than-humans, throughout the Great Lakes region and beyond, connecting ancestors and descendants.

It is this concept of souls, and particularly the idea of a doodem soul, which explains why the Anishinabek historically felt that it was important to return the dead to the country of their birth, as we saw in the example of the 1642 gathering discussed in the Introduction. While the soul that was the essence of the individual leaves the body after death and travels west to re-join other relatives who have died, there is another soul that remains with the body and resides within the bones and only leaves the bones when it is "recycled" into a descendant. An individual's soul could even depart before the death of the physical body, but the second, the body soul, would remain behind.[38] In 1639, the Jesuit Paul Le Jeune spoke with an Anishinaabe Elder who poignantly expressed to Le Jeune the grief felt by survivors whose loved ones have passed on: "They distinguish several souls in one and the same body. An old man told us some time ago that some ... have as many as two or three souls; that his own had left him more than two years before, to go away with his dead relatives, – that he no longer had any but the soul of his body, which would go down into the grave with him."[39] What remained to animate this Elder's still-breathing body was a "body-soul" that would be buried with his physical remains. As Father Le Jeune further observed of the same conversation, "One learns from this that they imagine the body has a soul of its own, which some call the soul of their Nation."[40] Nearly a century later, the French writer

---

37 Vecsey, *Traditional Ojibwa Religion*, 59–61. Vecsey distinguishes between the travelling "free soul" which lives in the brain, and the ego-soul, which lives in the heart. The ego-soul remains with the body. Johnston and I think this ego-soul is the doodem soul – residing in the heart, remaining with the body.

38 Johnston, "Litigating Identity," 78.

39 The ellipsis removes the word "Savages." *Sauvage* in the original French did not have the same extreme negative connation that Thwaites's translation gives. Le Jeune, "Relation of 1640–41," in Thwaites, *Jesuit Relations*, 16:191–3. See also the writings of Jean de Brebeuf, S.J., who observed that the Wendat believed in multiple souls as well, saying the Wendat "call the bones of the dead Atisken, or the souls"; de Brebeuf, "Relation of the Hurons, 1636," in Thwaites, *Jesuit Relations*, 10:287.

40 Le Jeune, "Relation of 1640–41," in Thwaites, *Jesuit Relations*, 16:191–3.

Pierre Charlevoix made a similar observation: "There are others who acknowledge two souls in men; to the one, they attribute every thing I have been just now speaking of, and pretend that the other never quits the body, unless it is to pass into some other."[41] More than three hundred years after Le Jeune's conversation with the Elder awaiting his passing, in 1992, Anishinaabe Elders from the Chippewa of Nawash First Nation expressed the same insight concerning the divisibility of souls and how body souls remained with the bones. They did so to Darlene Johnston, during their community's eight-day vigil to protect a burial ground located within the city limits of Owen Sound.[42] The bones buried within this cemetery were not simply human remains, but they were in fact *ensouled* remains – still possessing qualities of personhood and agency and still in relationship with the living.

Johnston explains that the body-soul to which Le Jeune referred – what he called the "soul of their Nation" – was in fact the soul of the doodem.[43] Johnston's interpretation makes complete sense; Anishinaabe practices and protocols for the treatment of the dead support this finding. Historically, people displayed doodem images prominently on grave markers. The deceased were, wherever possible, interred in the land of their birth, even if that meant carrying their bones considerable distances. These practices are old. In 1612, Samuel de Champlain visited an Anishinaabe cemetery on the Ottawa River at the summer council site of the ogimaa Tessouat. There, Champlain observed aboveground, wood-covered graves with marker posts ("in the form of shrines"). On those posts, people carved images to indicate the deceased person's doodem and accomplishments in life, particularly if the deceased had been a chief.[44] Recall too the evidence discussed in the Introduction – how at regional gatherings Anishinaabe returned home the bones of those who had died outside the land of their birth. Doodem remained important in Anishinaabe funeral practices. Nearly two hundred years after Champlain, in 1793, the British officer Major E.B. Littlehales reported seeing doodem-inscribed grave markers as he accompanied the new

---

41 Charlevoix, *Letters to the Duchess*, 2:153.
42 The community was successful in having the federal government recognize the land as part of an existing treaty, protecting it from development. See Darlene Johnston, *Connecting People to Place*.
43 Darlene Johnston, "Litigating Identity," 78.
44 de Champlain, *Works*, 2:279–80.

Lieutenant Governor of Upper Canada, John Graves Simcoe, on a tour of what is now southern Ontario. Littlehales observed aboveground burials of "raised earth ... wickered over," and beside the graves "a large pole with painted hieroglyphics on it, denoting the Nation, Tribe and achievements of the deceased, either as Chiefs, Warriors, or Hunters."[45] Inscribing the doodem of the deceased on a grave post (see Figure 12) allowed others of the same doodem to recognize the grave as that of one of their immediate kin, one who shared the same doodem soul.

These deep familial bonds created by the doodem tradition transcended certain binaries that exist in Western thought, such as living and dead, human and animal. Doodem is the source of metaphor describing what it means to be related to someone. To share a doodem is to be immediate kin. In contrast, Western Europeans define immediate kin though the metaphor of shared blood – the more blood one is presumed to share, the closer the relationship. This equally potent metaphor, used to describe descent-based relatedness, is an idea drawn from Aristotelian concepts of generation.[46] The Western tradition of patrilineal descent and family names, and of the social importance of the male "lineage" to create "blood ties," continues today, despite the knowledge that a foetus has an independent blood supply, separated from the mother's by the placenta, and blood isn't a substance that is typically shared between people outside the context of transfusion. If anything, the discovery of DNA and the modern focus on genetics as the connective force in family relationships has only strengthened older ideas about the importance of blood in defining who is kin, even though more precisely the link is through genetic material.[47] But for the Anishinabek, while some doodem kin would have close biological

---

45 Littlehales, "Journal from Niagara to Detroit, 1793," 289.
46 This is an over-simplification of complex and diverse metaphors pertaining to sex and sexual reproduction in early modern Europe, but it is significant in demonstrating its distinction from Anishinaabe worldview. See Laqueur, *Making Sex.*
47 French and English legal regimes had different, and changing, approaches to the problem of adoptive or fictive kin, as opposed to birth or "real" kin. In both societies, the adoption of children was a marked category distinct from family formation through birth. The question of "blood ties" was particularly important in determining inheritance rights and subjecthood (citizenship). See, for example, Gager, *Blood Ties and Fictive Ties.* English law made room for consideration of the national identity of the child's mother in determining subjecthood status until legislative changes in the nineteenth century – see Todd, "Mother's Blood."

relationships, other doodem kin would not.[48] Note that the blood metaphor sometimes appears in both colonial and Anishinaabe sources that discuss the doodem tradition. The Jesuit Louis Nicolas wrote in the late seventeenth century of the honour felt by members of the Hare doodem "to say that all their race was of this divine blood [referring here to Nanabozhoo] ... they say openly and in their right minds that they are directly descended from this majestic divinity ... For this reason they put in their escutcheon, as their arms, a great hare that makes the snow fall"[49] Nicolas here connects the writing or inscribing of the doodem image with the idea of relatedness to the doodem being. William Warren also used the blood metaphor extensively to discuss doodem kin, likening the doodem to a "blood relationship" and noting that "any individual of any one of the several Totems, belonging to a distinct tribe, as for instance the Ojibway, is a close blood relation to all the other Indians of the same Totem, both in his own and all other tribes, though he may be divided from them by a long vista of years, interminable miles, and knows not even of their existence."[50] In each case though the writers were consciously reaching for an analogy to explain this concept of relatedness to their Western audiences in terms that audience would understand. These are acts of interpretation rather than expressing an idea integral to Anishinaabe worldview.

Doodem identity was and is of such importance because of its connection to what Westerners would describe as the spiritual and the sacred. While doodem identities inscribed on treaty and other documents appear to be in a secular context, Anishinaabe readers of those images would also have recognized their spiritual significance. They were well versed in other narratives and other meanings associated with those doodem beings. Such narratives tied doodem identities to the very creation of the world, the emergence of the Anishinabek, and the creation of relationships between the living, the dead, and place. Doodem was also an assertion of responsibility for the lands and waters of one's doodem being. In the origin narratives told to the interpreter Nicolas Perrot by Anishinaabe Elders in the late seventeenth century, after the creation of the world the First Beings moved into the places

---

48 This idea is expressed in Bohaker, "*Nindoodemag*: The Significance of Algonquian Kinship Networks," 38.

49 Nicolas, *Codex Canadensis*, 313, 324. An escutcheon is a shield or other emblem on which a coat of arms is displayed.

50 Warren and Neil, *History*, 42–3.

best suited "for their pasture or prey."[51] In Perrot's retelling of the aadi-zookaanag, as Nanabozhoo (Michabous) brought forth the first human beings from the corpses of the First Beings, so subsequent generations of Anishinabek received their respective doodemag from the souls of their ancestors. I have found one seventeenth-century exception to the idea of repatriating the bones of the deceased that still fits the general principle, which is really about returning doodem souls to the lands to which they belong. For those Anishinabek who traced their descent from Michabous (the Great Hare), souls had to be repatriated through burning the bones of the deceased. This exception has a cultural logic grounded in core Anishinaabe beliefs because Michabous was from the Sky world. As the Jesuit Sebastian Râle was told in a passage previously cited, Michabous himself "directed that, when his descendants should die, their bodies should be burned, and their ashes scattered to the winds, so that they might be able to rise more easily to the Sky."[52]

In the case of the Hare doodem, burning the bones of the deceased was a practice still grounded in the logic of shared souls connected to a particular landscape. In this case, because the Hare doodem's place was the Sky world, the burning of bones was entirely consistent with the goal of repatriating the body-soul of the deceased.

Through the aadizookaanag that spoke of the creation of the doodem tradition, Anishinaabe people could situate themselves in the landscape of the Great Lakes, even if they were some distance from the place of their own birth. Those of the Hare doodem could look to the island of Mich-ilimackinac and know its special significance as the home of Michabous and, by extension, his many descendants. The descendants of the Great Beaver knew the final resting place of their ancestor was on the northeast-ern shore of Georgian Bay at the outlet of French River, while those of the Crane could look to Bawaating. Doodem origin narratives create a sense of both belonging to and responsibility for particular places. Doodem as metaphor could extend further to shape requests for aid, to request access to resources even by people who were not of that doodem. In the late seventeenth century, for example, Perrot was told that

If, when any stranger or poor widow in need near these Amikoüas [Amik-wag, or those who gathered at the council fire kept by the Beaver doodem

---

51 Perrot, "Mémoire," in Blair, *Indian Tribes*, 1:5–6.
52 Râle, "Lettre à Monsieur son Frère."in Thwaites, *Jesuit Relations*, 67:153–7.

ogimaa at Lake Nipissing or the eastern shore of Georgian Bay] or any one of their clan, they see a branch that has been gnawed at night by some beaver, the first person who finds it at the entrance of his tent picks it up and carries it to the head of the clan, who immediately causes a supply of food to be collected for this poor person, as a memorial of their ancestors; and those in the villages willingly club together to make a present to him who has done them the honour of recalling them to their origin. They do not practice this with the Frenchmen, since these deride them and their superstition.[53]

Doodemag are described within aadizookaanag narratives recorded by seventeenth- and eighteenth-century non-Anishinaabe observers in ways that reveal the doodem tradition to be an old one, with deep generational and historic roots. Such origin stories also describe the fundamental importance of gift exchange and reciprocity as a means of cementing relationships between beings, as the example from Perrot above suggests. But this understanding of doodem as a gift continues. As William Warren described it much later in his mid-nineteenth century text, the doodem tradition is itself a gift to the Anishinabek and, as a gift, it creates an obligation between humans and other-than-human beings of the same doodem to share resources and to assist one another as kin should do.[54]

Doodem origin stories reveal a political tradition that created interconnected communities spanning long distances while anchoring people to the places they called home. European observers of the tradition instead likened doodem to their own extended families. By calling doodem images "coats of arms," French colonists attempted to find a parallel practice from within their own culture. But the doodem tradition was developed within, and as a central part of, Anishinaabe worldview and understandings of the natural world. Bears, cranes, and caribou are all Anishinaabe doodemag and are also beings who/that inhabit (or inhabited, in the case of the caribou) the Great Lakes region. However, other beings, including the *animikiig* (thunderbirds), *nebaanaabeg* (mermen), and the *michi-bizhi* (underwater manidoog), are also doodemag. In Anishinaabe worldview, these beings are accorded the same

---

53 Perrot, "Mémoire," in Blair, *Indian Tribes*, 1:63–4.
54 Warren, *History*, 44. Warren uses the word "blessing" to describe the gift of the "totemic divisions."

potentiality for personhood as other flora and fauna. Collectively, then, all doodemag are drawn from Anishinaabe cosmology and Anishinaabe understandings of the world.

Anishinaabe doodemag are a small set of all life in the Great Lakes region, but they share common qualities that are metaphorically productive in terms of Anishinaabe cultural values. These metaphors, in turn, illuminate the political and social significance of each doodem and, in short, their relevance to law and governance. Doodem images functioned as a visual metaphor for Anishinaabe readers that were connected to a much larger set of cultural knowledge and allegorical associations. Doodem pictographs evoked additional, and often bi-directional, associations between the person and his or her doodem identity, further connecting that person to the larger Anishinaabe corpus of narratives featuring their doodem being. At the most basic level, these associations could refer to physical characteristics or shared behavioural qualities. The concept of an inheritable, shared doodem soul provided a descent-based explanation for common physical characteristics among people with the same doodem. Anishinaabe peoples understood that related people had similar appearances; they extended that logic to include a physical resemblance to their other-than-human ancestors. According to Perrot, the late seventeenth-century French fur trader, the Anishinabek suspected that the French, because of their beards, were related to the Bear family.[55] Nearly two centuries later, William Warren personally observed that members of the Bear doodem are "possessed of a long, thick coarse head of the blackest hair, which seldom becomes thin or white in old age." He also remarked that all those of who had various fish as doodemag were "physically noted for being long lived, and for the scantiness and fineness of their hair, especially in old age; if you see an old Indian of this tribe with a bald head, you may be certain that he is A-waus-e."[56] People felt that the soul of the doodem had agency over the individual and that it had the potential to shape one's physical form.

Several sources indicate how doodem as metaphor could also shape the trajectory of individual lives. Warren describes how the leadership role in councils that was undertaken by members of the Loon doodem was visually reinforced by the fact that the common loon has markings

---

55 Perrot, "Mémoire," in Blair, *Indian Tribes*, 1:309.
56 Warren and Neill, *History*, 43, 49.

around its neck, resembling the wampum shell collars that leaders wore to indicate their status and political role.[57] Anishinabek of the Loon doodem, then, could expect to step into leadership roles. As Anishinaabe teacher Basil Johnston explains in his 1976 *Ojibway Heritage*, "as these animals were endowed with certain traits of character, so did the Anishinabek endeavour to emulate that character, and make it part of themselves. Each animal symbolized an ideal to be sought, attained, and perpetuated."[58] While the Jesuits and other Catholic missionaries might look to the lives of saints, for example, the Anishinabek sought (and seek) the teaching and wisdom of the elder animals, through parable and metaphor, to guide them.[59]

People drew metaphors for leadership from doodem beings of all sizes and shapes. While the strength and size of an animal like the bear or eagle makes each seem an obvious choice to produce metaphors for leadership, smaller animals are also doodem beings and served similar purposes. The northern clear water crayfish, the most common species in the Great Lakes, is an assertive defender of its territory; the few doodem images I have of this species show it raising its claws to attack or defend.[60] The small muskrat plays a central role in the earth diver narrative in the creation story as the being who successfully returns a grain of sand to Michabous/Nanabozhoo so that he can fashion the earth. Consequently, as Basil Johnson points out, the muskrat "possesses and reflects" the quality of endurance, as do those who share that doodem. All doodem beings have different qualities connected with leadership characteristics: Johnston also notes that cranes have "eloquence for leadership," white-headed eagles have "foresight," bears "strength and courage," caribou "grace and watchfulness," pike "swiftness and eloquence," and catfish "breath and scope."[61]

Warren ascribes similar qualities to the five original doodemag, commenting on the strength of the Bears but also of their fondness for fighting, and the leadership qualities of the Crane and Loon because of their strong voices. Another contemporary Anishinaabe traditional

---

57 Ibid.
58 Basil Johnston, *Ojibwe Heritage*, 53.
59 Ibid., 46.
60 Page, "Crayfishes and Shrimps."
61 Basil Johnston, *Ojibway Heritage*, 53.

teacher, Edward Benton-Banai, explains in his 1979 book *The Mishomis Book: The Voice of the Ojibway* the distinctions between each doodem in terms of roles, in that "each of these clans was given a function to serve for the people."[62] Johnston, Warren, and Benton-Banai all describe doodemag serving as potent metaphors that can shape individual character and life choices of people, while also connecting through doodem identity to specific political roles and to places. This idea that one's doodem shaped one's physical form as well as one's character is evident in sources dating from the seventeenth century to the present day. And all of the beings discussed here appear as doodem images on Great Lakes treaties that were signed on documents beginning in 1671, providing a continuous chain of evidence of the importance of doodem to law and governance and the role of doodem in shaping how people defined their roles and responsibilities within councils and communities.

Basil Johnston provides some further insight into how doodemag and their connection to other-than-human beings are reflected in Anishinaabe worldview. He explains how human beings are dependent upon animal beings – their kin, or "elder brothers" – in three fundamental ways: first, and most obviously, physically, as these other-than-human beings fed Anishinaabe people with their bodies, and second, provided them with tools and clothing from their skins and bones. But there was another equally, if not more, important level of dependence: "for knowledge of the world, life and himself."[63] As Johnston explains, "There is in animals a unique capacity to sense the changes of the world, the alternation of the seasons, and the coming state of things. Man does not have the preknowledge possessed by bluebird or trout, or squirrel. For man to prepare, he looked to his elder brothers." And by this Johnston meant that the Anishinabek should look to what Western Europeans would call the animal world. As Johnston explains, because of their importance, because of humanity's dependence upon them, and because

---

62 Warren and Neill, *History*, 49: "It is a general saying, and an observable fact, amongst their fellows, that the bear clan resemble the animal that forms their Totem in disposition. They are ill-tempered and fond of fighting, and consequently they are noted as ever having kept the tribe in difficulty and war with other tribes, in which, however, they have generally been the principal and foremost actors"; Benton-Banai, *Mishomis Book*, 74.

63 Basil Johnston, *Ojibway Heritage*, 52.

humans needed these other-than-human beings to sacrifice themselves
so that they might live, "the Anishinaabe included them in almost all of
their stories."[64] As Basil Johnston's discussion suggests, some of these
beings were particularly productive in terms of metaphor; they all have
in common, as doodemag, some quality or qualities that resonated with
the Anishinabek.

Today, many continue to assert that doodem identities have particular social roles to fulfil because of the behavioural characteristics they
share with their doodem namesake. Thus, people with the Bear doodem are described as protectors and are likely to take up occupations in
policing, the military, and healing. Cranes and Loons are still regarded
in many communities as most likely to work in politics or leadership,
while people of the Marten doodem are particularly noted for their
work in mediation. Those having fish doodemag, identities associated
with wisdom and learning, are more likely to seek careers in teaching.
A member of the Sturgeon doodem, when a newly elected chief of his
First Nation, enumerated to me the many members of *his* Sturgeon doodem kin who all work in the education sector – logical career choices,
given the connection between fish doodemag, teaching, learning, and
wisdom.[65]

These comparatively more recent sources suggest that the relationship between humans and their doodem identities was and is limited
to metaphor. When these nineteenth- and twentieth-century authors
explain that people of the Pike doodem are *like* fish because they have
little body hair and that people of the Bear doodem are *like* bears in
that they have much body hair, they are employing metaphor. But
older sources, and some oral traditions that survive today, indicate
that people clearly understood these connections in terms of shared
souls and also saw the possibility of metamorphosis from one physical
form to another. One constant theme in Anishinaabe oral traditions is
the ability for people to move between human and non-human forms.
Doodem images support this insight: some writers, particularly those
of the Crane and Caribou doodemag, drew track marks to indicate
their doodem identities. After all, that is one important way in which

---

64 Ibid., 56.

65 Benton-Banai, *Mishomis Book*, 77; Basil Johnston, *Ojibway Heritage*, 59–61. On the
    Sturgeon doodem: Reg Niaganobe, Ogimaa, Misissauga First Nation, Blind River,
    Ontario, personal communication, fall 2011.

Table 2 Basil Johnston's chart of doodemag organized by social/governance function

Leadership	Defence	Sustenance	Learning	Medicine
Chejauk (Crane)	Noka (Bear)	Waubizhaezh (Marten)	Mizi (Catfish)	Makinauk (Turtle)
Wawa (Goose)	Myeengun (Wolf)	Amik (Beaver)	Kinozhae (Pike)	Negik (Otter)
Mong (Loon)	Pizheu (Lynx)	Moozo (Moose)	Numaebin (Sucker)	Medawaewae (Rattle snake)
Kaihaik (Hawk)		Addick (Caribou)	Numae (Sturgeon)	Muzundumo (Black Snake)
Peepeegizaence (Sparrow Hawk)		Wawashkaesh (Deer)	Addikmeg (Whitefish)	Mukukee (Frog)
Migizi (White-headed Eagle)		Wuzhushk (Muskrat)		Nebaunaube (Merman) or Nebaunaubequae (Mermaid)
Kineu (Black-headed Eagle)				
Makataezheeb (Brant)				
Kayaushk (Seagull)				

Source: Johnston, *Ojibway Heritage*, 60.

a caribou or a crane leaves behind an impression of itself. These statements of shared physicality express the Anishinaabe idea that the same ensouled being could inhabit different physical forms. These ideas continued to be expressed in the twentieth century; despite the impact of colonialism, missionization pressures, and residential schools, this worldview has survived. For example, the artist Selwyn Dewdney, who researched Anishinaabe *midewiwin* scrolls in the 1960s, was told by those he interviewed that they were aware when their doodem was hunted or fished, because they themselves were that being.[66] This understanding also explains some taboos that existed against hunting or eating other-than-human beings who shared one's doodem identity.

---

66 Dewdney, *Sacred Scrolls*, 30.

The potential for metamorphosis in Anishinaabe culture also existed in another, more destructive context: that of *wiindigoog*. A *wiindigoo* is a wild and dangerous being that travels alone and feasts on the unwary. People could become windigoog under certain conditions, and they presented a grave danger to the community.[67] In one narrative told by Elder Maude Kegg (1904–96), titled "When Aazhawakiwenzhiinh Almost Became a Windigo," she explains the connection between a person's doodem and the cannibal actions of a wiindigoo as follows: "he who is a windigo sees the other Indians as their totems. He sees anybody who has a Bear for his totem as a bear, and so he kills and eats him, and so with someone who has the Deer as his totem. If anyone has a Beaver as his totem, that's how he sees him and so he kills and eats him."[68] Kegg's account explains the violation of a taboo act in terms of the wiindigoo's vision: a wiindigoo commits a horrible act because they see the doodem soul and not the human person.

The physical connection between the Anishinabek and their doodemag was reinforced even further when people wore materials or marks on their bodies that proclaimed their identity. There is a remarkable continuity between descriptions of this practice from seventeenth-century sources through to the twentieth century. Louis Nicolas, observing in the second half of the seventeenth century, noted the eldest member of the Hare doodem was "always dressed or wrapped in the manner of the natives in a robe of the skin of hares, which had to be killed during the time of snows so that these rare skins would be all white, and so that this illustrious elder descended from the great hare god would always wear the livery and the colour of this divinity."[69] Nearly two centuries later, Peter Jones wore a coat that had his Eagle doodem embroidered on the lapel at his audience with Queen Victoria in 1844.[70] Even into the twentieth century, people

---

67 Basil Johnston explains that *wiindigoos* were invoked or discussed as punishment for excess: greed, gluttony, coveting, etc. See Johnston, *Ojibway Heritage*, 165–7; see also John Borrows, "Windigos," in *Drawing Out Law*, 216–27.

68 Kegg and Nichols, "When Aazhawakiwenzhiinh Almost Became a Windigo." My thanks to Alan Corbiere for bringing this source to my attention.

69 Nicolas, *Codex Canadensis*, 313.

70 Willmott, "Clothed Encounters," 477.

used both materials and symbols to communicate doodem identity.[71] It continues today, as people wear sometimes large and sometimes small images or material references to their doodem identities on dance regalia at powwows and in other formal settings such as present-day council meetings.

Doodemag as a System of Categories

While the doodem tradition connects people to their history and to each other as relatives, it is very much also a framework for thinking with and for organizing and making sense of the world. It provides a system of categories. Categories matter: they are "the building blocks in the creation of knowledge and in the application of knowledge to situations." To understand how and why people took the actions that they did across different periods, it is critical that we understand each culture's fundamental categories and how people of those cultures used those categories. For the Anishinabek, race, class, and social rank were far less relevant than doodem.[72] While it appears simplest to describe the doodem tradition as a kinship category, it is more accurate to describe it a "system of categories." Specific doodem such as Bear and Beaver are categories within the main set of doodemag in the same way in which

---

71 Jenness observed that "otter people worked an otter in beadwork on the front of the coat, and the loon people attached the head of a loon." Jenness, *Ojibwa Indians of Parry Island*, 8. The practice has continued in more recent years: as young girl growing up on the Bruce Peninsula, Professor Darlene Johnston's grandmother explained that her winter moccasins were dressed with otter fur because she was Otter doodem: "I was sitting at Grammie's round, claw-legged, table that was always covered with the white hand-crocheted cloth. She passed to me the most beautiful pair of moccasins, the ones that reach nearly to the knee. They were beaded, but it's not the beadwork that I remember. I was drawn to the dark, silky fur that trimmed the top. I remember asking her what kind of fur it was. She told me it was Otter. I probably asked her why, because the next thing I remember her saying was that she was Otter clan ... She said that she was Otter because her Father was Otter and her Father's Father before him and her Father's Father before him; that her father had been the last in a long line of hereditary chiefs from the Otter clan." Johnston, "Litigating Identity," 45.

72 Shoemaker, "Categories," 51.

"male" and "female" are categories within the larger set of categories that is gender.[73]

Kinship is a significant emic, or insider-based, category; so, for the Anishinabek, being Crane was and is a distinct category from being Loon. Historians have become increasingly aware of how kinship is a potent source of metaphors for defining political relationships in North American Indigenous societies. This awareness is crucial for understanding how Indigenous allies understood their relationships with each other and how these metaphors structured the practices of Indigenous-European diplomacy.[74] Such awareness is also important for understanding how the Anishinabek negotiated the experiences of encounter, missionization, and colonization from within their own worldview. The doodem tradition embodied a system of categories that had both social and political meaning – in the way that race, class, and gender continue to be socially and culturally significant in the world today. The doodem tradition is a set of categories embedded in Anishinaabe epistemology.

Like so many concepts used in ethnohistorical research, the problem with kinship as a category of analysis is that it can carry a great deal of unconscious baggage. We think we know what kinship means because all human beings, regardless of culture, find their lives shaped by kin and kin ties; as a result, we have a tendency to apply our own understanding of that category to the people or culture under study. But kinship as a category of analysis requires an understanding of how kinship operates in the culture in question. Within each cultural tradition, it is vital to consider how declarations of relatedness and belonging are made and how these have changed or remained consistent over time. It is certainly customary today for people to name their doodem first when introducing themselves and then to say the community where they are from. Historically, when people were wintering in small, extended

---

73 Ibid., 56.

74 The study of the way in which Anishinaabe peoples deployed kinship over time is a type of nonevent history. See Fogelson, "Ethnohistory of Events and Nonevents," 36. For important studies of kinship, see, especially, Brooks, *Captives and Cousins*; Brown and Peers, "There Is No End to Relationship"; Cook, "Onontio Gives Birth"; Nash, "Abiding Frontier"; Thorne, *Many Hands of My Relations*; Van Kirk, *Many Tender Ties*. For gender as a source of political metaphors, see Shoemaker, "Alliance between Men."

family groups, that place would have been the site of their common or local council, such as Bawaating, Mnjikaning, or Bkejwanong, where they would have gathered in the spring and fall, or the site of their summer base camp. By naming both doodem and place, speakers situated themselves in the web of their relations. They identified both the node of place and the lines of relatedness connecting them to their doodem kin.[75] Doodem in one's daily life operated as a set of categories that gave people a network of family in all four directions.

---

75 Kinship studies, once a cornerstone of anthropological fieldwork, nearly died in the 1970s when David Schneider declared kinship to be an artificial construct of anthropology, not a fact of human existence. Kinship studies have rebounded, however, as the next generation of anthropologists, freed from the strictures of biology and descent-based systems, were able to consider how human beings constructed themselves as related to others. This has proven to be a most useful line of inquiry. See Peter Schweitzer's overview of kinship studies in *Dividends of Kinship*, 2–5.

2

Family in All Four Directions

All those who are of the same mark or totem [doodem] consider themselves as relations, even if they or their forefathers never had any connexion with each other, or had seen one another before. When two strangers meet and find themselves to be of the same mark, they immediately begin to trace their genealogy, at which they even beat my countrymen, the Highlanders.

– Duncan Cameron, 1801[1]

In 1801, Scottish fur trader Duncan Cameron published his memoirs on his life as a fur trader working among Anishinaabe council fires in the western Great Lakes. Cameron started his career as a clerk in 1785, at the age of twenty-one, and he spent much of his time in the Lake Nipigon area. There he married an Anishinaabe woman of the Loon doodem; together they had children and raised their family.[2] She welcomed him into the world of Anishinaaabe family relations and taught him what

---

1 Cameron, "Nipigon Country, 1801," 247. My thanks to Sylvia van Kirk for bringing this source to my attention.
2 Cameron's experience was shared by many other French, English, and Scottish fur traders when they married into Anishinaabe and other Indigenous families. See especially Van Kirk, *Many Tender Ties*; Brown, *Strangers in Blood*. For a biography of Duncan Cameron, see Brown, "Cameron, Duncan." For more on the enduring Anishinaabe family, see Brown and Peers, "There Is No End to Relationship."

the obligations and reciprocal responsibilities of Anishinaabe bonds of kinship meant – to ancestors and descendants and to those kin now living – to one's own doodem kin and the doodem kin of one's spouse. She showed him the difference between the clan system of the Highland Scots and the doodem tradition of the Anishinabek. In the latter, each Anishinaabe person exists at the centre of four lines extending in the four directions: The vertical lines represent the generations of one's ancestors and descendants, while the horizontal lines extending perpendicular to the vertical represent the expansive network of kin in the present – through one's doodem and through the doodem of one's mother or spouse.[3] Cameron married a woman of a prominent and large family; a later census from 1850 shows sixty-nine members of the Loon doodem at Lake Nipigon, only behind the Moose and Catfish doodem in size.[4] Other doodemag at Lake Nipigon included Caribou, Kingfisher, and Bear. Cameron would therefore have a connection through marriage to his wife's Loon doodem father, uncles, brothers and sisters, and nieces and nephews. He also would have kin connections through the doodem of his wife's mother as well, as each Anishinaabe person was (and is today) suspended in a web of kin.

Alliances of marriage partners were lived both physically and metaphorically around the fire, in this case the fire of the *wigiwaam*, or family dwelling. The alliances they made were reinforced through the reciprocal work of caring for and raising children and taking care of the elders. Anishinaabe mothers modelled the reciprocal duties of treaty partners in the care of their children from the time of their birth. In Anishinaabe teachings around parenting and the mother–child bond, the quality of that bond must not be taken for granted. In order for the relationship to be successful, the relationship must be balanced, in that both parties (mother and child) must have their needs met. And in order for this to happen, other family members outside the mother-child pair must help to maintain the relationship.[5]

---

3 Cory Willmott calls ties made *between* doodem *through* marriage lateral alliances. "Clothed Encounters," 95.

4 Census of Population of Lake Nipigon, 1 June 1850, LAC RG10, Vol. 1728: 2.

5 Anishinaabe writer and poet Leanne Betasamosake Simpson calls breastfeeding "the very first treaty." At the time of her first child's birth, Simpson recalls Anishinaabe Elder Edna Manatowabi's teaching that "breastfeeding is where our children learn about treaties, the relationships they encode and how to maintain good treaty relationships." Simpson, *Dancing On Our Turtle's Back*, 106–8.

From such beginnings, children were educated in knowledge of the work required to maintain larger political relationships, as the fundamental principal of reciprocity shaped all alliances, large and small. In other words, the principles and practices that shaped Anishinaabe legal traditions around governance through alliance were grounded in the principles and practices that guided everyday family life in the pursuit of *mino-bimaadiziwin*. This phrase means both life itself and the rules for proper conduct – to live well, to achieve mino-bimaadiziwin, is to fulfil one's obligations to all one's relations, in all four directions.[6] By exploring the four directions of Anishinaabe families – through ancestors and caring for the deceased, with descendants and through alliances forged between marriage partners – this chapter demonstrates how doodem was a central organizing principle of Anishinaabe life, connected to the idea of mino-bimaadiziwin. The reciprocal obligations of families united through doodem and alliance created the foundational constructs for Anishinaabe governance. When an Anishinaabe person married a non-Anishinaabe partner, the council fire could adopt the new spouse into a doodem to ensure that they too could participate fully in Anishinaabe society. When Anishinaabe council fires entered into alliance relationships with non-Anishinaabe peoples, marriages not only served to strengthen the alliance but also ensured that the next generation understood their treaty obligations to each other, to their doodem beings, and to the other ensouled beings that comprised the life-world of the Great Lakes region.

Descendants

When children were born, the long-standing cultural practice was that they typically inherited the doodem of their fathers.[7] The traditional kinship terms in Anishinaabemowin provide evidence of the patrilineal descent of doodem identity, as there are separate terms for parallel and

---

6 As Michael Angel explains in his glossary, bimaadiziwin means life, but more specifically "a long, productive and healthy life – the goal of all Anishinaabeg." *Preserving the Sacred*, 231.

7 As Anton Treuer points out: "Throughout Ojibwe country, I have never encountered a knowledgeable elder, a reliable archival reference, or a tradition that claims patrilineal clan inheritance alters with introduction of a non-Indian father." *Assassination of Hole in the Day*, 18.

cross cousins.[8] Instead of using a generic equivalent such as "uncle" to address either their father's or their mother's brothers, Anishinaabemowin speakers historically called their father's brothers by one distinct term (*ninmishoomenh*) and their mother's brothers by another (*ninzhisbhenh*). Each person shared a doodem with their father's brothers and sisters but had a different doodem than their mother's brothers and sisters.[9]

The archival record, too, supports the idea that Anishinaabe doodemag historically followed the father's line, back in time from one father to another, to the First Being who shared the doodem. In all of the genealogies that I studied of Anishinaabe signatories to Great Lakes treaties made with British and American colonial officials from the 1760s to the 1860s, the pictorial evidence from the doodem images consistently demonstrate that the principle of patrilineal inheritance was widely upheld. This is not to say that other methods of inheritance are not valid. There are people today who know that their specific doodem came through the mother's line or through fasting and visions. There are also examples, especially beginning in the late nineteenth century, of doodemag acquired through ceremony.[10] Inheritance from the father's line is such an important basic principle there have been some contemporary statements that the right to call oneself Anishinaabe is only inheritable through the father's line and that those without Anishinaabe fathers are not Anishinabek.[11] However, not all Anishinabek agreed with or followed this practice. More specifically, people did not interpret "through the father's line" to mean through genetic inheritance. As I demonstrated in Chapter 1, blood is not an Anishinaabe metaphor for defining belonging. As this chapter will show, communities used a range of practices to ensure that children of Anishinaabe mothers and non-Anishinaabe fathers could still have their doodem soul, be part of Anishinaabe communities, and take up

---

8 As Anishinaabemowin linguist Rand Valentine has noted: "Historically, the Anishinaabe kinship system fundamentally distinguished between parallel and cross-cousins of aunts, uncles and cousins." *Nishnaabemwin Reference Grammar*, 108.

9 Ibid., 110–11.

10 See Willmott, "Anishinaabe Doodem Pictographs." However, I feel the evidence overwhelmingly supports patrilineal inheritance of the doodem among the Anishinabek in the nineteenth century and earlier.

11 Wub-e-ke-niew, *We Have the Right to Exist*.

their responsibilities in governance to all of their relations. These strategies included adoption into the doodem of one's mother and maternal grandfather, specific "adopting" doodemag, naming ceremonies, and the inclusion of new doodemag from other cultural traditions.

Ancestors

Given the expression of relatedness through the idea of shared souls, Anishinaabe peoples also placed, and continue to place, great significance on the maintenance of ongoing relationships with the deceased; as these relationships were integral to historic Anishinaabe conceptions of kinship and collective identity. As legal historian Darlene Johnston has so persuasively argued, Anishinaabe views of death, souls, reincarnation, and the obligations of the living toward the dead are a critical component of legal and political history.[12] The complex beliefs surrounding souls and burial locations play a significant part in any understanding as to why specific landscapes have such a deep pull on people having that associated doodem. Historic events could push some people out from the lands they called home for some time, but people continued to express their desire to return and to return the bones of their deceased to the land of their birth. As discussed in Chapter 1, the desire to repatriate remains was connected to the idea of the doodem soul.

The *Jesuit Relations* contain many examples of how Anishinaabe and other Indigenous peoples cared for the dead and returned them home for burial. In the spring of 1637, the bodies of seventy Anishinabek from Lake Nipissing (sometimes called the Nipissings), who had fallen ill and died while they were overwintering near a Wendat community on the Penetanguishene peninsula, were all carried home in seven canoes for burial, rather than being interred where they died. The Jesuits observed that these Nipissings had "embarked to return to their own country" with their deceased.[13] The paddlers were from the same council fire that hosted the late summer gathering in 1642 that opened this book. More than a century later, the French military engineer Pierre Pouchot noted in his observations of the Seven Years' War that if a man died while hunting, "even if it has been three or four months they will disinter him and carry him in their canoes to bury him in their

---

12 Darlene Johnston, "Litigating Identity," 72; *Connecting People to Place.*
13 le Mercier, "Relation of 1637," in Thwaites, *Jesuit Relations*, 14:37.

village."[14] The living needed to care for their dead relations; part of that care required people to return the dead home for burial to the country of their birth. Allowing bodies to decompose on platforms above ground, at least initially, enabled the soul that remained with the body to have the freedom to come and go as it wished. Once the bones had lost their flesh, people could then bundle the bones to return them to the place of the person's birth. By so doing, the soul of the nation could be properly recycled and passed on to subsequent generations. In the nineteenth century, the increased use of coffins and burial "six feet under" required the adaptation of Anishinaabe internment practices: when using a coffin, the lid would not be nailed down or instead holes would be drilled in the top of the coffin to allow the body-soul to leave and then return to the body.[15] Even as burial practices changed, the Anishinabek continued to have ongoing relations with their deceased. Their bones or, more properly, the soul of the nation housed within them, had agency and even personhood. In the 1920s, on Parry Island in Georgian Bay, the Anishinaabe community there considered digging up a grave to recover a medal that had been buried with a relative at Shawanaga. They consulted with a traditional medicine expert, who recommended that the medal be replaced with another offering (in this case, a mirror) "to avoid the shadow's displeasure."[16] These complex beliefs provided powerful motivation; the needs of the dead shaped the actions of the living.

Anishinaabe ancestors were also *remembered* and formed part of the ongoing social world of the living. As Duncan Cameron noted (quoted earlier in this chapter) he was deeply impressed by the ability of people to remember detailed genealogies and to know more ancestors than his own Scottish Highlanders, a fact he found remarkable.[17] In mid and late-nineteenth-century petitions presented to colonial officials in Upper Canada, Anishinaabe leaders provided impressive eight- and ten-generation genealogies to underscore the legitimacy of their political position.[18] In 1843, the Deputy Superintendent of

---

14 Pouchot, *Memoir*, 2:231–2. My thanks to Darlene Johnston for bringing this source to my attention.

15 Darlene Johnston, "Litigating Identity," 90–1.

16 Jenness, *Ojibwa Indians of Parry Island*, 107–8.

17 Cameron, "The Nipigon Country, 1801," 247.

18 Petition to The Honourable E. Dewdney, Supt. General of Indian Affairs, 4 April 1892, LAC RG10, Vol. 2568, file 125851, p. 1; my thanks to Reg Good for bringing this

Indian Affairs for Canada, Samuel Jarvis, received one such petition from Thomas Shilling on Snake Island in Lake Simcoe, listing both the genealogy of his own family and that of the current ogimaa, William Yellowhead. Both were Caribou doodem, but Shilling explained that it was his ancestor (his fourth-great grandfather) Nekike who was the first ogimaa at Lake Simcoe, having come from the Mississaugas on the north shore of Lake "before the war with the Mohawks"; that his third great-grandfather Oskabewis, a war chief, led the attacks on the Mohawk and defeated them; and that Oskabewis's son Mindameness made peace with the Mohawk – all events of the seventeenth century. Shilling's remarkable listing of two lineages in chronological order along with historical markers is documented evidence of what Duncan Cameron observed. Cary Miller also found that Anishinaabe leaders in the western Great Lakes also anchored their claims to leadership and to responsibility over land through genealogies of their lineage.[19] William Warren reported that the great ogimaa Tugwaug-aun-ay kept a "circular plate of virgin copper" on which was marked "the number of generations of the family who have passed away since they first pitched their lodges at Shaug-a-waum-i-kong [Chequamagon Bay]."[20] Warren observed eight marks for the eight ancestors who had died since Chequamagon's council fire was first established and five since the people at Chequamagon had first met Europeans.

When people were displaced or dislocated from the land of their ancestors, they expressed their intention to remain with or to be reunited with their deceased family members. Colonial records contain evidence of these desires; in 1642, an eighty-year-old Anishinaabe Elder told the Jesuit Jérôme Lalemant that his family had once inhabited the island of Montreal, in the mid-sixteenth century, but that they had been driven away by the Wendat. The Elder told Lalemant that he wished to return to the island of Montreal "to be buried in it, near my ancestors."

---

petition to my attention. Another family genealogy is in a petition by the Shilling family to re-establish their claim to the office of ogimaa: see Shilling to Jarvis, 9 May 1843, Office of the Chief Superintendent in Upper Canada, Samuel Peters Jarvis – Correspondence (S to T), Department of Indian Affairs, LAC, RG10, Vol. 138: 78951–3. My thanks to Darlene Johnston for introducing me to this source.

19 Cary Miller, Ogimaag, 200–2.
20 Warren and Neill, History, 89–90.

Lalemant heard similar wishes from other Anishinabek in the Montreal area.[21] In 1721, the Jesuit Pierre-François-Xavier de Charlevoix observed that the Anishinabek living at Trois Rivières refused to relocate to Chicoutimi, where other "Algonquins" were; the reason they gave was that "they could not resolve to quit a place where the bones of their ancestors rested."[22] In a later letter, Charlevoix explained that their "tombs are held to be sacred."[23]

More than two centuries later, in 1936, American anthropologist Charles Wisdom was dispatched to the Great Lakes region by the Office of Indian Affairs to find out why the Chippewa people in Minnesota and Wisconsin were so unwilling to relocate, despite cash incentives and other economic benefits for doing so. Wisdom noted that "they, or many of them, will not move merely because the new land has obviously greater economic value, for the simple reason that it has no emotional value for them. Their dead are buried in the old habitat; it is the birthplace of themselves and their ancestors; and a thousand emotional ties bind them to it."[24] For centuries, long-standing cultural protocols required that the dead not be left behind because of the deep meaning and attachment to place in the Anishinaabe world and the ongoing kinship relationships that they had with those who had died. People felt a deep sense of connection to their deceased relatives, cared for the dead long after their departure, fed them by burning food in fires, and sheltered their graves from the effects of the weather. Jesuit missionaries nodded approvingly overall at their care of the dead but attributed to superstition that which appeared to suggest that mortal remains had needs in common with the living.[25] Instead, the Anishinabek were including their ancestors within their social world and were continuing to be in relationship with them. Ongoing care of the dead was and remains an expression of that relationship.

---

21 Lalemant, "Relation of 1645–46," in Thwaites, *Jesuit Relations*, 28:173.
22 Charlevoix, *Letters to the Duchess*, 1:54. Charlevoix travelled through the Great Lakes in 1721. For a biography see Hayne, "Pierre-François-Xavier de Charlevoix."
23 Charlevoix, *Letters to the Duchess*, 2:153.
24 Wisdom, "Report on the Great Lakes Chippewa," 4.
25 Le Jeune, "Relation of 1634," in Thwaites, *Jesuit Relations*, 8:21–2; see also Le Jeune, "Relation of 1633," in Thwaites, *Jesuit Relations*, 5:131 for descriptions of burning food to feed the souls of the dead.

Marriage: Forging Alliances between Doodemag

Marriage relationships functioned as micro-alliances bringing different doodemag together. Most often, an Anishinabekwe (-*kwe* is the female suffix) married an Anishinaabe man, and the couple typically relocated to live with the husband's family after the birth of their first child. The Jesuits observed this practice of patrilocality (of women living with their husband's families) among Anishinaabe communities early on, noting in the 1630s that their "daughters have married with all the neighbouring Nations ... Your children live in the land of the Nipissiriniens, of the Algonquins, of the Atikameques, of the people of the Sagne and in all the other Nations."[26] Women made important social and political connections by marrying men from other doodemag, sometimes from quite considerable distances away. Such marriages, spread out geographically, created the Anishinaabe political world. It meant that travellers could then rely upon the hospitality of kin as they voyaged through the region. War leaders and warriors could count on the support of their spouse's relatives as allies. For example, the decision of the Sinago Ottawa to relocate west of Lake Michigan around 1650 was grounded in these sorts of kinship relationships. Chief Sinagos's wife was the sister of the chief of the Sakis. In 1665, Chief Sinagos was able to raise a large party to go to war against the Sioux by calling on his brother-in-law, while his brother-in-law in turned reached out to the Sakis' allies, the Potawatomis and Renards [Fox].[27] As one 1736 French report on the number of allied peoples in the Great Lakes noted, "all the Northern Nations have this in common; that a man who goes to war denotes himself as much by the device [doodem] of his wife's tribe as by that of his own, and never marries a woman who carries a similar device to his."[28] Such doodem ties created a thick web of relationships, multiplied access to support, and were historically important for providing allies in times of conflict.

In contrast to the automatic kinship ties that existed because of a shared doodem soul, bonds of alliance that included marriage ties were not automatic. Marriages, like all alliance relationships, had to

---

26   Le Jeune, "Relation of 1636," in Thwaites, *Jesuit Relations*, 9:219.

27   Perrot, "Mémoire," in Blair, *Indian Tribes*, 1:188.

28   Dénombrement des nations sauvages, 1736. ANF, fondes des colonies, S&ie C11A, vol. 66, fol. 236–256v.

be requested, arranged, and maintained between people, their families, and the council fires to which they belonged. Such relationships
required additional effort but they were crucial. Marriages created the
foundational alliances that connected council fires. At one level, the
practice of women marrying outside their natal family, coupled with
the principle of doodem exogamy, meant that families had kin spread
out over large geographic areas. But, examined in a different way,
these marriage practices created communities that were interlinked
by multiple kin ties and could be quite insular. Anthropologists call
the practice of marrying within one's family "endogeny." Anishinaabe
kinship practices were historically both exogamous *and* endogenous.
Since cross-cousins were seen not only as potential but as ideal marriage partners, sisters who had married men with different doodemag
could arrange matches between their children.[29] In Western kin practices, such marriages would be between first cousins. Beloved nieces
and nephews could thus become "in-laws," reducing potential strain
on close-knit family groups by having an "insider" step into the social
spot reserved for an "outsider" – that of spouse. One can easily envision
the conversations of grandmothers at gatherings conferring on which of
their respective grandchildren would be good matches and how those
matches would serve to strengthen the community.[30] Since women had
connections in both their birth community and the community into
which they married, they were well-placed to give advice on the types
of connections that would strengthen the alliances between council
fires, as such alliances kept the regional (general) council functioning
well. The preference for cross-cousins as marriage partners remained
well into the twentieth century in some places. When anthropologist
Irving Hallowell "asked his principal Ojibwa consultant, Chief William Berens, if a man could marry a woman he called *ninam* [*niinim*,
or "cross-cousin"], Berens gave a straightforward response: 'Who the
hell else would he marry?'"[31] Intimate preferences like these reinforced

---

29 Hallowell, *Contributions to Anthropology*, 8.
30 Elder Lewis Debassige of M'Chigeeng First Nation has told me that this practice
    continued well through the nineteenth and into the twentieth century on Manitoulin
    Island, where he was born. He describes the practice as more of "suggestions" than a
    system where marriages were formally arranged, but a wise person knew to listen to
    the good advice of Nokomis.
31 Hallowell, *Contributions to Anthropology*, 8; Peers and Brown, "There Is No End to
    Relationship," 533.

the ties between particular doodemag over the generations. Making and supporting marriages between young people was crucial political work, undertaken primarily by grandmothers and especially those "principal women" who would have comprised the leadership of the women's council.

The central importance of marriage as an alliance-making institution is evident in the rules around who and when one could marry. Since the principle of doodem exogamy was essential to the integrity of the political tradition, it was reinforced by an incest taboo against marrying someone with the same doodem. However, the evidence of social shaming for those who violated the social norm suggests that violations did occur from time to time. As Duncan Cameron noted, those with the same doodem "do sometimes marry, but it is against the will of the parents, and they are greatly despised by the others for it."[32] There was also flexibility around the question of when someone could remarry after the loss of a spouse. Since the work of ogimaawag was so dependent upon these alliance relationships, leaders could observe shorter periods of mourning before they could remarry than the general population (six months, instead of one or two years).[33]

The demands of hosting and travelling also meant that sometime polygamy was permissible. Ogimaawag could have more than one spouse to handle the additional responsibilities of hosting and gift-giving that they were obligated to perform as firekeepers. As Nicolas Perrot recorded in his memoirs of his late seventeenth-century Great Lakes fur trading career, ogimaawag were dependent upon the work of their wives. He wrote that they could not "get along without women to serve them, and to cultivate the lands which produce their tobacco and all that is necessary for them to be prepared to receive those who come to visit them."[34] Perrot interpreted the work women did through a seventeenth-century French lens and imagines Anishinaabe women as servants for their spouses. But as this book will discuss in later chapters, this "women's work" and their participation on the women's council was integral to the cultivation and development of alliances. From the preparation of gifts for allies to the care of sacred medicines such as tobacco (essential to the pipe ceremonies of treaty-making),

---

32 Cameron, "The Nipigon Country, 1801," 247.
33 Perrot, "Mémoire," in Blair, *Indian Tribes*, 1:74.
34 Ibid.

women were actively engaged in the art of forming and maintaining alliances.

Polygamy, in an Anishinaabe context, must therefore be read through the lens of alliance-making. In the early eighteenth century, Father Charlevoix also noted that polygamy was practiced among the Anishinabek and that families preferred in these cases that sisters married one man.[35] More than a century and a half after Perrot's and Charlevoix's observations, Peter Jones observed that polygamy was still being practiced among leading ogimaawag in what is now southern Ontario and that sister marriage was preferred in these cases too. Jones reported that the Credit River ogimaa Adjutant (also known as Captain Jim or James Adjutant) had two wives. An 1818 census at the Credit River shows Adjutant's family consisting of three adult men (Adjutant and two related men) and four adult women (most likely the wives of these men). Likewise the noted Otter ogimaa Assance, from the Lake Simcoe area, had three wives when he converted to Christianity in 1827.[36] Peter Jones, who knew Assance and Adjutant well, explained in his *History of the Ojebway Indians* that ogimaawag preferred to marry sisters "from the idea that they will be more likely to live together in peace, and that the children of one would be loved and cared for by the other than if the wives were not related."[37] Since these sisters shared the same doodem, the bond between the two doodemag in this family was further strengthened. Ogimaawag also took into their households those who needed care, including widows with children, to ensure they were provided for, as this was part of their responsibility to their community.[38] Polygamy here did not serve to subordinate women to male sexual or reproductive needs but instead was used to meet the political and social needs of all the members of the council fire, through supporting alliance-making work and ensuring that everyone had someone to hunt for them in the winter.

Doodem exogamy clearly is visible in the records that Peter Jones kept of the Mississaugas of the Credit River beginning in 1826. In the

---

35 Charlevoix, *Letters to the Duchess*, 1:197.
36 For a biography of Assance, see Sims, " Exploring Ojibwe History."
37 "Return of Indians Present ... at the River Credit," 20 October 1818, Canada and Lower Canada Requisitions, Estimates and Returns, LAC, RG 10 vol. 478:172548; Jones, *History*, 81.
38 Lewis Debassige, personal communication.

register of converted Methodists he not only listed the Anishinaabe and English names for each member of the congregation but also wrote the doodem identities for nearly all of the eighty individuals on it. The fact that this register gives the doodem identities of the female members of the community makes this a rare and important document. A comparison of that list against the marriage and baptism records also kept by Jones reveals that, of the twelve married couples I have been able to identify conclusively, all but one couple were doodem exogamous. Jones's records also reveal particular patterns in choice of spouse, indicating that at least some families were continuing to use the principle of doodem exogamy to strengthen alliances between specific doodemag. Jones's register, while admittedly a very small sample, reveals that the Eagle men on this list preferred to marry women of the Otter, Caribou, and Birch Tree doodemag, prominent doodemag in the nearby council fires of Rama and Rice Lake.[39]

Whether political alliances were made between council fires of Anishinabek, or between Anishinaabe and other peoples, over time these increasingly close relationships led to both marriage and, subsequently, children. For the Anishinabek, such marriages had the potential to challenge the doodem tradition if the father of the children was non-Anishinaabe. A doodem identity was a necessity.[40] This was true whether the non-Anishinaabe father was European, Dakota, Wendat, or Haudenosaunee. What the Anishinabek did was to work within their own cultural tradition to find a distinct set of solutions to ensure that the doodem tradition remained viable. These responses varied across the region and were the product of local creativity. At present, I do not have enough data to assess how consistently, and to what extent, each of these methods was in use and where across the Great Lakes region. However, the examples presented below do make a convincing case for the importance to the Anishinabek of ensuring that children had a doodem and for the various methods they used to do so when non-Anishinaabe fathers were involved. Some of these solutions, in the

---

39 Register, including births, 1776–1881, marriages, 1831–1855 (predominantly undated), deaths, 1840–1883, of the River Credit Indians; Record of Baptisms, 1802–1846 and Membership list of Methodist Society at the Upper Mohawk Grand River, 1826; New Credit Methodist Indian Mission (Ontario) fonds, F1434, United Church of Canada, Toronto.

40 Treuer, *Assassination of Hole in the Day*, 17.

end, also resulted in the appearance of new doodem identities within Anishinaabe communities.

If a non-Anishinaabe father came from a society with an analogous tradition of kinship networks, marriage could be a vehicle through which a foreign identity became an Anishinaabe one. Siouan or Iroquoian-speaking fathers, for example, could bring new identities from their own cultural traditions into Anishinaabe communities and the tradition of doodemag. The Kingfisher doodem came to be part of the Anishinaabe world through marriage between an Anishinaabe woman and a Dakota man in what is now Minnesota.[41] Similarly, William Warren was told how a chief of the Catfish doodem "died without male issue, and his only daughter married a Dakota chief who belonged to the Wolf Clan of his tribe." During a lengthy interval of peace between the ongoing series of wars with the Dakota, two sons were born, "who of course inherited their father's totem of the wolf. In this manner this badge became grafted among the Ojibway list of clans." Those belonging to the Wolf doodem from the St. Croix and Mille Lac communities, Warren went on to say, "are all descended from this intermarriage."[42]

The identity exchange could also go the other way to serve political and diplomatic purposes. Warren pointed out how the Merman, or Water-Spirit doodem, is known among the Dakota through marriage between Anishinaabe women of this doodem and Dakota men.[43] There is a significant and long history of Dakota–Anishinaabe conflict in the western Great Lakes area, which was underway by the sixteenth century (and lasted well into the nineteenth); these marriages and the alliances they produced were part of a series of diplomatic initiatives designed to keep the peace.[44] The forging of kin relationships like these

---

41 Anton Treuer recorded this information from his interview with Elder Vernon Whitefeather, who identified the marriage as having taken place in Ponemah, Minnesota. This fact, Treuer notes, helps "to explain the prevalence of that clan [kingfisher] at Red Lake and Turtle Mountain, as well as its scarcity east of Red Lake." Treuer, *Assassination of Hole in the Day*, 18–19; quotation on 231n26. Note that a census of Lake Nipigon Anishinabek (north of Lake Superior) counted sixty-nine members of the Kingfisher doodem. See Census of Population of Lake Nipigon, 1 June 1850, LAC RG10, Vol. 1728: 2.

42 Warren and Neill, *History*, 165.

43 Ibid., 43.

44 Michael Witgen discusses the long history of this conflict, and periods of peace, in *Infinity of Nations*.

did not prevent outbreaks of violence between the Dakota and western Anishinabek in the late 1730s, but it was, regardless, the mechanism that people used throughout the region to help alliances last. At peace negotiations and gatherings, those of the Merman and Wolf doodemag from both Anishinaabe and Dakota sides would acknowledge one another as kin on the grounds that, back in time, a Wolf leader from the Dakota had married a woman of the Catfish doodem.[45] In addition, Warren reports that the Merman doodem is related to the Catfish, as they are both part of *A-waus-ee* (*awaasii*), a larger grouping that includes both of these doodemag. Awaasii is a word in Anishinaabemowin that both refers to a specific species (bullhead catfish) and a larger "taxonomic" category that encompasses other inhabitants of the underwater world.

So when Anishinaabe women married French and English men, they were not doing something radically new or marrying "outside," because all Anishinaabe marriages served the important political function of making connections between different people. In fact, this question of what to do about non-Anishinaabe fathers existed long before contact with Europeans and the marriages that resulted from the fur trade. When the French first arrived in the Great Lakes region, they found that Anishinaabe peoples were already intermarried with their neighbours, including the Wendat. As Warren explain above, similar marriages were occurring between the Anishinabek and Siouian-speaking peoples like the Dakota. Following the Great Peace of Montreal in 1701, French officials observed that Anishinaabe peoples living in eastern Ontario also married people from the Haudenosaunee (Iroquois Confederacy), their former enemies.[46] As the French colonial official and historian Claude-Charles Le Roy De La Potherie observed in volume two of his 1722 *Histoire de l'Amérique septentrionale*: "they were mutually bound to give their daughters in marriage on both sides. That was a strong bond for the maintenance of entire harmony."[47] La Potherie also noted that women married into allied nations across the region.[48] French observers described women as being "exchanged" when they described

---

45 Warren and Neill, *History*, 165.
46 Chief Robert Paudash, "Testimony of Chief Robert Paudash on the Coming of the Mississauga," 9–13.
47 Claude Charles Le Roy, Sieur de Bacqueville de la Potherie, "Histoire de l'Amérique septentrionale," in Blair, *Indian Tribes*, 2:277.
48 Ibid., 2:301.

these practice to support the maintenance of the alliance. Such language suggests that women were pawns in this process and not active participants in the maintenance of alliance relationships. Yet the evidence that women, particularly grandmothers, were the primary arrangers of marriages suggests otherwise. Clearly, Anishinaabe families had developed strategies to manage the implications of cross-cultural marriage before French and English fur traders presented themselves as potential spouses. Marriage was the key mechanism through which council fires strengthened alliances with one another; when Europeans arrived in the region, they were simply incorporated into existing cultural and political practices.

Adoption into a Doodem

Adoption was an important means used to address the challenge of having children of non-Anishinaabe fathers. This could be done by adopting the non-Anishinaabe father into an Anishinaabe doodem or by adopting the children themselves directly into the doodem. Anishinaabe adoption practices in which a person is made a full member of the community are not the same as a ceremonial adoption (the equivalent of honorary citizenship) or Western-style legal adoption, in which the individual ceases to legally be the child of one set of parents and instead becomes the descendant of another. A child born to any non-Anishinaabe father would need to be adopted into a doodem – this was as true of a child born to a Haudenosaunee father as a French or English one. From the beginning of the fur trade with Europeans in the seventeenth century, there were certainly many children born of relationships between French, Scottish or English men and Indigenous women. By 1815, there were as many as ten thousand people primarily living around fur-trade posts who were descendants of these relationships and living culturally and politically distinct lives from their Anishinaabe kin. Others integrated more fully into Anishinaabe communities.[49] There were often strong kin ties between these distinct peoples. If the children were to be part of Anishinaabe communities, they would require a doodem. Children with French, Scottish, or English fathers might also be baptized or christened and receive a Christian name as well. Children could receive a doodem by being adopted as the children

---

49 Peterson, "Many Roads to Red River," 62.

of a particular person, by being assigned to the doodem of an "adopting clan," or by receiving the doodem through ceremony.

One common method was to adopt someone into a doodem. Consider the case of Peter Jones (Kahkewaquonaby), who was born in 1801 on the escarpment overlooking Burlington Bay on Lake Ontario. His mother was Tubinaquay, daughter of Wabenose, one of the principal gichi-Anishinaabe of the Mississauga-Anishinabek. Wabenose's family, in turn, had gathered each spring and fall since the late seventeenth century at the Credit River. Wabenose and his daughter Tubinaquay were both *migizi*, or Eagle doodem, while the baby's father, Augustus Jones, was a Welshman. Augustus Jones worked as the deputy surveyor for the British colonial government of Upper Canada, which had only been established ten years earlier. By the patrilineal practice of the doodem tradition, Kahkewaquonaby would in theory not have had a doodem. And yet he proclaimed his Eagle doodem identity throughout his life, and even after he converted to Christianity. As an adult, when acting in his capacity as an ogimaa of the Mississauga, he consistently signed documents with a migizi image. When he travelled to England in 1838 to meet Queen Victoria, he wore a coat with an embroidered migizi image on the lapel to his audience with the queen as part of his court dress.[50] Given his father's identity as a British subject, Jones's assertion of migizi identity seems to disaffirm the principle of patrilineal descent of doodem identity; and yet, it did not. Wabenose used the practice of adoption to welcome his grandson into the Eagle doodem by giving him the name of his own deceased son, Kahkewaquonaby. A name conveys the spirit of the person who had previously held it and aspects of their personhood and character. Through this act of naming, Kahkewaquonaby was given not only his maternal uncle's name but his doodem identity. Wabenose restored the principle of doodem inheritance through patrilineal descent by making his daughter's son his own.

The descendants of Lawrence Herkimer faced a similar situation. Herkimer was a Loyalist who married a Mississauga woman from Rice Lake after the American Revolution. Their children are all listed on the

---

50 Donald Smith, *Sacred Feathers*, 167–8. For a discussion of the suit, see Willmott, "Clothed Encounters," 477. The Credit River community elected Jones aanikeogimaa in 1829; he consistently signed treaties, letters, and petitions below the leading ogimaa, Joseph Sawyer. For a discussion of Mississauga-Anishinaabe leadership at the Credit River and Jones's roles, see Bohaker, "Anishinaabe 'toodaims,'" 109–12.

Methodist Society membership list as belonging to the Bear doodem, meaning either that Herkimer had been formally adopted into the Bear doodem himself or that Herkimer's Anishinaabe wife was of that doodem identity and the children had subsequently been given that doodem in their naming ceremony.[51] Regardless, once named in a naming ceremony, a person was unquestionably Anishinaabe, and to have an Anishinaabe name and doodem identity was, and is, to be fully Anishinaabe. Much as a citizenship ceremony makes one fully Canadian or American, there was no possibility of being "half blood" or "part Anishinaabe," because the doodem tradition does not use blood as a metaphor.[52] Understanding of this older Anishinaabe law of belonging persists in communities, despite settler colonial legal regimes in both Canada and the United States that have usurped responsibility for determining community membership. In his research on contemporary practices of adoption at Fort William First Nation, community member and adoptee Damien Lee explores how his aunt Iskigamizige-giizis expressed the right of her adopted nephew to belong to Fort William. As Lee noted, she did so using "a family's authority to claim individuals." Iskigamizige-giizis used a blood metaphor for belonging while subverting it at the same time in order to express an Anishinaabe concept of kin. As Iskigamizige-giizis explained, "I mean, you may not be blood, but you're blood, because you're family."[53]

There is also the well-documented practice of "adopting clans" – specific doodemag into which children born to non-Anishinaabe fathers were assigned by some Anishinaabe communities. Among many communities in Minnesota, children in this situation were assigned to the Eagle (migizi) doodem, whereas if the child lived in northwestern Ontario, he or she could be adopted into the Marten (waabizheshi) doodem.[54] In other cases, French voyageurs in the early days of the fur trade were actually adopted into the ba-bi-zha-shi'do-i'daym, or Marten doodem. By adopting these French men into the Marten doodem, Edward Benton-Banai (Anishinaabe from Lac Courte Oreilles) writes his *The Mishomis Book*, "it was possibly felt that the acceptance of the

---

51 Membership list of Methodist Society at the Upper Mohawk Grand River, 1826; New Credit Methodist Indian Mission (Ontario) fonds, F1434, United Church of Canada, Toronto.
52 See Damien Lee, "Adoption Constitutionalism," 785.
53 Cited in Ibid., 800. See also Lawrence, *"Real" Indians and Others*.
54 Treuer, *Assassination of Hole in the Day*, 16.

responsibilities of this clan would be a worthy test of the sincerity of the newcomers. The French traders must have impressed the Ojibway with their loyalty because they were accepted, for the most part, fully and completely."[55] As Benton-Banai explains, the Marten doodem have responsibility as warriors, providers, and hunters. So by accepting French men into the Marten doodem, their new Anishinaabe communities were giving the newcomers their adult roles. Likely, other doodemag in the categories of leadership, medicine, and teaching would have been less suitable for French newcomers due to their lack of childhood and adolescent training for those areas of responsibility.

In some Ontario communities, children of non-Anishinaabe fathers had their "adopting clan determined at a *jiisakaan* [shake tent]" ceremony of the Midewewin, or Grand Medicine Society, "where the practitioner divines the adopting clan."[56] This last practice may seem to be completely at odds with the principle of patrilineal descent, but in the context of Anishinaabe cosmology it is not. If a child received a doodem identity through such a ceremony, the child would also receive the soul of the doodem and would share with doodem relatives the connection back through their father's ancestors back to the original first doodem being. The doodem tradition, after all, reflects a metaphysical relationship. In fact, all of these diverse practices are united by a common purpose. They represent creative solutions to the challenge posed by non-Anishinaabe fathers to the principle of patrilineal descent, ensuring Anishinaabe children of their ability to fully participate in Anishinaabe society, including in Anishinaabe councils.

In other cases, Anishinaabe leaders looked to the visual symbols of French, British, and American political authority and deemed *those* to be doodemag in the context of Anishinaabe cosmology. In contemporary community sources, those whose fathers are American or whose ancestry is American are sometimes said to belong to the Eagle doodem because the United States government took the bald eagle for its symbol. This idea is expressed in some western Great Lakes Anishinaabe communities in both oral histories and, today, online community heritage sites.[57] In a similar way, those with British fathers were said to be

---

55 Benton-Banai, *Mishomis Book*, 105.

56 Treuer, *Assassination of Hole in the Day*, 16.

57 See, for example, "Do You Know Your Clan," Turtle Mountain Chippewa Heritage Center, 1 March 2012, http://www.chippewaheritage.com/1/post/2012/3/do-you-know-your-clan.html; see also Michelson, "Note on the Gentes," 338.

michi-bizhi or the great underwater manidoog, because of the similarity in appearance between the lion on the British coat of arms and the physical form in which the manidoog is most often depicted, that of a long-tailed cat.[58]

Children could also bring new doodem identities into Anishinaabe culture when they were adopted after being captured in warfare. Noted Anishinaabe artist Norval Morrisseau recounted a family oral history that explained how the Grizzly Bear doodem came to be adopted into the doodem of the western Anishinabek from the Stony (Assiniboine) people. Morrisseau was told by his maternal grandfather, Moses Nanakonagos of Beardmore, that his direct ancestors were Assiniboine (Stony) because of a war at some unspecified time in the past. During this conflict, "the Ojibways, being a great nation to be feared, went into the plains in the land of the Stonies to fight. The Ojibways passed a law [i.e., came to a consensus in council] that if a full-scale battle were fought and all the enemy killed, any surviving children should not be killed or mistreated but brought back to be adopted as children of the Ojibway." Morrisseau then revealed that two children of the Grizzly Bear doodem were brought back in this manner and that one of them became his ancestor on his mother's side. It is through these children that the Grizzly Bear doodem came to be an Anishinaabe doodem, as the Anishinabek did not require the children to forfeit their birth identity following adoption. Not only does Morrisseau use this story to explain how the Grizzly Bear doodem became an Anishinaabe doodem but he also uses it to explain how some western Anishinaabe art shows Assiniboine influence.[59] The story also reveals insights into Anishinaabe governance practices. The council considered the impact of war on non-combatants and also accepted their responsibility to take care of them afterwards.

Taken together, the examples discussed above reveal the diverse local and regional strategies that different council fires used to ensure that all Anishinaabe children, regardless of their fathers' identities, each had a doodem. The Anishinabek developed processes for incorporating newcomers into their families and societies using the doodem tradition and expanded it or adjusted it where required to fit new circumstances. The list of doodem identities given in Chapter 1 (Table 2), therefore, is both

---

58 Michelson, "Note on the Gentes," 338; Dewdney, *Sacred Scrolls*, 125–7.
59 Morrisseau, "Great Conjurers and Warriors," 87–8.

evidence of the tradition's antiquity and a reflection of change over time, as the list includes older as well as more recent doodem identities. Narratives that explain the inclusion of new identities (e.g., the Wolf, incorporated from the Dakota) and changes in the relationships between others (e.g., the Moose, whose descendants became cousins of the Marten doodem following a conflict between them) are evidence of the political history of the Anishinabek.[60] Children needed to have a doodem identity because one could not participate meaningfully in Anishinaabe civil, social, and political life without one. Adoption facilitated this and, by extension, fostered the kinds of family ties between allies that built connections over time.

Towards a Philosophy and Law of Alliances

With family in all four directions, Anishinaabe peoples lived suspended in a web of relations. The doodem tradition shaped self-conception and political actions, law, and governance practices. As an analytic category, doodem opens up ways to describe and explain the historical choices of individuals. The concept of shared doodem souls is a distinctly Anishinaabe source of metaphor and political allegory, used as metaphor in aadizookaanag from which the Anishinabek derived their laws. The ongoing relationships that the Anishinabek historically had with their dead reflected their sense of responsibility towards the land and the doodem beings that originated on it. Marriage, as an alliance-making institution, created unions between people having different doodem and served in its own way as a model for Anishinaabe self-governance – a practice of continual negotiation grounded in a set of ethical principles founded on the reciprocal duty to take care of the other. People expressed this reciprocal duty of care through the exchange of gifts, a long-standing practice demonstrated at the many regional gatherings as in the example of 1642 described in the first chapter. These principles created the structures for Anishinaabe polities and these principles which were extended to alliances with newcomers. The gifts exchanged in the context of formal councils were a key part of the Anishinaabe law of alliances as they were both symbol and evidence of understandings and undertakings (somewhat the equivalent of an oral contract)

---

60 For the story of the Wolf doodem from the Dakota, see Warren and Neill, *History*, 165; for the Marten/Moose doodem story, see 49–53.

to enter into and to maintain their relationships. When Anishinaabe council fires gathered to renew their alliances, they exchanged gifts of clothing, cooking implements, and weapons. Such items all did double work as both tangible and useful items and metaphors for the type of responsibility allies owed each other: to clothe the other, to feed the other, to protect the other.[61] These twin purposes were also echoed in the gifts exchanged between individuals and families as part of the work of making and maintaining relationships.

In Great Lakes regional diplomacy with the Haudenosaunee and the Wendat, and with French, English and other newcomers, leaders also exchanged gifts as part of the law of alliances. Orators in council described alliances metaphorically as paths, roads, or rivers that connected autonomous council fires. These culturally and political distinct peoples had developed formal council protocols for making or renewing alliance relationships, specifically to address the challenges of effective and long-lasting relationships between distinct peoples, where the emphasis was on co-existence. Alliances between council fires built on Anishinaabe philosophies and ethics of forming family relationships on the principle of interdependence. While the details of these practices did differ between different cultural traditions and throughout the region, there were common elements. These elements included opening ceremonies involving smoking the pipe together to place people in a "good mind"; offering prayers of thanksgiving that reminded listeners of the gifts they had received from creation and that, therefore, they had an obligation to return; giving speeches that invoked all creation as a witness to the proceedings; condolences offered for the deceased; and the exchange of gifts. Council members smoked *semma* (tobacco) together from sacred pipes. In these treaty councils, the semma accompanied prayers of thanksgiving and gratitude and carried messages to the manidoog in its smoke. Orators spoke on gifts, whether wampum or other items, or with the calumet (the pipe of peace) as being markers of truth and as evidence of the giver's capacity to care for the other in an alliance. Wampum strings and belts functioned as mnemonic devices, as a marker of truth, and as gifts; the speaker typically gifted wampum strings to the other party so that the words spoken would be remembered. Parties to an agreement made belts and exchanged them as records of

---

61 See especially Perrot for a description of the many gifts given and received during regional gatherings. Perrot, "Mémoire," in Blair, *Indian Tribes*, 1:87–8.

the alliance. Wampum played a critical role in Indigenous governance and law throughout the region. Wampum-made diplomatic items also embody Indigenous ontologies as they represent "the literal weaving together of thoughts from living human beings and materials from living marine, floral and faunal beings." Wampum, and by extension other diplomatic gifts given in council, both represent and are part of "social (and not just material) relationships with the non-human persons (e.g. flora, fauna, and mollusks) who provide the raw materials."[62] Gifts given in these contexts were more than just records of the alliance (although they were that too); these gifts were an integral part of the social relationships formed and maintained through each alliance.

When Great Lakes and eastern North American Indigenous nations made alliances with Europeans, they performed the same ceremonies and gave the same types of gifts, with the same meanings. The presents were assurances that each party understood the obligation to the other, as kin. Gifts always flowed both ways. The Anishinabek understood Europeans in terms of Indigenous political categories and integrated them into their thought worlds. The 1671 prise-de-possession ceremony discussed in the Introduction is an excellent example of this. In return for the goods brought to "purchase" the Great Lakes, the French received "an equal value" in beaver pelts and other gifts. This was no purchase but an alliance, founded on Anishinaabe law, in which the parties to the alliance have an obligation to care for the other. The reason Anishinaabe leaders used kinship terms in formal council with their allies is simply that Anishinaabe law used the metaphors of alliance and treaty within a family to structure their entire system of governance. In turn, the Anishinabek had every reason to feel that the both French and later British officials at the very least understood and respected their protocols – that allies had an obligation to each other – because representatives of imperial governments acted as if they understood. Empires and settler governments studied Great Lakes diplomatic protocols and participated fully in them. They hosted regional council meetings in which officials participated.[63] And, as hosts, they took on the responsibilities of ogimaawag and fed their guests.

These same colonial officials both distributed and *received* presents; in other words, they acted as a relative, an ally, and a leader should.

---

62 Bruchac, "Broken Chains of Custody," 69.
63 This practice continued into the numbered treaties negotiated after Confederation. See Craft, *Breathing Life into the Stone Fort Treaty*.

Sometimes the minutes of colonial councils contain descriptions of the pipes, wampum strings, and belts given to their colonial allies, but the full extent of gifts given by Indigenous peoples to Europeans is seldom listed in these documents. But give they did. Recall that at the 1642 gathering discussed in the Introduction that the Jesuits were given many gifts; this practice continued because it was a fundamental aspect of Anishinaabe law in which gifts were used to form and maintain social relations. While the recipient was supposed to maintain the gift as evidence of their alliance relationships, the reality is that many of these items have ended up in European and North American museum ethnographic collections following a sojourn in the family collection or curiosity cabinet of the representatives from imperial governments.[64] Not all the items in these ethnographic collections are diplomatic gifts. Some of these items came in to museums through collectors who purchased items from Anishinaabe and other Indigenous communities and others from contexts that are more dubious.[65] The story of museum collections of Anishinaabe material culture has its own complex history.[66] But certainly some wampum strings and wampum belts came into museum collections via former imperial diplomats, as well as other items from diplomatic contexts: pipes, war clubs, suits of clothing, and chiefly regalia such as headdresses. Many other items, such as furs that were given during councils, were simply sold off as part of the fur trade, and their importance as evidence of the alliance contract is only visible in council minutes or colonial accounts.[67]

---

64 On the expectation to keep the gift, see Cary Miller, "Gifts as Treaties," 225. As co-director of GRASAC, I have spent the past decade researching treaty gifts and other Great Lakes material culture in museums and archives in Europe, the UK, Canada, and the United States in collaboration with my colleagues, especially Ruth B. Phillips and Alan Corbiere. Their work on the significance of these collections has opened my eyes to their political and legal importance.

65 Wampum belts, strings, and politically significant items came into museum collections through dubious means in the late nineteenth century, or ended up sold by museums to private collectors. For a detailed study of the illegal removal from community and subsequent sales of just two belts, see Bruchac, "Broken Chains of Custody."

66 See for example, Phillips, *Trading Identities*; Hamilton, *Collections and Objections*.

67 For example, at the 1671 council at Bawaating at which the French claimed to have performed a prise-de-possession ceremony, the Sieur de St. Lusson reported that he received in exchange for the gifts he had brought, their equivalent value in beaver furs. See Talon to the King, 2 November 1671, Fonds des Colonies. Série C11A. Correspondence générale, Canada, vol. 3, fol.159–171v, ANOM.

Two specific examples of these types of diplomatic gifts are a council pipe given to Sir Francis Bond Head in 1836 when he was lieutenant governor of Upper Canada (see Figure 13) and a presentation bgamaa-gan given to Lord Elgin while he was Governor General of Canada during the period 1848–56 (see Figure 14). These are beautiful works of art, which would command high prices at auction today. The detailed porcupine quillwork and the quality of the carvings reflect the value that the Anishinabek who gave these gifts placed on maintaining their alliance relationship with the Crown. Such diplomatic gift-giving is a very old practice in the Great Lakes region – recall that the Jesuits at the gathering in 1642 discussed in the Introduction understood the diplomatic significance of these gifts and came prepared to give gifts of their own. As Father Lalemant recalled, "we strove to win the affections of the chief personages by means of feasts and presents."[68] It was in particular this participation in the cycle of gift exchange that the Jesuit priest Lalemant explained was the reason that the Jesuits were invited to travel to the gathering at Bawaating later in the fall of 1642. Anishinaabe council fires continued to give gifts to colonial leaders throughout the land surrender period. Following the signing of the Robinson-Huron treaty in 1850, for example, petitions and speeches sent to the colonial government and later the government of Canada concerning unfulfilled treaty obligations and concerns with the treaty were accompanied by pipes and pouches.[69]

The gifts of clothing given in council have particular meaning; they express the ability of the giver to meet the needs of the recipient. Specific items of clothing, such as headdresses, carried additional meaning, recognizing a leadership role. Military commanders at posts throughout the Great Lakes found themselves gifted with clothing when they attended councils hosted by their Anishinaabe counterparts. Recall from the Introduction how in 1642 the Nipissing leaders were formally recognized at the general council: they were called forward in their best robes and given the headdresses and neck ornaments that signified their new roles. So when Anishinaabe leaders first entered into alliance relationships with the French and later British, the Anishinabek treated their forts as council fires and their leaders as ogimaa.

68 Lalemant, "Relation of 1642–43," in Thwaites, *Jesuit Relations*, 23:221.

69 See for example, Speech of Way-ge-ma-keu (Beaver Doodem) and Pâpâsence (Beaver doodem), 17 August 1851, LAC, RG 10, vol. 323, 216151–5.

The Anishinabek recognized these commanders with suits of clothing and bestowed upon them headdresses and other chiefly regalia. This is different from but related to practices of adopting individuals. When Anishinaabe peoples adopted individuals, they also clothed them. For example, fur trader Alexander Henry described the experience of being ritually washed and given new clothing when he was rescued by the Anishinabek at Bawaating during Pontiac's War.[70] Anishinaabe councils took the same approach to recognizing the colonial leaders with whom they interacted.

French and later British colonial officials in turn reciprocated with these gifts of clothing, particularly headgear, which Anishinaabe leaders interpreted as acceptance of the terms of the alliance. At the regional peace agreement made at Montreal in 1701 (also known as the Great Peace of Montreal), clothing exchanges figured prominently. At the first assembly on 25 July, the visiting Great Lakes leaders presented their gifts to the French governor, Louis-Hector de Callière, as the host or ogimaa of the Montreal council fire.[71] In subsequent meetings, as was the regional practice, leaders spoke on gifts, requiring Callière to respond in kind.[72] In his first major speech of the negotiations, Callière spoke on and distributed thirty-four belts of wampum as part of the French gifts and as records of the peace. During the subsequent speeches from leaders of the Great Lakes council fires, the diversity of headdresses amazed the French delegates. One Jesuit remarked that the Indigenous delegates "put their main glory in the adornment of their heads." But this was not mere vanity or concern for appearance. Rather, each headdress communicated important cultural and community meanings. When orators in council wore headgear they had previously received as gifts in the context of an alliance relationship, they were honouring that alliance. At the Great Peace negotiations, the Fox orator Miskouensa provoked the governor and the French audience into laughter when he appeared wearing "an old wig" that he subsequently doffed "as if it was a hat." Given the importance of headdresses as marks of leadership in this cultural context, Miskouensa likely interpreted the wig as a headdress, which he wore to honour the French. He then removed the wig as if it was a hat because he had seen French colonial officials offer

---

70 Henry, *Travels and Adventures*, 72.
71 Havard, *Great Peace of Montreal*, 127.
72 Ibid., 138.

that gesture as one of respect to the each other. Certainly by 1701 the French were well aware of the significance of headdresses, as they gave their own headgear as diplomatic gifts in return. As the leaders left the assembly to return home, they received as parting gifts, in addition to musket and shot, "caps decorated with laces of gold braid."[73]

This practice of clothing exchange continued throughout the eighteenth and into the nineteenth century and occurred among the Haudenosaunee as well. It was part of regional diplomatic protocols; Superintendent of Indian Affairs Sir William Johnson frequently appeared in "Indian dress" at councils.[74] Figure 15 shows a red wool stroud "chief's coat" of the type given by the British to Anishinaabe leaders. Both fur traders and colonial officials presented coats to Indigenous leaders. This one was given to Oshawana of Walpole Island, during the War of 1812. Oshawana (Thunderbird doodem) was Tecumseh's aide.[75] While this coat looks at first glance like standard British military issue, the cut and placement of the chevrons is different.[76] These coats were made specifically to give to Indigenous leaders. Likewise, Indigenous leaders continued to receive and value gifts of European hats as they in turn bestowed headdresses on their European counterparts. Figure 16 is an ambrotype of Oshawana, taken in 1838, now, like his coat, in the collections of the Royal Ontario Museum. In this picture, Oshawana visibly affirms the alliance connections he is responsible for maintaining as an ogimaa by wearing the gifts he has received, including a top hat gifted to him by the British and the George III medal around his neck. The silver gorgets, hat bands, and wristlets were very likely also gifts given in council to commemorate alliances.[77]

---

73 Ibid., 140n134.

74 Shannon, "Dressing for Success," 13–42.

75 The coat is at the Royal Ontario Museum, 911.3.119; HD6294. Item photographed and described as part of a GRASAC team research trip to the Royal Ontario Museum, 15–19 December 2008, funded by a SSHRC Aboriginal Research Grant, of which I was a participant. Ozhawanoo signed a request for the Indian Department to forward £300 Halifax currency to the community for the purchase of agricultural implements alongside three other members of council. Requisition of Chippewas of Chenail Ecarte & St. Clair, 28 June 1843, Resident Agent, Montreal, Colonel D.C. Napier – Correspondence, 1843, LAC RG10, Vol. 141: 45525–27. The doodem signatures appear on page 45527.

76 These details were noted by GRASAC researchers during our conversations on site. See GRASAC item 1190.

77 Cumberland, *Oronhyatekha Historical Collection*, 54.

The King George III medal that Oshawana is wearing was also a typical gift given by the French and later the British to recognize Indigenous leaders. The medals signal visually that one's role as chief had been ratified by one's allies, in the same way that new leaders were affirmed at the 1642 general council and subsequent gatherings, with their "commissions." As French and British colonial officials first entered into the Great Lakes world, they responded to this practice of neck ornamentation by giving medals, which they distributed in recognition of those chiefs and councillors of council fires with which they were allied. The two shown in Figures 17 and 18 were commissioned expressly for the commemoration of alliances with Great Lakes nations, and they clearly convey the spirit of alliance. Both have the monarch on the reverse. The George II Peace Medal dated 1757 has the inscription: "Let us look to the most high who blessed our fathers with peace." The second medal, from the Treaty of Niagara, says "Happy While United 1764." The European-produced medals were limited in quantity and highly valued, passed down in families on hereditary lines.[78]

These reciprocal gifts of clothing and headdresses are particularly important because they underscore that such councils and alliances occurred within the framework of an Anishinaabe legal tradition. When French, British, and later American officials gave gifts, flags, and medals to chiefs, they may have thought they were exerting some control over their Indigenous allies by participating in these ceremonies. But if anything, the situation was the exact reverse – Indigenous leaders, through gifting chiefly regalia, were in fact legitimating the leadership of French and later British and American posts and recognizing those sites as council fires. Mutual recognition of leaders in alliance was an old regional practice. Similar to the case of wearing their allies' gifts of clothing, when Anishinabek wore medals or even flew the flags of their allies, they were recognizing and honouring their alliance relationships, not proclaiming their submission to imperial authority.[79] There are other

---

78 Distributing medals to Indigenous leaders was a practice that began in the late seventeenth century and continued until 1921, with the last treaty medal struck for Numbered Treaty 11. The United States government also issued its own treaty medals with similar images, beginning in 1777 and in earnest after 1789. France and Britain also gave medals in other imperial contexts. See Pickering, et al., *Peace Medals*, which includes discussion of medals distributed during the French regime; Jamieson, *Medals Awarded to North American Indian Chiefs*.

79 Cary Miller, "Gifts as Treaties," 230.

headdresses and ceremonial clothing in overseas museum collections like the ones discussed above. While further research is needed, their very presence in collections that came into museums through families with a record of military service in British North America raises significant interpretative possibilities, given the fact that such items would only have been given in the context of a formal council and bestowed upon someone recognized in a leadership role.[80]

The research of Ruth B. Phillips on two complete suits of clothing from the late eighteenth century given to British officers supports this interpretation, as does an 1850 photo showing the treaty negotiator William Beverly Robinson with leading treaty negotiators Nebanagoching and Shingwaukonce, in which Robinson wears a headdress, while the ogimaawag also wear their headdresses and medals. The images in Figures 20, 21, and 22 are all of British subjects who received recognition by Anishinaabe council fires and who received gifts of regalia as confirmation of their roles as ogimaawag. Sir John Caldwell was an Irish baronet who served at both Detroit and Niagara between 1774 and 1780. He so admired his regalia that he commissioned this formal portrait including his headdress. It now hangs in the Museum of Liverpool; the items themselves are now part of the collection of the Canadian Museum of History. In his portrait displaying the gifts he received, he is holding wampum and a pipe, indicating the status of an ogimaa and pipe carrier. Andrew Foster was likely gifted the outfit in Figure 21 during his service as an officer at Detroit, Michilimackinac, and Miami Rapids between 1793 and 1796.[81] Note the thunderbird motifs on the neck ornament, likely signifying that Foster was of the Thunderbird doodem. While not all images on Anishinaabe material culture correspond to the doodem of the wearer, Anishinaabe leaders did often wear an image of their doodem on their formal council regalia. In fact, many continue to do so today.

Figure 22 shows William B. Robinson on the left with Shingwaukonce and Nebanagoching. All three men are wearing regalia including marks of leadership. Shingwaukonce and Nebanagoching are wearing the same clothing that they wore when they visited Lord Elgin in 1849. The two leaders posed along with Menissinowenninne (The Great Warrior) for an image that was printed as a woodcut in the 15 September

---

80 Alan Corbiere, "Anishinaabe Headgear."

81 See Ruth B. Phillips' discussion of these suits as adoption clothing in "Reading Between the Lines," 115–19.

1849 edition of the *London Illustrated News*. Both Shingwaukonce and Nebanagoching are wearing the same regalia in this second image. Both also wear their King George medals, and Nebanagoching has a heart-shaped thunderbird pendant, which he wears below. Nebanagoching wears the same regalia in the portrait that was painted of him by Cornelius Krieghoff. Nebanagoching's crane doodem is also visible on his coat. Nebanagoching's coat has a large crane doodem image on it, just below his right shoulder. As with Oshawana, discussed above, these leaders were all wearing their alliance relationships with formal regalia. Robinson, too, is wearing the headdress of an ogimaa and a neck ornament, demonstrating continuity with the earlier practices. Robinson is also wearing a capote – the kind of wool blanket coat known well to historians of the fur trade. Given his career as a fur trader on Georgian Bay, it would not be surprising that he would own such a coat or even that the leggings and moccasins would belong to him. Note the detailed and beautiful beadwork on the apron and leggings of Robinson's clothing – this type of decorated clothing was very likely gifted to him and reflects a significant investment of time and women's labour. The material composition of the headdresses can reflect the doodem identity of the leaders; the feathers are earned for accomplishments and can have different meanings for the type of bird species. The position of the feathers is a metaphorical reflection of either calmness and peace, if flat or laid out to the side, typical of civil ogimaa headdresses, or, if stiff and pointing up, of vigilance or a metaphorical reference to war. There is no indication of how Robinson came to be wearing that headdress and whether or in what context it was gifted to him, but this would have not been done lightly. It is significant that Robinson sat with Nebanagoching and Shingwaukonce and posed in chiefly regalia with them, and particularly in a headdress, in clothing that was in all likelihood gifted to him.[82] By wearing his gifts, Robinson was honouring his relationship with the Lake Huron Anishinabek.

French and later British colonial officials gave medals as marks of leadership to the Anishinabek and gifted Anishinaabe leaders with suits of clothing, because that is how the Anishinabek treated them.[83]

---

82 Alan Corbiere, "Anishinaabe Headgear."

83 Bruce M. White has discussed the significance of gift exchange in the French fur trade. See "Give Us a Little Milk." Cary Miller found this practice of gift exchange between allies continued during Anishinaabe treaty-making with Americans: "Gifts as Treaties," 221–3.

The exchange of clothing signified the ability to care for the other. The exchange of the insignia of ogimaa and marks of leadership symbolized mutual recognition of the leadership roles of the other. While the word ogimaa was translated by the French as captain or chef, and by the English as chief, translation went the other way as well. The Anishinabek assigned the role of ogimaa to kings, queens (*ogimaakwe*), governors, and lieutenants-generals and post commanders – transforming these imperial officials into a recognizable Anishinaabe leadership category. And when these same colonial leaders or their delegates performed the expectations of their new role – by taking care of their allies as relatives – they provided tangible evidence to Anishinaabe eyes that their colonial allies understood Anishinaabe values and laws.[84]

Even after the War of 1812, when Anishinaabe communities really found themselves on the front lines of settler colonialism, material gifts still had legal meaning and material goods still functioned as metaphor. In 1829, for example, at a council at the British fort on St. Joseph's Island, the Crown announced its intention to relocate its council fire (where the British distributed presents) to Coldwater. The Crown had purchased the island in 1798 to build a military fort, and for thirty years a British council fire had been "lit" at this location. Anishinaabe council fires sometimes moved (as Chapter 3 will discuss, council fires could be covered, extinguished, or kindled), but this decision was worrisome because the British had not consulted their allies. In their remarks in response to this announcement, speakers expressed their concern about this unilateral action, but then invited the British to demonstrate to the Anishinabek that the British were still good allies (good relations).

In their speeches, the chiefs did not press the British with outrageous demands but rather requested that their allies demonstrate their continued capacity to care for the old, the young, and generations yet unborn. These were metaphorical demands: chiefs asked for kettles for the old women, weapons for the young men, and clothing for the unborn child of a young widow. The expectation was still that allies would be generous in meeting demands. And in turn, when allies had needs such as access to land or military aid, those needs would also be met – in the same way that they had always been. Some speeches from this council demonstrate this rhetorical device and invoked need in terms of what

---

84 Cary Miller, "Gifts as Treaties."

anthropologist Mary Black Rogers has called a pity speech, intended to invite one's relation to meet a need: Shingauch, the Menominee ogimaa, said, "This wampum is from the old women; some of them are very industrious and are good cooks, but they have no kettles to cook in. I beg you will give them some." He then gave a pipe and the wampum. Next, Kitchi Negou spoke and said, "There is a poor woman in our camp, who has no husband or means of clothing her unborn child. I beg you will give her a suit for it." These were requests asking for material confirmation of the alliance's terms – it is beyond belief that assembled leaders could not provide some kettles or some clothing to the individuals named. Each request was accompanied by a wampum string or a pipe – in other words, a gift to the Indian Department officials present. This was a performance of alliance and the demonstration of interdependence of allies. The speakers asked the British to continue following Anishinaabe principles in which allies and their leaders keep past, present, and future generations in mind at all times. Leaders exercised their responsibility to those generations by provisioning them so that they in turn could meet the needs of their allies. As the British provisioned the Anishinabek, they in turn would be generous with the British when the latter had need of military aid, land, or other resources.[85] Such ongoing gift exchanges in the context of alliance-making and renewal call for rethinking Canada's pre-Confederation treaties with Anishinaabe council fires as simply land purchase agreements. As Anishinaabe leaders performed Anishinaabe law in formal treaty councils, they invited their French and later British counterparts into the Anishinaabe practice of governance through alliance, into a network of relationships that were grounded in the structures of Anishinaabe families. By granting allies use of their land, they were meeting the needs of their allies, just as their allies in turn met their needs through the provision of rations in times of food shortages, or through the gifting of clothing, weapons, shot, and utility items.

While the purpose of this book is to describe historical political structures and systems of governance, it is instructive to bear in mind the larger moral principle that the Anishinabek conceptualized those political structures as serving: mino-bimaadiziwin. It is this principle that animated

---

85 Transcription of Speeches from council at St. Joseph's Island, 1829, transcribed and printed in the Appendix to the 6th vol. of the *Journals of the Legislative Assembly of the Province of Canada*. Printed by the Order of the Legislative Assembly, 1847. Appendix T.

the women who sheltered graves from heat and fed the dead, the people who placed offerings of semma (tobacco) along the French River in honour of the First Beaver, the willingness to provide shelter and food to doodem kin, and the decisions of the Anishinabek to fight alongside their allies in imperial conflicts. In other words, while each Anishinaabe person was indeed suspended in a web of kin relations that would serve to sustain them in times of need, the principle and goal of bimaadiziiwin required adult Anishinabek to be actively engaged in taking care of their relations in all four directions, through the giving and receiving of gifts. In turn, when individuals received gifts, including the gift of an animal giving its life for food, people offered their thanks in recognition of another being fulfilling its obligations. Through reciprocal gifts, Anishinaabe peoples maintained their relationships with their doodem kin and allies and with all of creation. These principles formed the basis for Anishinaabe governance, discussed in the next two chapters.

3

Anishinaabe Constitutionalism

On 22 January 1840, the Anishinaabe ogimaa Musquakie (William Yellowhead), Caribou doodem, rose to speak at a general council hosted at the Credit River council fire. A veteran of the War of 1812, he was by then in his seventies. Musquakie had travelled from his home on the Rama Reserve near Lake Simcoe, some 150 kilometres away, to attend this regional gathering at which two hundred assembled Anishinaabe and fifteen Haudenosaunee delegates sought to renew a long-standing alliance agreement.[1] As he began his oration, Musquakie held aloft a woven belt of white and purple shell wampum, "3 feet long and 4 inches wide." The belt "had a row of White Wampum in the centre, running from one end to the other, and the representations of wigwams every now and then, and a large round wampum tied nearly the middle of the Belt, with a representation of the sun in the centre."[2] As he displayed the belt, Musquakie began to speak, reciting the terms of the alliance agreement that had been made some 150 years earlier, after the eastern Anishinabek and the Haudenosaunee Confederacy had agreed

---

1 "Musquakie," *Dictionary of Canadian Biography Online*. Details of this council are richly discussed in Donald Smith, *Sacred Feathers*, 123–77.
2 Minutes of a General Council held at the River Credit, 16 January 1840, Paudash Papers, LAC RG10, Vol. 1011, Part B:60–92.

to a formal peace following a century or more of episodic conflict.[3] Four of the five images on the belt represented a council fire that had been created or an old fire that had been relit as the result of the alliance.[4]

According the minutes taken in translation by Peter Jones,

> Yellowhead stated that this Belt was given by the Nahdooways [the Haudenosaunee Confederacy] to the Ojebways [Anishinaabe] many years ago – about the time the French first came to this country. That the great Council took place at Lake Superior – That the Nahdooways made the road or path and pointed out the different council fires which were to be kept lighted. The first marks on the Wampum represented that a council fire should be kept burning at the Sault St. Marie.
>
> The 2nd mark represented the Council fire at the Manitoulin Island, where a beautiful White fish was placed, who should watch the fire as long as the world stood.
>
> The 3rd Mark represents the Council fire placed on an Island opposite Penetanguishene Bay, on which was placed a Beaver to watch the fire.
>
> The 4th mark represents the Council fire lighted up at the Narrows of Lake Simcoe at which place was put a White Rein Deer. To him the Rein Deer was committed the keeping of this Wampum talk. At this place our fathers hung up the Sun, and said that the Sun should be a witness to all what had been done and that when any of their descendants saw the Sun they might remember the acts of their forefathers.
>
> At the Narrows our fathers placed a dish with ladles around it, and a ladle for the Six Nations, who said to the Ojebways that the dish or bowl should never be emptied, but he (Yellowhead) was sorry to say that it had already been emptied, not by the Six Nations on the Grand River, but by the Caucanawaugas residing near Montreal.
>
> The 5th Mark represents the Council fire which was placed at this River Credit where a beautiful White headed Eagle was placed upon a very tall pine tree, in order to watch the Council fires and see if any ill winds blew upon the smoke of the Council fires. A dish was also placed at the Credit.

---

3 See the testimony of Elder Fred Pine Sr., in Conway, "Ojibwa Oral History"; "Testimony of Chief Robert Paudash on the Coming of the Mississauga," Paudash Papers, Ontario Historical Society, 1905, published in *The Valley of the Trent*, ed. Edwin C. Guillet (Toronto: Champlain Society, 1957), 9–13. For an excellent summary of these accounts, see MacLeod, "Anishinabeg Point of View."

4 While the location of the belt is not known, Figure 23 may be the wampum pouch in which the belt was stored; or it would have been held in a pouch very similar to this one. Note the caribou hoof motif, reflecting the doodem of the wampum carrier.

That the right of hunting on the north side of the Lake was secured to the Ojebways, and that the Six Nations were not to hunt here only when they come to smoke the pipe of peace with their Ojebway brethren.

The path on the Wampum went from the Credit over to the other side of the Lake the country of the Six Nations.

Thus ended the talk of Yellowhead and his Wampum.[5]

As he recited the terms of the alliance, Musquakie was performing Anishinaabe constitutionalism – by this, I mean that the sites of governance and their leaders were legitimated through meetings of Anishinaabe ogimaawag assembled in a regional council with their allies, just as the Nipissing leaders were recognized in 1642 at the regional gathering. The establishment of new common council sites required the sanction of the broader network of people within the alliance, so the new lands had to be constituted as responsibilities of named Anishinaabe council fires but ratified by all.[6] Decisions were ratified by regional ogimaawag, acting on the advice of councils of women and councils of warriors, coming to consensus in formal council. Such decisions always involved doodemag, as an ogimaa of a particular doodem would be assigned as the keeper of the newly constituted council fire. Anishinaabe constitutionalism required periodic renewal and reconfirmation of the terms of alliance agreements and renewal and reconfirmation of sites of governance; and this, in fact, is what Musquakie and the assembled ogimaawag were doing in 1840: hearing the full terms of the agreement prior to discussion of its renewal. This chapter explores how doodem was used as allegory to constitute and structure Anishinaabe governance and to claim, and reaffirm, Anishinaabe relationships to particular lands and resources. The doodem tradition, as a system of categories and a uniquely Anishinaabe kinship category, expressed their responsibility to the lands and waters of the Great Lakes.

Musquakie's 1840 recitation of the alliance that rekindled and founded two new eastern Anishinaabe council fires took place six months before the British Parliament would impose a new constitution on its colony

---

5 Minutes of a General Council held at the River Credit, 16 January 1840, Paudash Papers, LAC RG10, Vol. 1011, Part B:60–92.

6 Anishinaabe constitutionalism is an ongoing and dynamic practice. See for example the process for developing the Constitution of the White Earth Nation, ratified in April 2009 and discussed in Vizenor and Mackay, "Constitutional Narratives."

of Upper Canada: the Act of Union. Intended to quell dissent and promote French-Canadian political assimilation following the rebellions of 1837–8, this new act replaced the 1791 Constitution Act, another British statute that had created the separate jurisdictions of Upper Canada and Lower Canada in the wake of the American Revolution.[7] Both acts defined the terms of British settler governance for these territories. The Anishinabek, however, had their own constituting practices and assertions of jurisdictions for these lands, which long pre-dated those imposed by the British. The belt read by Musquakie is a constitution, akin to an act of parliament that creates a new province or territory within an existing polity. According to the agreement, the Haudenosaunee initiated the peace (they "made the road") and requested that the Anishinabek keep four council fires burning as sites of governance for the alliance. The political legitimacy of each was recognized and reaffirmed by the public reading of the terms. This required the physical presence of the belts, an audience of those who were party to the terms, and a speaker who recited the terms he had committed to memory.

This was an alliance agreement that, in its initial acceptance in the late seventeenth century, reshaped the political geography of the eastern Great Lakes region after the breakup of the Wendat Confederacy in 1649. Following a period of conflict, the parties came to agreement on the terms of peace. The Anishinabek entered into an alliance with the Haudenosaunee, who in turn formally recognized Anishinaabe responsibility for the lands that are now in southern Ontario. Recall that prior to 1649, Anishinaabe council fires were lit in what is now southern Ontario and that those council fires had been in alliance relationships with the Wendat. But after the breakup of the Wendat Confederacy, and as peace returned to the region, old council fires needed to be relit and new ones established, to restore old, and create new, jurisdictions in collaboration with allies. The Great Lakes practice of constitutionalism required public oration at regular intervals, which Musquakie was doing at this council. As he recited, Musquakie explained that each of the circles on the belt represented a council fire which was the responsibility of a particular doodem: Whitefish on Manitoulin Island, Beaver on Parry

---

7 Parliament of Great Britain, Constitutional Act, 1791 (31 Geo. III, c.31); 23 July 1840, Parliament of the United Kingdom, Act of Union, (3 and 4 Vict. C. 35). For an overview of the Rebellions, see Bernard, *Rebellions of 1837 and 1838*, or a standard university survey textbook in Canadian history.

Island in Georgian Bay, Caribou at Mnjikaning (the narrows where the waters of Lake Couchiching flow into Lake Simcoe), and Eagle at the mouth of the Credit River, where the river flows into Lake Ontario.

Musquakie spoke metaphorically of regional political changes that had happened more than a century and a half before. The circles representing Manitoulin Island and Parry Island were for fires whose slumbering embers were uncovered – that is, they represented places where previous council fires had burned. To describe the fire at Mnjikaning, Musquakie said that it had been "lighted up" – in other words, that it represented a new site of governance and that the Caribou doodem would therefore be the firekeeper. *Ishkode*, or fire, was used by Musquakie both metaphorically and literally to refer to the specific sites where councils were held and as the metaphor for Anishinaabe governance broadly. By explicitly naming the doodem responsible for each fire, he revealed the intertwined centrality of doodem and ishkode in Anishinaabe governance: each council fire that Musquakie named was a gathering place for a council where decisions regarding access to lands and resources were made. Each of the four doodemag that Musquakie associated with place identified the ogimaa who was responsible not only for maintaining the physical council fire when meetings occurred but also for the broader political responsibilities of that council. This record of Musquakie's speech is a rare and important archival record of Anishinaabe constitutionalism in action; it demonstrates Anishinaabe practices for creating new sites of governance and identifying the people responsible for those lands.

But there were old fires that were also referenced by this agreement: one Anishinaabe council fire, which met at Bawaating, and the multiple council fires of the Haudenosaunee Confederacy, which had initiated, or "made the road," for this alliance. Their homeland stretched across the Finger Lakes district of what is now upper New York State. The Haudenosaunee also used fire as metaphor for governance, though their languages and political systems were significantly different from Anishinaabe ones.[8] Bawaating is where the war council had first met in the early 1650s to plans its actions against Haudenosaunee attacks. All the Anishinaabe delegates listening to Musquakie speak that day would have known of the Crane doodem's long-standing role as the keeper of

---

8 See "Glossary of Figures of Speech in Iroquois Political Rhetoric," in Jennings, ed., *History and Culture of Iroquois Diplomacy*, 115–26.

the council fire at Bawaating, reaffirmed through widely shared oral histories. As is common with wampum belts, the symbols displayed on it can form a visual synecdoche – a metaphor where a part represents the whole – and this belt as described was no exception. Listeners could imagine the line of the alliance as the arced path connecting these fires, from Bawaating on the one end, through the new fires, and off the belt on the other end to the fires of the Haudenosaunee Confederacy then located south of Lake Ontario.

These implicit fires – Bawaating and those of the Haudenosaunee Confederacy – were already "lit" (i.e., established) before this late seventeenth-century agreement was made, and they had never been extinguished. The Haudenosaunee Confederacy was established much earlier through its own constitution and Great Law, as expressed in the Ayenwahta Wampum Belt.[9] The establishment of Bawaating is recorded in origin narratives that situate the Crane as the keeper of the council fire there dating back to time immemorial – back to the emergence of the First Crane, the ancestor being of the Crane doodem.[10] Such narratives that are set in "time immemorial" establish broad Anishinaabe Indigeneity to those places.[11] But, as this chapter will show, some Anishinaabe origin narratives also perform constitutionalism by using doodem allegory to assert the claim of particular doodem identities to governance responsibilities at specific places.

The agreement read by Musquakie is also significant because it explains why the pattern of doodem images on some eastern Ontario land sale agreements look the way that they do, particularly in locations for which there were multiple documents signed. Treaties and associated documents, such as receipts for annuity payments, consistently show Crane doodem images appearing first and with the highest frequency on documents pertaining to the lands and resources under the jurisdiction of Bawaating. Likewise, Caribou doodem images appear first, and with the highest frequency, on documents pertaining to the lands and resources under the jurisdiction of the Caribou at Mnjikaning. Eagle doodem images appear first, and with the highest frequency, on documents pertaining to the lands and resources under the

---

9 For a concise overview of the Great Lake and Ayenwahtha Belt, see Hill, *Clay We Are Made Of*, 31–5.
10 For one version of the founding of Bawaating, see Warren and Neill, *History*, 87.
11 Chamberlin, *If This is Your Land, Where Are Your Stories?*

jurisdiction of the Eagle at the Credit River. The peace agreement read by Musquakie established and asserted the Crane and Eagle doodemag as being responsible for the lands and resources in their respective jurisdictions. (See Figures 24 and 25.)

As Musquakie also explained through allegory, the second image on the belt represented the fire on Manitoulin Island, "where a beautiful White fish was placed, who should watch the fire as long as the world stood." The third image represented "the Council fire placed on an Island opposite Penetanguishine Bay, on which was placed a Beaver to watch the fire." While this alliance specifically identified council fires to be kept by Whitefish and Beaver doodem ogimaawag on Mnidoo Minising or Odawa Minising (Manitoulin Island) and Wasauksing (Parry Island) respectively, there are not the same number of documents with examples of these doodemag and these council fires as there are for Mnjikaning, Bawaating, and the Credit River to demonstrate the continuity of leadership. For example, the major land cession for Manitoulin Island, the north shore of Lake Huron, and eastern Georgian Bay was the 1850 Robinson-Huron Treaty. This treaty is an anomaly. It is the one major land cession negotiated between the British and the Anishinabek in the pre-Confederation period that did *not* contain doodem images.[12] Nevertheless, recorded oral narratives and doodem images on other treaties, annuity payments documents, letters, and speeches reveal that Whitefish and Beaver were both regionally significant identities with

---

12 There is also a smaller land cession, the Coldwater Road Allowance, signed in 1836, that also has X-marks. Significantly, both this cession and the Robinson Treaties of 1850 were negotiated by the same person: William B. Robinson. On this earlier cession, four of the leading ogimaawag signed with their doodemag, while the remaining gichi-Anishinaabek signed with x-marks. Chippewas of Lakes Huron and Simcoe - Surrender ..., 26 November 1836, LAC RG10, Vol. 1844/126. Robinson was not a member of the Indian Department and so this departure from standard protocol may have been his personal preference. However, in 1843 a member of the department, J.W. Keating, expressed frustration with the amount of time and ceremony involved in inscribing doodem images on treaty documents and receipts for annuity payments: "I had commenced by causing each Indian to make his totem but the amazing time each took would have occupied two or three days from their numbers & so they merely touched the pen as white people unable to write but before a witness who can swear to the genuineness of each signature." J.W. Keating to Samuel Jarvis, 13 September 1843, Office of the Chief Superintendent in Upper Canada, LAC RG10, Vol.134:76098–91.

long-standing ties to these places. The Beaver doodem in particular was identified in early seventeenth-century records and on seventeenth-century maps as the "Amikouais" or Beaver nation (People of the Beaver, an effort by French writers to spell "Amikwag"), located roughly in the northeastern corner of Georgian Bay.

The fourth mark on the belt read by Musquakie "represents the Council fire lighted up at the Narrows of Lake Simcoe, and at which place was put a White Rein Deer … the 5th mark represents the Council fire which was placed at this River Credit where a beautiful White headed Eagle was placed upon a very tall pine tree." Musquakie was the ogimaa from Mnjikaning. He was at the Credit River reading the belt in 1840 because, through this agreement more than a century and a half earlier, the Caribou doodem at Mnjikaning was given the responsibility of "the keeping of this Wampum talk." The first council at which this agreement was made was likely Mnjikaning itself because, as Musquakie explained, it was Mnjikaning where "our fathers hung up the Sun, and said that the Sun should be a witness to all what had been done and that when any of their descendants saw the Sun they might remember the acts of their forefathers." For the Anishinabek, the sun is both a manidoo and a grandfather: an ensouled being with qualities of personhood and also a relative and ancestor. By invoking the Sun as a witness, Musquakie was emphasizing the sacredness and importance of this constitution. Invoking the Sun as a witness to the agreement is akin to swearing an oath on the Bible. The fact that Musquakie situates the act of witnessing by the Creator as occurring at Mnjikaning underscores the continued legitimacy of the Caribou's role as the keeper of the talk and the central council fire of the alliance. By extension, this role included Mnjikaning's responsibility for being the alliance's archive – Musquakie not only kept the physical belt but was responsible for ensuring that the memory of the alliance was preserved and transmitted to the next generation.

This renewal in 1840, however, was being held at the Credit River, with attendees from the Six Nations of the Grand River. In his speech following his remarks about Mnjikaning, Musquakie explained the specific role of the Eagle doodem within the alliance. Recall that at the River Credit "a beautiful White headed Eagle was placed upon a very tall pine tree" – its purpose, Musquakie then explained, was "in order to watch the Council fires and see if any ill winds blew upon the smoke of the Council fires." The beautiful white-headed Eagle is, of course, a bald eagle. And the white pine, with its five needles representing the original five nations of the Confederacy, is one of the Haudenosaunee Confederacy's most potent central symbols.[13] There is a double reference here. The Haudenosaunee also described a white-headed eagle sitting on their great tree of peace (the white pine) while the bald eagle was also the doodem of the ogimaa who was the keeper of the council fire of the Credit River. Musquakie's allegory presented the Credit River council as being the one tasked with, in essence, relationship management, or external affairs.

This agreement also contained within it the roles and responsibilities of the allied council fires. Given that each council fire kept its autonomy in these types of alliances, neither the Credit council nor the Mnjikaning council could compel the actions of any of the other parties. An "ill wind" is a metaphor for a problem or threat; so in this alliance the Credit River council was tasked with being an early warning system for any potential threats to the alliance that might require additional negotiation to sort out. The longevity of this alliance, lasting more than 150 years, is a testament to their success. Musquakie's subsequent remarks also described additional responsibilities for the Credit River community within the alliance – to be the messenger between the Haudenosaunee and the rest of the allied Anishinaabe fires in the eastern Great Lakes and to notify the Caribou if and when renewal councils should be called. In so doing, the speech Musquakie recited reveals the use of nested metaphors for both Anishinaabe common and general councils. Every council had its ogimaa who met in consultations with his gichi-Anishinabek. Recall that ogimaa often had an identified aanikeogimaa, or step-below chief, who acted as both an assistant and a deputy. On treaty documents the doodem images of these individuals appear below that of the ogimaa, in the second position. In this larger alliance agreement, then, Musquakie stood in relation to the ogimaa of the other fires as a *chi-ogimaa*, as the ogimaa of a local council stood in relation to his own gichi-Anishinabek. And the Credit River ogimaa (the host of this particular event) filled this agreement's roles of both messenger and step-below chief in the larger alliance.

This record of the 1840 council is remarkable as a document of an alliance between the Anishinaabe and Haudenosaunee peoples and also for what it reveals about use of doodem and fire as metaphors through

---

13 Jennings, *History and Culture of Iroquois Diplomacy.* For an excellent recent study of the Haudenosaunee at Six Nation in Canada, see Hill, *Clay We Are Made Of.*

which Anishinaabe governance was constituted. The belt shows us how doodemag were used, allegorically, to enact new relationships between people and place by referring to new sites for councils; and, by extension, to identify the leaders who had responsibility for the lands and resources. It created jurisdictions by identifying which doodemag were the keepers of the respective council fires. In addition to alliance agreements such as the one above, Anishinaabe aadizookaanag (sacred stories) and dibaajimowin (histories) also use doodem as a political allegory to explain how particular people came to gather at different locations and what doodem identity was responsible for keeping the fire of each common council. Drawing from these understandings, one can then see Anishinaabe law in action and construct a dynamic political map of the Great Lakes region, one that captures the complexities of Anishinaabe governance, the continuities and changes in doodemag, the emergence of new council fires, and the webs of alliances which crossed the Great Lakes.

Doodem and the Founding of Council Fires in Deep Time

As the ogimaa Musquakie demonstrated so evocatively in his 1840 reading of an alliance agreement, the doodem tradition was a system of categories that did political work through metaphor and allegory. Chapter 1 discussed the origin narratives for the doodem tradition. Those same narratives that tell the history of the doodem tradition also consciously tied certain doodem identities to specific places, as the birthplace or site of emergence for human beings with that doodem. Such origin narratives not only explained the creation of the doodem tradition; they were also constitutional. Migration narratives form the other dominant strand of Anishinaabe origin stories, and they likewise contain both elements of Anishinaabe political histories (where people moved from, where to, and why) and how people came to have responsibility for lands in new locations.

Doodem narratives of origin are powerful political allegories. As the examples in Chapter 1 showed, late seventeenth- and early eighteenth-century doodem origin narratives that explain the emergence of the Beaver doodem along the French River or the Hare doodem at Michilimackinac use doodem as allegory to recognize and reaffirm longstanding doodem responsibility for particular territories and council fires. In another version, published in William Warren's *History*, Crane ogimaa Tugwaugaunay explains how the origins of Bawaating as a seat

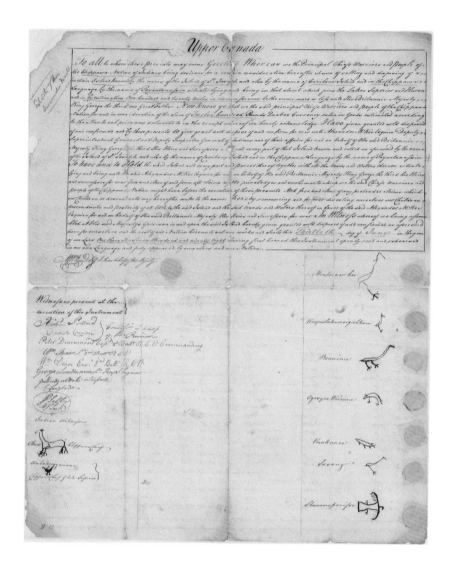

1. Treaty for the sale of St. Joseph's Island, 30 June 1798 to the British Crown, signed with doodem images by Ogimaa Meatoosawke (Crane), Aanikeogimaa Keegustakamsigishkam (Crane), Boanince (Crane), Ogasque Waiaune (Marten), Kaukonce (Pike), Sasong (Crane), Shawanapennisse (Thunderbird). Library and Archives Canada.

2. A large woven mat, made of basswood and bullrush or cattail, 126 cm wide × 206 cm long, "wrought as tapestries are in France." This example is from Leech Lake, Minnesota, and was made sometime before 1904. This and the following four images are examples of gifts given to a council fire host. Ethnologisches Museum Berlin, Germany.

3. An oval-shaped birchbark basket with a rim wrapped in split root and porcupine quills, 22.5 cm × 16.5 cm. Museo Civico di Scienze Naturali di Bergamo, Italy.

4. Strands of white wampum ("porcelaine beads"), bound as traditionally expected: bound on one end, loose at the other end. One end is tied with a blue silk ribbon tie. 40 cm long. Ethnologisches Museum Berlin, Germany.

5. A pair of moccasins given to British Army officer Major Andrew Foster (1768–1806) at Fort Miami or Fort Michilimackinac. Colours faded from their original bright blue, red (now orange), black, and white. © National Museum of the American Indian, Smithsonian Institution.

Portrait d'un homme de l'a
Nation des Noupiming dach=riniouek.

ouaRacouathache deguerre

6. Portrait of a man of the nation of the Noupiming-dach-iriniouek, *Codex Canadensis*, circa 1700. Gilcrease Museum, Tulsa, Oklahoma.

homme de La Nation des
amikouek dont sa nations. 17. fournit plusieurs Milliers
de castors pour la france.

7. Portrait of a man of the Amikouek nation, *Codex Canadensis*, circa 1700.
Gilcrease Museum, Tulsa, Oklahoma.

8. Ball-headed Otter war club carved from wood, with iron spike set into the ball, 60 × 23 × 9.5 cm, and close-up of the face. The artist has captured the wide-set eyes, whiskers, and the jaw line of the otter. Musée du quai Branly, Paris, France.

9. Fishing by the Passinassiouek, *Codex Canadensis*, circa 1700. These two men, from Bawaating, are both wearing headdresses. Compare these with images of headdresses in Figures 21 and 22, especially with Nebanagoching's headdress in Figure 22. The man in the bow of the canoe is playing a bibigwan (an end-blown flute). Anishinaabe peoples historically used flutes for many purposes, including fishing. Gilcrease Museum, Tulsa, Oklahoma.

10. George Catlin, *Canoe Race Near Sault Ste. Marie*, 1836–7. Catlin's painting captures the excitement and energy at the games and competitions during an Anishinaabe gathering at Bawaating. Men, women, and children enthusiastically cheered the racers as they lined the course while sitting (or standing!) in their brightly painted birchbark canoes. Smithsonian American Art Museum, Washington, DC.

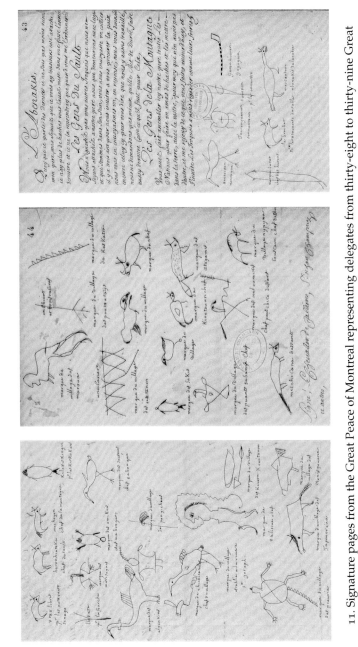

11. Signature pages from the Great Peace of Montreal representing delegates from thirty-eight to thirty-nine Great Lakes Indigenous nations. Anishinaabe pictographs appear in the top half of the middle page. Archives Nationales d'Outre Mer, Aix-en-Provence, France.

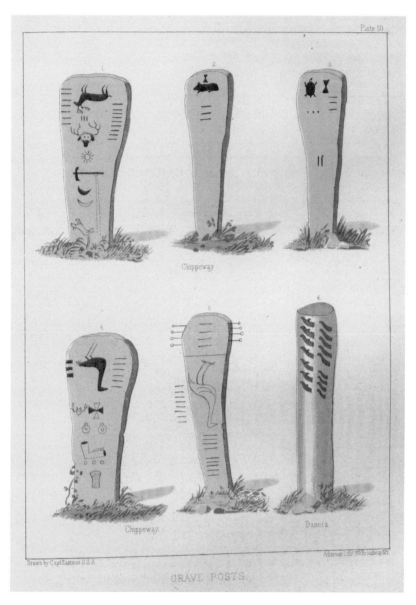

Plate 50

Chippeway

Chippeway

Dacota

Drawn by Capt Eastman U.S.A.

Ackerman Lith 379 Broadway N.Y.

GRAVE POSTS.

12. Grave posts with doodem images from Henry Rowe Schoolcraft, *Historical and statistical information, respecting the history, condition and prospects of the Indian tribes of the United States*, 1857.

13. Pipe presented to Sir Francis Bond Head as Lieutentant-Governor of Upper Canada at the 1836 Manitowaning Treaty. The pipe was used to open council between the British and 1,500 assembled Anishinaabeg. Overall length of pipe and stem: 47 5/8 inches. The pipe has been repatriated by the host council fire, Wiikwemkoong Unceded Territory, and is printed here with their kind permission.

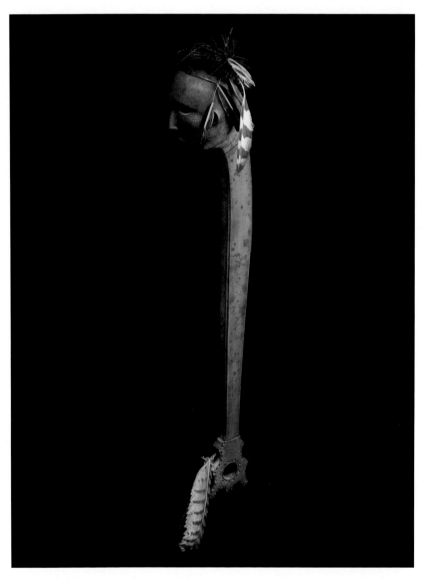

14. A bgamaagan, or war club, presented to Lord Elgin, while he was
Governor General of Canada (1847–54). National Museum of Scotland,
Edinburgh.

15. Chief's coat, issued by British Army, said to have belonged to Oshawana (John Naudee), Anishinaabeg (Ojibwa). Royal Ontario Museum, Toronto.

16. Ambrotype portrait of Chief Oshawana of Walpole Island, Tecumseh's aide de camp during the War of 1812, taken in 1838. Royal Ontario Museum, Toronto.

17. King George II Peace Medal, dated 1757. The inscription reads: "Let us look to the most high who blessed our fathers with peace." This and the medal in Figure 18 were commissioned to commemorate alliances between the British and Great Lakes nations. Gilcrease Museum, Tulsa, Oklahoma.

18. George III Indian Chief Medal, dated 1764, from the Treaty of Niagara. The inscription reads: "Happy While United." Library and Archives Canada.

19. 1764 Treaty of Niagara Covenant Chain belt. This belt is presumed to have been lost in a fire. The last known belt-carriers lived on Manitoulin Island. A sketch of the belt was made from the originals in the 1850s. Reproduction by Ken Maracle, Canadian Museum of History, Ottawa.

20. Sir John Caldwell wearing gifted regalia, circa 1780. National Museums Liverpool, United Kingdom.

21. Regalia given to Andrew Foster, gifted around 1790 when Foster was serving at Fort Michilimackinac. Note the thunderbird motifs on the neck ornament. National Museum of the American Indian, Washington, DC.

22. William B. Robinson (left), government treaty negotiator for the Robinson-Huron Treaty of 1850, with Shingwaukonce (centre) and Nebanagoching (right), the hereditary Crane ogimaa of Bawaating. All three men are wearing regalia including marks of leadership. Image taken in either Toronto or Montreal. Shingwauk Residential Schools Centre, Algoma University, Sault Ste. Marie, Ontario.

23. Pouch with Caribou doodem referenced by two caribou hoof images and
five representations of the four directions. The black and white quillwork also
evokes wampum. Canadian Museum of History, Ottawa.

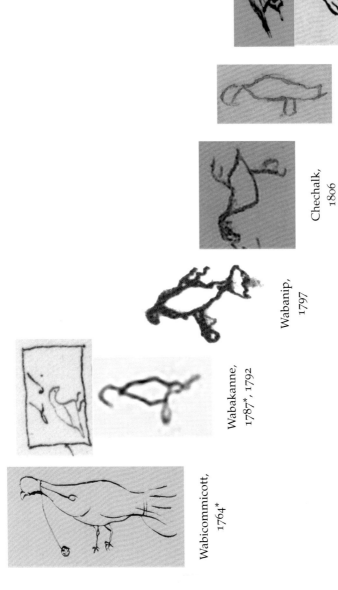

Joseph Sawyer,
1831, 1844

Adjutant,
1818

Chechalk,
1806

Wabanip,
1797

Wabakanne,
1787*, 1792

Wabicommicott,
1764*

24. Eagle ogimaag at the Credit River. Years given indicate the date when the pictograph was inscribed on the treaty document or petition. * indicates copy made by clerk.

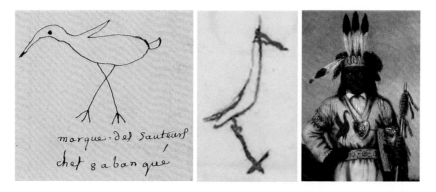

Bawaating: Marque des Sauteurs, 1701; Meatoowanakwee, 1798;
Nebanagoching, 1849

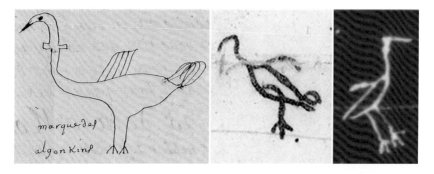

Marque des Algonquins, 1701; Pahtash, Rice Lake, 1818; George Paudash,
Rice Lake, 1856

25. The Crane doodem were keepers of multiple council fires throughout the
Great Lakes, including at Bawaating, Rice Lake, and in Algonquin territory
along the Ottawa River. Nebanagoching's portrait shows him wearing
his Crane doodem on his coat, in a posture indicating the intent to defend
one's territory.

Marque des   Shawanapenisse,   Peewaushemanogh,
Mississauges,   1798   Treaty of Detroit,
1701   1807

Wabinaship, Credit River, 1792

Chechalk, Credit River, 1806

Peter Jones (note the
bald head), on a petition
to Queen Victoria, 1844

26. Leadership qualities in Thunderbird and Eagle doodem images.

Sandhill crane, bowing | Wabanqué, Bawaating, 1701 | Kewukance, Treaty of Manitowaning, 1836

Sandhill crane, jumping

George Paudash, Rice Lake, 1856

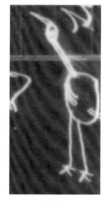

Sandhill crane, location call

Toquish, Windsor/ Detroit area, 1800

27. Leadership qualities expressed through the body postures of cranes in Crane doodem images.

Woodland caribou, note dewclaws visible above rear hoof,
reproduced on track mark below.

| Ningwason, Mnjikaning, and Ogaa, St. Joseph's Island, both 1798 | Mesquescon, Bay of Quinte, 1816; Maytoygwaan (partially covered by a wafer), 1819 | Annamakance, Caribou doodem represented by the track mark, London Township, 1796 |

Channel Catfish, note forked tail

| Kiskakons, 1701 | Mitchiwass, London Township, 1796 | Boquaquet, Treaty of Detroit, 1807 |

28. Representation of Caribou and Catfish doodem images.

shall and may at all times forever hereafter, Peaceably
and quietly have, hold Occupy, Possess and enjoy all and
Singular the said Tract or Parcel of Land, hereditaments an
Palmises aforesaid with the Appurtinances, and every Part or
Parcel thereof, without trouble, hindrance, molestation, interrup-
-tion or disturbance, of them the said Wabakanyne, the Sachems
&c their Heirs or Successors, or any Other Person or Persons Law-
fully claiming, or to Claim, by from, or under them, or any of
them, and that Sneed, Discharged and kept have
endemnified, of, from, and against all former and other
Gifts or Grants whatsoever. In Witness whereof we
have hereunto set our hands and Seals the Date and Date
above Mentioned

Witness Present   Signed   Wabaka   his   nyne   (Seal)
                                                      mark
Signed   Robt Mayes Majr 34 Regt   Nanne   his   boson   (Seal)
         D Forbes Capt 34 Regt   mark
    Joseph Brant Thayendanegea   Pokqu   his   an   (Sea
    David Hill Karonghyenta   mark
                                            Nanaghkay   washem   (Seal)
    P Wilkinson   Peapam   his   aw   (Seal)
    Act Secty Sip Nation Dyt   mark
                                            Jabeno   his   an   (Seal)
                                                      mark
                                            Sawa   his   manok   (Seal)
                                                     mark
                                            Peasa   her   nish   (Seal)
                                                     mark
    Montreal 23d March 1791   Wapanonus   her   II   (Seal)
    a True Copy of the   chiqua
    Orriginal Deed   Wapeanoyt   her   qua   (Seal)
    Joseph Grieu   mark
    SIA

An Assemblage of the Chiefs of the Mississauga Nation took place at York, 7 Octr. 1811 and the following Speech was made by them to His Excellency the Lieutenant Governor previous to his departure for England —

Father — We are grieved to see You leave us, because we have experienced the Constancy of Your Charity —

We Speak our own feelings and the feelings of our Brothers at Lake Simcoe — if they were here, they would Speak the Sentiments which we now speak — they and us have but one and the Same heart towards You — —

Father — We know the Charities which You have done to our Wives and Children, and we hope that he who is to take Your place, will be like You — and that You will recommend us to be considered by him — We shall be always ready to listen to him — and he will send us decided —

Father — Leave behind You further Marks of Your good heart, and tell him who takes Your place, to have Pity upon us when we are in Sickness, and to clothe our Children when they are naked — This is all we have to say, and we hope that You listen to us, and will not forget us —

Father — As you are about to embark, we wish that the Great Spirit will have his Eyes on you, that You may arrive Safe in Your Own Country, where our Great Father the King is —

Wabbanonay
Edjican
Yayassoway
Osawe
Nosins
Ayyabananse

J. B. te Cadotte
Indian Interpreter

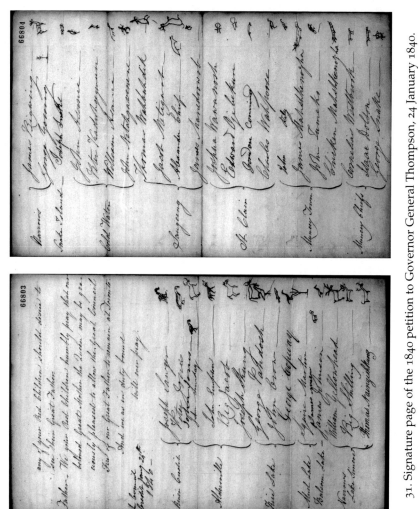

31. Signature page of the 1840 petition to Governor General Thompson, 24 January 1840. Library and Archives Canada.

32. Nipissing-Anishinaabe petition from 1848 showing a Caribou doodem affixed with sealing wax. Library and Archives Canada.

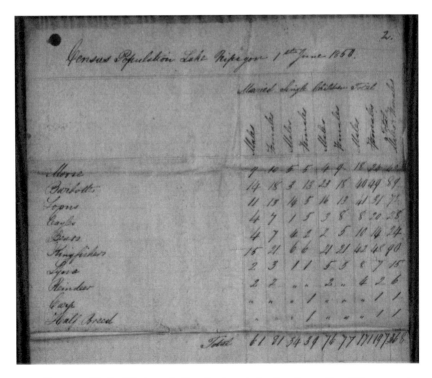

33. Census of Lake Nipigon *indinaakonigewin* by doodem, 1850. Library and Archives Canada.

SYMBOLIC PETITION OF CHIPPEWA CHIEFS,

presented at Washington, January 28th 1849, headed by Oshcabawis of Monomonecau, Wisconsin

34. Symbolic petition of Chippewa Chiefs, presented at Washington, 28 January 1849, headed by Oshkabawis of Wisconsin.

Ningwason, 1798   Big Shilling, 1835   David Abetung,
                                                                       1857

Chippewas of RAMA
First Nation

Deer Sun Logo of the Chippewas of Rama First Nation

35. Representation of Caribou doodem images changing to Whitetail Deer at
Mnjikaning (Chippewas of Rama)

Marque du Village,   Neace, 1787
1701

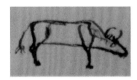   

Moses Pahdequong, 1831   James Smoke, 1837

36. Representation of Bison, changing to Domestic Cattle.

of governance led by a Crane doodem ogimaa dates back to the creation of the Anishinaabe world. In Tugwaugaunay's recounting, after the Great Spirit first made the Crane, "it circled slowly above the Great Fresh Water Lakes ... looking for a resting place, 'til it lit on the hill overlooking Boweting [Bawaating/Sault Ste. Marie]."[14] That hill was the site of councils at Bawaating and the location where St. Lusson had held his 1671 prise-de-possession ceremony, as described in the Introduction. Such narratives demonstrate the use of doodemag as a source of law that gives the parameters of jurisdictions – of who had rights and responsibilities in each place.

Establishing New Council Fires

While French, British, and later American officials may have struggled to appreciate the political significance of doodem identity, they did record enough Anishinaabe narratives to give insights into how doodem governance operated both locally and regionally. Those who did have more intimate, first-hand knowledge of the teachings of Elders are crucial sources, especially those Anishinaabe authors who wrote about the tradition, particularly Peter Jones and William Warren. Such stories like those concerning the origin of the Beaver, Hare, and Crane doodemag explained how humans with those doodem identities could claim precedence in a region due to their in-situ origin or establishment by a First Being. But what about those times when the Anishinabek needed to establish new council fires? On what stories would they draw? As the example of the wampum talk that opened this chapter demonstrates, Anishinaabe ogimaawag also used doodem to constitute new councils. In the absence of origin narratives, on what basis would they have decided that the Caribou should host the council fire at Mnjikaning, for example, or the Eagle at the Credit River? Why one doodem and not another? I suggest that here doodem as an ontological category also worked to create certain kinds of political possibilities and to limit others. In other words, there is doodem logic at work here.

With their knowledge of the characteristics, behaviours, and preferred habitats of particular doodem beings, the Anishinabek understood that only certain doodemag were culturally logical choices for this kind of leadership role. Specifically, the doodem identity chosen to

---

14 Warren and Neill, *History*, 87.

be the keeper of a fire also needed its other-than-human counterpart to exist in the habitat where the new fire was established. This problem arose for the people from the north shore of Lake Huron, some of whom moved into the southern Ontario peninsula in the late seventeenth and very early eighteenth century. On the signature page of the 1701 Peace of Montreal, these "Mississaugas" of the north shore of Lake Huron signed with a clear representation of a thunderbird image. Allied with and led by chiefs of the Crane and Beaver doodem across the north shore region from Sault Ste. Marie to the French River, the Mississaugas had taken part in a campaign to push the Haudenosaunee Confederacy out of what is now southern Ontario. Following their victory and subsequent peace treaty with the Confederacy, some of the north shore people returned home, while others moved south. However, those Anishinabek who came to the mouth of the Credit River signed later treaties not with the thunderbird but with an eagle doodem image. What led to this change?

These different images express a related idea and communicate a political history. The Eagle doodem image from the Credit River is actually a visual metaphor that served to connect the new community with their relatives from the north shore of Lake Huron. Recall that the belt read by Musquakie established the council fire at the Credit River as being cared for by the Eagle doodem; but the bald eagle refers allegorically to the thunderbird. As Peter Jones, who was from the Credit River community, explains, he was dedicated by his grandfather as an infant, "to the eagle, i.e., to the thundergod."[15] Later in his narrative, Jones related a teaching he received as a young man: that the animikiig (thunderbirds) were beings who nested and raised their young on the tops of the white flint rock hills on the Michigan peninsula. When these hills were viewed "from a distance they have all the appearance of snow-capped mountains," resembling the heads of bald eagles.[16] The north shore of Lake Huron has the same sort of geology. Viewed from the water on a sunny day, the quartz in the north shore hills glistens like snow. The Credit River location, and other important sites on the north shore of Lake Ontario, did not have the hills of white quartzite where animikiig dwelled. However, Lake Ontario was home to hundreds of bald eagles that gathered, as the Anishinabek did, at river mouths to

---

15 Jones, *History*, 12.
16 Ibid., 43.

fish. How could the Credit River people express themselves as thunder beings if they were no longer in the country of the animikiig? The lands and waters of the Credit River had no quartzite hills. The lands, waters, and ecology were different here. However, by representing themselves as bald eagles, the Anishinabek who came to establish a council fire at the Credit River could express a historic relationship with the home of their ancestors. The white head of the mature bald eagle was a reminder of their former home, and it expressed a shared quality of "eagleness" with the mighty animikiig who dwelt there. In the late seventeenth century the Credit River location would not have been a logical choice for the people of the Caribou doodem to be keepers of a council fire, as the habitat of the woodland caribou extends only as far south as the bottom extent of the Canadian Shield. The location of the Caribou council fire established at Mnjikaning is at the southern edge of the Shield and, by extension, the southern edge of the woodland caribou's range.

The Eagle doodem was also a logical choice for the Credit River location, given the characteristics and behaviours of eagles as a species and the responsibilities held by the maintainers of the Credit River council fire under this treaty. Recall that in the terms of the agreement recited by Musquakie, which opened this chapter, the Eagle was charged with two additional responsibilities: to keep a watchful eye on the behaviour of the Haudenosaunee Confederacy to the south and to act as the messenger for the Caribou at Mnjikaning, calling people together in council when required. Logic pointed to the Eagle doodem as much better suited to this role than the Caribou. There is quite a bit of poetry in positioning a far-seeing "beautiful White headed Eagle ... upon a very tall pine tree" – one that resonates with Haudenosaunee cultural symbolism as well, with the white pine being the tree of peace and the symbol of the Confederacy. Neither the Crane nor the Caribou doodem had the physical qualities that would enable them to serve as such a potent political allegory. It is no accident that the Eagle doodem came to be the leading doodem at the Credit River, as the Caribou did at Mnjikaning. These were deliberate choices made in council by ogimaa from the various doodemag who had participated in the war against the Haudenosaunee, and they were choices that also resonated deeply with the cultural logic of the doodem tradition.

Around the same time the Credit River fire was first kindled, some other Anishinabek returned to eastern Ontario – particularly in the region known as the Kawartha Lakes district, about three hundred kilometres west of Ottawa. But this was a homecoming. As the fur trader

Nicolas Perrot reported in a manuscript written not many years after the Great Peace, "Algonkins" had lived long before the French arrived "along the river of the Outaoüas, at Nepissing, on the French River, and between this last and Taronto [Toronto]."[17] Anishinaabe peoples from a council fire on the Ottawa River signed the Great Peace of Montreal as the Algonquins, with the Crane doodem. And on later treaties signed with the council fire at Rice Lake to the west, a Crane doodem always signed first. Other doodem images on nineteenth-century eastern Ontario treaties include Pike, Bison, and Birch. Champlain reported meeting fifteen canoes of people called "Quenongebin" (Ginoozhe, or Pike people) along the Ottawa River in 1613.[18]

Examples of Anishinaabe use of doodem as political allegory are found elsewhere in the Great Lakes region and demonstrate the use of doodem as a political metaphor specifically to assert the claim of a council fire to a particular territory. In his memoirs, Perrot recalled being told that:

> the Nepissings (otherwise called the Nipissiniens), Amikoiis, and all their allies claim that the Amikoiis, which means descendants of the beaver, took their creation from the corpse of the Great Beaver, from where emerged the first man of that nation; and that this beaver left Lake Huron, and entered the stream which is called the French River. They say that as the water became too low for him, he made dams, which are now rapids and portages. When he reached the river which takes its origin from the Nepissing, he crossed it, and followed [the course of] many other small streams which he passed ... And so having spent some years in his travels, he wanted to fill the country with children whom he left there, and who multiplied wherever he had passed.[19]

Perrot's account makes it clear that he was told multiple times about the origin of the Beaver doodem and its connection to the Anishinaabe council fires of eastern Georgian Bay and Lake Nipissing region. The story describes the territory fully (it is even today rich beaver habitat, full of dams and lodges) and asserts the long claim of the Beaver doodem

---

17 Perrot, "Mémoire," in Blair, *Indian Tribes*, 1:42–3. By Algonkin, Perrot is referring to Anishinaabe peoples, not specifically the Algonkin nation today.
18 Champlain met the Kinouchespirini in 1612 in what is now eastern Ontario and included them on his 1613 map. See Champlain, *Works*, 2:264.
19 Perrot, "Mémoire," in Blair, *Indian Tribes*, 1:62–4.

and the council fire of the Amikouais to that region. People recognized that territorial right throughout the region, as Perrot noted that "all their allies" also supported the claim of this origin narrative. And perhaps Perrot was told the story so many times to remind the French whose lands they were on.

In the 1820s, the Crane ogimaa Tugwaugaunay of La Pointe, Wisconsin, used a doodem origin story to depress the political pretensions of the Loon doodem ogimaa who was challenging his precedence. Embedded within that story is also a history of how·the Crane doodem first became the keeper of the fire at Bawaating and, subsequently, how it was the members of the Crane doodem who had moved west to kindle new fires, including the one at La Pointe. Tugwaugaunay's narrative, like the belt read by Musquakie, reveals how Anishinaabe governance in the Western Great Lakes was also defined through doodem and ishkode. In addition, it demonstrates the ways in which Anishinaabe leaders mobilized doodem characteristics to make political claims. As Tugwaugaunay explained to Warren: "Pleased with the sand point," the Crane,

circled over it and viewed the numerous fish as they swam about in the clear depths of the Great Lake. It lit on Shaug-ah-waum-ik-ong,[20] and from thence again it uttered its solitary cry. A voice came from the calm bosom of the lake, in answer; the bird, pleased with the musical sound of the voice, again sent forth its cry, and the answering bird made its appearance in the wampum-breasted Ah-auh-wauh (Loon). The bird spoke to it in a gentle tone "is it thou that gives the answer to my cry?"

The Loon answered "it is I" the bird then said to him "thy voice is music-it is melody, it sounds sweet in my ear, from henceforth I appoint them to answer my voice in council." Thus continued the chief, the Loon became the first in council, but he who made him chief was the Businasee or Crane. These are the words of my ancestors, who from generation to generation, have repeated them into the ears of their children.[21]

The Crane ogimaa was making an argument, through his telling of these stories to Warren, that it was not the French who made the Loon

---

20 Warren here is referring to a location on Chequamegon Bay of Lake Superior, located in what is today the northern tip of Wisconsin.
21 Warren and Neill, *History*, 86–9.

doodem ogimaa; it was the council fire at Bawaating where the Crane doodem ogimaa was the fire keeper. This is also a reference to the regional alliance. Bawaating was at this time the fire keeper for the alliance of Lake Superior council fires, and it was at the Bawaating council, according to this account, that kindled the council fire at Chequamegon and therefore constituted its government and recognized its leaders. Furthermore, by naming the Loon as the one to "answer [the Crane's] voice in council," Tugwaugaunay was reminding the Loon ogimaa that his role in the larger alliance was that of a speaker and not the fire-keeper. Tugwaugaunay was pushing back against what he saw as the Loon ogimaa's effort to use the alliance with the French to advance his own agenda. The Anishinabek not only recorded their political history through doodemag but drew from that tradition to explain or justify their politics and to shape their choices, by invoking doodemag to make political arguments. As with the wampum read by Musquakie that opened this chapter, the narratives recorded by Perrot and Warren demonstrate how doodem identity was used in both metaphor and allegory for constitutional and political purposes.

The Metaphor of Fire

When Anishinabek spoke about their councils, they used the word fire, or ishkode, as a metaphor for governance. It was a regionally significant political symbol that the Haudenosaunee and Wendat also used, and it is important to unpack this metaphor as well because doodem and ishkode were used together in allegories about governance. Fire was used to evoke acts of governance, councils and alliances, and, by extension, the polities constituted by their deliberations. Fire appears as a metaphor in diplomatic negotiations with Europeans from the earliest days of the seventeenth century.[22] As political scientist Heidi Kiiwetinepine-siik Stark demonstrates, fire is such a potent metaphor in Anishinaabe political discourse because it draws meaning from aadizookaanag that explain how the culture hero Nanabozhoo acquired fire for the Anishinabek. In the story, Nanabozhoo transformed himself into a hare (through the power of metamorphosis) in the hope that he would be captured by two young human girls, who would bring him to their home and next

---

22 "Glossary of Figures of Speech in Iroquois Political Rhetoric," in Jennings, *History and Culture of Iroquois Diplomacy*, 118.

to their fire. Once inside, their father realized quickly that Nanabozhoo was a *manidoo* (an ensouled spirit being) who wanted to steal the fire that he guarded. About to be caught, Nanabozhoo, thinking quickly, set his own fur on fire with a spark before running across the frozen lake to escape. Upon returning to his home, Nanabozhoo's grandmother successfully captured some of the fire before putting out the fire in his fur. However, Nanabozhoo's formerly all-white fur was now scorched. The Anishinabek had fire, but Nanabozhoo's appearance had been changed in the process of obtaining it.[23]

This story not only serves to explain why the fur of the hare changes colour from brown in the summer to white in the winter, but it also functions as a political allegory. As Stark explains, while fire serves as a metaphor for a discrete polity (she uses nation), the hare's changing fur colour (marked by fire), "illustrates how nations are defined and are in turn marked by their treaties and alliances. When a nation enters into an alliance or treaty, it retains its separate distinct identity in the same way that the hare retains his white fur in the winter. Nonetheless, a nation is also marked or shaped by its alliances with other nations in the same way that the hare in this story is marked by the quest for fire, having brown fur in the summer."[24]

Nanabozhoo's quest for fire is an expression of the desire to be in alliance with others and of the benefits that come from making alliances with other people. There are multiple lessons that listeners can draw from this story, but for Anishinaabe political purposes the message is that, through treaties and alliances, one is both simultaneously changed and yet still the same. In the Anishinaabe worldview, one can belong to or meet around multiple fires. By extension, one does not lose either identity or autonomy by entering into a treaty or an alliance relationship. And one most certainly does *not* become the subject of a foreign power through treaty or alliance.

While Stark and others have equated council fire with nation, fire as a political metaphor was used to describe any Anishinaabe polity ranging from a small gathering of several extended families to large confederacies of multiple smaller fires. One could call all of these polities "nations," and many historians have done so. But, as Michael Witgen notes in *An Infinity of Nations*, "the idea of nation, as either a political

---

23 Stark, "Marked by Fire."
24 Ibid., 121–2.

construct or a description of collective identity, was the misapplication of a European social category onto a Native social formation."[25] I suggest more precisely that the idea of nation as expressed in European political discourse has been, and continues to be, mapped inappropriately onto more than one "Native social formation," masking the social and political gradations that the Anishinaabe and other Great Lakes peoples understood when they spoke of "fires." Sometimes both historians and the authors of source documents have also used the word "nation" to describe doodem identities, and sometimes they applied the term to people who met at a particular council location. On the land surrender treaties, Anishinaabe signatories are identified as either "nations" or "tribes," but the patterns of doodem images on each reveals polities not covered by either word. As this book demonstrates, the pattern of doodem images in such treaties actually reflected the leadership of the local council fire that had responsibility for the land in question. As the examples of treaty documents in this book show, people having multiple doodem identities could belong to one council fire while people with the same doodem identity lived in different council fires spread throughout the region.

Colonial writers often referred to the locations of council fires as villages, but this is another inaccurate term for describing historic Anishinaabe gatherings. When early visitors to the Great Lakes region saw hundreds and up to two thousand people congregating to conduct councils, visit with one another, trade, arrange marriages, and discuss issues of common concern, these Europeans reached for the closest analogy to their own terms for settlements. "Village" seemed to be the nearest equivalent, in an effort to convey the permanency they saw in the semi-annual return of people to the same location. However, there are crucial distinctions: French and English villages in the seventeenth and eighteenth centuries were places inhabited year-round by families living in permanent dwellings in an otherwise rural area. Furthermore, the word "village" connotes a particular population concentration that was bigger than a hamlet (a concentration of a few families) but smaller than a town. Villages had differentiated spaces: there was usually a church and at least a few small shops, for example. Villages lacked the larger markets

---

25 Witgen, *Infinity of Nations*, 75.

and major churches or cathedrals of towns, whose populations of one to several thousand were supplemented by people coming in to access the regional markets and more specialized services that towns offered. The word "village" conjures up in the mind a certain small size of human settlement, of minor to no political importance, in a rural area.

In contrast, the Great Lakes Anishinaabe gathering sites that European visitors called "villages" looked nothing like their English and French namesakes and were often highly significant political sites. Prior to the establishment of French or English missionary stations, trading posts, or military forts at these locations, people left these sites during the winter months when families headed out into their hunting territories. And they were often densely inhabited during annual or semi-annual gatherings. Examples from the *Jesuit Relations* give some further insight into these geographic patterns, which were well-established in the early seventeenth century. In 1626, the Jesuit Charles Lalemant observed that two or three related families travelled together for six months of the winter, "erecting their cabins together in one place." Families consisted of anywhere from ten to twenty people, typically a group of brothers with their wives and children. In summer, Lalemant described how families would come together at specific locations on the St. Lawrence to fish and socialize, as did families who gathered at Bawaating and other locations throughout the Great Lakes. As discussed in the Introduction, Lalemant's brother Jérôme described the same pattern in 1640 among the people who gathered on the shore of Lake Nipissing. He noted that in the spring, some of the Nipissing people were busy with fishing on the Lake while others spent a month travelling to James Bay for trade, and then another month returning. The entire community came together in the late summer for a gathering before heading out in the fall to their hunting camps. The Nipissing chose to hunt on Wendat territory. From there they could trade with their meat for the corn and other produce of their allied Wendat winter neighbours.[26]

---

26 Lalemant, "Relation of 1640–41," in Thwaites, *Jesuit Relations*, 21:239–41.

Nicolas Perrot's description of "village life" at Bawaating in the late seventeenth century reveals the continuity of practice:

> Those who have remained at the Saut [sic], their native country, leave their villages twice a year. In the month of June they disperse in all directions along Lake Huron ... This lake has rocky shores, and is full of small islands abounding in blueberries. While there they gather sheets of bark from the trees for making their canoes and building their cabins. The water of the lake is very clear, and they can see the fish in it at a depth of twenty-five feet. While the children are gathering a store of blueberries, the men are busy in spearing sturgeon. When the grain [that they have planted] is nearly ripe, they return home. At the approach of winter they resort to the shores of the lake to kill beavers and moose, and do not return thence until the spring, in order to plant their Indian corn.[27]

This pattern was not changed significantly until the nineteenth century, when Anishinaabe families were forced onto reserves and settler colonialism imposed a new political geography and new subsistence strategies upon them.

In the Great Lakes region, imported labels such as "nation," "tribe," "band," and even "village" do not accurately describe the distinctive political shape of Anishinaabe polities, with their web-like political geometries consisting of nodes of seasonally occupied council fire sites connected by overlapping, intersecting, and mobile networks of doodem relations and allied kin.[28] Recall that in 1642 the council at Bawaating was part of the eastern Anishinaabe alliance – the council farthest to the west in the alliance. But it was also part of other alliances too, including alliances of Lake Superior council fires. In the agreement recited by Musquakie, the council fire at Bawaating was part of the alliance, but it was not the central fire, where the talk was kept and the agreement first made. Mnjikaning had that responsibility. However, Bawaating *was* the historic constituting fire for Chequamegon, according to Tugwaugaunay's history as told to William Warren. Each council fire could be part of multiple and differing alliances and each council was free to choose its own path and allies. However, once the alliance was recognized in formal council, with the sun as a witness, the

---

27 De la Potherie, "Histoire de l'Amérique septentrionale," in Blair, *Indian Tribes*, 1:279–80.
28 Ferris, *Archaeology of Native-Lived Colonialism*, 4–6.

alliances became binding, and allies took on the responsibility to care for each other. These alliances thus shaped the political geography of the Great Lakes region.

Mapping Anishinaabewaki

A central claim of this book is that alliances were the framework through which the Anishinabek defined their relationships with other Indigenous societies and, in turn, with European newcomers. Alliance-making was a long-standing legal and political tradition that met social and cultural needs. The region is full of examples of long-lasting agreements constructed between council fires of Great Lakes Indigenous peoples – between the Anishinabek and the Wendat, the Haudenosaunee, the Sioux, and others. These international alliances demonstrate the centrality of alliance-making to the construction of the region's political geography: the Wendat Confederacy, for example, and the coalition between the eastern Anishinabek and the Wendat, the Haudenosaunee Confederacy, the Three Fires Confederacy of the Anishinabek, and the western Anishinaabe–Sioux alliance.[29] In all of these alliances, the constituting council fires maintained their distinctive identities and political autonomy, even as they were strengthened and changed by their alliance relationships.

Evidence for the rough locations of long-standing Anishinaabe council fires are in the colonial archives, but they are not always obvious. Seventeenth-century French colonial records, particularly maps, are a useful source of names. One can almost read from the names covering the map that European travellers were asking one of the most basic of human questions in encounter situations: "Who are you?" But the question (and the anticipated answer of national identity or country of origin) varied greatly in different cultural contexts. As Anishinaabe teacher and Elder Basil Johnston explains, historically, Anishinaabe "men and women preferred to regard themselves as members of a totem [doodem] and then a community. Strangers, when they met, always asked one another, 'Waenaesh k'dodaem?' (What is your totem?);

---

29 For the Wendat–eastern Anishinaabe alliance see Labelle, *Dispersed but Not Destroyed*; for the Haudenosaunee Confederacy as an alliance, see Parmenter, *Edge of the Woods*; for the Three Fires Confederacy, see Belfry, *Three Fires Unity*; for the western Anishinaabe–Sioux alliance see Witgen, *Infinity of Nations*.

only afterwards did they ask, '*Waenaesh keen*?' (Who are you?)." The maps and memoirs produced by early seventeenth-century French travellers are not surprisingly populated with names of Anishinaabe polities that answer Johnston's primary question, "*Waeneash k'dodaem*? – What is your doodem?"[30]

Of course, travellers and traders from across the Atlantic were really asking, "What is the name of your/that nation?" It is clear from answers that these visitors recorded on their maps and in their documents that the Anishinabek often were answering with the doodem identities of the keepers of specific council fires. For decades now, scholars have recognized that at least some of the names of "nations" in early seventeenth-century sources – names such as the Amikouai, or Beaver (amik-wag) people; Outchagi, or Heron (*shagi*) people; and Sinago (Squirrel) people – were clearly connected to Anishinaabe doodem names. In other cases, the names of "nations" were references to the gathering of people at places, such as Baouichtigouian, or the People of the Rapids (Bawaating), or Kitchisipirini, the Nation or People of the Great River (the Ottawa River). Still others refer to the name of a hereditary ogimaa, such as the Nassauakueton.[31] To date, the conventional understanding has been that each of these names referred to a distinct polity. As historian Michael Witgen has noted, both seventeenth-century observers and subsequent generations of historians saw in these many different names a Great Lakes region populated by "an infinity of nations." According to the conventional narrative, these many nations then collapsed in the wake of mid-seventeenth-century wars, epidemics, and depopulation, before reforming by the eighteenth century into the people we recognize today as nations, such as the Ottawas, Ojibwes, Potawatomis, and Mississaugas.[32] But, as Witgen demonstrates, such a characterization masks the significance of Anishinaabe alliances, which do not conform to Western understandings of what a "nation" is. Doodem images on treaty documents provide the key for reinterpreting the observations of seventeenth-century observers, allowing us to now see what was really there: a world of interconnected alliances of kin made through marriage and doodem relations.

---

30 Basil Johnston, *Ojibwe Heritage*, 59.
31 McDonnell, *Masters of Empire*, 98.
32 Witgen, *Infinity of Nations*, 20–1.

By recovering the centrality of doodem and fire to Anishinaabe culture, the "nation" names that I have cited resolve themselves into the names of council sites, some of which are referred to locally by the doodem of the hosts, others by the place at which they were held, less commonly but sometimes by the name of their leading ogimaa, and by other metaphors in Anishinaabemowin that refer to doodem identity. A doodem is not a polity itself; rather, it is the crucial category through which Anishinaabe governance was constituted and defined. Council fires were hosted by an ogimaa of the named doodem, but the fire itself created a point of intersection that brought different doodemag together – including those of the spouses of the council fire hosts, who, because of the principle of doodem exogamy, always had different doodemag. It is possible now to identify many different Anishinaabe council sites throughout the region and the doodem that hosted each.

To reconstruct a map of Anishinaabe polities, therefore, we have to begin by imagining a political order enmeshed in networks of doodem alliances. We can identify major council fire locations as the places where Anishinaabe governance was enacted through the networks of relations who came together in annual or semi-annual gatherings. There were many council sites throughout the Great Lakes region, some of which routinely saw much larger gatherings than others. They were places well-resourced with food, especially fish, as councils and the group activities associated with these gatherings could last several weeks. Places where waters narrowed, forcing fish as they moved between lakes to swim closer together, were particularly well suited. To facilitate the fish harvest, people also constructed fish weirs. The timbers of the fish weirs at Mnjikaning are still visible today.[33] It is no accident that long-standing council sites such as Bawaating, Mnjikaning, the Credit River, and Bkejwanong were all locations where large quantities of food could be readily provided to council attendees.

One of the earliest sources of names for council fires is found in the *Jesuit Relation* of 1640. In this document mission superior Paul Le Jeune expressed the "hope we have for the conversion of many" by enumerating names and approximate locations of all the "nations" that the French in Quebec had some knowledge of, either through the

---

33 See Parks Canada, "Mnjikaning Fish Weirs National Historic Site," n.d., https://www.pc.gc.ca/en/lhn-nhs/on/mnjikaning, accessed 14 April 2020.

reporting of interpreter Sieur Jean de Nicolet or from collected scraps of information that had made their way to Le Jeune's ear, such as Amikouai – amikwag (beavers), Kinounchepirini – *ginoozhii* (Pike) people, or Outchogai – ashagiwag (Great Blue Heron) people.[34] Recording in print what others had been told, early colonial authors assumed that these were names of nations or tribes and in so doing mapped European understanding onto an Indigenous political tradition for which there was no direct translation or comparison.

Some of the names in Le Jeune's list are very clearly names for the doodem of the council fire hosts: in addition to those above, Le Jeune's list includes Nikoquet (Otters), Maroumine (Catfish) and Roquai (*noka*, or female Bear). Other names either clearly refer to place: Kichesipirini, or the Great River people, whose council fire was on what is now known as Calumet island in the Great (Ottawa) River and who signed the 1701 Great Peace with a Crane doodem image; Baouichtigouian (People of the Sault, Sault Ste. Marie); and Oumisagai, whose name refers to the wide river delta of the Mississagi River where it enters Lake Huron from the north shore. For others, the irregular and phonetic spelling make it harder to determine what word he intended. After listing all known names for polities from the north shore of the St. Lawrence to the southwestern shores of Lake Michigan, Le Jeune reported that "we have been told this year that an Algonquin, journeying beyond these peoples, encountered nations extremely populous. 'I saw them assembled,' said he, 'as if at a fair, buying and selling, in numbers so great that they could not be counted; it conveyed an idea of the cities of Europe."[35] Note that, in referring to "nations" in the plural, Le Jeune was likely to be commenting on the status of Indigenous peoples as not Christian, rather than making any sort of comment on the type of polity.

While the purpose of Le Jeune's report was to convey the extent to which North America was "a glorious field for Gospel laborers," it is actually an important historical source of geopolitical data. Le Jeune managed to collect significant information about the extent to which the region was populated with many different council sites and, by extension, the size of gatherings of people (from several hundred to several thousands), even if his informant, Sieur Nicolet, was uncertain

34 Le Jeune, "Relation of 1640 – Hurons, Quèbec," in Thwaites, *Jesuit Relations*, 18:231.
35 Elizabeth Fenn says these were likely the Mandan: see her *Encounters at the Heart of the World*.

about what type of polity to which each name referred. Nicolet would have asked people who they or others were; when they replied, Nicolet in turn would have passed those terms on to Father Le Jeune for the first sweeping survey by Europeans of the geopolitics of the Great Lakes region.[36]

It is also possible to decipher doodem names in other sources through an understanding of how people employed metaphor to refer to this identity. William Warren, in his *History of the Ojibways*, explained that "Bus-in-aus-e" was the name used in the western Great Lakes region to mean the Crane doodem, as it means "Echo-maker" and evokes "the loud, clear, and far reaching cry of the Crane."[37] Likewise, while the name *maang* is Anishinaabemowin for loon, the doodem name given by Warren is "Ah-ah-wauk," which is a reference to the call of the loon. Other metaphorical names were collected by the anthropologist William Jones, who interviewed Anishinaabe people in Minnesota in the 1920s. Jones found significant evidence that metaphorical references to doodem beings' behaviours and habitats were used to refer to peoples of that identity. For example, moose prefer swampy habitat. Jones noted that his informants called people of the Moose (*moos*) doodem *miciwaa-naantag*, "because he lives in a big swampy place there." Jones's informants also told him that "Pamaangik, or they that pass by singing" was a metaphor for the *wawa* or Swan doodem identity; for wolf (*maingan*), it was *wawaonog*, "the barker crier"; the beavers (*amik*) were *pimaawidaasi-wag*, or "carriers." Bald eagles, Jones noted, were called "otoonipi" [*sic*] or "belly of fish," because of the tendency of these birds (and by logical extension, their relatives in human form) to overeat during annual salmon spawning runs.[38]

Multiple metaphors could be applied to the same place. This is true of Bawaating, listed in seventeenth-century sources as "Passinassiouek." This name appears on Louis Nicolas's circa-1670s map of the Great Lakes region near Bawaating. The spelling is a reflection of Nicolas's effort to

36 Le Jeune also consulted a Huron map of the region south of the Great Lakes, provided by Father Paul Ragenau, which included people Le Jeune thought might be "at the North of Virginia, Florida, and perhaps even new Mexico." Le Jeune, "Relation of 1640 – Hurons, Quèbec," in Thwaites, *Jesuit Relations*, 18:233.
37 Warren and Neill, *History*, 39; Darlene Johnston, *Connecting People to Place*.
38 William Jones, Ethnographic and linguistic field notes on the Ojibwa Indians, William Jones fonds, folder 1, APS.

render the name Bus-in-aus-e (Baswenaazhi), or Echo-Maker (referring metaphorically to the Crane doodem), into French.[39] Nicolas, following French practice, added "ouek" at the end to mean the animate plural suffix – *wag*.[40] But earlier in the 1640s, the Jesuits had, in two separate reports, recorded first Baouichtigouian and then "Pauoitigoueieuhak" as names of "nations" also living at the Sault.[41] Le Jeune translated Baouichtigouian as the "name of the people of the Sault."[42] Different polities? Different council fires? No – the same. Baouichtigouian and Pauoitigoueieuhak are both attempts to spell *Baawaatigirini* – the people who gathered at the Sault – while Passinassiouek is a metaphor for the Crane doodem that was the keeper of the council fire there. All three names refer to the same gathering of people and the same place – those who met each spring and fall in council at what is now Sault Ste. Marie. A Crane doodem image represents "the Sault" on the Great Peace of Montreal, and the Crane doodem was the leading doodem image on treaties for lands around Bawaating from 1763 through the 1850s. People with other doodem identities met in council at Bawaating too, but Bawaating was known by the Crane doodem who were the keepers of the fire. Anishinaabemowin speakers appear to have used these different names for the same place, just as today we use alternative names like "the City of Lights," "the Big Apple," or "the Six" to refer to Paris, New York, and Toronto, respectively.

This pattern continued in French and later British sources and reflects Anishinaabe practices of using multiple metaphors. Names in these documents refer to council fires sometimes by place and sometimes by the doodem responsible for the territory. When one takes a closer look at the pattern of names, it is clear that the same Anishinaabe councils were continuing to meet and to exercise their responsibilities for the lands regardless of what names they were labelled with in French-authored sources. In 1681, Jacques Duchesneau (the Intendant of New France from 1675 to 1682), conducted another enumeration. He described the eastern Anishinaabe as those who came to trade at Montreal, consisting

---

39 For a biography of Louis Nicolas and a history of his manuscript, see Warkentin, "Aristotle in New France."

40 Nicolas, *Codex Canadensis*, overleaf one.

41 Le Jeune, "Relation of 1640," in Thwaites, *Jesuit Relations*, 18:229; Lalemant, "Relation of 1642–1643," in Thwaites, *Jesuit Relations*, 23:223.

42 Pierre Radisson recorded "Pauoesligonce" as his version of "people from the Sault": see Radisson, *Voyages*, 227.

of "Ehemistamcies [Temiskaming], Nepisserinens [Nipissing], Missisa-
kis [Mississaugas], Amicoües [Amikwa], Sauteurs, Kiskacons [Kiska-
kons], et Ehionontatoronons."[43] This last name is in the Wendat language and refers to Weskarini of eastern Ontario. They are sometimes
called the Iroquet in French records, after their ogimaa Iroquet, who
welcomed Champlain in 1609.[44] The Weskarini are also Anishinabek.
What Duchesneau shows is that these council fires were again active in
the same areas where earlier sources indicated that they had been prior
to the wars and dislocations of the late 1640s. Duschenseau then identified the following people as those who traded with the eastern Anishinaabe for furs – living north and west of Lake Superior: "the people of
the woods [Northern Anishinabek], Kislistenons [Omukshego/Cree],
Assinbouels [Assiniboine], and the Nadouessioua [Dakota/Lakota],"
and living on the south side of the lakes: the "Sakis, Poutouatamis,
Puants, Oumalominers or of the wild rice [Menomini], the Outagami or
Renards [Fox], Mascoutens, Miamis, and Islinois [Illinois]."[45] While the
arrangement of council fires and communities in the post-1650 world
of the Great Lakes region experienced change, they did not change *significantly*. Furthermore, and even more importantly, change was neither
random nor ad hoc but in keeping with Anishinaabe law. The structure
of Anishinaabe governance did not change. New sites of governance
still required the approval and ratification of other constituting councils
for the area concerned.

Another enumeration taken of the Great Lakes region in 1736, almost
fifty years later, reveals the continuing presence of Anishinaabe council fires in the southeastern Great Lakes, with Anishinaabe governance
clearly re-established or (in the case of the Caribou at Mnjikaning and
Eagle at the Credit) more recently established. This manuscript (now in
the French Colonial Archives) was authored most likely by Philippe-
Thomas Chabert de Joncaire and titled "the Enumeration of the Sav-
age Nations that are related to the government of Canada, the warriors belonging to each one of them and their coats of arms (or armorial

---

43 Mémoire du Duchesneau au ministre, 13 November 1681, ANF, fondes des colonies,
    Série C11A, vol. 5, f.307; on diffusion microfilm: LAC, Reel C-2376.
44 Champlain, *Works*, 2:68.
45 Mémoire du Duchesneau au ministre, 13 November 1681, ANF, fondes des colonies,
    Série C11A, vol. 5, f.307.

bearings)" – by which the author means their doodemag.[46] This census distinguishes between place-based names such as the Sauteurs, Mississaugs, and Nepissingues, and the respective doodemag associated with each. This document is further evidence of how doodem and council fire together define the Anishinaabe political world. The list names only one or two doodem identities for each council, indicating the doodem of the hereditary ogimaa and/or leading doodemag at each location. Given that people kept their doodem when they married, each of these locations would have included people from other doodemag, people who had "married in" to that community. Joncaire was therefore only identifying the council fire keepers or the doodem of the ogimaa. What the document also reveals is that some doodemag were either more numerous or more influential in governance than others: the Cranes, for example, were listed as the "arms" of eight "nations," from eastern Ontario to western Lake Superior.[47] The Bear doodem is listed at four sites; the Beaver is listed at three.[48]

The real purpose of the document was military – the report was commissioned to get an accurate count of the number of warriors who could be counted on to fight for the French in the wake of the Fox Wars and at the onset of a new western Anishinaabe–Dakota conflict.[49] It was also a time of rising tensions with the British, and the westward population pressure from Anglo-American expansionism meant that the French-held interior was at increased risk. France was dependent upon its Anishinabek and other Indigenous allies in this region to protect its

---

46 Dénombrement des nations sauvages, 1736, ANF, fondes des colonies, Series C11A, vol. 66, fol. 236–256v. Schoolcraft identifies the author as M. Chauvignerie; Newbigging identifies him as Joncaire. See Newbigging, "Ottawa-French Alliance," 346. The "enumeration" has been published both in Schoolcraft's *Historical and Statistical Information*, 3:553–8, and in O'Callaghan, *Colonial History of the State of New York*, 1:17–23. However, the manuscript in C11A actually consists of two copies back to back. The first version appears to be a draft and contains the interesting notes about the visual ways in which Anishinaabe peoples communicated their identities (231–41). The second version appears to be the one published by Schoolcraft and in O'Callaghan's edited volume, although neither published version is a faithful transcription of the original.

47 The voice of the Crane clearly travelled a great distance. See Schenck, *Voice of the Crane*.

48 Dénombrement des nations sauvages, 1736, Fondes des colonies, ANF, Series C11A, vol. 66, fol. 236–256v.

49 Witgen, *Infinity of Nations*, 306–12; McDonnell, *Masters of Empire*, 126.

claim; Joncaire, who in 1736 had just been appointed the Indian agent to the Iroquois (a position his father had held), had been sent out to learn what he could.[50] The census was as comprehensive as Joncaire could make it but only in terms of covering Indigenous peoples who were allies of New France. Joncaire documented different Indigenous polities from New England, the north, and the Great Lakes – all regions where the French were known and had allies.

The census supports the finding by historians Michael Witgen and Michael McDonnell that the French imperial hold on the Great Lakes region was far more tenuous than has been previously thought and that even after a century of engagement in the Great Lakes region, French colonial officials still struggled to understand the people with whom they were dealing.[51] The manuscript census in the French Colonial Archives reveals two enumerations, one apparently a draft of the other. The draft reveals additional important commentary about the multi-faceted reality of collective identity in the Great Lakes. Again, in an effort to work within comfortable categories, Joncaire attempted first to enumerate by geographic region and then by name of nation in that region and to list the "coats of arms" or "armorial bearings" of the principal families, if known. But he quickly ran into difficulty with this method, as he noted that people from the same place could have the same or a different "coat of arms." He then interrupted his own draft to note, "at this point one can object and ask how to distinguish a Sauteur from a Mississauga who has the same coat of arms?" He responded to his own question first by noting that a person was known both by the place they were from – "by the arms of his Nation" – and second by the arms "of his family," or doodem. And the Anishinaabe, he then explained, were "raised to distinguish each nation by the way of doing its mark, of making the huts, of cutting their hair, by the differences in their weapons, the arrows … by the snowshoes, by the canoes, by the paddles and by other indications that they leave on their routes." In other words, it took a lifetime of knowledge to be able to read these signs; Joncaire doubted whether even a full study would provide a thorough understanding.[52]

---

50 Newbigging, "Ottawa-French Alliance," 346–7, 346n21.
51 Witgen, *Infinity of Nations*; McDonnell, *Masters of Empire*.
52 Dénombrement des nations sauvages, 1736, ANF, fondes des colonies, Series C11A, vol. 66, fol. 236–56v.

These colonial sources reveal the fundamental continuities of Anishinaabe governance through doodem and ishkode. *Together*, these categories were the mechanism through which Anishinaabe peoples negotiated and articulated their responsibilities for and connections to specific places, lands and sources. People were known both by the council fire community to which they belonged *and* by their doodem. One can see now how councils were places of significant ontological difference between the Anishinabek who gathered there and the Europeans who came to visit. The impact of such divergent worldviews has continued to the present, affecting contemporary interpretations of treaties and alliances, because subsequent generations of political actors from Western European countries could not comprehend Indigenous thought worlds or chose to dismiss them as irrelevant. Because these same individuals produced the primary sources upon which historians have to date almost exclusively relied, our interpretations have been necessarily limited and one-sided. This is not to say that, over time, local colonial officials on the ground did not come to some understanding about the importance of doodemag; and they certainly learned the diplomatic protocols of Anishinaabe councils and the locations of regionally significant council fires.

Consistently, Anishinaabe leaders meeting in council signed colonial documents with images representing their doodem identities, as an inscribed representation showing which doodem was the firekeeper at each council site. In so doing, these leaders emphasized the importance of kin and family in understanding how the Anishinabek recognized relationship to and responsibility for lands and resources. An examination of doodem images produced on treaty and other documents over more than three centuries also shows that there was a significant change in what – or, more precisely, who – the image represented. On the few extant seventeenth- and eighteenth-century documents from the French colonial period, a single image would represent an entire council fire. As La Potherie explained in 1671, "leaders made the mark of their families," and as was the case with doodem images on rock art, one doodem image could represent all the individuals in a canoe. On the Peace of Montreal of 1701, while specific leaders were sometimes identified by name, there was only one doodem image per council fire.[53]

---

53 Ratification de la paix, 4 August 1701, ANOM, Fonds des Colonies. Série C11A. Correspondence générale, Canada, vol. 19, fol. 41–4.

Following the Seven Years' War in 1763, British colonial officials entered into a new treaty relationship with Anishinaabe peoples at the Treaty of Niagara in 1764.[54] The Proclamation of 1763, which was effectively Britain's constitution for the new colonies it acquired after the Peace of Paris, also contained provisions for the purchase of Indigenous land, to be conducted at a public council called for that purpose.[55] The inclusion of this reference to public councils is no accident. Formal councils were places where decisions of the broader communities were ratified. These were the sites where Anishinaabe law was performed. Following the Proclamation, when British colonial officials sought to purchase land, they used their own title deeds but had them signed at these public councils. And on these title deeds, Anishinaabe leaders signed with their doodem images, which British officials considered as equivalent to their signatures. They were not, but officials acted as if they were. Regardless of what officials thought at the time, the Anishinabek knew what their doodem images meant and consistently wrote them on documents that pertained to the work of governance, to reflect the alliances between doodemag that comprised their councils. In turn, Anishinaabe leaders also wrote their doodem images on petitions sent to colonial governments. These petitions were also the product of deliberations in council. The consistent and enduring presence of doodem images on political documents embodies the relationship between council fires and doodem identity, a relationship best described as doodem constitutionalism. Through doodem identity the Anishinabek articulated their relationship to particular landscapes and their responsibility for the beings who lived in those lands. But the doodem tradition, much as it drew its political legitimacy from narratives that connected the identity to particular locations, did not define that land as exclusively the property or bounded territory of a single doodem. Instead, Anishinaabe peoples made decisions about governance in council that comprised representation of multiple doodem beings, reflecting the broader areas of

---

54 Parmenter, "Pontiac's War"; John Borrows, "Wampum at Niagara."
55 United Kingdom, Royal Proclamation of 1763, reprinted in R.S.C. 1985, App. II, No. 1, 1 at 4–5. For a discussion of the clear recognition of Indigenous title, which legal scholars now accept is embedded in the Royal Proclamation, see Walters, "Brightening the Covenant Chain," 89.

doodem responsibility as defined in Anishinaabe teachings. The next chapter analyzes these doodem images on treaty and other documents as sources for Anishinaabe governance in action. Despite the impact of settler colonialism during this period of dispossession, the practice of Anishinaabe governance through alliances of doodem and council fire continued.

4

Governance in Action

"Among the Indians there have been no written laws. Customs handed down from generation to generation have been the only law to guide them ... They would not as brutes be whipped into duty. They would be as men persuaded to the right."

– George Copway, 1851[1]

Anishinaabe missionary George Copway included the statement above in his *Traditional Sketches of the Ojibwe*. Like his contemporary Peter Jones, Copway had been raised in Anishinaabe tradition; he too wrote for a non-Indigenous audience. "Customs," he noted, were "the only law to guide them." For a Western audience, "no written law" has too often been read as "no law." But yet, as Copway went on to discuss in his chapter on traditional government, regular meetings of Anishinaabe councils ensured that customary laws were both enacted and followed after fulsome discussion within the community. Copway's statement can also be read as praise for a system of government that was consensus-based and a rebuke to authoritarianism. Both Jones and Copway attended councils; Jones was an aanikeogimaa who knew from first-hand experience how Anishinaabe governance worked and how

1 Copway, *Traditional History*, 141.

it reflected and was answerable to the community. As Copway (who was Crane doodem, from Rice Lake) noted, anyone (including an ogimaa) acting "different from what was considered right" would "bring upon him the censure of the Nation, which he dreaded more than any corporeal punishment that could be inflicted upon him ... This fear of the Nation's censure acted as a mighty bond, binding all in one social, honourable compact."[2] This is an idealized statement, of course, and Anishinaaabe leaders were as capable as any others of disagreeing with one another or coming to different interpretations of "what was considered right." Nevertheless, Anishinaabe councils were sites where Anishinaabe law was put into action, whether at the common councils or regional gatherings, with advice from advisory councils and the entire community. Anishinaabe governance was direct and participatory, and the "censure of the Nation" was a powerful check on leaders who forgot their responsibilities to the people in their care.

As earlier chapters have demonstrated, Anishinaabe consensus-based governance practices through alliances and councils are old. Origin narratives and other oral histories describe these practices through political metaphor and allegory. When leaders met in council, they brought the specific knowledge and attributes of their doodem beings with them, which in turn informed both governance practices and decision-making. To understand Anishinaabe governance in action, I look first at leadership, to see the relationships between doodem and governance. Evidence for the historical practice of governance through alliance comes from a study of recorded Anishinaabe oral histories and colonial documents. Analysis of the differing composition of common and general councils and their areas of responsibility comes from treaty and land sale/purchase documents. The role of women in governance is harder to see in the colonial record, given the near invisibility of Anishinaabekwe in archival documents. But again, a combination of recorded oral histories and evidence drawn from treaty documents and council minutes brings their presence, power, and importance to light. French, and later British, American, and Canadian government officials recognized Anishinaabe governance structures. Colonial officials came to learn which councils had jurisdiction in different places; they also successfully made alliances and renewed them. Through the reciprocal exchange of gifts, the same colonial officials demonstrated at least some

---

2 Ibid.

understanding of the binding obligations they had co-created through the performance of alliance ceremonies in council. Colonialism and particularly settler colonialism did have a significant impact on Anishinaabe governance practices over time. Historically, the general councils occurred on a regular – annual if not semi-annual – basis and were part of the Anishinaabe seasonal round. But the arrival of colonists in significant numbers during the first half of the nineteenth century increasingly made off-reserve travel both unsafe and expensive. Increasingly, general councils were attended only by ogimaa and aanikeogimaa, with only the people of the host community to bear witness to the council's deliberations. Despite these challenges, leaders continued to exercise their responsibilities according to the practices of earlier centuries and to assert those values in their speeches and writing to colonial officials.

Anishinaabe Leadership

As legal scholar John Borrows has noted, Anishinaabe histories are a potent source of law. They model governance "best practices," and demonstrate through allegory how consensus-based, consultative decision-making worked.[3] Anishinaabe oral histories consistently model consultative and consensus-based leadership models. These narratives define leaders as those who are responsible for the welfare of others. This is evident also in the doodem origin story recounted to French fur trader Nicolas Perrot in the late seventeenth century and discussed in Chapter 1. While the animals of the earth floated on a raft following a flood, the Great Hare, as leader of the animals, asked for volunteers to dive in search of soil; he did not compel or order them.[4] As leader of the animals, the Great Hare acted on his responsibility to provide for those under his care – in this case, to provide the very earth on which his people needed to live. But the Great Hare could not achieve this objective on his own – all the animals who could dive had to contribute their skills. And in the achievement of the muskrat, who died in his successful effort to return to the surface with soil, listeners learn how the smallest and seemingly insignificant make crucial contributions to the well-being of the community, even at the cost of their own lives. So this

---

3 John Borrows, *Drawing Out Law*, 216–27.
4 Perrot, "Mémoire," in Blair, *Indian Tribes*, 1:32.

story, like many Anishinaabe oral histories, is also a parable intended to teach fundamental principles of Anishinaabe law and leadership and to model the ethical principles for members of the community.

Drawing from many examples in the aadizookaanag (sacred stories), Anishinaabe peoples recognized multiple categories of leadership. For civil governance, leadership roles for men (and occasionally women) ranged from leaders of a family group (indinaakonigewin) to ogimaawag of council fires, to regional gitchi-ogimaawag. Women's councils and warriors' councils also had leaders. Gichi-ogimaawag were highly respected individuals whose talent for leadership and demonstrated excellence in managing spiritual power were widely known. Because of their record of accomplishments, the words of a gichi-ogimaa carried extra weight in councils, but their authority was limited to the power to persuade. Many prominent leaders whose names appear frequently in the archival record of French and British colonial officials were gichi-ogimaawag, and colonial officials counted themselves fortunate when they had these leaders on their side as allies.[5] Beyond civil governance, people could assume leadership roles in other ways. People (generally men) stepped forward to lead war parties; any adult could be a spiritual leader, knowledge keeper, or healer.[6] Individuals could, and did, have more than one leadership role over their lifetimes. Someone who became ogimaa of a council fire or who achieved recognition as gichi-ogimaa showed leadership skill in other roles first. They could demonstrate their fitness for civil leadership through the recognition they gained as hunters and warriors. As skilful hunters, they would have met the Anishinaabe leadership test of being a good provider for their people; as excellent warriors, they would have demonstrated their ability to protect their people. Future ogimaawag also spent time in other leadership positions,

---

5 For Anishinaabe leadership roles see Treuer, *Assassination of Hole in the Day*; Cary Miller, *Ogimaag*; Chute, *Legacy of Shingwaukonse*, especially 1–7.

6 Most scholarship on Anishinaabe leadership focuses on the nineteenth century, when the political tradition was under significant stress and experienced colonial pressure to change. To reach back earlier, the broad brush strokes of what historically constituted "traditional" Anishinaabe governance has to be gleaned from oral traditions, colonial texts, and Anishinaabe-authored sources from the mid-nineteenth century, particularly the writings of William Warren, Peter Jones, George Copway, and Francis Assiginack.

acting as messengers or as aanikeogimaawag (step-below chiefs). All Anishinaabe leaders were expected to be generous with material wealth; good leaders accumulated wealth in order to give it away, indicating further their ability to lead by being a good provider, and through gifting, creating, and renewing the alliance relationships that ensured security for the community.

Despite the fact that responsibilities ranged from the local to the regional, Anishinaabe leadership was not hierarchical. A regionally known gichi-ogimaa would, at the same time, be the headman of his own family hunting group. While council fires did follow a hereditary principle for the keeper of the council fire, it was the doodem that defined the role. In other words, the ogimaa of Bawaating would historically have belonged to the Crane doodem; at the Credit River, the Eagle doodem; at Mnjikaning, the Caribou doodem. In some cases, the successor was the child of the incumbent (as for example in the case of Mahiingan in 1670, who the Jesuits reported succeeded his father as the ogimaa of the Amikwa council on Georgian Bay). But this was not by any means a hard and fast rule. What mattered was that the new ogimaa for that council be of the same doodem as the prior incumbent, well suited for the role, and ratified by the general council. People looked for leaders who had the training and ability to take on the role. When communities looked to fill the ogimaa position of a particular council, the new leader needed to be of the doodem that represented that council. People having other doodem identities filled other leadership roles on council. Anishinaabe governance structures were flexible.

Visual analysis of doodem images signed by Anishinaabe leaders on treaty documents strongly suggests that the choices people made in how to represent themselves were shaped by these conceptions of leadership characteristics, specifically that leaders were those who took responsibility for their community through provisioning and protecting them. (See Figures 26 to 28.) Leaders were *stewards* – they took care of the people and land.[7] The eagle doodem images that I have observed, for example, all show the eagle either perching or in the act of catching prey. No other eagle behaviour, such as eating, nesting, or courting, is reflected in these images. As Eagle ogimaawag and gichi-Anishinabek, these leaders represented themselves as either in the act of hunting, and therefore provisioning their

---

7 Lindsay Borrows, *Otter's Journey*, 26.

people, or as sitting vigilant and watchful in a perched position. Even images of the pike demonstrate the quality of provisioning; some show an image of a pike with its head higher than its tail, as one would visualize the pike lying in wait camouflaged by reeds in the water, watching to grab a duckling on the surface. The leadership quality of vigilance is reflected in many other categories of doodem images. In the crane images, most show elevated tail feathers, indicating arousal and heightened awareness. The thunderbird with its wings outstretched is preparing to do battle with the underwater manidoog, protecting the Anishinabek from dangerous lake storms.[8] Most of the caribou pictographs embody the quality of vigilance by showing the raised tail the caribou uses as a threat warning. One doodem image of a bull caribou appears to be demonstrating an excitation leap, which caribou undertake to communicate a possible danger ahead to the herd behind them by leaving a scent warning in their tracks as they kick out with their hind legs.[9] The pictographs of catfish are drawn with their barbels extended. While this could simply be intended as an aid to identify this doodem, it is through the barbels that catfish, having the keenest sense of smell and taste of any vertebrate, sense their food.[10] Beaver doodem images are consistently drawn showing the tail as the key diagnostic feature, as the beaver uses its tail as a communication device, slapping the water to warn others of approaching danger. Several of the crayfish, admittedly from a tiny sample size, are shown rearing up in a defensive posture employed by this tiny crustacean.[11]

The Anishinaabe artists who drew these images on treaties, speeches, and petitions had an infinite range of possibilities when it came to choosing how to best draw their doodemag; and what they chose to

---

8 For a discussion of the ongoing cosmological significance of the animikeek, see Theresa Smith, *Island of the Anishinaabeg*.

9 Russell, *World of the Caribou*, 27; Caton, *Antelope and Deer*, 241. I made this interpretation originally in Bohaker, "Reading Anishinaabe Identities," 19.

10 Caprio, et al., "Taste System of the Channel Catfish."

11 One possible interpretation of this emphasis on the communication of danger or warning signs is that, through these postures, the writers were attempting to warn others of possible problems with the treaty process, but I do not think this is the correct interpretation. Any warning signals indicated by doodem images can also be interpreted as expressions of vigilance by leaders on behalf of their people, a quality that good Anishinaabe leaders were expected to demonstrate. See Chute, *Legacy of Shingwaukonse*, 19.

do, consistently, was to reflect central qualities of Anishinaabe leadership in their graphic vocabularies. In so doing they also reflected ideas of leadership embedded in their aadizookaanag, in which their doodem beings were the central actors in narratives that taught how governance should be conducted in the human world: through deliberative discussions in councils, in which people negotiated resolutions to problems and strengthened their economic security and social safety net through the formation and renewal of alliances.

Women's Councils and Women's Political Work

Women's councils were a central component of Anishinaabe governance.[12] Not only were women historically highly respected by Anishinaabe men for their crucial contributions to social and societal well-being, but women had clearly defined political roles. During gatherings, women met in councils to discuss issues of importance; one woman, an *ogimaakwe*, or chief woman, then presented the results of the women's council findings to the men. Women's councils contributed advice on matters of both peace and war.[13] Significantly, several late eighteenth- and very early nineteenth-century land sale agreements with the British in the eastern Great Lakes region also recognize this consultative structure of Anishinaabe governance and in particular the involvement of women. Three early British–Anishinaabe treaties, all signed between 1792 and 1796, describe the constitutive elements of Anishinaabe political councils, stating in the preambles that the treaties were with "Sachems, War Chiefs and Principal Women," as does one early agreement with the Six Nations on the Grand River.[14] And on a 1784 land cession signed by the Mississauga-Anishinabek to grant land to the Crown to create a territory for the Six Nations, the presence of the women as signatories is clear – three women (Peawamah, Wapamonessychoqua, and Wacanoghaqua) affixed their doodem images, next to the clerk's works "her mark." Inclusion of women in these texts indicates that the British clerks who preparted the documents and the officials who hosted these councils had at least some understanding that Anishinaabe women had political roles and responsibilities. Women

---

12 Cary Miller, *Ogimaag*, 66–9.
13 Ibid., 67–8.
14 Canada, *Indian Treaties and Surrenders*, 61, 64, 65–6.

are no longer mentioned specifically in the preambles to treaties after 1800, as the description of the parties changes to "Principal Chiefs, Warriors and People," but it would be a mistake to conclude from this that Anishinaabe women ceased to be politically relevant in their communities merely because the British stopped mentioning them. It is possible that other Anishinaabe women signed later treaty documents, but it is hard to say with certainty. Personal names can sometimes indicate gender. The suffix "kwe" is used to indicate a woman; "inni" or "nabe" a man. Kwe was often written in colonial records as "quay" or "qua." But the 1784 document described above has the only two such suffixes that I have been able to find.[15] Anishinaabe personal names are just as likely to not be gendered, however, so without further genealogical research it is difficult to know for sure.

The advice of the women's council and council of warriors is also visible in the minutes of an 1805 common council held at the Credit River to discuss a prospective land sale to the British Crown. In this case, both advisory councils disagreed with the government's proposal. The colonial government of Upper Canada was asking to purchase a "Tract of Land on the Lake Ontario from the River Etobicoke to the head of the Lake," which would have included the Credit River itself. The common council first said no, and the Crown then asked for the Credit River Anishinabek to consider selling part of their lands. Quenepenon (Otter doodem), the aanikeogimaa and orator, rose in council to explain their response. He began by reminding the Crown of purchases made under previous administrations and how the Crown had promised that the settlers would benefit the Mississauga. Instead, the reverse happened: "The inhabitants drive us away instead of helping us, and we want to know why we are served in this manner ... the farmers call us Dogs and threaten to shoot us." But at the same time, Quenepenon noted that the Mississaugas were still allies of the King and must honour their obligations to their relatives to provide them with more land. Yet the councils were split. As Quenepenon went on to explain: "The Young Men & Warriors have found fault with so much being sold before; it is true we are poor & the Women say we will be worse, if we part with any more." The naming here specifically of the warriors and women accords with Miller's findings for the presences of these councils in the

---

15 Surrender of land by the Ottawa, Chippawa, Pot-to-wa-to-my, and Huron Indian Nations of Detroit, 19 May 1790, LAC RG10, Vol. 1840/IT002.

Western Great Lakes. In the end the ogimaa, aanikeogimaa, and gichi-Anishinabek who comprised the formal council followed Anishinaabe law and agreed to the land sale, fulfilling their commitment to their allied council fire, the British, against the advice of the other two councils but not before noting their differences for the record. These leaders, after listening to all the advice, placed the needs of their allies over their own. The fulfilment of obligations to an ally in these interdependent alliance relationships was a cornerstone of Anishinaabe law.[16]

The role of women's councils in land sale agreements appears to have been advisory, and this practice may have been rooted in historic Anishinaabe marriage practices. Because women kept their doodem identities when they married, and because they typically married outside of their own and moved to their husband's communities, they brought other doodem perspectives and insights with them. These women served to connect their husbands' council fires with the council fires on the lands where they were born, strengthening the alliances between them.[17] But the marriage alone was not the sum total of their political work. It was not as if following their marriages Anishinaabe women retreated to a domestic sphere. Through participation in the women's council, advising on decision-making involving both internal matters and external relations, Anishinaabekwe did important political and community-building work. The political significance of doodem exogamy among the Anishinabek is therefore connected to the political work that women did through the alliances that they made and reinforced and the knowledge that they brought with them from the communities of their births.

It was possible for a woman to be an ogimaa (ogimaakwe).[18] For example, in 1892, the "Kettle Point and Sauble Indians" from Sarnia township in southwestern Ontario submitted a petition in which they included a genealogy of their leadership in support of a proposition. This genealogy indicated that, at one time, the people from the Kettle Point and Sauble communities had an ogimaakwe. In this document, Mahmahwegeahego was identified as the Chief "when Montreal was the headquarters of the French government." Mahmahwegeahego was succeeded by Inashiquay, who was followed in that position by her son

---

16 See especially Mills, "What is a Treaty?"; Stark, "Changing the Treaty Question."
17 Cary Miller, *Ogimaag*, 67–73.
18 McCallum, "Miss Chief."

Pewash. The author of the document described Pewash as "successor to his mother" and Inashiquay as an "Indian Queen."[19] Not only was Inashiquay acting as ogimaa, her son Pewash moved into that role after her, further evidence that she was an ogimaakwe and firekeeper, not the head of the council of women. As an ogimaakwe in this capacity, Inashiquay would have had responsibility for the entire common council community.

The rarity of women's doodem images on treaty documents should not detract from understanding their historical significance. Anishinaabe women, unlike their settler counterparts, were not less favoured by law. Rather, Anishinaabe women participated fully in the crucial political work of binding council fires and communities together through alliances. The 1784 Niagara sale/purchase agreement discussed above has three doodem images; they provide evidence of the work Anishinaabe women did maintaining alliances between the council fires of their birth and marriage. This sale agreement was between the Mississauga-Anishinabek and the British Crown and then permitted the subsequent granting of the Haldimand tract along the Grand River to the Haudenosaunee in the aftermath of the American Revolution. On that document (Figure 29), principal women are listed as signatories. Beside the names of Peawamah, Wapamonessychoqua, and Wacanoghaqua the clerk wrote "her mark,"[20] and beside each name is a doodem image. Unfortunately, the only known versions of this document are clerks' copies and clerks generally did a poor job reproducing doodem images; this case is no exception. However, I have a high degree of confidence that Peawamah and Wapamonessychoqua's doodemag were both Crane. The clerk managed to capture the bow posture of the Crane and tail "bustle" in both cases.[21] I am reasonably confident, based on my visual analysis and comparison with thousands of other images, that Waconoghaqua was likely Beaver doodem.[22] Significantly, in 1784 Wapamonessychoqua (or Wapanatashiqua) was the widow of Wabbicomicott, the former

---

19 Petition to The Honourable E. Dewdney, Supt. General of Indian Affairs, 4 April 1892, LAC RG10, Vol. 2568, file 125851, pp. 1–3; my thanks to Reg Good for bringing this petition to my attention.

20 Indenture for the sale of lands along the Grand River, 23 May 1784, Archives of Ontario, Crown Lands, RG1–1v2p145–6. True copy of the original deed.

21 Happ and Yuncker-Happ. Sandhill Crane Display Dictionary.

22 Bohaker, "Reading Anishinaabe Identities."

ogimaa of the Credit River. Her daughter Peshinaniqua or Margaret Ball was born, according to Peshinaniqua's baptismal record, "about Lake Huron, 1746." Peshinaniqua was an elderly woman when she was baptized by the Reverend Alvin Tory in 1825.[23] The fact that she reported being born "about Lake Huron" suggests strongly that her mother Wapanatashiqua was from an Anishinaabe community whose council fire site was on that lake. While Anishinaabe women typically moved to live and raise their children in their husband's community, the young couple would often stay with the wife's family until the first child was born. In the 1740s, Anishinaabe council fire sites were all around Lake Huron and on Lake St. Clair and the Detroit River. But the facts that, first, Wapanatashiqua was Crane doodem, and second, that she married the ogimaa of a regionally important council fire (Credit River) suggests a smaller set of council fires that she would have been from. A French census of Great Lakes French allies in 1736 locates a significant council site kept by a Crane doodem ogimaa at the base of Lake St. Clair, where the lake enters the Detroit River.[24] The prominent Crane doodem ogimaa Wasson, who signed the adhesion to the 1764 Treaty of Niagara in September at Detroit, was from the council fire at Saginaw Bay on Lake Huron.[25] Wapanatashiqua was likely from Saginaw Bay or perhaps Lake St. Clair. Regardless, she would have considered Crane doodem ogimaa at both of these council fires as her immediate kin. When she moved to the Credit River with her husband Wabbicomicot, she was doodem kin and therefore the key connection to the prominent Crane families and leaders of the Detroit and Saginaw Bay council fires. She would have had responsibilities to her doodem kin and they to her.

---

23 Record of Baptisms, Baptisms, 1802–57, New Credit Ontario Indian Mission, United Church Archives, Reel 77.202L 1830, f.27.

24 Dénombrement des nations sauvages, 1736, ANF, fondes des colonies, Series C11A, vol. 66, fol. 236–256v. See also "The French Era, 1720–1761," in Tanner, *Atlas of Great Lakes Indian History*, Map 9.

25 Kelsey, "Wasson"; Item 4, Copy of "Transaction of a Congress held with the Ottawas and Chippewa Nations with several others," 7 September 1764 (U1350 O48/4); Item 5, Copy of an acknowledgement by the Indians that they accept what has been written down, 11 September 1764 (U1350 O48/5), Centre for Kentish Studies (CKS), Unit 1350 (Amherst Mss.), Series 48 (Indian Affairs). Wasson signed a land cession for the lands of south-western Ontario north of Lake Erie as the ogimaa of the "Chippewas" with the track marks of the Crane: Surrender of land by the Ottawa, Chippawa, Pot-to-wa-to-my, and Huron Indian Nations of Detroit, 19 May 1790, LAC RG10, Vol. 1840/IT002.

This glimpse into the life of Wapanatashiqua is rare, but it reminds us about the political importance of Anishinaabekwe. The reality is that the bulk of records produced in colonial settings were by French, British, and American men recording their encounters with Anishinaabe men in formal councils. The importance of the political roles played by women was seldom seen or acknowledged by European observers.[26] When leading male ogimaawag are credited with negotiating treaties and alliances, we do not see the essential work their spouses did in making the alliances possible. Wabbicomicot, for example, is credited with bringing the Detroit Anishinabek into the Covenant Chain relationship in September of 1764. It is hard to imagine Wabbicomicot succeeding in this endeavour without the pre-existing and strong kinship ties between the Credit River council fire and the Crane doodem ogimaa Wasson, maintained by Wapanatashiqua.

Likewise, officials in the British Indian Department followed the British practice of privileging men in their records of Anishinaabe families who claimed annuity payments under treaty provisions. Only the names of heads of families were given; the names of women appear only if they were widows and, therefore, heads of households. Nevertheless, Cary Miller found that as Anishinaabe societies faced significant assimilative pressures in the second half of the nineteenth century, women during this same later period continued to be active politically. They used collective work groups as a political forum or as a type of women's council; such work continued into the twentieth century, through homemakers' clubs and other "social" activities that were really about community-building and the maintenance of relationships between families.[27] The relative invisibility of Anishinaabe women in the French, British, and American archival record must therefore not prevent us from being aware of the political work they did, especially in creating and reinforcing regional networks of alliance and information exchange. Both genders participated as Anishinaabe leaders, and both were essential to the decision-making that took place within formal councils.

---

26 Note that shifts in discourses around women's roles did not really change married or single women's legal status much in either the common law or the civil law traditions prior to Confederation. See Girard, Phillips, and Brown, *History of Law in Canada*, 683–701.

27 Cary Miller, *Ogimaag*, 67–8. See also Howard-Bobiwash, "Women's Class Strategies."

Alliance-Making through Council

Records of formal councils are everywhere in the colonial archives and from the earliest colonial records of encounter. These records are crucial as they reveal that the practices of governance through alliance, and alliances made through a process of formal governance in council, were old. Although there are far fewer records of councils involving only Indigenous participants (such as the alliance renewal ceremony discussed in Chapter 3), these colonial records demonstrate that Anishinaabe governance was conducted in a formal, structured setting that placed binding obligations on the participants; the regular meetings of these councils ensured that those binding obligations were fulfilled. Alliances between Anishinaabe council fires, and alliances made between non-Anishinaabe peoples and Anishinaabe council fires, had to be made in formal council, and following Anishinaabe long-established legal protocols for creating those alliance relationships. The French cartographer and later governor of the Quebec settlement, Samuel de Champlain, wrote frequently in his accounts of regular council meetings. His early descriptions of council structures reveal common protocols that have much in common with those described by Jones and Copway in their respective works on Anishinaabe governance more than two centuries later.

Champlain's experiences with alliance-making in council occurred very early in his ventures into the eastern Great Lakes region. The process he describes began in 1608, when the French and allied Wendat and eastern Anishinabek exchanged youth to overwinter with one another and learn each other's language. Savignon travelled with Champlain to France, and Etienne Brulé overwintered with the Wendat. The next summer, the parties came together again for a second meeting. The parties expressed pleasure at seeing how well their countrymen looked. Brulé, Champlain reported, "was well pleased with the treatment received from the Indians," and "had learned their language well," while Savignon "spoke well of the treatment [Champlain] had given him in France," and also "of the strange things he had seen, wherat they all wondered." Brulé explained to Champlain that the Wendat and eastern Anishinabek now wanted to make an alliance with Champlain. Since Champlain had treated Savignon so well, the Wendat explained to Champlain that this had "placed them under such obligations to be kind to me in anything I might desire of them." After several speeches, they exchanged gifts. Champlain had clearly already been briefed on this protocol, for he reported receiving "a gift of one hundred beaver skins," and he gave them in return "other sorts of merchandise."[28] Through ceremony and regionally established protocols, these parties were now allies.

The result of this alliance is that later that summer Champlain travelled with the Wendat and eastern Anishinabek to attack the Mohawk. Both the alliance and the attack loom large in Canadian history, and the engraving that Champlain produced of the battle has long been a staple in Canadian history textbooks. But this over-focus on a military alliance misses the objective that the Wendat and eastern Anishinabek were trying to achieve through establishing an alliance relationship of interdependence with Champlain and the men under his command. During the council at which the alliance was ratified, the Indigenous orators expressed significant concern about the other French traders who had followed Champlain up the river, who they feared might do them harm. Several days later, Champlain reported being called to their lodges "about midnight," where he found the leaders "all sitting in council, and they made me sit down beside them, saying that their custom was, when they wished to meet to discuss some matter, to do so at night, in order not to have their attention diverted by any objects; for at night one thought only of listening, whilst daylight distracted the mind."[29] Then and there Champlain's new allies again expressed concerns about these other Frenchmen, that these traders, "were not very friendly towards one another ... they also said that some of their people had been beaten." They wanted Champlain's assurances that these other Frenchmen would not come back, as "they much mistrusted the others." Champlain was invited to return with more people, "as many people as [he] liked, provided they were under the leadership of one chief." In return they were willing to show Champlain their country and permit him to live there if he wished. They also then gave Champlain a gift of another fifty beaver pelts and four wampum belts ("which they value as we do gold chains") to be shared with Champlain's "brother (meaning Pont-Gravé, since we were together)." These gifts came from other council fires not present, who nonetheless extended the hand of friendship to the French. Champlain observed

---

28 Champlain, *Works*, 2:188–9.
29 Ibid., 2:193.

both deliberative decision-making in action and the role of gifts in signalling formal intent or acceptance of terms. These Anishinaabe and Wendat leaders were also symbolically demonstrating, through gifts, their ability to take responsibility for Champlan.

Of course, what Champlain observed was nothing new. The Anishinabek shared diplomatic language, metaphors, and protocols with their Indigenous neighbours; these practises were simply extended to European newcomers. The Haudenosaunee Confederacy, for example, used the Covenant Chain to describe an alliance negotiated between the Mohawk Nation and the Dutch in the early seventeenth century. The initial metaphor was a rope, signifying that the two peoples were still distinct, yet bound together. When the British captured Albany from the Dutch in 1664, they became allies of the Mohawk Nation, using an iron chain as the metaphor, intended to indicate the strength of the relationship. But iron rusts, and so by the late seventeenth century a new metaphor, silver, was used to define the alliance relationship between the British and the Haudenosaunee Confederacy, one that in time would come to include Anishinaabe council fires after the Seven Years' War. Silver proved a highly suitable metaphor, as it tarnishes and turns black (the colour associated with war in Great Lakes colour symbolism) unless it is polished regularly (i.e., unless regular meetings are held to address grievances).[30] The Haudenosaunee used silver because what they wanted to emphasize in their choice of metaphors was the regular work needed by both sides to maintain the relationship represented by the image of a covenant chain. It was this Covenant Chain relationship that was extended in 1761 to the Anishinabek in the central and western Great Lakes, who had been French-allied during the Seven Years' War, and was reconfirmed at the Treaty of Niagara in 1764 as defining the relationship between all Great Lakes peoples, the British, and the Haudenosaunee Confederacy, a "tri-partite alliance."[31]

While the treaty relationship itself was defined by a different metaphor, the enacting body for this agreement was a council fire and, specifically, the leaders from many diverse Great Lakes communities, representing the people of their own fires, who met around the large

---

30 There is a significant body of literature on the Covenant Chain. See, for example, Jennings, *Ambiguous Iroquois Empire*.
31 Parmenter, "Pontiac's War"; John Borrows, "Wampum at Niagara."

council fire at Fort Niagara. This flexibility and variability in the size and scale of the polities was defined through the metaphor of fire discussed in Chapter 3; the fact that fires as polities or alliance agreements could themselves be comprised of other fires is part of what makes Great Lakes political history so challenging to interpret. Council fires were not exclusive, nor were they hierarchical jurisdictions. Further, smaller fires did not lose their autonomy when they joined a larger fire: they maintained their complete independence in policy and decision-making. At the same time, larger fires could not represent the wishes or needs of their constituent parts unless permission was granted, again in council, on a very specific basis.[32]

Anishinaabe governance was enacted at both common and general council fires. Doodem identity played a central political role in these larger general councils, as Jones explained: the "head chief of the tribe in whose territory the council is convened, generally takes the lead."[33] As the general council convened in 1642 exemplified, general councils provided a place for allied Anishinaabe council fires to convene and discuss issues of common concern. It was at general councils that larger military actions were agreed to and planned on a scale that impressed French, British, and American officials and seemed to them to reflect effort on a "national scale," such as the series of attacks on British-held forts in the summer of 1763 often called Pontiac's War.[34] These major differences in the types of council fires are what make it hard to understand the differences between the parties who entered into alliance agreements at a general council and the parties who entered into land sale or land use agreements, which were transacted with common councils.

However, British colonial officials certainly seemed reasonably well informed of the political distinction between the two types of councils and the respective jurisdiction (areas of responsibility) of each. In October of 1763, King George III issued a proclamation setting up the rules for governing the new territories he had acquired through Britain's victory over France in the Seven Years' War, including France's claim to the Great Lakes region. By that proclamation, the British Crown reserved for itself the sole right to purchase land from Indigenous peoples in

---

32 Stark, "Marked by Fire," 124.
33 Jones, *History*, 106.
34 Eid, "'National' War"; see also Dowd, *War Under Heaven*.

order to make land available for colonists.[35] But from whom specifically would the Crown purchase land? By the Treaty of Niagara in 1764, the British Crown, through the negotiations of Sir William Johnston, entered into a Covenant Chain relationship with "twenty-four nations" who gathered at Niagara.[36] This was an alliance and peace relationship, and the "twenty-four nations" represented distinct regional council fires, each of which had sent representatives to Niagara. Significantly, when it came time to make land purchases on behalf of the Crown, Sir William Johnson and subsequent generations of Indian Department officials did not reconvene the general council that had entered into the Covenant Chain relationship. For land purchases with the Anishinabek, the British made separate agreements with the common councils who were responsible for the lands under consideration. This fact alone tells us that when the land surrender period in Upper Canada began in earnest after 1791, local Indian Department officials knew exactly with whom, and where, responsibility for land surrender agreements rested – and it was with the local or common council.

According to Anishinaabe governance principles, both general and common councils were consensus-based deliberative bodies that were expected to receive and consider advice from the people they represented. All maintained alliances. At common councils, leaders were accountable to all adults in a community. They took advice from the council of women and the council of warriors about what do about everything from where and what to hunt (resource management), to where family groups would be (a winter safety net), to the settling of internal conflicts and external disputes. Alliances here were made between families. General councils, in contrast, were places at which alliances between common councils were established and renewed, and ties between doodem lineages reinforced between council fires.

---

35 The proclamation was also the first British constitution for the former French colony of Quebec as well as Grenada and East and West Florida, but it gave significant attention to the question of the Crown's relationship with Indigenous peoples west of the proclamation line. It also laid out the rules that would permit non-Indigenous people to settle on Indigenous land. His Majesty the King, George III, "A Proclamation," 7 October 1763, Mark Baskett, Printer to the King's most Excellent Majesty; and by the Assigns of Robert Baskett.

36 John Borrows, "Wampum at Niagara."

The work that councils did is also evident in other types of documents they produced and signed with doodem images, including speeches and petitions. One beautiful example is an address that was commissioned by Anishinaabe peoples living near Amherstburg, Upper Canada, in 1809. It was presented to Colonel Jasper Grant on the occasion of his permanent return to Ireland. This document now resides in the National Library of Ireland in Dublin. Grant, who was Anglo-Irish, had been the commanding officer at Fort Amherstburg (near the mouth of the Detroit River) from 1806 to 1809. Both he and his wife had developed good relationships with the Anishinabek who visited the fort and had received many gifts, including at least six pipe bowls and one pipe and stem, wrapped in porcupine quills – the kind of gifts given in the context of a formal council. Grant's wife was also an avid collector of Anishinaabe material culture and quite likely also a receiver of these gifts; she returned to Ireland with a sizeable collection of women's artistry, including beaded moccasins and woven baskets.

At a council held prior to the Grant family's departure, Wabionishkoubi (Eagle doodem) made a formal presentation to the Colonel, bestowing upon him a single parchment carried on a bed of scarlet goose down, along with sixteen strings of white wampum. The strings of white wampum signified peace and prosperity, while the red goose down communicated deep emotion and the great sense of their loss.[37] On the parchment page were recorded the words of the orator: "Father, Since you have been here we have always found you kind and friendly to us on all occasions and We cannot allow you to leave us without expressing our regret at the loss of such a good Commanding Officer. We pray the Great Spirit to smooth the Watery way for you to conduct you and your family home in safety over the Great Waters where we wish you may find your Relations and friends in Prosperity and Peace."[38]

---

37 For the Jasper Grant collection, see Phillips, *Patterns of Power*, an exhibit catalogue produced when the Jasper Grant collection travelled to Ontario to mark the provincial bicentennial. In April 2002 I visited the National Library of Ireland, where the letter and goose down are held. The downy feathers are packaged with the address, while the wampum strings are stored nearby in the vaults of the ethnography department of the National Museum. The feathers are small, about four inches long, delicate, and a vivid, bright scarlet.

38 Letters of Col. Jasper Grant, MS 10, 178, Box 3, Address of the Ottawas, National Library of Ireland, Dublin.

Ten individuals signed the address; beside each name, the signatories drew images of their respective doodem identities. Jasper Grant, or his wife Isabella at the very least, evidently returned the feelings of affection. She kept the letter after Grant's death in 1812, together with the wampum strings and goose down and along with beautiful examples of Anishinaabe ceremonial clothing, pipe bowls, weapons, and other items that she left to the care of her daughters after her death. These items were treasured in the family and well taken care of before the collection was donated to the National Museum of Ireland in 1902.[39] Other council fires also gave letters of thanks to departing vice-regal dignitaries.[40] (See Figure 30.) Addresses and gifts such as the one given to Jasper Grant are also evidence of the deep personal and familial relationships that Anishinaabe peoples and colonial officials and post commanders made with one another. Alliance relationships transcended politics and over time created enduring family ties. The doodem images on the documents, along with many other petitions produced in council, can also be read along with treaty documents signed between 1781 and 1862 for what are now lands in the province of Ontario to reconstruct the composition of those councils and the doodem alliance connections between them.

Councils and Doodemag

As Peter Jones explained in his *History*, the reason that Anishinaabe peoples negotiated land transactions at the level of the common council is that this is how the Anishinabek, as a whole, recognized who had responsibility for particular lands and territories. The specific function of the common council, was, according to Jones, to be responsible for "local affairs," which included "the sale and division of their lands, settling disputes, adopting other Indians into their own body, and the transaction of business with the British government."[41] The right to engage in land transactions also belonged at this level because it was at the common councils where Anishinaabe leaders historically determined who would hunt in which winter territory and how and under

---

39 Phillips, *Patterns of Power*, 20n2.
40 For another example of a letter of thanks, also signed with doodem images, see Address of the Chiefs of the Mississauga ... to His Excellency the Lieutenant Governor, 7 October 1811, LAC, RG10 Vol. 27:16316–8.
41 Jones, *History*, 107.

what terms councils negotiated access to other limited resources, like a sugar bush or a fishery.[42] While a majority of male common council members may have had the same doodem as the fire-keeper, common councils could and did have an aanikeogimaa and gichi-Anishinabek from other doodem identities, whose long-time residency in the region ensured that they too had a voice in council. These multi-doodem common councils are not evidence of some earlier "tradition" of single doodem councils being changed or disrupted; instead, they reflect marriage practices and long-standing relationships that had developed between specific doodemag. As I explained earlier in Chapter 2, the names of Anishinaaabe polities in seventeenth-century records such as "Amikouais (Beavers) and Niquoquet (Otters)" do *not* reflect council fires where every male and female member had the same doodem. The name instead refers to the doodem that had responsibility as the keeper of that council fire. Every council comprised people from multiple doodemag.

Peter Jones's description of the common council can be seen in action in the pattern of doodem images that appear on treaty documents covering what is now eastern and southern Ontario (illustrated in Tables 3 and 4). These documents were signed by the ogimaawag and gichi-Anishinabek of the common councils. The first example (Table 3) from the Credit River shows the changes and continuities in the council there over thirty years. The 1796 Mississauga-Anishinaabe cession of lands at the western end of Lake Ontario, which the British negotiated with the council fire of the Credit River, contains six doodem images: four Eagles, one Pike, and one Caribou. On this, and subsequent, land sales signed by the Mississaugas in council at the Credit River, the Eagle doodem always signed first and appeared most frequently. Each doodem image represents a principal leader of an extended family of that doodem identity. The ogimaa of this council was always of the migizi, or Eagle, doodem. It is in this sense only that we can think of traditional governance as "hereditary," as there was no requirement for first-born sons to follow fathers as in a system of primogeniture.

At Mnjikaning (the narrows between Lake Couchiching and Lake Simcoe, today known as Rama), Table 4 shows that it is the Caribou doodem image that always occupies the top position on the vertical

---

42 See Cary Miller, *Ogimaag*, 34–6, for more specific discussion of how local councils regulated hunting territories.

Table 3 Changes and Continuity of Doodem Identities on Treaty Documents Signed at the Credit River (the Common Council)

1792	1795	1797	1 Aug 1805	2 Aug 1805	1806	1818	1820
Eagle	Eagle	Eagle	Eagle	Eagle	Eagle	Eagle	Eagle
Eagle	Eagle	Otter	Otter	Otter	Otter	Eagle	Eagle
Otter	Otter	Caribou	Eagle	Eagle	Eagle	Otter	Eagle
Eagle	Eagle	Eagle	Eagle	Eagle	Eagle	Otter	Otter
Caribou	Eagle	Eagle	Eagle		Eagle	Pike	Pike
	Caribou		Eagle		Eagle		
			Eagle		Eagle		
					Eagle		
					Caribou		
					Pike		

Sources: Deed of Feoffment, Niagara to the Thames River (Between the Lakes Purchase), 7 December 1792, RG10, Vol. 1840/IT005; Sale of Lands to Captain Brant, Burlington Bay, 10 October 1795, RG10, Vol. 1840/IT008; Sale of lands at Head of the Lake (Burlington Bay), 21 August 1797, RG10, Vol. 1841/IT029; Toronto Purchase, 1 August 1805, RG10, Vol. 1841/IT039; Agreement to Surrender Peel and Halton reserving Credit River, 2 August 1805, RG10, Vol. 1841/IT041; Sale of Lands (Lease and Release) from Etobicoke to Burlington Bay, 6 September 1806, RG10, Vol. 1842/IT042; Adjetance Purchase (Sale of 624,000 acres), 28 October 1818, RG10, Vol. 1842/IT059; Cessions of 12 Mile Creek, 16 Mile Creek and Credit River Reserves, RG10, Vol. 1842/IT071; all Indian Treaties and Surrenders collection, Library and Archives Canada.

Table 4 Changes and Continuities of Doodem Identities on Treaty Documents Signed in the Common Council at Mnjikaning

1798	1818	1836	1852	1856
Caribou	Caribou	Caribou	Caribou	Caribou
Otter	illegible	Otter	Caribou	Caribou
Pike	Otter	Caribou	Caribou	Birch
Caribou	Pike	Caribou	Birch	Catfish
Caribou	Catfish (very poor quality)	*9 men signed with X-marks	Catfish	Otter
			Otter	Otter
			Illegible	
			Otter	

Sources: Conveyance of the Harbour at Penetanguishene, 25 May 1798, RG10, Vol. 1840/IT008; Sale of 1.5 million acres in the Home District, 17 October 1818, RG10, Vol. 1842/IT055; Sale of the Coldwater Road Allowance, 26 November 1836, RG10, Vol. 1844/IT126; Surrender of 20 Acres in Orillia, 17 June 1852, RG10, Vol. 1845/IT152; Sale of Islands in Lake Simcoe, 6 June 1856, RG10, Vol. 1845/IT188; all Indian Treaties and Surrenders collection, Library and Archives Canada.

column of doodem images, and it is the Caribou doodem that occurs with the greatest frequency, along with Otter, Catfish, Pike, and Bison doodem images. While these council fires were "multi-doodem," one doodem was still recognized as the respective keeper of the fire (the hosts of that council): the Cranes at Bawaating and Rice Lake, the Caribou at Mnjikaning, the Eagle at the Credit River.

The Credit River Council Fire

The council fire of the Mississaugas of the Credit was established through the alliance discussed in the opening of Chapter 3.[43] The rich archival record for this council fire makes it possible to reconstruct the composition of this common council from that founding, in the late 1690s, and pictographically on treaty documents from 1764 through to the extinguishment of the council fire in 1847. From this we can see how this common council participated in larger regional agreements and the ways in which doodem ties connected the Credit to other council fires. The council fire of the Mississaugas of the Credit River was part of an alliance with the British-allied Haudenosaunee Confederacy since the early eighteenth century; the French enumeration of 1736 acknowledged as much when it provided no census information about the Anishinabek of the north shore of Lake Ontario, noting only that they were already trading with the British.[44] The council fire may have been temporarily covered during the Seven Years' War, as one document in the papers of Sir William Johnson refers to Wabbicomicot and his community coming back to their location near Toronto at the war's end from the Detroit area.[45] Wabbicomicot first met William Johnson at Fort Niagara in 1761 and agreed to come with him to Detroit, where he introduced Johnson to the council as his brother.[46] Following the outbreak of Pontiac's War in 1763, Wabbicomicot opposed the action and spoke against it to, as he put it, "convince the bad Indians at and about Detroit

---

43 This peace agreement was renewed in 1840. Peter Jones recorded the minutes. See Minutes of a General Council held at the River Credit, 16 January 1840, Paudash Papers, LAC RG10, Vol. 1011, Part B:60–92.

44 Dénombrement des nations sauvages, 1736, ANF, Fondes des colonies, Series C11A, vol. 66, fol. 236–256v.

45 "An Indian Congress, Niagara July 17–August 4, 1764," in Johnson, *Papers*, 11:307.

46 See Graham, "Wabbicommicot."

of their error" and to remind them of the council the British had held with them two years earlier and their peaceful intentions.[47]

Wabbicomicot was then one of the ogimaa invited to attend the Treaty of Niagara in 1764, along with all of the former French-allied "Western Indians," to discuss a peace agreement and to formalize their new alliance. Over the two weeks of meetings, Johnson received many wampum belts from attending ogimaawag, as they and their orators spoke about the conflict. In a separate meeting with Johnson in the evening of 29 July, Wabbicomicot came to see Johnson with "six others of his People" for a private council. This was still a formal affair, as Wabbicomicot brought a pipe to the meeting; the Mississaugas and officers present smoked together. At this meeting Wabbicomicot informed Johnson of what he had been doing at Detroit to make peace; he also gave Johnson a belt of purple wampum with five white circles on it. Johnson did not record the meaning of this belt, but the circles would typically refer to other council fires in an alliance, perhaps the very alliance discussed in Chapter 3. Johnson then responded with two belts for Wabbicomicot, including one described in detail: "a large Belt with a Figure representing Niagara's large House, and Fort, with two Men holding it fast on either side, and a Road through it, and desired that he, Wabbicomicot, and his People would come, and settle at their old Place of Abode near Toronto, and have a carefull Eye always over said Fort, and Carrying Place."[48] Johnson was asking Wabbicomicot to uncover the slumbering fire at the Credit, to protect the main portage route from the Humber River to Mnjikaning. Johnson then distributed medals to the Mississauga leaders.

Two days later, Sir William Johnson addressed all the Nations together "in their Camp" – across the river from Fort Niagara (Mississauga Point). Johnson invited all of the Nations into "the great Belt of Covenant Chain that we may not forget our mutual Engagements." Employing the visual metaphors of a road and two council fires, one at each end, Johnson said "I desire that after you have shewn this Belt to all Nations you will fix one end of it with the Chipaweigs [Anishinabek] at St. Mary's [Bawaating] whilst the other end remains at my House [Niagara] ... if you will strictly observe this, you will enjoy the favor of

---

47 "An Indian Congress, Niagara July 17–August 4, 1764," in Johnson, *Papers*, 11:307–8.
48 Ibid., 11:307.

the English, a plentiful Trade, and you will become a happy People."[49] Johnson's decision to name Bawaating as the anchor point may very well have been influenced by Wabbicomicot, and the existing eastern Anishinaabe alliance, as Bawaating was one of the "anchors" for that agreement. But not all agreed. One ogimaa arose and suggested instead that the "Belt of the Covenant Chain" should be kept at Michilimackinac, "as it is the Centre, where all our People may see it."[50] (See Figure 19.) In these early days of the British alliance with the former French-allied Anishinabek, Johnson still had much to learn of the region's deep history and Michilimackinac's significance as the place where Nanabozhoo began to remake the world. The eastern alliance could not be the keeper of a belt for the nations of the entire region. In the end, the belt was entrusted to the Ottawa and made its way with them back to the Michigan peninsula and, eventually, to Manitoulin Island.[51]

Following the exchange of the Covenant Chain belt in July and the formal founding of the new alliance, Wabbicomicot travelled back to Detroit alongside Colonel Bradstreet, who was commanding British forces in the area. He then helped to persuade the council fires there to accept the peace and come into the Covenant Chain alliance. While there were only wampum belts exchanged at Niagara, at Detroit Bradstreet had the ogimaawag sign a document agreeing to the peace. It was signed by members of the "Chippeways, Ottawa, Miamis, Wyandot, Potawatomies and Sakis," all of whom had not been at Niagara.[52] All of the Anishinaabe delegates signed with doodem images (while representatives from other political traditions such as the Wendat represented their own kinship systems with images). Wabbicomicot also signed as a witness with his doodem.[53] As Figure 24 shows, Wabbicomicot chose to underscore his close and deep relationship with Johnson and the British council fire by showing his Eagle doodem while wearing a King George

---

49 Ibid., 11:310.
50 Ibid., 11:311.
51 Ibid., 11:309–10.
52 Item 4, Copy of "Transaction of a Congress held with the Ottawas and Chippewa Nations with several others," 7 September 1764 (U1350 O48/4); Item 5, Copy of an acknowledgement by the Indians that they accept what has been written down, 11 September 1764 (U1350 O48/5), Centre for Kentish Studies (CKS), Unit 1350 (Amherst Mss.), Series 48 (Indian Affairs).
53 Richard White, *The Middle Ground*, 288–9; "Journal of Colonel Croghan's," in O'Callaghan, *Colonial History of the State of New York*, 7:779–88.

medal, the one he received from Johnson on 29 July, just before travelling to Detroit to bring the remaining fires into the Covenant Chain.[54]

As discussed above, Wabbicomicot's capacity to be a strong voice at Detroit was made possible by his marriage to Wapanatashiqua, the Crane doodem woman from a council fire located at the southern end of Lake Huron. As a young adult he already would have starting training for a leadership role of the Credit River council fire. Wabbicomicot's grandmothers would have suggested a suitable partner from an allied council fire. It was this doodem connection to the important Crane council fires of the Detroit area and Saginaw that proved so useful to both Wabbicomicot and Johnson and gave Wabbicomicot the ability to influence the council at Detroit. But there would also have been the additional and to date unacknowledged influence of Wabbicomicot's wife. Behind the scenes reported by colonial officials, the women's council would have met, and Wapanatashiqua would have given her assessment of the British as potential allies. She could speak convincingly to her Crane doodem kin of her own experiences with the British and her travels with Wabbicomicot to Johnson Hall and her assessment of British behaviour respecting the Covenant Chain.

With the war ended and the alliance with the British confirmed, the Mississauga could return to a more peaceful existence, at least for a few years. However, unlicensed traders continued to flood into the region; Wabbicomicot promised Johnson to try to stop the trading, but as an ogimaa, he could not compel people. Wabbicomicot continued to visit Niagara and send news to Johnson (who lived further east along the Mohawk River) until Wabbicomicot's death in August 1768. In 1781, his successor, Wabakayne, attended a large regional council at Niagara. The leading ogimaawag of the council fires attending signed a treaty confirming a 1764 transfer of the west bank of the Niagara River to the British, for the consideration of three hundred suits of clothing. Four signed with their doodem, reproduced and labelled on a clerk's copy of the original: Nanibisure (Swan) from west of the Grand River, who is identified by the clerk as "Chipwewigh"; the other three were identified as Misssissaga: Paghquan (Bear), Wabakinnie (Wabakayne/

---

54 Wabbicomicot's loyalty to Johnson has been well established. See Graham, "Wabbicommicot."

Eagle), Minaghquat (Duck).[55] Here were four very important Mississauga ogimaawag renewing their alliance with the British, granting the British use of their land, and receiving gifts in return.

Then, in 1784, the British asked the Mississaugas to create space in their territory for Britain's Haudenosaunee Confederacy allies. They did so, granting lands along the Grand River. Wabakayne signed first, with Wabanip (also Eagle doodem) and five other gitch-Anishinabek. Within a few short years after the end of the American Revolution, the influx of Loyalist Americans wanting to settle in what is now the province of Ontario sent the British to ask their Mississauga-Anishinaabe allies of the Credit River council fire for more land. The treaties (seven land sales and one lease) signed between 1787 and 1820 all represent agreements between the British crown and the Anishinabek of the north shore of Lake Ontario. Specifically, these transactions were with the council fire of the migizi, or Eagle, doodem at the Credit River. The pattern of doodem reflects the composition of the common council. The leading image on each document is of the ogimaa of the Credit River (just west of the present-day city of Toronto). On the treaties signed in 1792 and 1795 Wabakayne signed as the ogimaa of the council.[56]

Wabakayne was murdered in 1796 by a British soldier after an altercation defending his wife's sister from sexual assault.[57] Wabanip, also Eagle doodem, took his place. He had served as Wabakayne's aanikeogimaa, or step-below chief. This person could be a son, or another worthy individual, who was preparing to take on the role of ogimaa in the future. But this was not always the case, especially if the aanikeogimaa was of a different doodem. For example, while Wabanip was ogimaa, the Otter doodem gichi-Anishinaabe Quenepenon ("Golden Eagle") was his aanikeogimaa. In this role Quenepenon took the responsibility of speaking on behalf of ogimaa Wabanip in

---

55 Surrender of land by Chipeweigs and Mississagas, 9 May 1781, LAC RG10, Vol. 1850/IT396.

56 Deed of Feoffment – The Messissague Nation to His Britannick Majesty, 7 December 1792, LAC RG10, Vol. 1840/IT005, and Captain Brant's purchase near the outlet in Burlington Bay, 10 October 1795, LAC RG10, Vol. 1840/IT008.

57 "Letter From Peter Russell to J.G. Simcoe, Niagara, 28th September 1796," in *Russell Papers*, 49.

council. Wabanip died sometime between 1797 and 1805. However, Quenepenon did not become ogimaa. He continued as aanikeogimaa under the new ogimaa, Chechalk (Eagle doodem). Chechalk died in 1810 and was replaced by Adjutant. Quenepenon then died in 1812.[58] The position of Adjutant's aanikeogimaa went to Weggishgomin, also known as Ogimaa-Bineseh (Okemapenesse) or "Chief Little Bird." Born in 1764, Weggishgomin (He Who Is Like the Day) was also Eagle doodem. He took on his new name when he became aanikeogimaa.[59] The influx of settlers, the spread of disease, and the War of 1812 and its aftermath were, as Donald Smith has described, very hard for the Credit River people.[60] The final surrender in 1820 left the Credit River community control over their reserve only. Weggishgomin then died in 1828 and Adjutant in 1829. Following this crucial loss of leadership, the Credit River leaders in council elected Nawahjegezhegwabe ("Sloping Sky Man," or Joseph Sawyer) their ogimaa and Kahkewahkonaby (Peter Jones) the aanikeogimaa.[61] Both men were by this time converted Christians, but they remained Eagle doodem. They participated fully in Anishinaabe political tradition, meeting in council and respecting the consultative, consensus-building process that characterized Anishinaabe politics. At the same time, they demonstrated the adaptability of Anishinaabe governance as they worked to find a way forward for the greatly diminished Mississaugas of the Credit, to rebuild the community, and to maintain their autonomy. They did so by changing aspects of their practices to resemble the norms of settler governments, including the keeping of minutes and the establishment of some of the apparatus of a formal justice system, but such changes were self-directed and represented adaptation instead of assimilation.[62]

Even as the Credit River fire began to change, they still maintained the centrality of their doodem identities to governance. On the documents they produced and signed we can see evidence of the continuing interconnected world of Anishinaabe governance through alliance. For

---

58 Quenepenon was elderly by 1812. He died from a gunshot wound (but not in combat) after fasting to acquire spiritual power to protect against such weapons. See Donald Smith, "Kineubenae (Quinipeno, Quenebenaw)."
59 Donald Smith, "Ogimauh-Binaessih."
60 Donald Smith, *Sacred Feathers*, 34–5.
61 Ibid., 104; Donald Smith, "Nawahjegezhegwabe."
62 Walters, "According to the Old Customs."

example, the Eagle doodem gichi-Anishinaabe Wabenose from Burlington Bay, who sat at the Credit River council fire, signed a treaty in 1797 as part of a land sale agreement for lands at the western end of Lake Ontario.[63] Wabenose (who was Peter Jones's maternal grandfather) was on this document as both a gichi-Anishinaabe of his own extended family from Burlington Bay and someone who participated in governance decisions and land transactions affecting all those who met in council at the Credit River. Because of this, Wabenose and his extended family were also, by extension, a party to the alliance agreement between the Anishinabek and Haudenosaunee that began in the 1690s, through which treaty the very fire at the Credit River to which Wabenose belonged was established. As a result of that agreement, Wabenose was also part of the alliance agreement with other Anishinaabe council fires that stretched in an arc north first to Mnjikaning, where the Caribou were the keepers, to Wausauksing (Parry Island) where the Beaver kept their fire, then to Odaawaa-minising (Manitoulin Island), where the Whitefish doodem watched the fire, and finally to Bawaating at today's Sault Ste Marie, the fire kept by the Crane doodem. Wabenose would also have thought of himself as part of the Treaty of Niagara and the Covenant Chain relationship with the British. Furthermore, Wabenose would also have kin through his wife Naishenum (although I do not yet know her doodem). Following Heidi Stark's argument, we can understand the Mississaugas of the Credit River as being "marked by fire," in that their alliance relationships defined the multiple polities to which each member of the community belonged.[64] However, as will be discussed in Chapter 5, Wabenose's children would find that settlers and the colonial government of Upper Canada would disrupt these lines of alliance and make these connections much harder for communities to maintain.

The Credit River council fire makes a particularly excellent case study for the composition of the local or common council because of the rich records that exist for this community. Not only did this council fire sign multiple land sale agreements – eight – in the period from 1792 to 1820 but further information is available on the number of extended families who received annuity payments as a result of these treaties.

---

63 Deed of the Sale of Land at the head of Lake Ontario in Upper Canada from the Mississaga Nation to William Claus Esq, 21 August 1797, LAC RG10, Vol. 1841/IT029.
64 Stark, "Marked By Fire," 128–9.

Baptism, marriage, death, and members' records of the Methodist church to which many of the community came to belong by 1826 further contribute to the demographic portrait. The turnover in leadership and the rearrangement of the composition of the council that the treaties suggest (see Table 3) can be explained by the set of circumstances facing the Mississaugas between the end of the American Revolution and the War of 1812. First, they suffered the impact of several epidemics. At the start of the 1790s, the total population of the community who gathered at the Credit River in the spring and fall of each year was around 500. By 1800, more than a quarter of the population was dead due to disease. The resulting grief and social dislocation had a negative effect on the community and on continuity of leadership. At the same time, Loyalist settlers displaced by the American Revolution and economic opportunists seeking free grants of land were encroaching on Mississauga-Anishinaabe land. This combined assault of colonialism and disease prompted some, including Weggishgomin, to engage in some measure of assimilation, or at least accommodation, to cope with this new reality. Weggishgomin began to learn English, built a log cabin, took up some farming, and changed his clothing to match that of the newcomers.[65] Yet he continued to participate in and respect traditional civil governance, and he accepted the position of aanike-ogimaa in 1805.

The War of 1812 had a significant impact on the Mississauga-Anishinabek, as it did on other Indigenous peoples living in what is now southern Ontario. The opposing armies marched right through Mississauga territory, devastating their lands. Furthermore, Mississauga warriors were among those defending Upper Canada from invasion and they were on the front lines when American soldiers landed at York on 26 April 1813. Many warriors died, including two chiefs – ogimaawag or gichi-Anishinabek – whose names were not identified.[66] At the same time, the doodem images on the set of land sale documents indexed in Table 3 provide remarkable examples of political continuity as well as change. The Eagle doodem was the keeper of the fire at the Credit and this fact is acknowledged in all of these agreements; the eagle doodem is consistently in the first place, as it was more than twenty years later on the petition that Peter Jones delivered to Queen Victoria in 1844,

---

65 See Donald Smith, "Ogimauh-Binaessih."
66 Sheaffe to Prevost 5 May 1813 in Word, *Select British Documents*, 93.

when Joseph Sawyer signed first with his Eagle doodem.[67] The presence of Otter, Caribou, and Pike doodem images is also not surprising. The Eagle doodem was in alliance relationship with the Caribou at Rama, and members of each community were also intermarried with one another. Likewise, Otter and Pike women were intermarried with Eagle men. The gichi-Anishinabek who headed these families never became the leading ogimaa while the council fire was lit at the Credit River, as that position was consistently held by those of the Eagle doodem. However, these men had been intermarried long enough to be part of the common council and to assume important political roles, as Quenepenon did in 1797, becoming the speaker in council for the Eagle ogimaawag Wabanip and Chechalk.

As headmen of local families, these gichi-Anishinabek of the Otter, Caribou, and Pike doodemag also had the responsibility to speak about land issues, and to sign treaty documents. By the time the first land sale documents were signed, the council fire at the Credit River had been lit for one hundred years. Family contingencies and close ties may have drawn brothers to be near sisters who had married into the Eagle doodem; sons-in-law may have formed close relations with their in-laws after marriage and may have stayed on in the area after the birth of their first child. Or an ogimaa, having only daughters, may have wished his sons-in-law to stay around to hunt for his family.[68] These are all reasons that would explain how the composition of common councils would change over time and add members from different doodemag.

By 1824, government census of those receiving annual presents at the Humber River reveals that the Credit River community consisted of other doodemag beyond the Eagle, Caribou, Pike, and Otter who comprised the common council. There were men with Birch, Goose, Bison, and Bear doodemag. While these doodem identities did appear on an 1835 petition on behalf of the Credit River community to ban liquor on the reserve and again on the 1844 petition to Queen Victoria, Birchbark,

---

67 Petition to Queen Victoria, 19 October 1844, Peter Jones fonds, Box 1 Folder 9: Indian Petitions and Addresses, Pratt Library Special Collections, Victoria University at the University of Toronto.

68 As discussed in Chapter 2, this was exactly the situation facing an Anishinaabe ogimaa in present-day Wisconsin. It was through this type of invitation that William Warren explained the origin of the Wolf doodem among the Anishinabek, as the son-in-law in that case was Sioux. Warren and Neill, *History*, 165.

Table 5 Transcribed Census showing Doodem of indinaakonigewin ogimaag and gichi-Anishinabek of the Credit Community in 1824*

	Men	Women	Boys			Girls		
			10–15	5–9	1–4	10–14	5–9	1–4
Bark Tribe	4	7	1	2	1	0	1	1
1 Eagle Tribe	2	4	0	2	2	1	1	0
2 Eagle Tribe	4	5	0	0	2	0	2	2
3 Eagle Tribe	3	12	0	2	2	1	4	2
4 Eagle Tribe	3	4	3	0	0	0	0	0
5 Eagle Tribe	14	20	5	4	1	2	0	0
Goose Tribe	2	0	0	1	0	1	0	0
Otter Tribe	7	3	1	1	1	0	1	0
Rein Deer Tribe	9	6	1	1	1	2	2	1
Pike Tribe	7	6	1	6	0	0	1	1
Total	55	67	12	19	10	7	12	7

* Recall that adult women who were spouses of the ogimaawag and gichi-Anishinabek would have had different doodemag.

Source: Return of the Missessague Indians Taken August 26th 1824 at the River Humber, NAC RG 10, Volume 42, p. 22671.

Goose, Bison, and Bear doodemag never appear on the land surrender documents. This is not because they were not seen as members of the community. As Table 5 demonstrates, the "Messissagua Indians" comprised families from a range of doodemag. However, it was only those recognized by the larger community as having responsibility for the lands in question who signed the land sale agreements. The common council determined who was a member of the community and how resources should be allocated to these other families. Marriage records reveal, though, that these other doodemag were related to common council doodemag.[69] In other words, the Bark and Goose "tribes" listed on the 1824 were kin.

---

69 Register, including births, 1776–1881, marriages, 1831–1855 (predominantly undated), deaths, 1840–1883, of the River Credit Indians; Record of Baptisms, 1802–1846 and Membership list of Methodist Society at the Upper Mohawk Grand River, 1826; New Credit Methodist Indian Mission (Ontario) fonds, F1434, United Church of Canada, Toronto.

Mnjikaning Council

The long history of the Mnjikaning council at what is now the Chippe-was of Rama can also be reconstructed from multiple treaty documents, as Table 4 shows. Recall from Chapter 3 that Musquakie indicated that the Caribou doodem was the keeper of the council fire at Mnjikaning and was also the fire keeper and wampum keeper for the entire east-ern Great Lakes Anishinaabe alliance. The first land cessions for this area involved the lands around Penetanguishene in 1798, to support the building of a British Naval Base. But after the War of 1812, new settlers also began to pressure the Anishinabek at Rama for their lands. They signed a series of cessions, eventually ending up with the small reserve that is Rama today.

In 1840, Musquakie was the ogimaa and wampum keeper. In 1846, he responded at a general council hosted in his own community to the proposed removal of Anishinaabe peoples to the Saugeen peninsula and the creation of manual labour schools to be funded by one-quarter of each community's treaty annuity payments. Musquakie spoke strongly against the proposed removal: "I am not willing to leave my village, the place where my Forefathers lived, and where they made a great encampment; where they lived many generations; where they wished their children to live while the world should stand, and which the white man pointed out to me, and gave me for my settlement. This is about all."[70] When the votes were taken on the question of funding schools from band annuity funds, only Musquakie (Caribou doodem) and ogimaa John Assance (Otter doodem) of Beau-Soleil Island were opposed. One short day later, they reversed their decisions in response to the wishes of their own common councils. Indeed, Captain Ander-son of the Indian Department received a signed memo from "a large majority of the Rama [Mnjikaning] Indians" approving of the Indian Department's proposals. It was signed by two others identified as chiefs, Thomas Nanegishkung (Caribou) and Big Shilling (Caribou), who signed with their doodem images, while the other adult men in the community signed either with their own signatures (5) or by X-marks (21).[71] Nanegishkung and Big Shilling were councillors. Neither was an ogimaa. But they carried forward the wishes of the larger community.

---

70 *Minutes of the General Council of Indian Chiefs*, 20.
71 Ibid.

Musquakie had no authority to act on his own. And Assance, too, was overruled by his own community. Because this particular council was held in Musquakie's community, the people also had the opportunity to hear what was proposed and to make their own decisions about the choice of action preferred. Musquakie had just a year earlier complained that missionaries were encouraging people to overrule their chiefs, but even if that was the case here the principles of Anishinaabe leadership meant that the ogimaawag had to respect the wishes of the community.

The leadership of Mnjikaning passed to Thomas Nanegishkung, but the council still remained under the leadership of the Caribou doodem. In 1856, the council was asked to cede all its islands: three in Lake Simcoe, one in Lake Couchiching, and all the islands in Georgian Bay and Lake Huron. Thomas Nanegishkung "signed by his son" Joseph Nanegishkung, and James Bigwind signed with one Caribou doodem.[72] George Young was next with a Birch tree, followed by Joseph Snake (Catfish), John Assance (Otter), and Peter Gadequaquon (Otter).[73] The ogimaa, an aanikeogimaa, and gichi-Anishinabek who signed this cession in council were still following the practices of Anishinaabe governance – even as their daily lives had been significantly changed as settler colonists moved on to their land. Most were now farming, had converted to Christianity, and were living on reserves. But this did not mean that people wanted to abandon their culture, language, laws, and values.

As these examples demonstrate, the interpretive potential of doodem images goes well beyond being able to identify a signatory to a treaty as belonging to a specific kinship network. They help us to see beyond the documents to the communities of people who lived in the Great Lakes region. Doodem images on treaty and other documents create in council provide visual evidence of Anishinaabe leadership values expressed in oral histories and provide a window into doodem governance. They are evidence for the continuity of Anishinaabe political practices from the seventeenth through the nineteenth century and help us to understand that council fires and doodem identities – not nations, bands, or tribes – were how Anishinaabe policies were organized. The doodem images on

---

72 Thomas Nanegishkung signed an 1836 cession with a Caribou doodem. "Chippewas of Lakes Huron and Simcoe - Surrender ...," 26 November 1836, LAC RG10, Vol. 1844/126. James Bigwind signed the 1856 cession with a Caribou doodem (cited below).

73 Surrender by the Chippewas of Lakes Huron and Simcoe of certain Islands..., 5 June 1856, LAC RG10, Vol. 1845/IT189.

treaty documents represent specific Anishinaabe council fires, providing evidence of continuity between Anishinaabe identities documented in the seventeenth century with the presence of Anishinaabe community members having those same identities, living in the same locales, some two hundred years later. To be sure, there were movements and relocations in the region – including some that occurred before the seventeenth century. But these identities, and the treaties and narratives associated with them, go a long way to explain Anishinaabe choices to protect particular sites in treaty negotiations as reserves in the face of settler colonialism. The doodem images also speak to relative political cohesiveness during a period when changing European ethnonyms for Indigenous peoples give an impression of constant political change and ethnogenesis.

While doodem identities reach back to deep time and are described as gifts from the Creator, council fires are human creations to which the Creator is witness.[74] As Chapter 3 demonstrated, council fires were lit, covered, or extinguished as local and regional needs determined, decisions ratified at general councils and regional gatherings. As this chapter has shown, once constituted, each council fire was kept by an ogimaa of a particular doodem. Hereditary doodem governance was then based on the position of ogimaa being transferred to doodem kin for as long as that fire continued to burn. The council fire at Sault Ste. Marie (Bawaating) is very old. It has been led by a Crane doodem ogimaa certainly since before the arrival of Europeans. The establishment of the Caribou doodem as keeper of the council fires at Mnjikaning (Rama) and the Eagle doodem as the keeper of the fire at the mouth of the Credit River can be dated to the 1690s, when they were kindled (established) through the regional peace treaty negotiated with the Haudenosaunee discussed in Chapter 3. Members of Caribou, Crane, and Eagle doodemag from the north shores of Lake Superior and Lake Huron relocated to establish the new fires or uncover slumbering embers, while maintaining ties with their former communities. While the Crane doodem may have led the most council fires in the region (eight according to a French enumeration in 1736), ogimaawag of Thunderbird, Pike, Beaver, Sturgeon, Whitefish, Sucker, Loon, Moose, and others kept their own council fires throughout the Great Lakes, while

---

74 Aimée Craft describes the spiritual dimension of council fires in *Breathing Life into the Stone Fort Treaty*.

people from multiple doodemag met around those fires and conducted their governance through alliances.

The council fire at Mnjikaning has metaphorically never been extinguished since it was first kindled; however, chief and council of the Chippewas of Rama First Nation now meet around a boardroom table on the second floor of a building which houses the band offices. The Credit River fire was formally extinguished in 1847, when the community of roughly 200, under duress from the rapidly growing non-Aboriginal population of Upper Canada that was nearing one million, relocated to a new reserve on the southwest corner of the Six Nations Reserve near Brantford, Ontario. The Mississaugas of the Credit, as they are known, re-established their council at their new home and then built the meeting-house that still stands on the reserve today. As a measure of comparison, the Rama council fire is more than 300 years old while the council fire at Bawaating is centuries, if not millennia, old. The Dominion of Canada, enacted by British statute in 1867, is younger than all three. Nevertheless, as the dispossession and relocation of the Mississaugas at the Credit attests, settler colonialism disrupted doodem governance and compromised the ability of the Anishinaabe peoples to practice their own legal, political, cultural, and spiritual traditions. The next chapter discusses the changes and continuities in Anishinaabe governance – in the doodem tradition and to council fires – as settler society worked to dispossess and assimilate the Anishinabek and to eventually replace their traditional governance structures with an elected model under the control of Indian Affairs, one that disenfranchised women and isolated common councils from one another.

5

Doodem in the Era of Settler Colonialism

Shortly before his premature death in 1853 at the age of 29, William Warren, author of the *History of the Ojibways*, had come to believe that the doodem-based system of Anishinaabe civil governance was "entirely broken up." In his view, the complex web of alliance networks and marriage and kin relationships that had historically structured Anishinaabe law and governance in the Great Lakes region was no longer effectively operational. For Warren, the first cracks appeared in 1826, at the negotiations for the Treaty of Fond du Lac on the southwest shore of Lake Superior. At that event, confident and expansionist American officials felt they could ignore Anishinaabe protocol with respect to the recognition of ogimaawag and instead distributed medals and recognition to those Anishinaabe men who had been sponsored by traders and who would be supportive of American interests. Those Anishinabek who were singled out for such attention not only claimed the medals for themselves; they also acted as if they had authority over people and their lands. In a damning indictment of what happened at Fond du Lac, Warren claimed that one young man in particular had received his medal "solely for the strikingly mild and pleasant expression of his face." It was to this treaty negotiation, Warren felt, that one could date "the commencement of innovations which have entirely broken up the civil polity of the Ojibways."[1]

---

1 Warren and Neill, *History*, 394.

Imperial and colonial officials had been trying to interfere in Anishi-naabe governance practices and laws since the early days of the fur trade in seventeenth-century New France. Some of the evidence for earlier interference in the Great Lakes region comes from Warren him-self, who describes specific incidents from the fur trade era in which the French tried to manipulate Anishinaabe councils, although less suc-cessfully than by the Americans at Fond du Lac. For example, War-ren recounted an example of how a Loon ogimaa from Chequamegon Bay challenged a Crane ogimaa at Chequamegon Bay for precedence in council and used as support for his claim the fact that the French had recognized some Loon leaders as ogimaawag. Such efforts attempt-ing to manipulate Indigenous polities though did not affect doodemag as a political tradition. Instead, these actions created points of tension, which Anishinaabe leaders responded to from within. In the conflict between the Loon and Crane ogimaawag, the Crane ogimaa told an allegory that made it clear to all that while the Loon ogimaa's ances-tor had in fact negotiated with the French and been recognized by the French, it was the Crane ogimaa's ancestor who had placed the Loon chief in the orator's role.[2] In other words, the Crane ogimaa reminded the Loon ogimaa that recognition by the French alone was not suffi-cient to support his political claims – recognition of leadership required wider ratification and regional support.

As Warren realized, the interference on the part of American officials and traders at Fond du Lac would have come to naught had those lead-ers who were given medals refused to accept them and instead insisted that American officials acknowledge their hereditary leaders. But this did not happen here. Direct confrontation was considered quite rude in Anishinaabe councils. And at Fond du Lac, a leading Crane ogimaa had recently died.[3] Instead, Warren felt that the political tradition was subverted from within, as those without hereditary doodem claims to leadership assumed those responsibilities and then subsequently signed treaties. By the late 1820s, the shift in the regional balance of power meant that neither the British nor the Americans needed Great Lakes Indigenous peoples as military allies. The British, for example, moved management of Indian Affairs from the War Depart-ment to the control of civil government in 1830. By this time, they did

---

2 Ibid., 88.

3 Treuer, *Assassination of Hole in the Day*, 46.

not consider Indigenous peoples to pose any real threat to their expansion plans in the region.[4] In this changed and charged environment, in which the Anishinabek were now outnumbered, Anishinaabe leaders faced tremendous external pressures that caused some to consider new approaches, such as working with the colonizers in an effort to protect what they could of their way of life as settlers flooded onto their land.

Settler colonialism is a well-studied phenomenon by which a colonizing power takes possession of the lands of others through the settlement of its own surplus population or of other peoples over which it can exercise jurisdiction.[5] American and British settler colonialism of the Great Lakes region operated in slightly different ways from each other but with the same clear intentions: (1) to take possession of the land from Indigenous peoples by legal instrument, transferring sovereignty and jurisdiction to the colonizer; (2) to produce monetary wealth from the land through logging, mining, and, where possible, turning it into farmland; and (3) to transform Indigenous people into socially inferior (i.e., not-quite-white) Christian farmers, domestics, and labourers. American leaders negotiated their treaties with Great Lakes peoples in some cases at the point of a sword. The British, hoping to avoid the expense of military deployments, negotiated treaties more in keeping with older alliance practices and maintained the practice of distributing presents until the 1850s.[6] Nevertheless, the end result was the same. On both sides of the new international border, older Indigenous ideas of shared jurisdictions and network alliances were repudiated by the newcomers and replaced instead by clearly demarked borders between lots, counties, provinces, and states.

Over their lifetimes, William Warren and other mid-nineteenth-century Anishinaabe writers such as Peter Jones and George Copway all experienced the impact of land-hungry colonists coming into their homelands and the subsequent consequences for the health and well-being of their communities as they were left to subsist on marginal lands

---

4 Richard White, *Middle Ground*, 517.
5 See, for example, Hixson, *American Settler Colonialism*, a recent synthesis on the subject for the North American context; and Ferris, *Archaeology of Native-Lived Colonialism*, a detailed study for southwestern Ontario.
6 For Canadian treaty history, see James Miller, *Compact, Contract, Covenant*; for the United States, see Prucha, *American Indian Treaties*; and for a more recent interpretation, see Harjo, *Nation to Nation*. For Indian Department policy in British North American see Allen, *History of the British Indian Department* and *His Majesty's Indian Allies*.

in reserves (Canada) and reservations (United States). The reserve/ reservation communities of today were created after the War of 1812 in the eastern side of the Great Lakes region. The demographic growth following the end of the War of 1812 was truly staggering. By 1851, there were more than three million new non-Indigenous peoples in the US territories and states that bordered the lakes; on the British North American side, a million newcomers called the colony of Upper Canada, which would become the province of Ontario, home. By 1900, following the Confederation of Canada in 1867 and the completion of railway networks on both sides of the border, the population had become even larger. In contrast, the Indigenous population of the region remained small, an increasingly tiny fraction of these new settler societies, confined to reserves or reservations. By 1900, there were across the Great Lakes region some fifty-six reserves in Canada and twenty-five reservations in the United States. These reserves or reservations were not large, some as small as a few hundred acres, on which these formerly independent peoples now had to dwell.[7]

This final chapter begins the work of assessing the impact of settler colonialism on doodem governance and law by broadly tracing some of the impacts of British, American, and later Canadian government policies and actions on Anishinaabe political and legal traditions. The demographic and ecological transformations in the Great Lakes region of the nineteenth century challenged and changed Anishinaabe political traditions and, by the end of the century, replaced it by legislatively enforced elected band councils in Canada and tribal councils in the United States. The massive influx of settlers and their urbanization of historic Anishinaabe gathering sites such as Bawaating, Bkejwanong, and at the Credit River displaced Indigenous peoples from those places that had deep and long-standing meaning. Programs of missionization and Christianization affected marriage patterns and choice of spouse. The people who led these programs also renamed and reorganized families according to Christian norms with new Christian names; marriage ceased to be about creating alliances between doodemag. Colonial laws that permitted only men to vote and to stand for band elections robbed Anishinaabe women of their historical roles in Anishinaabe governance and as lawmakers.[8]

---

7 Danziger, *Great Lakes Indian Accommodation and Resistance*, frontispiece map.
8 The 1876 Indian Act only permitted men to vote in band council elections. Women did not get the right to vote until the Act's 1951 amendments.

Recent scholarship offers a complex and nuanced understanding of Anishinaabe reactions to these challenges. Their choices included acts of political resistance and strategic adaptations in the face of pressures to assimilate to the ways of the newcomers, pressures that became codified in settler laws by the second half of the nineteenth century.[9] For example, Anishinaabe and other Great Lakes Indigenous peoples engaged in the new settler economy by selling fish, game, and maple sugar; by acting as guides for Euro-American hunters; and by producing art for tourists both to supplement family incomes and to maintain traditional knowledge.[10] Efforts at regional governance through alliance continued, but these were now increasingly shaped by the line of the international border. In Ontario, Anishinaabe leaders continued to meet in general council and tried to coordinate some responses to government legislation, with mixed results.[11] Preference for Anishinaabe values and cultural practices remained strong. Archaeological research has revealed that Anishinaabe families maintained significant continuities between eighteenth- and nineteenth-century practices in such everyday things as the arrangement of internal living space in their homes and their continued reliance upon seasonally available gathered and hunted foods, even when "settled" in reserve communities and surrounded by colonists in southern Ontario.[12]

Even as waves of newcomers moved into Anishinaabe lands, the Anishinabek continued to draw on historic governance practices in their efforts to secure a better future for themselves and their children. Doodem and ishkode continued to be important categories through

---

9 Laws passed to define and regulate Indigenous peoples and control their lands include, for Canada and its colonial predecessors, An Act to Encourage the Gradual Civilization of the Indian Tribes in the Province (20 Victoria, c. 26 Province of Canada); An Act for the Gradual Enfranchisement of Indians, the Better Management of Indian Affairs, and to Extend the Provisions of the Act 31st Victoria, Chapter 42 (Statutes of Canada 1869 c. 6); and the much amended but still in force "Indian Act": An Act to Amend and Consolidate the Laws Respecting Indians (S.C. 1876, c. 18). In the United States, see historic legislation such as the Dawes Severalty Act (U.S. Statutes at Large, Vol. 24, p. 38, 1887), and Title 25 (Indians) of the current United States Code.

10 Phillips, *Trading Identities*; Evans, "The People's Pageant"; Donald Smith, *Mississauga Portraits*; Ferris, *Archaeology of Native-Lived Colonialism*, 32–78.

11 Murdoch, "Mobilization of and against Indian Act Elections."

12 Ferris, *Archaeology of Native-Lived Colonialism*, 35–7.

which Anishinaabe peoples not only defined themselves but thought about how civil governance and law should work. This remained true as long as people were still speaking and thinking in Anishinaabemowin, because the language itself is a potent source of Anishinaabe law.[13] The residential school system and the twentieth-century attack on Indigenous languages posed the biggest existential crisis to Anishinaabe political tradition and indeed to other Indigenous polities. Residential schooling was a direct assault on corporate memory and knowledge of Anishinaabe law. Nevertheless, in places where assimilative pressures were not overwhelming, the doodem tradition maintained its capacity to innovate while retaining its central role in Anishinaabe identity. The case studies discussed in this chapter push back against the idea that settler colonialism completely disrupted Anishinaabe capacity for self-government, Anishinaabe identity, or the doodem tradition. During the first half of the nineteenth century, Anishinaabe leaders and communities engaged in self-directed change.[14] But these case studies also reveal nineteenth-century colonialism's harsh impact on the lives of Indigenous peoples and their cultural and political traditions. The fact that people were able to draw on their own laws, customs, and practice to weather transformative changes as best they could should not be an "alibi" for programs of forced assimilation that were imposed on them by outsiders.[15]

Rivers and Reservations: "Native-Lived Colonialism" and the Extinguishing of Council Fires

As settlement pressure began to build in southern Ontario after the War of 1812, Anishinaabe leaders consolidated their efforts around maintaining land rights in an effort to preserve their access to key council sites and significant rivers and lakes important to their fisheries. These actions expressed the Anishinaabe principles of duty of care for their lands and the other-than-human ensouled beings with whom they were in relationship. But access to the fisheries was also crucial for maintaining political and cultural integrity. Annual gatherings to participate in fishery remained important because the collective fishery harvest was

---

13 Lindsay Borrows, *Otter's Journey*, 12.
14 Chute, *Legacy of Shingwaukonce*; Jones, *History*.
15 This is the central thesis of Brownlie and Kelm, "Desperately Seeking Absolution."

also a time when important governance and legal discussions occurred. In addition, the Anishinabek also wanted to secure their right to hunt and to continue to be able to use their winter hunting territories.[16] This is what leaders hoped to achieve when they entered into treaties to let newcomers settle on some of their lands. Council fires were also seeking to preserve existing alliance relationships in keeping with Anishinaabe law. Offering land to newcomers in this context is part of historic practices of gift exchange in which the gift was an expression of responsibility to others in alliance. By this time Anishinaabe leaders were certainly well aware that newcomers changed the land and altered entire ecosystems through their agricultural and forestry practices.[17] In making land cessions, Anishinaabe leaders sought to create space for both societies to co-exist and for the Anishinabek to continue to exercise their responsibility for the land and its beings. But settler colonialism proved relentless. For the Mississauga-Anishinabek of the Credit River council fire, the pressures from settler colonists meant being forced off their lands. The council fire at the Credit was extinguished in 1847 and the remaining members relocated to the southwestern corner of the Six Nations of the Grand River reserve in what is now the province of Ontario.

How the Mississaugas negotiated this pressure for their land reveals much about the priorities of their leadership to protect and preserve their way of life. When the land cession era began following the American Revolution, the first lands the Mississauga-Anishinabek were willing to allow newcomers to settle on were those from Niagara west to the Thames River, well away from the Credit River.[18] Those lands remained important to the Mississauga-Anishinabek; baptism records reveal that most members of the Credit River community in the 1830s had been born on the watersheds stretching from Niagara to what is now Hamilton today.[19] They had regularly gathered at Mississauga Point on the Canadian side of the Niagara River across from Fort Niagara. In 1793, the British relocated their seat of colonial government from

---

16 Surtees, *Indian Land Surrenders*, 111.

17 The best general study of the significant environmental change wrought by newcomers remains Cronon, *Changes in the Land*.

18 Deed of Feoffment – The Messissague Nation to His Britannick Majesty, 7 December 1792, LAC RG10, Vol. 1840/IT005.

19 Baptisms, 1802–1857, New Credit, Ontario, Indian Mission, Reel 77.202L M1830, United Church Archives.

Niagara-on-the-Lake to York (now Toronto) and brought with them a few hundred white settlers. These newcomers did not respect Anishinaabe law or protocols for resource sharing. That same year the Mississauga-Anishinabek petitioned Lieutenant-Governor Simcoe for redress because incoming settlers were digging up and stealing apple and other fruit trees they had planted on the valley flats of the rivers along Lake Ontario and were stealing their fish.[20]

As discussed in Chapter 4, the colonial government of Upper Canada expressed interest in purchasing all of the remaining Mississauga lands along Lake Ontario in 1805. The ogimaa Cheechalk and the gichi-Anishinabek of the Credit River council fire were understandably reluctant to accede to this request. They clearly explained to the Indian Department the need to protect access to their fishery and the site of their council fire. In the provisional agreement signed at the Credit River on 2 August 1805, the leaders agreed to sell the land in question but reserved "to ourselves and the Mississague Nation the sole right of the fisheries in the Twelve Mile Creek, the Sixteen Mile Creek, the Etobicoke River, together with the flats or low grounds on said creeks and river, which we have heretofore cultivated and where we have our camps. And also the sole right of the fishery in the River Credit with one mile on each side of the River." In his speech at the council, Quenepenon, the Otter gichi-Anishinaabe from Twelve Mile Creek, reminded William Claus, the deputy superintendent of the Indian Department, that at previous councils, "our old Chiefs at the same time particularly reserved the fishery of the River."[21] Not only were fish a crucial part of their diet in this period but the annual salmon runs drew large numbers of bald eagles to the mouth of the Credit. The council was also looking out for the needs of the Credit community's doodem beings by seeking to protect that fishery.

But within a generation, the overwhelming increase in the settler population meant the British colonial government no longer felt the necessity of attending to its historic alliance relationships with Indigenous

---

20 A memoreal [sic] of Different familys of Massesagoes Unto his Excellency the Governor, 1793, Papers of John Graves Simcoe, Canadian Loose Documents, Envelope 17, Archives of Ontario. My thanks to Donald Smith for bringing this document to my attention.

21 Lieutenant-Governor's Office, Upper Canada, vol. 1:288–309, Proceedings of a meeting with the Mississaugas at the River Credit, 31st July, 1805: 96.

peoples.[22] In the case of Upper Canada, Quenepenon's descendants found it increasingly difficult to resolve their concerns about settler encroachments on their lands. However, they continued to raise those issues with Indian Department officials in their meetings at the council fire grounds that represented the alliance relationship, which were physically located west of Fort York. After the War of 1812, the colony of Upper Canada focused more on internal political debates concerning the need for political reform.[23] Indian Affairs moved to the back burner of colonial priorities. Mississauga-Anishinabek nevertheless continued to meet regularly with Indian Department officials at the colony's council fire site. From the department's perspective, the Anishinabek were gathering to receive the gifts of a benevolent colonial government and their annual annuity payment for lands sold (also paid in goods). From the Mississaugas' perspective, these gatherings were occasions where their alliance relationships were renewed through the giving and receiving of gifts, just as other Anishinaabe allies of the Crown continued to meet annually for similar purposes at other posts and forts, such as at Drummond Island (1815–28), St. Joseph's Island (1829), Penetanguishene, near Rama (1830–35), and Manitoulin Island (1836–58).[24]

In 1837–8, simmering internal tensions about oligarchical privilege and the exercise of overbearing executive control erupted in the British North American colonies of Upper and Lower Canada. While Upper Canada experienced a minor rebellion that was quickly quashed, the neighbouring colony of Lower Canada broke out into armed conflict, led by French-Canadian bourgeois who had grown increasingly frustrated by being effectively shut out of real political power. When the dust settled, the British government responded to the concerns of French-Canadians by merging the colonies of Upper and Lower Canada into one, with the intention of neutralizing French-Canadian dominance in the Lower Canadian legislature and thereby promoting the assimilation of

---

22 As Neal Ferris has noted, "as the context that touched on and began to constrain the daily lived experiences of Native people, colonialism did not fully emerge until the colonial state really began to *ignore* the autonomy of Aboriginal nations through indifferent acts of transforming the region into a world of and for the colonizer." *Archaeology of Native-Lived Colonialism*, 28 (emphasis in original).

23 On the maturation of Upper Canada, see the essays in Greer and Radforth, *Colonial Leviathan*. For a discussion of the rebellion in Lower Canada, see Greer, *The Patriots and the People*.

24 Sims, "Algonkian-British Relations," 1.

French-Canadians into an English-speaking colony in which the anglophone population would come to dwarf the francophone.

Since the merger of the two colonies required the merger of two legislative bodies, the Crown proposed moving the seat of government to new location "within the present limits of Upper Canada" but further east. Some members of the legislative council protested the decision, as it would involve moving the legislative assembly "a ruinous distance from the Western extremity"[25] of Upper Canada and deprive Toronto of its importance as a government town. But for the Anishinabek of southern Ontario, this decision was a catastrophe. The unilateral decision of the British government to relocate their seat of government in Upper Canada was, from an Anishinaabe perspective, the unilateral decision to extinguish a council fire. The Anishinabek living in southern Ontario convened a regional council in January of 1840, at which the ogimaawag and gichi-Anishinabek from all the Anishinaabe council fires in the region crafted and signed a petition explaining to the governor-general why the consolidation of the legislature and its movement to Kingston was so profoundly disturbing to them. In their petition (see Figure 31), the Anishinaabe leaders of what is now Ontario drew on the metaphor of ishkode (fire) in an effort to explain to the Governor General why they opposed the move:

> Father – We have heard that a Union of Upper and Lower Canada is about to take place, and that in all probability the Great Council Fire, which was lighted at Menesing now called Toronto will be removed towards the sun rising. Father – We beg to inform your Excellency that the great body of your Red Children have been happy and contented to live within sight and reach of the smoke of your Great Council Fire, to which our forefathers and ourselves have resorted for wisdom, protection, and assistance. Father – It fills our hearts with fear and sorrow when we think of the difficulties and expenses that may attend the journey when any of your Red Children should desire to see their Great Father. Father – We your Red Children humbly pray that our beloved Great Mother the Queen may be graciously pleased to allow the Great Council Fire of our Great Father to remain at Toronto.[26]

25 Phillip VanKoughnet, William Allan, and Alexander McDonnell, Dissentients, http://www.canadiana.ca/view/oocihm.9_00940, Saturday 14 December 1839, *Journal of the Legislative Council of Upper Canada* (fifth session of the thirteenth provincial Parliament), (Toronto J. Carey, 1840), 25.
26 Chief Superintendent's Office, Upper Canada (Colonel S.P. Jarvis) – Correspondence, Petition to Thompson, January 1840, LAC RG10, Vol. 72, 66801–4.

By their unilateral action, the Crown was repudiating their responsibilities in the alliance. This petition fell on deaf ears; the docket indicates "no reply" was given. And so the "Great Council Fire" at Toronto was extinguished as the government of the now united Canadas moved to Kingston. Without this fire at Toronto, how was the alliance relationship to be maintained? By 1840, Indigenous travel through southern Ontario was an increasingly complicated and costly undertaking, with former trails now bisected by fences and tolls along the coach roads of the colony. Just as settler colonists worried that the new location of government would be a "ruinous distance from the Western extremity," so too were Indigenous leaders, especially those from Toronto and points west, concerned about their ability to maintain their relationships with the Crown. The move also meant that the Credit River Mississaugas would no longer be the host community for Anishinaabe leaders coming to meet with government officials.

The petition sent to Thompson also remains a stunning example of the continuity of doodem governance in southern Ontario at a time when the Anishinabek were becoming rapidly outnumbered. It was signed 24 January 1840, just two days after Musquakie read the belt that opened Chapter 3. That reading of the alliance belt at the opening of the council was in effect the renewal of Anishinaabe law of the land. Two days later, the attendees dealt with a contemporary political problem – their colonial allies – who in extinguishing their council fire were repudiating their long-time allies. The signatories appealed to the gichi-ogimaakwe of the British, Queen Victoria, to overturn this decision. They knew all too well that only the political power of the monarch or her representative in Canada could check the ever-present pressure of settlers on their lands.

The signatories represented at least the ogimaa and aanikeogimaa of each common council across what is now southern Ontario – the governments of what settlers now called bands. Some sent three or four delegates. Those who were literate in English signed their own signatures, but each gave his doodem. The host council fire, Credit River, signed first and in rank order: ogimaa Joseph Sawyer (Eagle), aanikeogimaa Peter Jones (Eagle), gichi-Anishinaabe John Jones (Eagle). The remaining council fires signed in order as the communities were located from east to west across the territory: Alderville (ogimaa John Sunday, Bison), Rice Lake (ogimaa George Paudash, Crane), Mud Lake (ogimaa Squire Martin, Birch), Balsam Lake (ogimaa James Johnson, Crane), Narrows of Lake Simcoe (ogimaa William Yellowhead, Caribou), Snake Island (ogimaa Joseph Snake, Catfish); Coldwater (ogimaa John Assance, Otter), Saugeen (ogimaa Thomas Waubahdik, Caribou), St. Clair (ogimaa Joshua Wawanosh, Caribou), Muncey Town (ogimaa John Riley, Eagle or Hawk, of the Chippewas of the Thames), and finally Muncey Chiefs at Moraviantown or Moravian of the Thames Reserve (Cornelius Westbrook, Wolf clan of the Lenape [Delaware] Nation).[27]

So here in 1840, both the common and general councils of the Anishinabek were continuing to function as a system of government. The councils constituted by the belt read by Musquakie are here: the Credit River and Mnjikaning (the narrows of Lake Simcoe). The other communities named were older council fires or ones that had been constituted or recognized by general councils held in the intervening century and a half. And there were newer council fires, too. The Muncey Chiefs represented a community of Delawares who had relocated to the Thames River Valley with their missionary in 1792 and the permission of the Chippewas of the Thames. Coldwater had been established only ten years before in 1830 by Lieutenant Governor John Colborne as a new site for the distribution of presents. Even as settlers were pushing them off their lands, the Anishinabek continued to meet in council to discuss critical issues, draft and sign petitions, and meet with colonial leaders in their efforts to have the Great Council Fire of the British honour its commitments to them. In other words, the Anishinabek were self-governing.

By 1840, the Credit River reserve was completely surrounded by white settlement. Nevertheless, they had recovered from the losses during the War of 1812 and by 1840 were thriving. They were nearly self-sufficient in their own bread, butter, potatoes, beef, pork, and milk. They had built their own timber mill and had built piers out into the Credit River harbour for a schooner that could sell their milled lumber. Most of the men were farmers, several were carpenters, and one was a shoemaker. Most could read and write in English (something not true of many white settlers) and twenty-four members of the community had been employed as missionaries around the Lakes. While the Credit River community had made many accommodations and changes to be more like their settler neighbours, they were trying to

---

27 Note that Thomas Wahbahdick's caribou is only partially complete on this document and is hard to confirm from this document alone. His identity as Caribou is clear on the Sale of the Saugeen Peninsula, 13 October 1854, LAC RG10, Vol. 1845/178.

navigate through these accommodations while maintaining themselves as a distinct people.[28] But in 1840 the Credit River community faced many challenges. They experienced significant pressure from the settlers who lived around them to sell their land. As Smith has described, the Credit River leadership had tried unsuccessfully for years to get title to their reserve land outright, rather than relying on the Indian Department to protect it.

By the 1840s, they had nearly run out of timber and they estimated less than a decade's worth remained. Their timber had been stolen, settlers had taken their fish without permission or compensation, and the Credit River fishery was mostly ruined in any case due to lack of access to spawning because of the great number of mills erected upstream of the reserve. They had no legal basis to pursue squatters and no land security. But this had not stopped their determination to survive as a distinct council of the Anishinabek. However, the lack of land security and concern for their future prompted them to think about moving. Credit River leaders considered moving to the Bruce Peninsula, but an initial survey deemed it too rocky. And after 1840, the Credit River community no longer had the benefit of proximity to the colonial government. So in 1847, the Credit River community accepted the invitation of the Six Nations to relocate to the southwestern corner of Six Nations reserve. The Mississaugas extinguished their fire at the Credit and re-established themselves as the community of the New Credit.[29] The pressures experienced by the Mississaugas of the New Credit also faced other council fires in southern Ontario. The Indian Department continued to sell off parts of other reserves, leading to the small size of many communities today.[30]

Challenges to Doodem Governance and Legal Traditions in the Age of Settler Colonialism

The experience of the Credit River Mississauga-Anishinabek raises important questions about how the traditional civil governance of the Anishinabek adapted to and co-existed with settler colonialism.

---

28 See Donald Smith, *Sacred Feathers*; Walters, "According to the Old Customs."

29 Donald Smith, *Sacred Feathers*, 203–7, 212.

30 Danziger, *Great Lakes Indian Accommodation and Resistance*; Donald Smith, *Sacred Feathers*; Chute, *Legacy of Shingwaukonse*.

Following the end of the War of 1812, it is certainly true that colonists were intent on displacing and marginalizing Indigenous peoples. But did these acts of dispossession mean that the doodem tradition was completely broken, as William Warren suggests? Not necessarily; the doodem tradition was open to innovation and did change – in no small part because the process of dispossession and marginalization was not immediate but took place over more than a half century. This gave time for people to adapt the tradition to fit changing circumstances. By the mid-nineteenth century, many Anishinaabe leaders in what is now southern Ontario were meeting in wood frame buildings, taking minutes of their deliberations, and corresponding in writing with colonial officials (and some cases, in Anishinaabemowin, with each other).[31] On the surface, changes like these may appear more as evidence of assimilation than as adaptation. However, a closer look at documents produced in these meetings reveals that doodem and council fire continue to be important for Anishinaabe governance and law. Older forms adapted to new circumstances. Until colonial legislators imposed band councils on the Anishinabek and other First Nations, Anishinaabe civil governance based on the doodem tradition was flexing before the assault of the colonial reality, but it was not broken. Even after settler governments imposed elected band councils on Indigenous peoples, doodem and iskhode continued to be potent political metaphors for the Anishinabek, while doodem continued to have meaning as part of Anishinaabe identity, even if its role in governance was diminishing.

As discussed in the vignette that opened this chapter, William Warren based part of his claim for the decline of traditional Anishinaabe doodem governance on that fact that, by 1826 at Fond du Lac (in what is now Wisconsin), American officials felt confident enough to ignore hereditary leaders and promote their own claimants for leadership. They interfered directly in Anishinaabe governance by recognizing individuals who would be more accommodating to their demands. Certainly the social and cultural dislocation that occurred in the nineteenth century made some communities open to other non-traditional models of leadership. This could mean the emergence of new leaders who did not ground their claim to office in hereditary title or doodem identity but who could (or were perceived to) deal more effectively

---

31 Walters, "According to the Old Customs"; Alan Corbiere, "Exploring Historical Literacy."

than traditional leadership did with aggressive colonial officials. In some cases, the success of these individuals came through a measure of fluency in spoken and written English and/or their relationships with – or strategies for dealing with – the new settler society governments. Such strategies proved effective, at least for a short period of time. Different ways in which new individuals could move into these formerly hereditary leadership roles in this period can be seen in the biographies of three Anishinaabe leaders of this time: Bugone-giisk, Kakewaquonaby, and Shingwaukonse. While Bugone-giisk's rise supports Warren's assertion that traditional doodem governance was damaged, Kakewaquonaby's and Shingwaukonse's path to leadership came through strategies that creatively flexed the doodem tradition.

Bugone-giisk (Hole in the Day), although Bear doodem by birth, took on an increasingly central role in regional politics of the southwestern Great Lakes following the death of the childless Crane ogimaa Babiizigindibe (Curly Head) in 1825.[32] A Crane doodem man should have followed Babiizigindibe, but Bugone-giisk became ogimaa instead. As Anton Treuer explains in his remarkable dual biography of Bugone-giisk and his son (who assumed the same name and leadership role following his father's death in 1827), the social disruption caused by war between the Ojibwe and Dakota coupled with growing American expansionism, created a set of circumstances that facilitated the rise of Bugone-giisk the Younger in particular to prominence and influence – despite the fact that he could make no hereditary claim to civil leadership. Bugone-giisk the Younger was charismatic, ambitious, and materialistic. Although William Warren was a close friend of Bugone-giisk the Younger, he was critical of Bugone-giisk's tactics.

Treuer describes Bugone-giisk the Younger as displaying qualities that were the opposite of those expected by Anishinaabe leaders: he was arrogant rather than humble, seemed to be working for his own interests as much as for his community, and claimed sole authority to sell land and enter into treaty, authority that he did not have. Nevertheless, his skills as an orator and his willingness to confront American officials directly (in contrast with the traditional non-confrontational

---

32 These council fires are in the present-day state of Minnesota. See Treuer, *Assassination of Hole in the Day*, especially Chapter 1, "The Nature of Ojibwe Leadership," for a discussion of mid-nineteenth century changes in Anishinaabe leadership practices. For the death of Babiizigindibe, see page 43.

style of leadership) were effective. At the age of only nineteen, he dominated the council that led to the 1847 Treaty of Fond Du Lac. As Treuer notes, the other assembled leaders must have been shocked by Bugone-giisk's aggressive claims, but they did not publicly challenge him, as that would have been contrary to established Anishinaabe political protocols. From William Warren's perspective, what Bugone-giisk did was seize political power in a way that would force other leaders to violate their own deeply held values in order to challenge him. This is what led Warren to conclude that the traditional system had been system had been "entirely broken up," since, from his perspective, Bugone-giisk the Elder in claiming leadership that was not his to claim in 1826, and his son through demonstration of behaviour that violated the standards of Anishinaabe leadership, bore at least part of the blame for subverting the traditional system.[33]

In two other cases, though, the new leaders respected the historic principles of doodem governance and Anishinaabe law. For example, in 1829, the Mississauga-Anishinabek of the Credit River made the twenty-seven-year-old Kahkewaquonaby (Peter Jones) one of their leaders. As discussed earlier, Jones was the son of an Anishinaabe Eagle doodem woman named Tubinaquay and Augustus Jones, a surveyor of Welsh ancestry. He was adopted by his grandfather, Wabenose, into the Eagle doodem and then again by Adjutant, hereditary ogimaa of the Eagle doodem at the Credit River prior to being made a gichi-Anishinaabe himself. What was unusual about Kahkewaquonaby's case was not any subversion of the doodem tradition; if anything, his double adoption confirmed the legitimacy of his position. It was his young age that made his appointment stand out. His elevation to the role of aanikeogimaa was due to his fluency in written and spoken English and his strong relationship with the Methodist missionary William Case. Jones's connections enabled him to leverage resources for the Credit River community. In addition, he was admired for his spiritual leadership of the Mississaugas, many of whom converted to Methodism following his example. Kahkewaquonaby and Bugone-giisk the Younger both rose to positions of power and influence at a young age, both in circumstances that reveal how the challenges of settler colonialism were necessitating

---

33 Anton Treuer, in *Assassination of Hole in the Day*, was able to corroborate Warren's statements and expand upon them in forty-seven interviews he undertook with respected regional Elders, all first-language speakers of Anishinaabemowin.

creative adaptations by the Anishinabek in response. But in Kahke-waquonaby's case, his elevation was supported and confirmed by the community and his behaviour conformed to Anishinaabe expectations of leaders. He remained humble and dedicated his life to the service of his community. Moreover, he did not ever assume the role of ogimaa at the Credit, remaining the deputy or aanikeogimaa for his entire career.

The life and leadership of Shingwaukonse is another example of changes and challenges to hereditary doodem governance in this period. Like Kahkewaquonaby, Shingwaukonse was born to an Anishinaabe mother, this time of the Crane doodem, and a white father. Shingwau-konse himself then married a Crane doodem woman. This in itself did not pose the problem of violating the taboo of marrying within one's doodem, as there is no evidence that Shingwaukonse was adopted into a Crane lineage. His descendants in interviews asserted that Shingwau-konse was Plover, a doodem identity that he had acquired through a dream. Historically the Anishinabek used vision quests, particularly at puberty, to acquire guardian beings that were distinct from one's doo-dem. Shingwaukonse appeared to be blending the two and, as anthro-pologist Cory Willmott has suggested, "perhaps due to his question-able descent narrative, he based his leadership claims upon his personal spiritual and military accomplishments," which were considerable.[34] A noted veteran of the War of 1812 and a charismatic spiritual leader who claimed the sun as a protective manidoo, Shingwaukonse also devel-oped a strong personal relationship with American Indian Agent Henry Rowe Schoolcraft and proved adept at negotiating with colonial authori-ties.[35] In adopting the Plover as his doodem (a small shore bird that in outline and track mark resembles the Crane), Shingwaukonse was able to connect with the idea of "crane-ness" without claiming a Crane iden-tity for himself – a strategy that could also make possible his marriage to a Crane doodem woman. As Willmott has explained, "in Shingwau-konse's case we can see a shift towards the rising power of achieved leadership roles, which his sons could nevertheless appropriate back into leadership claims that were based on ascribed doodem descent."[36]

What the examples of Bugone-giisk (Elder and Younger), Kahkewa-quonaby, and Shingwaukonse all demonstrate is that doodem continued

---

34 Willmott, "Anishinaabe Doodem Pictographs," 140.
35 Chute, *Legacy of Shingwaukonse*.
36 Willmott, "Anishinaabe Doodem Pictographs," 141.

to be a crucial category in Anishinaabe political thought during the first half of the nineteenth century. While each of these leaders may be said to have achieved leadership that at first glance appears to be outside of the conventional descent-based path, each still asserted their right to lead within a doodem framework. Other examples of conflict over leadership in the nineteenth century indicate that doodem continued to be highly relevant to Anishinaabe politics. Shingwaukonse's biographer Janet Chute found evidence of other doodem-based political conflict in 1853, following the decision of the colonial government in Canada West to merge the Batchewana and Goulais bands on the north shore of Lake Superior near Sault Ste. Marie and to place them under the leadership of Nebanagoching, the Crane ogimaa at the Sault. Nebana-goching supported this move. At the same time, someone placed "a wooden standard bearing the 'doodem' of the Crane" at the southern boundary of the Batchewana Bay reserve. However, members of the Bear doodem at Batchewana tore it down and explained their actions to the local government surveyor, John Keating, by saying that the Cranes did not have authority over them. Another unrelated doodem dispute occurred on Parry Island in 1860. The issue was who would replace Megis as ogimaa there: James Pagahmegabow of the Caribou doodem or Ahwahquagezick of the Birch Tree doodem? The now very elderly Musquakie of Rama spoke in favour of Pagahmegabow.[37] Note that Musquakie was also Caribou; he supported his doodem kin, as one would have expected, in the claim.

In these disputes, Anishinaabe leaders involved colonial officials through the petition process, attempting to educate colonial officials in the Indian Department about which ogimaa from which doodem was the proper ogimaa of the common council and drawing officials in as potential arbiters of these disputes. What these disputes also reveal is that the doodem tradition continued to be politically relevant and important for Anishinaabe peoples on the northern shores of the Great Lakes during the same period when William Warren thought the traditional governance was no longer operating in the southwestern Great Lakes. However, by the last quarter of the nineteenth century in both settler states, increasingly coercive colonial governments passed legislative regimes that forcibly disrupted Anishinaabe law by imposing elected band councils and elected tribal councils that were effectively

---

37 Chute, *Legacy of Shingwaukonse*, 154, 295n67.

controlled and managed by the respective government departments in charge of "Indian Affairs." These actions, along with residential schooling that disrupted the teaching of language, history, and politics to future leaders, were the real cause of the system's breakdown.

Writing Doodem in the Broader Great Lakes

Despite the imposition of programs of assimilation, the doodem tradition remained important to the Anishinabek, and in Canada leaders continued to sign with doodem images, on petitions in particular, into the twentieth century. These examples show the persistence of doodem identity and doodem governance outside of the Ontario Peninsula. The first two examples come from Nipissing, the host council fire of the 1642 gathering described in the Introduction. In 1848, Cabojijak (Caribou doodem ogimaa and a later signatory to the Robinson-Huron Treaty) from the Lake Nipissing Anishinabek dictated a petition to the community priest, who wrote the petition in Anishinaabemowin. The petition asked for lands on which to garden, a request that mystified the Crown, given that no land surrender had yet been signed for these lands. Cabojijak then cut out his doodem on a separate piece paper and affixed with sealing wax to the document, the only known example of this practice that I have seen (see Figure 32).[38] Two other caribou with ribs showing were also drawn in ink, with no names attached, and a pike and loon were outlined in pencil. By asking that they be granted lands to cultivate the Nipissing Council was seeking security of land title at a time when the allied north shore of Lake Huron council fires (of which the Nipissing were a part) were dealing with the increasing encroachment of settlers staking mining claims. The caribou doodemag with ribs showing is another telling detail. The petition was dated the 3 August 1848, a time of year when the caribou should be fat. By showing their doodem images in this way, the Nipissing Council was reminding their allies of their obligations under the Covenant Chain alliance – visually expressing their need.

The doodem tradition remained important to the Nipissing. In the early twentieth-century the Nipissing Council sent another petition,

---

38 Indians of Lake Nipissing ... 3 August 1848, LAC Executive Council Office of the Province of Canada fonds (formerly RG 1), Land submissions to the Executive Council, series RG1 E5, vol. 9:1168.

undated but addressed to Prime Minister Robert Borden (1911–20) and written sometime between 1915 and 1920. The council, protesting the imposition of game laws in Ontario in 1915 that significantly infringed upon their hunting rights, undertook to write a petition to the superintendent of Indian Affairs, Duncan Campbell Scott. Although only a copy now exists in the department's files, the clerk who produced it copied the doodem images from the original. This document demonstrated the continuity of doodem governance and the composition of the Nipissing Council some sixty-plus years after the 1848 petition was written. It is signed with doodem images of two pike, two beaver, five caribou, and a loon. People with the Caribou, Loon, and Pike doodemag continue to form the Nipissing Council. But the Beaver doodem has a long tradition at Lake Nipissing as well. Recall that evidence for the Beaver doodem at Lake Nipissing dates back to the early seventeenth century and that oral histories recorded by Nicolas Perrot put the emergence of the First Beaver (or Great Beaver) along the "French River" and Lake Nipissing itself.[39] The signatories of both these documents were ogimaawag and gichi-Anishinabek, communicating government to government, as Anishinaabe councils had historically always done.

While Anishinaabe doodem images do not appear on American treaties after 1817, visual petitions recorded by Henry Schoolcraft are evidence of the continuity of Anishinaabe graphic practices in the United States. In 1849, several Anishinaabe delegates travelled to Washington at their own expense to petition for a return of some lands in Wisconsin that had previously been sold to the Americans. As Schoolcraft explained, their leader knew that they lacked letters of introduction to meet with American government officials and so produced this example, which Schoolcraft called "primitive letters of credence" on birch bark, as a means of gaining admission to the halls of government and a hearing. This petition, shown in Figure 34, was presented to President James Polk and shows seven leaders represented as their respective doodem identities: one Crane, three Martens, one Bear, one Merman, and one Bullhead Catfish. The lines represent the unity of the delegates' hearts and minds and their connection to a series of rice lakes

---

39 Petition to the Honourable Robert Laird Borden, Premier of the Dominion of Canada, n.d., p. 3, LAC RG10, Vol. 6743, file 420–8; Perrot, "Mémoire," in Blair, *Indian Tribes*, 1:62–3.

in Wisconsin, where they wanted a guaranteed reserve.[40] Schoolcraft, in his work, also reproduced four other petitions with doodem images that he said had been submitted by different Anishinaabe leaders coming to Washington to have their grievances addressed.[41] Despite the lack of American treaties with Anishinaabe doodem images after 1817, this petition is also evidence of the enduring significance of doodem identity to governance in the US-controlled portion of Anishinaabe historic territories.

While the border between the United States and British North America was fixed by the Rush-Bagot Agreement of 1817, these "lines drawn upon the water" did not stop the movement of Anishinaabe peoples through their traditional territories and the continuity of cultural practices in the Great Lakes region.[42] However, despite these continuities, the creation of reserves (in Canada) and reservations (in the United States) did ultimately create a special set of problems for the viability of the doodem tradition and its role in Anishinaabe governance and law. Doodemag, as I discussed in earlier chapters, created a set of relationships that connected kin over long distances and a set of ethical obligations towards those kin that functioned as a social safety net. It was a system that suited the needs of a highly mobile people. The reserve and reservation system fundamentally disrupted this way of life and eliminated much of the crucial social safety net that the tradition had earlier provided. Once again, the tradition remained capable of innovation and was able to adapt to new circumstances.

But what strategies did people adopt to deal with these changing circumstances? One solution may have come in the form of the types

---

40 Symbolic Petition of Chippewa Chiefs, presented at Washington, 28 January 1849, headed by Oshkabawis of Wisconsin. Pictograph A. Plate 60. Drawn by S. Eastman, USA, Printed in Color by P.S. Duval, Philadelphia, in Schoolcraft, *Historical and Statistical Information*, 416–17.

41 Schoolcraft, *Historical and Statistical Information*, 416–21. Gerald Vizenor has questioned whether this document was in fact a petition. Vizenor points out that William Warren, who knew the Anishinaabe leaders supposedly responsible for this petition, did not discuss this document or the claim itself in his *History of the Ojibways*. Instead, Vizenor interprets these documents differently: "The visual stories of the totemic cranes, and other creatures eye to eye, and heart to heart, set as a union of views, are native scenes in visual cartography" – in other words, maps and stories. Vizenor, *Fugitive Poses*, 176–7.

42 Hele, "Introduction," viii–xxiii.

of roles ascribed to specific doodem identities. In more contemporary works published in the 1970s by Basil Johnston and Edward Benton-Banai, the doodemag themselves are assigned specific occupational roles: for example, Cranes as civil leaders, Bears as defenders, fish doodemag as teachers. These specific social roles, I suggest, are an innovation on the older idea that the physical characteristics and behavioural qualities of doodem beings (specifically through the shared doodem soul) shaped the person who bore that identity. These articulations of Bears as policemen, for example, or those of the various fish doodemag as teachers, draw from much older understandings about the ways in which one's doodem being shapes one's character and personality. Both nineteenth- and twentieth-century sources suggest that members of the makwa (Bear) doodem had a particular association with war, for example, and were more likely to be made war leaders in the past. Warren even suggests that members of this doodem kept the war-pipes and clubs for each community and "often denominated the bulwarks of the tribe against its enemies."[43] However, it is important to remember that enumerated lists of warriors who served with the British in the first part of the nineteenth century show that, during that time period, warriors were drawn from all the doodemag known in the area – Caribou, Eagle, Crane, Otter, and others – each of whom took their war leaders from among members of their own doodem.[44] Each doodem had its own civil leaders as well.[45] By re-associating doodem with related but new adult social roles, the doodem tradition remained relevant to the Anishinabek in the reality of reserve or reservation life, as people increasingly participated in the wage economy. Such changes to the function of the doodem tradition retain an Anishinaabe cultural logic and reflect continuity with the past.[46]

The impact of Christianity on forms of doodem expression must also be taken into consideration. Peter Jones, the Anishinaabe Methodist

---

43 Warren and Neill, *History*, 49.

44 See for example: List of Chiefs and Indian Warriors ... at the Holland Landing, 22 December 1838, Office of the Chief Superintendent in Upper Canada, LAC RG10, Vol. 124: 69964–70; Shilling to Jarvis, 9 May 1843, Office of the Chief Superintendent in Upper Canada, LAC RG10, Vol. 138: 78952–3. My thanks to Darlene Johnston for bringing these two documents to my attention.

45 See Basil Johnston, *Ojibway Heritage*, 53; Benton-Banai, *Mishomis Book*, 75–7.

46 Too often such changes are seen as "inauthentic." For a discussion of this problem and its impact on Indigenous peoples, see Raibmon, *Authentic Indians*.

missionary, did not find doodem incompatible with his new faith; he wore his Eagle doodem with pride and passed on the identity to his children. But, as a professed Christian and devout believer, it is highly unlikely he personally believed in having an other-than-human being as his ancestor. In both his private and public communications, he quite clearly distances himself from such "superstitions," and it is clear that he wishes his congregation, and all Anishinaabe peoples, to leave these ideas behind. Other members of the Mississauga-Anishinabek also continued to sign petitions and documents with doodem identities long after both they and their children had converted to Christianity and other prominent Anishinaabe religious leaders, including John Sunday and George Copway, also made no secret of their respective identities. The evidence is clear that doodem identities – on twentieth-century documents signed with doodem images and on doodem images woven or embroidered on to ceremonial regalia – remained important for many Anishinabek. Even as their role in governance and law decreased, knowing one's doodem and displaying it was still a means by which one could demonstrate connection to other-than-human beings and express being Anishinaabe.

Ecological Changes and Changes in the Representations of Doodem Beings

The influx of settler colonists into the Great Lakes region did not just dramatically increase the area's population; the newcomers came intent on remaking the area into an income-generating agricultural landscape. In Upper Canada, this included clear-cutting and intensive wheat farming.[47] As the newcomers radically transformed the land, changing forests into farms, local ecologies were rapidly changed as well. Some species were locally extirpated or rendered nearly or totally extinct, including the woodland caribou and woodland bison. Settlers introduced new and invasive species, like starlings, house sparrows, and dandelions.[48] The newcomers chopped down trees, dammed rivers, and fundamentally altered the ecosystem of the Great Lakes region. Rapid environmental change on its own created challenges for the doodem tradition, which historically had been predicated upon a fundamental relationship between a doodem being, a particular landscape, and people who shared that identity. Given the

---

47 See McCalla, *Planting the Province*; John McCallum, *Unequal Beginnings*.
48 See Cronon, *Changes in the Land*.

belief that ensouled beings are connected to the animals or plants that give Anishinaabe doodem kin their name and their existence, a habitat needed to be able to support all of the beings bearing that identity, both human and other-than-human. In this situation; what happens to the doodem tradition when there is rapid environmental change?

I have found two specific examples where environmental changes were clearly reflected in the ways in which doodem images were drawn on treaty and other documents. Woodland caribou, for example, were extirpated from the eastern Great Lakes region by the 1780s. By the 1850s, some sixty years later, some people with known Caribou identities, especially in southern Ontario, were drawing pictographs that resembled the white-tailed deer; as Figure 35 illustrates, they no longer emphasized the distinct hoof shape and antlers of the caribou in the images that they drew. As members of the Caribou doodem of this period found themselves restricted to reserves, their opportunities to hunt limited by settlers, and the caribou long gone, their knowledge of what their doodem being looked like began to recede from community memory. With the deaths of any remaining Elders who remembered what caribou looked like, treaty signatories in the 1850s and later had to draw their Caribou doodem images from remembered descriptions and by looking to the closest available analogues. As the caribou retreated northward, white-tailed deer migrated up into the same habitat. It is not surprising then that, over time, Anishinabek from the Lake Simcoe area would come to draw a white-tailed deer and then, later, use the image of the deer as a symbol of their people. Today, a stylized leaping deer is now the logo on the casino located on the lands of the Chippewa-Anishinabek of Rama (Chippewas of Rama First Nation). While the doodem tradition remained relevant to the community, the specific identity of some doodemag shifted to adapt to the changing ecosystem, and for some, the Adik or Caribou doodem changed as well.

A similar problem occurred for those who had the Bison as their doodem (see Figure 36). The woodland or eastern bison (*Bison bison pennsylvanicus*) used to range well into eastern North America. By the early nineteenth century, the woodland bison had been extirpated from the lands east of the Mississippi as, like the caribou, it experienced significant habitat destruction with the arrival of Euro-American colonists and their radical transformation of the land into farms.[49] The loss of the

---

49 Rezendes, *Tracking and the Art of Seeing*, 279–301.

woodland bison, in turn, affected later representations of the doodem image by those belonging to the Bison doodem. While there was an image of a distinct bison on the 1701 Peace of Montreal, bison images begin to look more like an ox or a cow on documents signed in the late eighteenth century and into the nineteenth. Neace's 1787 bison in Figure 36 was drawn as a cow by the clerk who reproduced the image (as British clerks in Upper Canada at this time would also have little or no awareness of the by then extirpated bison). As with the caribou, it is not surprising that Anishinaabe artists turned to a new local analogue – the domestic cow – for visual inspiration when those Elders with knowledge of the bison were no longer alive to advise their grandchildren on what a bison actually looked like. The Mississauga-Anishinabek in southern Ontario drew their Bison doodem as a cow when there ceased to be extant bison in southern Ontario; the Chippewa-Anishinabek of Mnjikaning (Rama) substituted a white-tailed deer for the caribou. In each case, when a species representing an Anishinaabe doodem identity was regionally extirpated, people adapted their traditions to accommodate the new reality by selecting a related species that had recently made the region its home. By doing so they could continue to emphasize the inter-relationships between doodem beings in human and other-than-human form and their mutual interdependence in a shared ecosystem. In other words, these changes remained consistent with Anishinaabe worldview.

Missionaries and Marriages

While the doodem tradition remained important during the nineteenth century, the use of doodem exogamy to create alliances between different doodemag was significantly eroded by century's end. As Anishinaabe peoples transitioned from relocating seasonally to living year-round on the same reserve, the frequency of regional gatherings dropped greatly, and populations came to contain a nearly static set of doodemag belonging to those families present when the reserve was created. By the 1840 council at the Credit River, only ogimaawag and gitchi-Anishinabek travelled to attend. These facts had a significant impact on the historic practice of doodem exogamy and by extension weakened the formerly very strong ties that historically were woven between different council fires through marriage practices. The pool of potential spouses shrank to those on reserve or in nearby settler communities.

Furthermore, nineteenth-century missionaries to Anishinaabe communities worked hard to change marriage practices and, by extension, to make Anishinaabe kinship categories conform to Western Christian models. In this model, doodem exogamy and even doodem identity, had no place. While missionary efforts were not universally successful, their work, when combined with the changes wrought upon Anishinaabe lifeways by the reserve system, meant that marriage and kinship practices did change. Over time, Anishinaabe kinship vocabulary more closely aligned with Western norms, which came into more common use by the twentieth century. Increasingly, the distinction between parallel cousins (formerly akin to a sibling) and a cross-cousin (a potential marriage partner) was lost.[50] And sometimes people married within their doodem.

Marrying within one's doodem eroded a fundamental purpose of the identity: providing two axes of doodem-kin support for each married couple. It is also a reflection of the fact that people traveled less (and travel was more difficult through now colonized lands), so a widespread safety net was no longer needed. Breaking the taboo had been an occasional societal problem that Anishinaabe people had dealt with prior to the reserve and reservation era. One contemporary teaching equates the disappearance of the Deer doodem to the violation of the taboo against intra-doodem marriage. According to Edward Benton-Banai, "The people of the Deer Clan once violated this natural law and began marrying within their clan. The Deer Clan people were sent warnings. Their children started to be born with defects and abnormalities. They made no correction in their ways. Finally, the Creator was so disturbed by this departure from the way of harmony that he destroyed the Deer Clan in its entirety."[51] Violating this taboo may have become more common, though, with the onset of the reserve/reservation era and the loss of mobility for Anishinaabe peoples.

By the twentieth century, the use of doodem tradition to regulate marriage was not only breaking down but that breakdown was also being interpreted as a cause of the hardships caused by settler colonialism. Anthropologists in the early twentieth century found Elders from Parry Island on Georgian Bay to Walpole Island near Detroit, from the

---

50 Valentine, *Nishnaabemwin Reference Grammar*, 107–112; Willets, "Correlated Changes in Ottawa Kinship."

51 Benton-Banaii, *Mishomis Book*, 77.

Michigan Peninsula and west to Thunder Bay, who all independently expressed the opinion that the violation of the incest taboo against intra-doodem marriage had been a significant factor contributing to their current state of poverty and isolation.[52] This idea was expressed more recently by Benton-Banai, who wonders how much stronger the Anishinabek would be had this taboo not been violated.[53] Doodem identity was so strong even then, and so central to Anishinaabe conceptions of self, that it retained the ability to act as an explanatory agent for social change, even as the historic governance, legal, and social roles of tradition itself were weakened. That these Elders would isolate the violation of the doodem taboo as an agent responsible for settler colonialism and the cultural and physical dislocation imposed by settlers on them, is both poignant and powerful evidence that the Anishinabek have continued, throughout the centuries since the arrival of Europeans, to look within their own cultural tradition to understand and negotiate changes in their world.

One significant innovation to the doodem tradition in the twentieth century has been the practice of acquiring a doodem identity through dream revelations. Anthropologist Cory Willmott has investigated this route of doodem acquisition, as it seems to depart significantly from the historical evidence for patrilineal descent of doodem identity. She was especially surprised to meet siblings with different doodem identities, which seemed at first to her to be a major difference from her historical understanding of doodem identity as one acquired through patrilineal descent. But what Willmott found in her detailed study is that this method of doodem acquisition is entirely consistent with older Anishinaabe practices of dreams and visions as important sources of knowledge, as the example of Shingwaukonse and his Plover doodem discussed earlier shows. By the mid-nineteenth century, the Anishinabek and other Indigenous peoples were under increasingly coercive state and missionary pressure to assimilate to settler society and to forsake their worldview, language, and belief system. Missionaries were keen to disrupt any aspects of Anishinaabe spiritual practices that were seen as "pagan," including the fasting rituals through which people had traditionally acquired helper beings. The Anishinaabe belief in two souls, discussed previously, persisted, though, and what Willmott

---

52 J.B. Peuessie, "Fort William, John Perrot, Fort Francis" in William Jones, Ethnographic and linguistic field notes on the Ojibwa Indians, folder 1, APS; Jenness, *Ojibwa Indians of Parry Island*.

53 Benton-Banaii, *Mishomis Book*, 77.

found is that the "shadow soul" or *jiibay*, historically associated with the doodem being as the soul that remains with the body after death, increasingly took on the role of the helper or guardian being.[54] Doodem was a public or civic identity well known to colonial officials and not perceived to be in conflict with Christianity, especially when people disavowed descent from other-than-human beings. While on the surface this seems a significant change, the reality is that doodem remained central to Anishinaabe identity. And what Willmott has found is that reliance on dreams and visions by Anishinaabe people to reveal a doodem identity lost to them through the activities of settler colonialism is not a departure from Anishinaabe tradition but, rather, draws directly from it.[55] Dream revelation as a source of doodem identity is also not connected to the idea of "blood" inheritance.

Despite challenges and changes, and also in response to them, the doodem tradition has endured. It is in the oral histories of the Anishinabek that evidence of political change was and is preserved through the doodem tradition, providing explanations of how disputes and conflicts arose between people and how those disputes were resolved. Anishinaabe Elder and cultural teacher Basil Johnston has said that "the totem [doodem] was probably the most important social unit taking precedence over the tribe, community and immediate family."[56] Additionally, in the rich narrative tradition of the Anishinabek, doodem beings provided a central source of metaphor that shaped and explained both social and political change. There can be no doubt that the activities and actions of settler colonists in the nineteenth and twentieth century radically disrupted Anishinaabe governance practices and the role of doodemag in law. The newcomers also had no room in their worldview for the concept of shared jurisdictions or alliances of interdependence. As a result of the land surrender process, colonial legislation, residential schools, and other policies, the networks of doodem relations connecting nodes of Anishinaabe governance were nearly severed from one another. In their place is an international border that bisects four of the five Great Lakes, within which are the enclosed polygons of state/provincial and municipal boundaries. Reserves or reservations created isolated enclaves of Anishinabek and fixed the composition of those resulting spaces to the descendants of those assigned to that

---

54 Willmott, "Anishinaabe Doodem Pictographs."
55 Ibid., 165–6.
56 Johnston, *Ojibway Heritage*, 59.

particular polygon at the time each reserve was created. Nevertheless, doodem remained important to being Anishinaabe, even if communities reshaped fundamental aspects of the tradition to adjust to the reality of settler colonialism.

The historic role of doodem identity in Anishinaabe civil governance and law itself was initially eroded under the influence of British and American colonial officials. It was eventually pushed aside in the late nineteenth century by twin legislative regimes, in both Canada and the United States, that replaced Indigenous governments with imposed elected band or tribal council systems. The impact of missionization programs and targeted assimilation projects also affected the practice of the doodem tradition. The belief in a kinship connection to a particular other-than-human ancestor was lost for some and suppressed by others, and, by the late nineteenth century, kinship terminology in Anishinaabemowin began, more and more, to parallel Western categories.[57] The most significant harm was done by the residential school system, which moved children out of their parents' care and custody, disrupted the teaching roles of parents and grandparents, and actively sought to suppress culture and political traditions by punishing students for speaking their own language.[58]

The knowledge and practice of the doodem tradition survived and continued to have meaning in the nineteenth century and into the twentieth, although that meaning, and the social and political work that doodem did, changed. While the network of relationships created by the intersection of councils connected through doodem relations was significantly disrupted during the nineteenth and twentieth centuries, the nodes and networks of the Anishinaabe world remained visible. There has been continuity between doodem identities documented in association with particular places in the seventeenth century and descendants with the same identities in the twentieth and twenty-first centuries. The importance of doodem to being Anishinaabe continues to this day, as communities work to revitalize their historic governance practices and imagine their future as a nation of Anishinaabe people.

---

57 Valentine, *Nishnaabemwin Reference Grammar*, 107–12.
58 Milloy, *A National Crime*; Truth and Reconciliation Commission of Canada, *Honouring the Truth*.

Conclusion

"The way I think of it is, every time we forget something from the past, that's an alternative future that's lost ... If you pick it back up, you're actually opening another future. The more that we do that, the more it allows some people to have their future."

– Wanda Nanibush, Curator of Indigenous Art
at the Art Gallery of Ontario, 2016[1]

Attend a summer gathering at Anishinaabe communities in the Great Lakes region today and the recovery and resurgence of the doodem tradition is clearly visible. Young dancers might wear their doodem image on their regalia. Many speakers now begin their speech with at least a few phrases in Anishinaabemowin. Before giving their name, each gives the place they are from and, if the speaker knows it, their doodem identity. Where families have become disconnected from their doodem identities as a result of the assimilative programs of the nineteenth and twentieth centuries, people are undertaking genealogical research or are consulting with Elders and Medicine People.[2] In some families, there is partial knowledge. Professor Darlene Johnston of the University

---

1 Berry, "How the AGO is Finally Paying Tribute."
2 Willmott, "Anishinaabe Doodem Pictographs," 155–6.

of British Columbia's Faculty of Law learned about her connection to the Otter doodem through her father's mother; her paternal grandmother relayed that information and much more during their winter conversations. But it was not until Johnston studied treaties signed by her father's grandfathers that she discovered her own identity as a Marten. Only by working with both Anishinaabe and Western record-keeping traditions could Johnston begin to fully approach the study of her family and broader Anishinaabe history.[3]

As cultural and political revitalization efforts continue, doodem identity is re-emerging as a system of categories relevant for law and governance today. First Nations are revitalizing old alliance relationships with each other and renewing practices of annual gatherings. Since 2010, the Mississaugas of the Credit have been hosting an annual three-day historical gathering, where community and academic researchers come together to share what they know about local and broader Mississauga history and sources for that research. And on 29 October 2016, the six Mississauga First Nations – Alderville First Nation, Curve Lake First Nation, Hiawatha First Nation, Mississauga 8 First Nation, Mississaugas of the Credit First Nation, and Mississaugas of Scugog Island First Nation – signed what they describe as a "historic relationship accord." The accord is a contemporary alliance, creating the framework for collaboration on areas of shared interest.[4] In September of 2016, on the anniversary of the treaty signing, the Robinson-Huron Treaty First Nations gathered at Whitefish Island in Sault Ste. Marie, the site of the original treaty negotiations. While the chiefs and councillors of these nations had collaborated in the past, this was a much larger gathering of several thousand people to both learn about the treaty and its history and to revitalize and celebrate Anishinaabe culture and history, with feasting, music, dancing, and games. This initial gathering was in conjunction the launch of the Robinson-Huron and Robinson-Superior court case, *Restoule v Canada*, concerning the question of annuities in the treaty.[5] The treaty gatherings have continued, with Atikameksheng Anishinabek First Nation hosting in 2017, Shawanaga (at Shawanaga

---

3 Darlene Johnston, "Litigating Identity," 45.
4 "Mississauga Relationship Accord," 20 October 2016, https://www.mississauganation.com/accord.html.
5 Restoule v. Canada (Attorney General), 2018 ONSC 7701 Reasons for Judgement, 21 December 2018.

and co-hosted with Wausauksing) in 2018, and Wiikwemkong in 2019. These multi-day celebrations invite members of all treaty signatory First Nations and interested guests to attend. They are inclusive, multi-generational gatherings where the host nation provides feasts and where there are a range of activities for young and old, in addition to formal conversations about governance. Both the Mississaugas and the Robinson-Huron Treaty signatories have innovated, too, using social media, livestreaming, and podcasting to ensure that those who cannot attend can witness the proceedings, hear their leaders speak, and keep abreast of current challenges, the treaty litigation process, and events in an open and transparent way. The Anishinaabe general council and with it the broader principles and structures of Anishinaabe governance are being reactivated.

The research project that produced this book began more than sixteen years ago. My intention has been to contribute to restoring a past once envisioned as fragmentary and beyond recovery.[6] Although I began this work before the rise of scholarship that critically examines what Patrick Wolfe has described as the "logic of elimination" embedded in settler colonialism,[7] it was clear to me that conventional academic scholarship on Indigenous peoples in what has become Canada and the United States has also contributed to discourses that have marginalized and erased Indigenous peoples. As the descendant of long-time settler colonists (my own paternal ancestors were Loyalists), I grew up hearing and being told histories that reflected my settler ancestors' experiences and those of other subsequent generations of newcomers. It is as if they had laid a drop cloth over the Indigenous landscape and built their own historical narratives on top. However, the outlines of Indigenous historical experiences have remained visible; we just have to choose to see them and to understand what it means that Indigenous peoples are still here, that they, in the words of Hawaiian scholar Kēhaulani Kauanui, "exist, resist, and persist."[8] As someone born in Oshawa, in the province of Ontario, in the country of Canada – all names derived from Anishinaabe and Haudenosaunee languages – I could not help but wonder about the deeper history behind those names. Fortunately, the rich and dynamic scholarship produced in the last two decades, including much

---

6 Richard White, *Middle Ground*, 1.
7 Wolfe, "Settler Colonialism."
8 Kauanui, "A Structure, Not an Event."

contributed by Indigenous researchers, is making these histories more visible, as they weave together evidence from oral histories and archival records in innovative ways.[9]

Recovering these histories and rethinking our understanding of the past in the Great Lakes region is important for all of us who live on these lands; it is the only way we are really going to meaningfully grapple with the implications of settler colonialism. While the Indigenous historiography has been marginalized by past practices, histories of settler experiences have also been distorted by these erasures. To fully understand our shared histories we must remove that metaphorical drop cloth, so that Indigenous and settler histories inform each other and the relationships that we have had and continue to have with each other. What was the spirit and intent of original treaty relationships?[10] How can they be meaningfully reactivated in the twenty-first century? How can we reconcile the significant differences in worldviews between Indigenous peoples and the settlers who came here from overseas? The Anishinaabe peoples' relationship to the land and waters of the Great Lakes region structured not only the doodem tradition but their broader practices of governance and law derived from doodem, which defines them as a distinct people, as a distinct society, and as a civilization, with its own legal tradition and an expanded concept of personhood, all anchored in deep time.

At a more abstract level, this book asks us to think more carefully and critically about applicability of outsider or etic categories to the writing of Indigenous histories. Do categories such as band, tribe, nation, and village distort Indigenous histories? Instead, do historians need to understand and then make use of Indigenous categories of social, political, and geo-spatial organization when writing history? The short answer is yes, to both questions. It is difficult to understand Anishinaabe history without using doodem as a category of analysis or without thinking about council fires – places that were sites of seasonal gatherings, for tens, hundreds, or even thousands of years. The Anishinaabe practice of governance, through alliance relationships between

---

9 In particular, see Witgen, *Infinity of Nations*; Cary Miller, *Ogimaag*; Treuer, *Assassination of Hole In the Day*; Stark, "Marked by Fire"; Child, *Holding Our World Together*; Whetung, "(En)Gendering Shoreline Law."

10 For an influential model of one collaborative answer to this question in a different treaty context, see Treaty 7 Elders and Tribal Council, et al., *True Spirit and Original Intent of Treaty 7*.

human and other-than-human beings, connected doodem beings across the region. Doodem shaped the composition of Anishinaabe political institutions from the nuclear family to widespread regional alliances. It was through their doodem that people articulated their relationship to place. Doodemag explain patterns of seasonal travel and choices in relocation. Doodemag were and are at the heart and soul of Anishinaabe conceptions of collective identity. Alliances between doodem created Anishinaabe families, defined local and regional polities, and were expressions of Anishinaabe law. Doodem defined the responsibilities that one had to doodem kin, to allies, and to the land.

Anishinaabe governance also happened in a place, around a council fire. By bringing the concept of doodem together with the regionally significant metaphor of ishkode, or fire, the political geometry of the Anishinabek becomes visible. The contrast between Anishinaabe practices and Western ones is stark. Settler colonists brought with them ideas of jurisdiction as bounded, enclosed, and ideally exclusive polygons (which could be nested, one within another, but were still clearly defined). The political geometry of the Anishinabek consisted of nodes or sites of governance and law, represented metaphorically and figuratively as circles connected by intersecting lines of doodem relations. Such a system created negotiated, overlapping, and shared jurisdictions. It was possible for the Anishinabek to imagine a world in which French and English newcomers were relatives who maintained their own council fires and had their distinct political identities; by the nineteenth century, it was nearly impossible for colonists to imagine that they too could inhabit such a world. Instead, what they offered the Anishinabek, and other Indigenous peoples of North America, was assimilation and the effective annihilation of their distinct societies, because settlers couldn't imagine a different kind of legal and political practice that would permit mutually respectful and beneficial co-existence.

This work recovers a political tradition that has a very long history. The existence of doodemag can be inferred from linguistic evidence and by reading against the grain of primary source documents authored by Europeans. Doodemag met the social, political, and diplomatic needs of people who traveled widely, gathering in the warmer seasons, dispersing in the winter. Through exogamous marriage practices (marrying outside of one's doodem), families created lateral alliances that secured access to the resources and support of their spouse's families, as well as ensuring the hospitality of those families when travelling. Over time, families developed long-standing and deeply embedded ties between particular doodemag. Cross-cousins married cross-cousins, further deepening these ties. The development of a political tradition founded on reciprocal alliances explains how Anishinaabe people could survive as a distinct people in the face of epidemics and the violent conflicts in the mid-seventeenth century and subsequent imperial wars. While some Anishinaabe families were undoubtedly affected directly, others were well removed from both contagion and conflict. Lived historical experiences varied widely. Kinship networks provided the basis for cohesion and continuity of cultural tradition, even in the case of temporary relocations. At times of crisis, people knew where to move, with whom to stay, and how to negotiate access to resources. They knew their law. Anishinaabe relocations within the Great Lakes region must be understood within this context of doodem kin, as doodem informed the demographics and movements of Anishinaabe people and communities.

The documentary record of doodem imagery is ironically richest during the land dispossession process from 1783 through to 1867, as that is how Anishinaabe leaders represented themselves on treaty documents. This evidence is most visible at the very time their distinct system of governance was under attack. The political tradition of doodemag was only eroded by late nineteenth and twentieth-century colonialist practices. Language loss, coupled with legislative interference in Anishinaabe politics, contributed to the weakening of the tradition, a process that parallels the experiences of other colonized peoples around the globe. However, aspects of the doodem identity have at least been partially handed on in some families. Today, there is a revival of interest in doodem identity and in restoring traditional systems of governance. This book may contribute to this process.

With respect to the state of the European-authored documentary record on the Great Lakes region, it is fair to say that these sources remain highly problematic for writing Indigenous histories. Colonial records disproportionately record the actions and experiences of adult men. As scholars of imperial archives have made clear, reliance on that record alone will continue to disappoint – and will continue to produce historical narratives dominated by war and description of violence.[11] Yes, Anishinaabe men were sometimes warriors, but they were primarily hunters and providers. The work of Elders and adult

---

11 Burton, "Introduction"; Stoler, *Along the Archival Grain*.

women, the laughter of children, and the daily and seasonal rhythms of Anishinaabe life appear far less often in the colonial archives. While the holdings of libraries and archives that historians are typically trained to work with are useful and valuable for many reasons, they do not house the knowledge of this land, its waters, or the aadizookaanag of the Anishinaabe peoples. But centuries of contact, missionization, population loss, residential schooling, and the oppressive weight of colonization have also disrupted many Anishinaabe oral traditions and that route of cultural transmission for Anishinaabe people as well.

The way forward may be to continue to weave these different sources together in collaboration with Anishinaabe communities to address the problem of fragmentation. Such collaboration is not only a gesture of respect (which it is) but also as a critical methodology. The opportunity exists now for teams of researchers (both Indigenous and non-Indigenous) to work together with Elders and community members in a cooperative manner to stitch the human history in the Great Lakes back into a coherent whole. Such a record will serve as the basis for more accurate understandings of the complex world Anishinaabe peoples built and the impact of settler colonialism upon them and their political traditions. It also will serve as a basis for reinterpretation of Anishinaabe–Crown relations and the pre-Confederation treaties and will have implications for contemporary international law.

It is my hope that this book, in picking up some pieces of the past, lets them contribute to shaping the future.

Bibliography

Archival Sources

Archives Nationales de France, Paris (ANF)
    Fonds des colonies. Série C11A, Correspondence générale, consulted on microfilm at Robarts Library, University of Toronto.
Archives Nationales d'Outre Mer, France (ANOM).
Archives of Ontario, Toronto, Canada
    RG 1 Crown Lands.
American Philosophical Society, Philadelphia, United States (APS)
    William Jones, Ethnographic and linguistic field notes on the Ojibwa Indians, ca. 1903–1905.
Centre for Kentish Studies, Maidstone, Kent, England
    Amherst Manuscripts (U1350).
Canadian Museum of History
    Ethnological Records.
Library and Archives Canada, Ottawa (LAC)
    Executive Council Office of the Province of Canada fonds, formerly RG 1, Land submissions to the Executive Council series.
    Department of Indian Affairs and Northern Development fonds, formerly RG 10 (DIAND fonds)
        Colonel D.C. Napier – Correspondence.
        Office of the Chief Superintendent in Upper Canada, 1831–1850.
        Paudash Papers, 1825–1849.
        Treaties and Surrenders, 1680–1956.

National Archives and Records Administration, College Park, Maryland,
    United States of America
    General Records of the United States Government, Record Group 11.
    Ratified Indian Treaties, 1722–1869.
National Library of Ireland, Dublin
    Letters of Colonel Jasper Grant (MS 10, 178).
United Church of Canada
    New Credit Methodist Indian Mission (Ont.) fonds, 1776–1887
        Baptisms, 1802–1846.
        Membership list of Methodist Society at the Upper Mohawk Grand
            River, 1826.
        Register, including births, 1776–1881, marriages, 1831–1855 (predomi-
            nantly undated), deaths, 1840–1883, of the River Credit Indians.
Victoria University Library and Special Collections, Toronto, Canada
    Peter Jones fonds – Series 1
        Indian Petitions and Addresses, 1826–44.

Published Primary Sources

Assiginack, Francis. "Legends and Traditions of the Odahwah Indians." *The
    Canadian Institute* 3 (1857).
Blackbird, Andrew J. *History of the Ottawa and Chippewa Indians of Michigan:
    A Grammar of Their Language, and Personal and Family History of the Author.*
    Ypsilanti, MI: Ypsilanti Job Printing House, 1887.
Blair, Emma Hellen, ed. *The Indian Tribes of the Upper Mississippi Valley and
    Region of the Great Lakes as Described by Nicolas Perrot, French Commandant in
    the Northwest.* 2 vols. Cleveland: Arthur H. Clarke Co., 1911.
Cameron, Duncan. "The Nipigon Country, 1801." In *Les Bourgeois de la Compagnie
    du Nord Ouest*, ed. Louis Masson, 231–300. Quebec: Imprimerie générale, 1890.
Canada, *Indian Treaties and Surrenders*. Ottawa: Queen's Printer, 1901.
Champlain, Samuel de. *The Works of Samuel de Champlain.* 7 vols. Ed. H.P.
    Biggar. Toronto: Champlain Society, 1922–36.
Charlevoix, Pierre. *Letters to the Duchess of Lesdiguieres; Giving an Account of a
    Voyage to Canada and Travels Through That Vast Country and Louisiana.* 2 vols.
    London: Printed for R. Goadby, 1763.
Copway, George. *Indian Life and Indian History by an Indian Author, Embracing
    the Traditions of North American Indians Regarding Themselves, Particularly
    of that Most Important of All the Tribes, the Ojibways.* Boston, MA: A. Colby,
    1858.

– *The Traditional History and Characteristic Sketches of the Ojibway Nation.*
Boston: B.F. Mussey & Co., 1851.

Davin, Nicholas Floyd. *Report on Industrial Schools for Indians and Half Breeds.*
Ottawa: n.p., 1879.

Henry, Alexander. *Travels and Adventures in Canada and the Indian Territories:
Between the Years 1760 and 1776.* New York: I. Riley, 1809.

Jamet, Denis. "Relation du Père Denis Jamet ... au Cardinal de Joyeuse." In
Nouveaux documents sur Champalin et son époque, ed. René Baudry and Robert
Le Blant. Ottawa: Public Archives of Canada, 1967.

Johnson, William. *The Papers of Sir William Johnson.* Ed. Alexander Clarence
Flick. 14 Vols. Albany: University of the State of New York, 1921–65.

Jones, Peter. *History of the Ojebway Indians, with Especial Reference to their
Conversion to Christianity; with a Brief Memoir of the Writer.* London: A.W.
Bennet, 1861.

Littlehales, E.B. "Journal from Niagara to Detroit, 1793." In *The Papers of
John Graves Simcoe*, vol. 4, ed. E.A. Cruikshank Toronto: Ontario Historical
Society, 1923–31.

*Minutes of the General Council of Indian Chiefs and Principal Men: held at Orillia,
Lake Simcoe Narrows, on Thursday the 30th and Friday, the 31st July 1846, on the
Proposed Removal of the Smaller Communities and the Establishment of Manual
Labour Schools.* Montreal: Printed at the Gazette Canada Office, 1846.

Nicolas, Louis. *The Codex Canadensis and the Writings of Louis Nicolas.* Ed.
François-Marc Gagnon and Nancy Senior. Montreal: McGill-Queen's
University Press, 2011.

Paudash, Chief Robert. "Testimony of Chief Robert Paudash on the Coming
of the Mississauga." From Paudash Papers, Ontario Historical Society,
1905, published in *The Valley of the Trent*, ed. Edwin C. Guillet. Toronto:
Champlain Society, 1957.

Pouchot, Pierre. *Memoir upon the Late War in North America between the French
and English, 1755–60.* Vol. 2. Roxbury, MA: Printed for W.E. Woodward, 1866.

Province of Canada. Bagot Commission Report of 1844 (Report on the
Affairs of the Indians in Canada), Laid Before the Legislative Assembly,
20th March, 1845, Sect. I and II. In Appendix to the Fourth Volume of the
Journals of the Legislative Assembly of the Province of Canada, Session
1844–1845, Appendix E.E.E.

– The Pennefather Commission of 1858: Richard T. Pennefather, Thomas
Worthington, and Froome Talfourd. "Report of the Special Commissioners
Appointed on the 8th of September, 1856 to Investigate Indian Affairs
in Canada." Appendix to the Sixteenth Volume of the Journals of the
Legislative Assembly of the Province of Canada, 1858.

- Report on the Affairs of the Indians in Canada, Laid Before the Legislative Assembly, 20th March, 1845, Section III. In Appendix to the Sixth Volume of the Journals of the Legislative Assembly of the Province of Canada, 1847, Appendix (T.).
Radisson, Pierre. *The Voyages*. Vol. 1 of *The Collected Writings of Pierre Radisson*, ed. Germaine Warkentin. Toronto: Champlain Society, 2012.
Russell, Peter. *The Correspondence of the Honourable Peter Russell: With Allied Documents Relating to His Administration of the Government of Upper Canada during the Official Term of Lieut.-Governor J. G. Simcoe, While on Leave of Absence*. Toronto: Ontario Historical Society, 1932–6.
Thwaites, Reuben Gold, ed. *Jesuit Relations and Allied Documents*. 73 vols. Cleveland: Burrows Brothers, 1898.
Warren, William Whipple, and Edward Duffield Neill. *History of the Ojibways, Based Upon Traditions and Oral Statements*. St. Paul: Minnesota Historical Society, 1885.
Word, William, ed. *Select British documents of the Canadian War of 1812*. Vol. 2. Toronto: Champlain Society, 1920–8.

Statutes

Canada. House of Commons. An Act for the gradual enfranchisement of Indians, the better management of Indian affairs, and to extend the provisions of the Act 31st Victoria, Chapter 42 (Statutes of Canada 1869 c. 6).
- An Act to amend and consolidate the laws respecting Indians (S.C. 1876, c. 18).
Parliament of Great Britain, Constitutional Act, 1791 (31 Geo. III, c.31); July 23.
Parliament of the United Kingdom, Act of Union, 1840 (3 and 4 Vict. C. 35).
Province of Canada. An Act to Encourage the Gradual Civilization of the Indian Tribes in the Province (20 Victoria, c. 26), 1859.

Secondary Sources

Allen, Robert S. *A History of the British Indian Department in North America (1755–1830)*. Ottawa: Department of Indian Affairs and Northern Development, 1971.
- *His Majesty's Indian Allies: British Indian policy in the Defence of Canada, 1774–1815*. Toronto: Dundurn Press, 1992.
Anderson, Benedict. *Imagined Communities: Reflections on the Origin and Spread of Nationalism*. New York: Verso, 1991.
Angel, Michael. *Preserving the Sacred: Historical Perspectives on the Ojibwa Midewiwin*. Winnipeg: University of Manitoba Press, 2002.

Baraga, Frederic. *A Dictionary of the Otchipwe Language.* Cincinnati: J.A. Hemann, 1853.

Bauerkemper, Joseph and Heidi Kiiwetinepinesiik Stark. "The Trans/National Terrain of Anishinaabe Law and Diplomacy." *Journal of Transnational American Studies* 4, no. 1 (2012): 1–21.

Bauerschmidt, Frederick Christian, and James J. Buckley. *Catholic Theology: An Introduction* Chichester, England: Wiley Blackwell, 2017.

Bedos-Rezak, Brigitte Miriam. "Medieval Identity: A Sign and a Concept." *American Historical Review* 105 (2000): 1489–533.

Belfry, Phil. *Three Fires Unity: The Anishinaabeg of the Lake Huron Borderlands.* Lincoln: University of Nebraska Press, 2011.

Benton-Banai, Edward. *The Mishomis Book: The Voice of the Ojibway.* St. Paul, MN: Indian Country Press, 1979.

Bernard, J.P. *The Rebellions of 1837 and 1838 in Lower Canada.* Ottawa: Canadian Historical Association, 1996.

Berry, David. "How the AGO is Finally Paying Tribute to the Indigenous Art it Previously Didn't Appreciate." *National Post*, 25 October 2016. https://nationalpost.com/entertainment/how-the-ago-is-finally-inviting -indigenous-artists-into-the-conversations-of-whats-constituted-toronto-art.

Bishop, Charles. "The Question of Ojibwa Clans." In *Actes du Vingtième Congrès des Algonquinistes*, ed. William Cowan, 43–61. Ottawa: Carleton University, 1988.

Blair, Peggy. *Lament for a First Nation: The Williams Treaties of Southern Ontario.* Vancouver: UBC Press, 2008.

Bohaker, Heidi. "Anishinaabe 'toodaims': Contexts for Politics, Kinship and Identity in the Eastern Great Lakes." In *Gathering Places: Aboriginal and Fur Trade Histories*, ed. Laura Peers and Carolyn Podruchny, 93–118. Vancouver: UBC Press, 2010.

– "Indigenous Histories and Archival Media in the Early Modern Great Lakes Region." In *Early American Mediascapes*, ed. Matt Cohen and Jeffrey Glover, 99–140. Lincoln: University of Nebraska Press, 2014.

– "*Nindoodemag*: Anishinaabe Identities in the Eastern Great Lakes Region, 1600–1900." PhD diss., University of Toronto, 2006.

– "*Nindoodemag*: The Significance of Algonquian Kinship Networks in the Eastern Great Lakes Region, 1600–1701." *William and Mary Quarterly* 63, no. 1 (2006): 23–52.

– "Reading Anishinaabe Identities: Meaning and Metaphor in Nindoodem Pictographs," *Ethnohistory* 57, no. 1 (Winter 2010): 11–33.

Bohaker, Heidi, Alan Corbiere, and Ruth B. Phillips. "Wampum Unites Us: Digital Circulation, Interdisciplinarity and Indigenous Knowledge

– Situating the GRASAC Knowledge Sharing Database." In *Translating Knowledge: Global Perspectives on Museum and Community*, ed. Ray Silverman. London: Routledge, 2015. https://doi.org/10.4324/9781315766935.

Borrows, John. *Canada's Indigenous Constitution*. Toronto: University of Toronto Press, 2010.

– *Drawing Out Law: A Spirit's Guide*. Toronto: University of Toronto Press, 2010.

– "Wampum at Niagara: The Royal Proclamation, Canadian Legal History, and Self-Government." In *Aboriginal and Treaty Rights in Canada: Essays on Law, Equity, and Respect for Difference*, ed. Michael Asch, 155–72. Vancouver: UBC Press, 1997.

Borrows, Lindsay Keegitah. *Otter's Journey through Indigenous Language and Law*. Vancouver: UBC Press, 2018.

Brooks, James F. *Captives and Cousins: Slavery, Kinship, and Community in the Southwest Borderlands*. Chapel Hill: University of North Carolina Press, 2002.

Brown, Jennifer S.H. "Cameron, Duncan." In *The Dictionary of Canadian Biography Online*. Article published 1998, revised 2001. http://www.biographi.ca/en/bio/cameon_duncan_7E.html.

– *Strangers in Blood: Fur Trade Company Families in Indian Country*. Vancouver: UBC Press, 1980.

Brown, Jennifer S.H., and Laura Peers. "'There Is No End to Relationship among the Indians': Ojibwa Families and Kinship in Historical Perspective." *The History of the Family* 4, no. 4 (1999): 529–55.

Brownlie, Robin Jarvis, and Mary Ellen Kelm. "Desperately Seeking Absolution: Native Agency as Colonialist Alibi?" *Canadian Historical Review* 75, no. 4 (1994): 543–56.

Bruchac, Margaret. "Broken Chains of Custody: Possessing, Dispossessing, and Repossessing Lost Wampum Belts." *Proceedings of the American Philosophical Society* 162 no. 1 (2018): 56–105.

Burton, Antoinette. "Introduction: Archive Fever, Archive Stories." In *Archive Stories: Facts, Fictions, and the Writing of History*, ed. Antoinette Burton, 1–24. Durham, NC: Duke University Press, 2005.

Campbell, Lyle. *Historical Linguistics: An Introduction*. Cambridge, MA: MIT Press, 2013.

Caprio, John, Joseph G. Brand, John H. Teeter, Tine Valentincic, D. Lynn Kalinoski, Jun Kohbara, Takashi Kumazawa, and Sandra Wegert. "The Taste System of the Channel Catfish: From Biophysics to Behavior." *Trends in Neurosciences* 16, no. 5 (1993): 192–7. https://doi.org/10.1016/0166-2236(93)90152-C.

Caton, John Dean. *The Antelope and Deer of America*. New York: 1974 (originally published in 1877).

Chamberlin, J. Edward. *If This is Your Land, Where Are Your Stories? Finding Common Ground*. Toronto: Knopf, 2003.

Charland, Thomas. "Rale, Sébastien." In *The Dictionary of Canadian Biography Online*. Article published 1969, revised 1982. http://www.biographi.ca/en /bio/rale_sebastien_2E.html.

Child, Brenda. *Holding Our World Together: Ojibwe Women and the Survival of Community*. New York: Viking, 2012.

Chute, Janet. *The Legacy of Shingwaukonse: A Century of Native Leadership*. Toronto: University of Toronto Press, 1998.

Clark, James A., et al. "A Model of Surface Water Hydrology of the Great Lakes, North America During the Past 16,000 Years." *Physics and Chemistry of the Earth* 53–4 (2011): 61–71. https://doi.org/10.1016/j.pce.2010.12.005.

Conway, Thor. "Ojibwa Oral History: Relating to Nineteenth Century Rock Art." *American Indian Rock Art* 15 (1992): 1–26.

– *Spirits on Stone: Lake Superior Ojibwa History, Legends and the Agawa Pictographs*. Sault Ste. Marie, ON: Heritage Discoveries, 2010.

Cook, Peter. "Onontio Gives Birth: How the French in Canada Became Fathers to Their Indigenous Allies, 1645–73." *Canadian Historical Review* 96, no. 2 (June 1, 2015).

Corbiere, Alan. "Anishinaabe Headgear: Symbolic, Cultural and Linguistic Meanings." *Americana Indian Art* 37, no. 3 (Summer 2012): 38–47.

– "Anishinaabe Treaty-Making in the 18th- and 19th-Century Northern Great Lakes: From Shared Meanings to Epistemological Chasms." PhD diss., York University, 2019.

– "Dbaad'dang Wiigwaaskeng: Talking about Working with Birch." Paper presented at the Second GRASAC Research Conference, Brantford, ON, 14 June 2014.

– "Exploring Historical Literacy in Manitoulin Island Ojibwe." *Papers of the Algonquian Conference* 34 (2003): 57–80.

– "Gchi-Ogaa: 'The Great Pickerel." In *Kinoomaadiwag Cultural & Historical Research* 3, no. 2 (2005): 1–5.

Corbiere, Mary Ann. "Flying Blind over Strange Terrain, or Ezhi-mkoshnang kweji-aan'kinoosjigeng: Issues in English-Nishnaabemwin Translation." In *Papers of the 39th Algonquian Conference*, ed. K.S. Hele and R. Darnell, 518–30. London: University of Western Ontario, 2008.

Corbiere, Mary Ann, and Rand Valentine. *Dictionary of Nishnabewin Database*. Trans. Daphne Odjig Miznibii'ganan. Publication pending.

Craft, Aimée. *Breathing Life into the Stone Fort Treaty*. Saskatoon: Purich Publishing, 2013.

Cronon, William. *Changes in the Land: Indians, Colonists, and the Ecology of New England*. New York: Hill and Wang, 1983.

Cumberland, F. Barlow. *Catalogue and Notes of the Oronhyatekha Historical Collection*. Toronto: Independent Order of Foresters, 1904.

Danziger, Edmund J. *Great Lakes Indian Accommodation and Resistance during the Early Reservation Years, 1850-1900*. Ann Arbor: University of Michigan Press, 2009.

Deloria, Vine, Jr. *God is Red: A Native View of Religion*. Golden, CO: Fulcrum Publishing, 2003.

Dewdney, Selwyn H. *The Sacred Scrolls of the Southern Ojibway*. Toronto: University of Toronto Press, 1975.

Doerfler, Jill, Niigaanwewidam James Sinclair, and Heidi Kiiwetinepinesiik Stark, eds. *Centering Anishinaabeg Studies: Understanding the World Through Stories*. East Lansing: Michigan State University Press, 2013.

Dowd, Gregory Evans. *War Under Heaven: Pontiac, the Indian Nations and the British Empire*. Baltimore: The Johns Hopkins University Press, 2002.

Doxtator, Deborah. "Inclusive and Exclusive Perceptions of Difference: Native and Euro-Based Concepts of Time, History and Change." In *Decentering the Renaissance: Canada and Europe in Multidisciplinary Perspective, 1500–1700*, ed. Germaine Warkentin and Carolyn Podruchny, 33–47. Toronto: University of Toronto Press, 2001.

DuVal, Kathleen. *The Native Ground : Indians and Colonists in the Heart of the Continent*. Philadelphia: University of Pennsylvania Press, 2006.

Eid, Leroy. "'National' War Among Indians of Northeastern North America." *Canadian Review of American Studies* 16, no. 2 (1985): 125–54.

Evans, Katy Young. "The People's Pageant: The Stage as Native Space in Anishinaabe Dramatic Interpretations of Hiawatha." *MELUS (Multi-Ethnic Literature of the United States)* 41, no. 2 (2016): 124–46.

Farrell Racette, Sherry. In conversation with Alan Corbiere and Crystal Migwans. "Pieces Left along the Trail: Material Culture Histories and Indigenous Studies." In *Sources and Methods in Indigenous Studies*, ed. Chris Andersen and Jean M. O'Brien, 233–7. London: Routledge, 2017.

– "Shaataahaa: Indigenous Methodologies for Collection Based Research." GRASAC, 8 December 2017. https://carleton.ca/grasac/2017/shaataahaa/.

Fenn, Elizabeth A. *Encounters at the Heart of the World: A History of the Mandan People*. New York: Hill and Wang, 2014.Ferris, Neal. The *Archaeology of Native-Lived Colonialism: Challenging History in the Great Lakes*. Tuscon: University of Arizona Press, 2009.

Fisher, John F. "The Ojibwa Creation Myth." In *Imagine Ourselves Richly: Mythic Narratives of North American Indians*, ed. Christopher Vecsey, 64–93. New York: Crossroad, 1988.

Fogelson, Raymond. "The Ethnohistory of Events and Nonevents." *Ethnohistory* 36 (1989): 133–47.

Gadd, Nelson R., ed. *The Late Quaternary Development of the Champlain Sea Basin*. St. John's, NL: Geological Association of Canada, 1988.

Gager, Kristin. *Blood Ties and Fictive Ties: Adoption and Family Life in Early Modern France*. Princeton, NJ: Princeton University Press, 1996.

Geniuz, Wendy Makoons. *Our Knowledge Is Not Primitive: Decolonizing Anishinaabe Botanical Teachings*. Syracuse, NY: Syracuse University Press, 2009.

Gidigaa Migizi (Doug Williams). *Michi Saagiig. This is Our Territory*. Winnipeg: ARP Books, 2018.

Gingras, Janick, Serge Couturier, Steeve D. Côté, and Jean-Pierre Tremblay. "Opposite Responses of Body Condition and Fertility in Adjacent Moose Populations." *The Journal of Wildlife Management* 78, no. 5 (2014): 830–83.

Girard, Phillip, Jim Phillips, and R. Blake Brown. *A History of Law in Canada*, vol 1. Toronto: Osgoode Society for Canadian Legal History and University of Toronto Press, 2018.

Glover, Jeffery. *Paper Sovereigns: Anglo-Native Treaties and the Law of Nations, 1604–1664*. Philadelphia: University of Pennsylvania Press, 2014.

Graham, Jane E. *The Patriots and the People: The Rebellion of 1837 in Rural Lower Canada*. Toronto: University of Toronto Press, 1993.

– "Wabbicomicot." *The Dictionary of Canadian Biography Online*. Article published 1974. http://www.biographi.ca/en/bio/wabbicommicot_3E .html.

Greer, Allan, and Ian Radforth, eds. *Colonial Leviathan: State Formation in Mid-Nineteenth-Century Canada*. Toronto: University of Toronto Press, 1992.

Hallowell, A. Irving. *Contributions to Anthropology: Selected Papers of A. Irving Hallowell*. Chicago: University of Chicago Press, 1976.

– "Ojibwa Ontology, Behavior and World View." In *Culture in History: Essays in Honor of Paul Radin*, ed. Stanley Diamond, 19–52. New York: Columbia University Press, 1960.

Hamilton, Michelle A. *Collections and Objections: Aboriginal Material Culture in Southern Ontario, 1791–1914*. Montreal: McGill-Queen's University Press, 2010.

Happ, George, and Christy Yuncker-Happ. *Sandhill Crane Display Dictionary: What Cranes Say with Their Body Language*. 2nd ed. Phoenix, AZ: Waterford Press, 2012.

Harjo, Suzan Shown, ed. *Nation to Nation: Treaties Between the United States and American Indian Nations*. Washington, DC: Smithsonian Institution, 2014.

Havard, Gilles. *Empire et métissages: Indiens et français dans le pays d'en haut, 1660–1715*. Sillery, QC: Septentrion, 2003.

– *The Great Peace of Montreal of 1701: French–Native Diplomacy in the Seventeenth Century*. Trans. Phyllis Aronof and Howard Scott. Montreal: McGill-Queen's University Press, 2001.

Hayne, David M. "Pierre-François-Xavier de Charlevoix." *The Dictionary of Canadian Biography Online*. Article published 1974. http://www.biographi .ca/fr/bio/charlevoix_pierre_francois_xavier_de_3E.html.

Hele, Karl S. "Introduction." In *Lines Drawn Upon The Water: First Nations and the Great Lakes Borders and Borderlands*, ed. Karl S. Hele, viii–xxiii. Waterloo, ON: Wilfrid Laurier University Press, 2008.

Hickerson, Harold. *The Chippewa and their Neighbors: A Study in Ethnohistory*. Rev. and expanded ed. Ed. Jennifer S.H. Brown and Laura Peers. Prospect Heights, IL: Waveland Press, 1988.

– "The Feast of the Dead Among the Seventeenth Century Algonkians of the Upper Great Lakes." *American Anthropologist* (New Series) 62, no. 1 (1960): 81–107.

Hill, Susan M. *The Clay We Are Made Of: Haudenosaunee Land Tenure on the Grand River*. Winnipeg: University of Manitoba Press, 2017.

Hixson, Walter L. *American Settler Colonialism: A History*. New York: Palgrave Macmillan, 2013.

Howard-Bobiwash, Heather. "Women's Class Strategies as Activism in Native Community Building in Toronto, 1950–1975." *The American Indian Quarterly* 27, nos. 3–4 (2003): 566–82.

Hutchison, Abigail. "The Whanganui River as a Legal Person." *Alternative Law Journal* 39, no. 3 (2014): 179–82. https://doi.org/10.1177/103796 9X1403900309.

Jamieson, Melville Allan. *Medals Awarded to North American Indian Chiefs, 1714–1922, and to Loyal African and Other Chiefs in Various Territories within the British Empire*. London: Spink & Son, 1936.

Jenness, Diamond. *The Ojibwa Indians of Parry Island: Their Social and Religious Life*. Ottawa: Canada Department of Mines, 1935.

Jennings, Francis. *The Ambiguous Iroquois Empire: The Covenant Chain Confederation of Indian Tribes with English Colonies from its Beginnings to the Lancaster Treaty of 1744*. New York: Norton, 1984.

–, ed. *The History and Culture of Iroquois Diplomacy: An Interdisciplinary Guide to the Treaties of the Six Nations and Their League*. Syracuse, NY: Syracuse University Press, 1985.

Johnston, Basil. "Is that All There Is? Tribal Literature." In *Centering Anishinaabeg Studies: Understanding the World Through Stories*, ed. Jill Doerfler, Niigaanwewidam James Sinclair, and Heidi Kiiwetinepinesiik Stark, 3–12. East Lansing: Michigan State University Press, 2013.

– *Ojibway Ceremonies*. Toronto: McClelland and Stewart, 1987.
– *Ojibway Heritage*. Toronto: McClelland and Stewart, 2003.
Johnston, Darlene. "Connecting People to Place: Great Lakes Aboriginal History in Cultural Context, Report prepared for the Ipperwash Commission of Inquiry of the Government of Ontario, Mount Forest, Ontario," August 2004, http://www.attorneygeneral.jus.gov.on.ca /inquiries/ipperwash/index.html.
– "Litigating Identity: The Challenge of Aboriginality." LLM thesis, Faculty of Law, University of Toronto, 2003.
Jones, David S. "Virgin Soils Revisited." *William and Mary Quarterly* 60 (2003): 703–42.
Kauanui, J. Kēhaulani "'A Structure, Not an Event': Settler Colonialism and Enduring Indigeneity." *Lateral: The Journal of the Cultural Studies Association* 5, no. 1 (2016). https://csalateral.org/issue/5-1/forum-alt-humanities -settler-colonialism-enduring-indigeneity-kauanui/.
Kegg, Maude, and John D. Nichols. "When Aazhawakiwenzhiinh Almost became a Windigo." *Nookomis Gaa-inaajimotawid: Oshkaabewis Native Journal* 1 (1990): 14–15.
Kennedy, Patricia. "Treaty Texts: When Can We Trust the Written Word?" *Social Sciences and Humanities Aboriginal Research Exchange* 3 (1995): 1–24.
Kimmerer, Robin Wall. *Braiding Sweetgrass: Indigenous Wisdom, Scientific Knowledge and the Teachings of Plants*. Minneapolis: Milkweed Editions, 2015.
Konkle, Maureen. *Writing Indian Nations: Native Intellectuals and the Politics of Historiography, 1827–1863*. Chapel Hill: University of North Carolina Press, 2004.
Konrad, Victor. "An Iroquois Frontier: The North Shore of Lake Ontario during the Late Seventeenth Century." *Journal of Historical Geography* 7, no. 2 (1981): 129–44
Labelle, Kathryn Magee. *Dispersed But Not Destroyed: A History of the Seventeenth-Century Wendat People*. Vancouver: UBC Press, 2013.
Laqueur, Thomas. *Making Sex: Body and Gender from the Greeks to Freud*. Cambridge, MA: Harvard University Press, 1990.
Lawrence, Bonita. *"Real" Indians and Others: Mixed-Blood Urban Native Peoples and Indigenous Nationhood*. Vancouver: UBC Press, 2004.
Lee, Damien. "Adoption Constitutionalism: Anishinaabe Citizenship Law at Fort William First Nation." *Alberta Law Review* 56, no. 3 (2019): 785–816.
Lee, James Jaehoon. "John Donne and the Textuality of the Two Souls." *Studies in Philology* 133, no. 4 (2016): 879–918.
Lévi-Strauss, Claude. *Elementary Structures of Kinship*. Boston: Beacon Press, 1969.

MacLeod, D. Peter. "The Anishinabeg Point of View: The History of the Great Lakes Region to 1800 in Nineteenth-Century Mississauga, Odawa and Ojibwa Historiography." *Canadian Historical Review* 73, no. 2 (1992): 194–210.

– "Microbes and Muskets: Smallpox and the Participation of the Amerindian Allies of New France in the Seven Years' War." *Ethnohistory* 39, no. 1 (Winter 1992): 42–64.

Mallery, Garrick. "Picture Writing of the American Indians." In *Tenth Annual Report of the Bureau of Ethnology to the Secretary of the Smithsonian Institution, 1889–89*, ed. J.W. Powell. Washington, DC: Government Printing Office, 1893. Reprinted unabridged as *Picture-Writing of the American Indians*. 2 vols. New York: Dover, 1972.

McCalla, Douglas. *Planting the Province: The Economic History of Upper Canada, 1784–1870*. Toronto: University of Toronto Press, 1993.

McCallum, John. *Unequal Beginnings: Agriculture and Economic Development in Quebec and Ontario Until 1870*. Toronto: University of Toronto Press, 1980.

McCallum, Mary Jane Logan. "Miss Chief: The Obscure History of First Nations Female Suffrage and Leadership." Public lecture and keynote address, Annual Graduate History Symposium, Department of History, University of Toronto, 12 May 2017.

McDonnell, Michael A. *Masters of Empire: Great Lakes Indians and the Making of America*. New York: Hill and Wang, 2015.

Michelson, Truman. "Note on the Gentes of the Ottawa." *American Anthropologist*, new series 13 (1911): 33.

Migwans, Mikinak (Crystal). "Naaknashk miinawaa Naaknigewin: Art, governance, and bulrushes." Invited Guest Lecture Series, Department of Art History, University of Toronto, 28 October 2019.

Miller, Cary. "Gifts as Treaties: The Political Use of Received Gifts in Anishinaabeg Communities, 1820–1832." *American Indian Quarterly* 26, no. 2 (2002): 221–45.

– *Ogimaag: Anishinaabeg Leadership, 1760–1845*. Lincoln: University of Nebraska Press, 2010.

Miller, James R. *Compact, Contract, Covenant: Aboriginal Treaty-Making in Canada*. Toronto: University of Toronto Press, 2009.

Milloy, John Sheridan. *A National Crime: The Canadian Government and the Residential School System, 1879 to 1986*. Winnipeg: University of Manitoba Press, 1999.

Mills, Aaron. "What is a Treaty? On Contract and Mutual Aid." In *The Right Relationship: Reimagining the Implementation of Historical Treaties*, ed. John Borrows and Michael Coyle, 208–74. Toronto: University of Toronto Press, 2017.

Morito, Bruce. *An Ethic of Mutual Respect: The Covenant Chain and Aboriginal-Crown Relations.* Vancouver: UBC Press, 2012.

Morrisseau, Norval. "The Great Conjurers and Warriors of the Mighty Ojibway." In *Legends of My People: The Great Ojibway,* ed. Selwyn Dewdney, 87–8. Toronto: Ryerson Press, 1965.

Murdoch, Chandra. "Mobilization of and against Indian Act Elections on Haudenosaunee Reserves, 1870–1924." Paper presented at the Annual Meeting of the Canadian Historical Association, Ryerson University, May 31 2017.

"Musquakie." In *Dictionary of Canadian Biography Online.* Article published 1976. http://www.biographi.ca/en/bio/musquakie_9E.html.

Nahwegahbow, Alexandra Kahsenniio. "Springtime in n'Daki Menan, the Homeland of the Teme-Augama Anishnabai: Babies, Cradleboards and Community Wrapping." MA thesis, Carleton University, 2013.

Napoleon, Val. *Thinking about Indigenous Legal Orders.* Ottawa: National Centre for First Nations Governance, 2007.

Nash, Alice. "The Abiding Frontier: Family, Gender and Religion in Wabanaki History, 1600–1763." PhD diss., Columbia University, 1997.

Newbigging, Bill. "Ottawa–French Alliance." PhD diss, University of Toronto, 1995.

O'Callaghan, E.B., ed. *Documents Relative to the Colonial History of the State of New York.* Albany, NY: Weed, Parsons and Company, 1857.

Page, Lawrence M. "The Crayfishes and Shrimps (Decapoda) of Illinois." *Illinois Natural History Survey Bulletin* 33, no. 4 (1985): 406–12.

Parmenter, Jon. *The Edge of the Woods: Iroquoia, 1534-1701.* East Lansing: Michigan State University Press, 2010.

– "Pontiac's War: Forging New Links in the Anglo–Iroquois Covenant Chain, 1758–1766." *Ethnohistory* 44, no. 4 (1997): 617–54.

Peers, Laura L. *The Ojibwa of Western Canada, 1780 to 1870.* Winnipeg: University of Manitoba Press, 1994.

Perrault, Claude. "Perrot, Nicolas." In *Dictionary of Canadian Biography Online.* Article published 1969, revised 1982. http://www.biographi.ca/en/bio/perrot_nicolas_2E.html.

Peterson, Jacqueline. "Many Roads to Red River: Métis Genesis in the Great Lakes Region, 1680–1815." In *The New Peoples: Being and Becoming Métis in North America,* ed. Jennifer S.H. Brown and Jacqueline Peterson, 37–71. Winnipeg: University of Manitoba Press, 1985.

Phillips, Ruth B. "Dreams and Designs: Iconographic Problems in Great Lakes Twined Bags." In *Great Lakes Indian Art,* ed. David Penny, 26–37. Detroit: Detroit Institute of Arts, 1984.

‒ *Patterns of Power: The Jasper Grant Collection (Housed in the National Museum of Ireland) and Great Lakes Indian Art in the Early Nineteenth Century.* Kleinburg, ON: McMichael Canadian Collection, 1984.

‒ "Reading Between the Lines: Soldiers, Curiosities, and Indigenous Art Histories." *Winterthur Portfolio* 45, nos. 2‒3 (2012): 107‒23.

‒ *Trading Identities: The Souvenir in Native North American Art from the Northeast, 1700‒1900.* Seattle: University of Washington Press, 1998.

Pickering, Robert B., et al. *Peace Medals: Negotiating Power in Early America.* Tulsa, OK: Gilcrease Museum, 2011.

Pitawanakwat, Kenn, and Jordan Paper. "Communicating the Intangible: An Anishinaabeg Story." *American Indian Quarterly* 20, nos. 3‒4 (1996): 451‒65.

Pouliot, Léon. "Lalemant, Jérôme." In *The Dictionary of Canadian Biography Online.* Article published 1966, revised 1979. http://www.biographi.ca/en /bio/lalemant_Jérôme_1E.html.

Prucha, Francis Paul. *American Indian Treaties: The History of a Political Anomaly.* Berkeley: University of California Press, 1994.

Radin, Paul. *Some Myths and Tales of the Ojibwa of Southeastern Ontario.* Ottawa: Government Printing Bureau, 1914.

Raibmon, Paige. *Authentic Indians: Episodes of Encounter from the Late-Nineteenth-Century Northwest Coast.* Durham, NC: Duke University Press, 2005.

Rezendes, Paul. *Tracking and the Art of Seeing: How to Read Animal Tracks and Sign.* New York: Collins Reference, 1999.

Rhodes, Richard A. *Eastern Ojibwa/Chippewa-Ottawa Dictionary.* Ann Arbor, MI: Mouton de Gruyter, 1993.

Richter, Daniel. *The Ordeal of the Longhouse: The Peoples of the Iroquois League in the Era of European Colonization.* Chapel Hill: University of North Carolina Press, 1992.

Rickard, Jolene. "Visualizing Sovereignty in the Age of Biometric Sensors." *South Atlantic Quarterly* 110, no. 2 (2011): 465‒82.

Rogers, Edward S. "The Algonquian Farmers of Southern Ontario." In *Aboriginal Ontario: Historical Perspectives on the First Nations,* ed. Edward S. Rogers and Donald Smith, 122‒66. Toronto: Dundurn Press, 1994.

Russell, H. John. *World of the Caribou.* San Francisco: Sierra Club Books, 1998.

Schenck, Theresa M. "The Algonquian Totem and Totemism: A Distortion of the Semantic Field." In *Papers of the 28th Algonquian Conference,* ed. David H. Pentland, 341‒53. Winnipeg: University of Manitoba Press, 1997.

‒ *The Voice of the Crane Echoes Afar: The Sociopolitical Organization of the Lake Superior Ojibwa, 1640‒1855.* New York: Garland, 1997.

Schoolcraft, Henry Rowe. *Algic Researches: North American Indian Folktales and Legends*. New York, NY: Harper & Brothers, 1839. Reprint edition: Mineloa, NY: Dover Publications, 1999.

– *The American Indians: Their History, Condition and Prospects, from Original Notes and Manuscripts*. Vol. 1. Buffalo, NY: G.H. Derby, 1851.

– *Historical and Statistical Information, Respecting the History, Condition and Prospects of the Indian Tribes of the United States*. 6 vols. Philadelphia: Lippincott, Grambo, 1851–7.

Schweitzer, Peter, ed., *Dividends of Kinship: Meanings and Uses of Social Relatedness*. London: Routledge, 2000.

Seed, Patricia. *Ceremonies of Possession in Europe's Conquest of the New World, 1492–1640*. Cambridge: Cambridge University Press, 1995.

Seeman, Erik R. *The Huron-Wendat Feast of the Dead: Indian–European Encounters in Early North America*. John Hopkins University Press, 2011.

Shannon, Timothy J. "Dressing for Success along the Mohawk Frontier: Hendrick, William Johnson, and the Indian Fashion." *William and Mary Quarterly* 53, no. 1 (1996): 13–42.

Shoemaker, Nancy. "An Alliance Between Men: Gender Metaphors in Eighteenth-Century American Indian Diplomacy East of the Mississippi." *Ethnohistory* 46 (1999): 239–64.

– "Categories." In *Clearing a Path: Theorizing the Past in Native American Studies*, ed. Nancy Shoemaker, 51–74. New York: Routledge, 2002.

Simpson, Leanne Betasamosake. *Dancing On Our Turtle's Back: Stories of Nishinaabeg Re-Creation, Resurgence and a New Emergence*. Winnipeg: ARP Books, 2017.

– "Looking after Gdoo-naaganinaa: Precolonial Nishnaabeg Diplomatic and Treaty Relationships." *Wicazo Sa Review* 23, no. 2 (2008): 29–42.

Sims, Catherine. "Algonkian–British Relations In The Upper Great Lakes Region: Gathering To Give And To Receive Presents, 1815–1843." PhD diss., University of Western Ontario, 1992.

– "Exploring Ojibwe History Through Documentary Sources: An Outline of the Life of Chief John Assance." In *Gis Das Winan: Documenting Aboriginal History in Ontario*, ed. Dale Standen and David McNabb, 35–47. Toronto: Champlain Society, 1996.

Smith, Donald B. "Kineubenae." In *The Dictionary of Canadian Biography Online*. Article published 1983. http://www.biographi.ca/en/bio/kineubenae_5E.html.

– *Mississauga Portraits: Ojibwe Voices from Nineteenth-Century Canada*. Toronto: University of Toronto Press, 2013.

- "Nawahjegezhegwabe." In *Dictionary of Canadian Biography Online*. Article published 1976. http://www.biographi.ca/en/bio/nawahjegezhegwabe_9E .html.
- "Ogimauh-Binaessih." In *Dictionary of Canadian Biography Online*. Article published 1987. http://www.biographi.ca/en/bio/ogimauh_binaessih_6E .html.
- "Peter Jones." In *Dictionary of Canadian Biography Online*. Article published 1985. http://www.biographi.ca/en/bio/jones_peter_8E.html.
- *Sacred Feathers: The Reverend Peter Jones (Kahkewa-quonaby) and the Mississauga Indians*. Toronto: University of Toronto Press, 1987.
Smith, Theresa S. *The Island of the Anishinaabeg: Thunderers and Water Monsters in the Traditional Ojibwe Life-World*. Moscow: University of Idaho Press, 1995.
Stark, Heidi Kiiwetinepinesiik. "Changing the Treaty Question: Remedying the Rights Relationship." In *The Right Relationship: Reimagining the Implementation of Historical Treaties*, ed. John Borrows and Michael Coyle, 247–76. Toronto: University of Toronto Press, 2017.
- "Marked by Fire: Anishinaabe Articulations of Nationhood in Treaty Making with the United States and Canada." *The American Indian Quarterly* 36, no. 2 (2012): 119–49.
Stoler, Ann Laura. *Along the Archival Grain: Epistemic Anxieties and Colonial Common Sense*. Princeton, NJ: Princeton University Press, 2006.
Surtees, Robert J. *Indian Land Surrenders in Ontario, 1763–1867*. Ottawa: Indian and Northern Affairs Canada, 1984.
Tanner, Helen Hornbeck. *Atlas of Great Lakes Indian History*. Norman: University of Oklahoma Press, 1987.
Taylor, Alan. *The Divided Ground: Indians, Settlers and the Northern Borderland of the American Revolution*. New York: Alfred A. Knopf, 2006.
Thorne, Tanis C. *The Many Hands of My Relations: French and Indians on the Lower Missouri*. Columbia: University of Missouri Press, 1996.
Todd, Barbara. "Mother's Blood: Inheritance and Women's Nationality in Early Modern English Law." Unpublished paper, Feminism and Law Workshop Series, Toronto, 2001.
Treaty 7 Elders and Tribal Council with Walter Hildebrandt, Dorothy First Rider, and Sarah Carter. *The True Spirit and Original Intent of Treaty 7*. Montreal: McGill-Queen's University Press, 1996.
Treuer, Anton. *The Assassination of Hole in the Day*. St. Paul, MN: Borealis Books, 2011.
Trigger, Bruce G. *The Children of Aataentsic: A History of the Huron People to 1660*. Montreal: McGill-Queen's University Press, 1987.

Truth and Reconciliation Canada. *Honouring the Truth, Reconciling for the Future: Summary of the Final Report of the Truth and Reconciliation Commission of Canada*. Winnipeg: Truth and Reconciliation Commission of Canada, 2015.

Valentine, J. Randolph. *Nishnaabemwin Reference Grammar*. Toronto: University of Toronto Press, 2001.

Van Kirk, Sylvia. *Many Tender Ties: Women in Fur-Trade Society in Western Canada, 1670–1870*. Winnipeg: Watson & Dwyer, 1980.

Vastokas, Joan. "History without Writing: Pictorial Narratives in Native North America." In *Gin Das Winan: Documenting Aboriginal History in Ontario*, ed. Dale Standen and David McNab, 48–64. Toronto: Champlain Society, 1996.

Vecsey, Christopher. *Traditional Ojibwa Religion and Its Historical Changes*. Philadelphia: American Philosophical Society, 1983.

Vizenor, Gerald. *Fugitive Poses: Native American Indian Scenes of Absence and Presence*. Lincoln: University of Nebraska Press, 1998.

Vizenor, Gerald, and James Mackay. "Constitutional Narratives: A Conversation with Gerald Vizenor." In *Centering Anishinaabe Studies*, ed. Jill Doerfler, Niigaanwewidam James Sinclair, and Heidi Kiiwetinepinesiik Stark, 133–48. East Lansing: Michigan State University Press, 2013.

Walters, Mark D. "'According to the Old Customs of Our Nation': Aboriginal Self-Government on the Credit River Mississauga Reserve, 1826–1847." *Ottawa Law Review* 30, no. 1 (1998): 1–45.

– "Brightening the Covenant Chain: Aboriginal Treaty Meaning in Law and History After Marshall." *Dalhousie Law Journal* 24 (2001): 75–82.

Warkentin, Germaine. "Aristotle in New France: Louis Nicolas and the Making of the *Codex Canadensis*." *French Colonial History* 11 (2010): 71–107.

Whetung, Madeline. "(En)Gendering Shoreline Law: Nishnaabeg Relational Politics Along the Trent Severn Waterway." *Global Environmental Politics* 19, no. 3 (2019): 16–32.

White, Bruce. "'Give Us a Little Milk': The Social and Cultural Meanings of Gift Giving in the Lake Superior Fur Trade," *Minnesota History* 48, no. 2 (1982): 60–71.

– "The Woman Who Married a Beaver: Trade Patterns and Gender Roles in the Ojibwa Fur Trade." *Ethnohistory* 46, no. 1 (1999): 109–47.

White, Richard. *The Middle Ground: Indians, Empires, and Republics in the Great Lakes Region, 1650–1815*. Cambridge: Cambridge University Press, 1991.

Willets, Jane Esther. "Correlated Changes in Ottawa Kinship & Social Organization." Master's thesis, University of Pennsylvania, 1948.

Willmott, Cory Silverstein. "Anishinaabe Doodem Pictographs: Narrative Inscriptions and Identities." In *Together We Survive: Ethnographic Intuitions,*

Friendships, and Conversations, ed. John S. Long and Jennifer S.H. Brown, 130–66. Montreal: McGill-Queen's University Press, 2016.

– "Beavers and Sheep: Visual Appearance and Identity in Nineteenth-Century Algonquian-Anglo Relations." *History and Anthropology* 25, no. 1 (2014): 1–46.

– "Clothed Encounters: The Power of Dress in Relations Between Anishinaabe and British Peoples in the Great Lakes Region, 1760–2000." Ph.D diss., McMaster University, 2000.

Willmott, Cory, and Kevin Brownlee. "Dressing for the Homeward Journey: Western Anishnaabe Leadership Roles Viewed through Two Nineteenth-Century Burials." In *Gathering Places: Aboriginal and Fur Trade Histories*, ed. Laura L. Peers and Carolyn Podruchny, 48–90. Vancouver: UBC Press, 2010.

Wisdom, Charles. "Report on the Great Lakes Chippewa." Washington, DC: Office of Indian Affairs, 1936. Manuscript copy filed at the Peabody Museum Library, Harvard University.

Witgen, Michael. *An Infinity of Nations: How the Native New World Shaped Early North America*. Philadelphia: University of Pennsylvania Press, 2012.

– "The Rituals of Possession: Native Identity and the Invention of Empire in Seventeenth-Century Western North America." *Ethnohistory* 54, no. 4 (2007): 639–68.

Wolfe, Patrick. "Settler Colonialism and the Elimination of the Native." *Journal of Genocide Studies* 8, no. 4 (2006), 387–409.

Wub-e-ke-niew. *We Have the Right to Exist: A Translation of Aboriginal Indigenous Thought: The First Book Ever Published from an Ahnishinahbæótjibway Perspective*. New York: Black Thistle Press, 1995.

Illustration Credits

From left to right, the doodem images on the first page of the Preface are:

Marque des Mississaugues (Thunderbird doodem), 1701: Archives nationales d'outre-mer, France (hereafter ANOM), Aix-en-Provence, "Ratification de la paix," 4 August 1701, Fonds des Colonies. Série C11A. Correspondence générale, Canada, vol. 19, fol.41v – Tous droits réservés.

Pahtash (Crane doodem), 1818: Library and Archives Canada (hereafter LAC), "Provisional Agreement with the Rice Lake Chiefs for the surrender of 1,951,000 Acres of Land," 5 November 1818, RG10, Vol. 1842/IT061.

Kitchi Negau (Caribou doodem), 1798: LAC, "Indian Deed of Sale for the Island of Michilimakinac," 12 May 1781, RG10, Vol. 1840/IT001.

Penise (Birch Tree doodem), 1818: LAC, "Provisional Agreement with the Rice Lake Chiefs for the surrender of 1,951,000 Acres of Land," 5 November 1818, RG10, Vol. 1842/IT061.

Kaukonce (Pike doodem), 1798. LAC, "Deed of Conveyance of the Island of St. Joseph from the Chippawa Nation to His Majesty," 30 June 1798, RG10, Vol. 1841/IT035.

Photo Section

1   LAC, "Deed of Conveyance of the Island of St. Joseph from the Chippawa Nation to His Majesty," 30 June 1798, RG10, Vol. 1841/IT035.

2   Ethnologisches Museum Berlin (Staatliche Museen zu Berlin), IV-B-6508.

3   Beltrami Collection, Museo civico di Scienze naturali di Bergamo, Italy.

4   Ethnologisches Museum Berlin (Staatliche Museen zu Berlin), IV-V-7587.

5   National Museum of the American Indian, Smithsonian Institution (24/2012).

6   GM 4726.7.009, Gilcrease Museum, Tulsa, Oklahoma.

7   GM 4726.7.013, Gilcrease Museum, Tulsa, Oklahoma.

8   © musée du quai Branly - Jacques Chirac, Dist. RMN-Grand Palais / Art. 71.1917.3.10 D. Photo: Patrick Gries.

9   GM 4726.7.015, Gilcrease Museum, Tulsa, Oklahoma.

10   Smithsonian American Art Museum, Gift of Mrs. Joseph Harrison, Jr.

11   ANOM, Aix-en-Provence, "Ratification de la paix," 4 August 1701, Fonds des Colonies. Série C11A. Correspondence générale, Canada, vol. 19, fol.41v) – Tous droits réservés.

12   Schoolcraft, *Historical and statistical information, respecting the history, condition and prospects of the Indian tribes of the United States* (Philadelphia: Gambo, 1857) vol 5: Plate 50. Image Courtesy Fisher Rare Book Library.

13   Images © Bonhams. Printed with the permission of Wiikwemikoong Unceded Territory.

14   Image © National Museums Scotland (A.1989.208).

15   Courtesy of the Royal Ontario Museum © ROM. 911.3.119, Dr. Oronhyatekha Ethnology collection.

16   Courtesy of the Royal Ontario Museum © ROM. 911.3.179, Dr. Oronhyatekha Ethnology collection.

17   GM 65.19, Gilcrease Museum, Tulsa, Oklahoma.

18   © Government of Canada. Reproduced with the permission of LAC (2020), inventory no. 200519.

19   1764 Niagara Covenant Chain Wampum Belt, reproduction by Ken Maracle, Canadian Museum of History, LH2016.48.2, IMG2016-0267-0250-Dm.

20   © National Museums Liverpool, Museum of Liverpool, 58.83.16.

21   The Andrew Foster Collection, National Museum of the American Indian, Smithsonian Institution (24/2000, 24/2001, 24/2002, 24/2003, 24/2004, 24/2006, 24/2012, 24/2016, 24/2022, 24/2034). Photo by NMAI Photo

Services. Assembled in this form for the exhibit Infinity of Nations: Art and History in the Collections of the National Museum of the American India.

22 Shingwauk Residential Schools Centre, Algoma University.

23 Pouch, Eastern Great Lakes, middle 18th century, Canadian Museum of History, III-X-374, S82-4211.

24 Wabicommicott, 1764: Kent Archives Service.

Wabakanne, 1787: LAC, "Indenture made at the Carrying Place, Head of the Bay of Quinty," 23 September 1787, RG10, Vol. 1841/IT040.

Wabakanne, 1792: LAC, "Deed of Feoffment - The Messissague Nation to His Britannick Majesty," 7 December 1792, RG10, Vol. 1840/IT005.

Wabanip, 1797: LAC, "Surrender of Land at the head of Lake Ontario by the Mississague Nation," 21 August 1797, RG10, Vol. 1841/IT030.

Cheechalk, 1806: LAC, "Lease and Release from the Mississagua Indians," 6 September 1806, RG10, Vol. 1842/IT042.

Adjutant, 1818: LAC, "Provisional Agreement with the Mississagues of the River Credit, for the surrender of 648,000 Acres of Land," 28 October 1818, RG10, Vol. 1842/IT059.

Joseph Sawyer, 1831 and 1844: Peter Jones fonds, Victoria University Library (Toronto).

25 Marque des Sauteurs, chef Wabanqué, 1701: ANOM, Aix-en-Provence, "Ratification de la paix," 4 August 1701, Fonds des Colonies. Série C11A. Correspondence générale, Canada, vol. 19, fol.41v – Tous droits réservés.

Meatoowanakwee, 1798: LAC, "Deed of Conveyance of the Island of St. Joseph from the Chippawa Nation to His Majesty," 30 June 1798 , RG10, Vol. 1841/IT035.

Nebanagoching: "Aboriginal Chief, Chippewa, the Eclipse or Wabumagoging," M1878 © McCord Museum

Marque des Algonquins, 1701: ANOM, Aix-en-Provence, "Ratification de la paix," 4 August 1701, Fonds des Colonies. Série C11A. Correspondence générale, Canada, vol. 19, fol.41v – Tous droits réservés.

Pahtash, 1818: LAC, "Provisional Agreement with the Rice Lake Chiefs for the surrender of 1,951,000 Acres of Land," 5 November 1818, RG10, Vol. 1842/IT061.

George Paudash, 1856: LAC, "Surrender by the Mississagas of Rice, Mud and Skugog Lakes of the Islands in Rice Lake...," 24 June 1856, RG10, Vol. 1845/IT195.

26 Eagle with fish and perched eagle: Shutterstock.com

Marque des Mississauges, 1701: ANOM, Aix-en-Provence, "Ratification de la paix," 4 August 1701, Fonds des Colonies. Série C11A.

Correspondence générale, Canada, vol. 19, fol.41v – Tous droits réservés.

Shawanapenisse, 1798: LAC, "Deed of Conveyance of the Island of St. Joseph from the Chippawa Nation to His Majesty," 30 June 1798, RG10, Vol. 1841/IT035.

Peewaushemanogh, 1807: Library of Congress.

Wabinaship, 1792: LAC, "Deed of Feoffment - The Messissague Nation to His Britannick Majesty," 7 December 1792, RG10, Vol. 1840/IT005.

Chechalk, 1806: LAC, "Lease and Release from the Mississagua Indians," 6 September 1806, RG10, Vol. 1842/IT042.

Peter Jones, Eagle doodem, 1844: Peter Jones fonds, Victoria University Library (Toronto).

27   Sandhill crane, bowing, location call posture, and jumping: Shutterstock. com.

Marque des Sauteurs, chef Wabanqué, 1701: ANOM, Aix-en-Provence, "Ratification de la paix," 4 August 1701, Fonds des Colonies. Série C11A. Correspondence générale, Canada, vol. 19, fol.41v – Tous droits réservés.

Kewukance, 1836: LAC, "Provisional Agreement for the Surrender of the Manitoulin Islands...," 9 August 1836, RG10, Vol. 1844/IT120.

George Paudash, 1856: LAC, "Surrender by the Mississagas of Rice, Mud and Skugog Lakes of the Islands in Rice Lake...," 24 June 1856, RG10, Vol. 1845/IT195.

Toquish, 1800: LAC, "Copy of Deed No. 12, the surrender of part of the Huron Church Reserve," 11 September 1800, RG10, Vol. 1841/IT037.

28   Woodland caribou: Shutterstock.com.

Ningwason, 1798: LAC, "Conveyance of the Harbour of Penetanguishene...," 22 May [1798], RG10, Vol. 1840/IT017.

Ogaa, Witness, 1798: LAC, "Deed of Conveyance of the Island of St. Joseph from the Chippawa Nation to His Majesty," 30 June 1798, RG10, Vol. 1841/IT035.

Mesquescon, 1816: LAC, "The Chiefs of the Mississague Nation of Indians to His Majesty George III," 5 August 1816, RG10, Vol. 1842/IT051.

Maytoygwaan, 1819: LAC, "Provisional Agreement with the Chippawa Nation to Surrender lands," 9 March 1819, RG10, Vol. 1842/IT065.

Annamakance, 1819: LAC, "Deed of the Sale of lands on the North side of the River Thames or La Tranche in Upper Canada from the Chippewa Nation to Alexander McKee," 7 September 1796, RG10, Vol. 1840/IT021.

Channel Catfish: Shutterstock.com.

Kiskakons, 1701: ANOM, Aix-en-Provence, "Ratification de la paix," 4 August 1701, Fonds des Colonies. Série C11A. Correspondence générale, Canada, vol. 19, fol.41v – Tous droits réservés.

Mitchiwass, 1796: LAC, "Deed of the Sale of lands on the North side of the River Thames or La Tranche in Upper Canada from the Chippewa Nation to Alexander McKee," 7 September 1796, RG10, Vol. 1840/IT021.

Boquaquet, 1807: Treaty of Detroit, 1807, Library of Congress.

29   © Government of Ontario. Reproduced with the permission of the Archives of Ontario (2020). Archives of Ontario, Crown Lands, RG1-1v2p145-6. True copy of the original deed.

30   LAC, RG10, Vol. 27:16317.

31   © Government of Canada. Reproduced with the permission of LAC (2020). Image courtesy Canadian Institute for Historial Microreproductions.

32   LAC, "Indians of Lake Nipissing ...," 3 August 1848, RG1 E5, vol. 9:1168.

33   Census of Population of Lake Nipigon, 1 June 1850, LAC, Census Records, Department of Indian Affairs. Image courtesy Canadian Institute for Historical Microreproductions.

34   Pictograph A. Plate 60. Drawn by S. Eastman, USA, Printed in Color by P.S. Duval, Philadelphia, in Schoolcraft, *Historical and Statistical Information*, 416–17. Image courtesy Fisher Rare Book Library.

35   Ningwason, 1798: LAC, "Conveyance of the Harbour of Penetanguishene..," 22 May [1798], RG10, Vol. 1840/IT017.

Big Shilling, 1835: LAC, "Request for Payment," 3 June 1835, RG10 Vol. 58, 59705 © Government of Canada. Reproduced with the permission of LAC (2020).

David Abetung, 1857: © Government of Canada. Reproduced with the permission of LAC (2020).

Deer Sun Logo: Courtesy Chippewas of Rama First Nation

36   Marque du village, 1701: ANOM, Aix-en-Provence, "Ratification de la paix," 4 August 1701, Fonds des Colonies. Série C11A. Correspondence générale, Canada, vol. 19, fol.41v – Tous droits réservés.

Neace, 1787: LAC, "Indenture made at the Carrying Place, Head of the Bay of Quinty," 23 September 1787, RG10, Vol. 1841/IT040 © Government of Canada. Reproduced with the permission of LAC (2020).

Moses Pahdequong, 1831: Peter Jones fonds, Victoria University Library (Toronto).

James Smoke, 1837: LAC, "Record of council decision to pay John Sunday, Alderville," 28 December 1837, RG10, Vol. 67:64216. © Government of Canada. Reproduced with the permission of LAC (2020).

Index

aadizookaanag (sacred stories),
37–8, 42–3, 43, 53; creation story,
44; ideas of leadership in, 141; on
origin of doodem tradition, 41–2,
45–9, 59–60, 137; origin of humans,
45–6, 47; re-creation story, 44–6,
47; as source of law, 138
aanikeogimaa/-wag (second chief,
deputy): appointing of, 11, 86;
individuals serving as, 135, 142,
160–1, 167, 185–6, representatives
of doodemag, 154; role in
leadership, xvii, 111, 137, 139, 143
Abenaki, 42, 46
absolutism, 26
Act of Union (1840), 106
Adjutant, James, 81, 161, 185
adoption: adopting clans, 87;
into doodemag, 73–4, 85–90;
in European tradition, 57n47,
85; of French voyageurs, 87; of
outsiders, 18, 21, 95
Agawa Canyon, 22, 24

Ahwahquagezick, 187
Algonquian languages, xvn5, xviii
allegory: of alliance, 119; doodem
as, 38, 61, 112, 116, 117–18,
171; doodem souls as, 90; in
oral histories, xvi, 119, 136–7;
in reading of wampum, 109,
111, 112; use in constituting
governance, 105
alliances: Anishinaabe
understanding of, xxi, 8, 28–30,
68, 119; as basis for political
relationships, 26, 123; British
abandoning of, 177–8, 180;
ceremonies used in, 7, 91–2;
colonial performance of, xx, xxi;
comparison of Anishinaabe and
European understanding of,
29–30, 148, 178; as consensual
relationships, 11; between
doodemag, xv; examples of,
123; governance through, xvii,
xx, 29–30, 147–53; leading to

marriages, 82; metaphorical descriptions of, 91; renewal of, 6, 14, 151

American Revolution, xvi, 31, 86, 106, 144, 160, 163, 176

Americans: adoption into doodemag, 88; expansionism, 130; gift-giving, 97; treaties between Anishinabek and, 31, 35, 99n83, 170–1, 172, 183, 189–90

Amikwa council fire, 12, 16, 21–2

analogies: between Anishinaabe and settler governance, 19, 25, 27, 58, 120; need to avoid, 44

ancestors: other-than-human, 46, 59, 61, 110, 192, 198; remembrance of, 60, 75–6; ties to, 38, 55, 71, 72, 74–7

Anderson, Benedict, xvn6

Anderson, Captain, 166

André, Father Louys, 22

Angel, Michael, xivn3, 72n6

animals: human relation with, 43, 46, 54; responsibility towards, xviii, 27; stories about, 44–6, 52, 137. See also other-than-human beings and individual animals

animikii. See thunderbird

Anishinabek/Anishinaabeg: burial practices, 4, 14, 55–6, 59, 74–7; calendar, 3n2; Christianity, comparison of worldview with, xiiin1, 46, 50, 53–6, 62, 195; Haudenosaunee, alliances with, 103–4, 106, 149, 156, 162, 168; Haudenosaunee, conflict with, 21–2, 107, 114, 115, 148, 204; migration of, 37, 51, 69, 112, 121, 204; peoples identifying as, xv; in relation with Jesuits, 15; response to social and political change, 53; response to settler colonialism, 174–5; use of term, xivn4, xvn6; views of death, 74; Wendat, coexistence with, 14. See also governance; law; leadership; Mississauga-Anishinabek; Ojibwe; Potawatomis

Anishinaabe studies, xixn16, xxv

Anishinaabemowin: grammar of, xivn2, 45n11; importance of using, xxvii; speakers of, 17, 42, 138; as source of law, 175; terms in, 72–3, 84, 127; writing in alphabetic script, xxviin42

Aquinas, Thomas, 54

archival sources: bias in, 30, 132; as source of council fire locations, 123–5, 128–9; as sources for treaty-related documents, xxii; sources of doodem images, 30ff

Aristotle, 53, 57

Asimettic, 33

Assance, 81, 166–7

Assiginack, Francis, xvn6

Assiniboine, 89, 129

Atlantic Ocean, 51, 53

Babiizigindibe, 184

Batchewana Bay, 187

Bawaating, 8, 16, 21, 22, 32, 47, 95, 104, 107, 121, 122, 125, 157–8; 1671 general council at, 22–3, 29, 93n67; connection to Crane doodem, 59, 107–8, 112–13, 127–8, 139, 154, 162, 168; in doodem origin narrative, 51; establishment of, 108; fire-keeper for Lake Superior council fires, 117; French names for, 128; Jesuit visit to, 17, 94; leaders from, 12

beadwork, 67n71, 99, 152

Bear doodem, 16, 33, 47–8, 49, 71, 87, 126, 130, 159, 164–5, 184, 187, 189; characteristics of, 61, 62, 63n62, 64, 191

Beardmore, 89

beaver: hides, 5–6, 12, 23, 92, 148; Great Beaver, 59, 102, 116; in aadizookanag, 47, 113

Beaver doodem, 16, 21, 33, 59–60, 114, 130, 140, 144, 168; association with Parry Island, 106–7, 109–10, 162; connection to French River, 59, 102, 112, 116, 189; connection with Lake Nipissing, 189

Beishlag, John, 49n22

Benton-Banai, Edward, 63, 87–8, 190, 195–6

Berens, William (Chief), 79

Big Shilling, 166

Bigwind, James, 167

birch tree: as animate, 27; as material, 12, 13, 189

Birch Tree doodem, 82, 164–5, 167, 180, 187

bison: extirpation from Great Lakes, 192, 193–4

Bison doodem, 164–5, 180

Bkejwanong, 69, 125, 173

Blackbird, Andrew, xvn6

blood: as European political metaphor, 57–8, 87

Bond Head, Sir Francis, 94

Borden, Robert, 189

Borrows, John, xviin12, xixn16, xxvi, 137

Borrows, Lindsay, 45n11

Bradstreet, Colonel, 158

Bradstreet's Treaty, 146

Brant, Joseph, 33

British: adoption into doodemag, 89; Anishinaabe business with, 18; attempts to relocate council fires, 100; comparison of polities to Anishinaabe, 120–1; concern with authorship in treaty documents, 34–6; gifting of clothing, 96–7; imposition of Upper Canada constitution, 105–6; misunderstanding of Anishinaabe governance, 28–9; performance of Anishinaabe protocols, 92–3; treaties with Anishinabek, 98, 101, 151, 172. *See also* Treaty of Niagara *and individual treaties*

British colonial officials: participation in ratification of ogimaawag, 12

Bruce Peninsula, 53, 67n71, 182

Bruchac, Marge, xxvi

Brulé, Etienne, 147

Bugone-giisk (Older and Younger), 184–5

bulrushes, 13

burial practices, 4, 59, 74–5; connection to landscape, 74; as expression of relationship with ancestors, 77; protection of burial grounds, 56; re-burial, 14, 55, 76–7; Wendat, 4n3

Burton, Antoinette, 5n6

Cabojijak, 188

Caldwell, Sir John, 98

Callière, Louis-Hector de, 95

calumet ceremony, xviiin14, 91

Calumet Island, 126

Cameron, Duncan, 70–1, 75, 80

caribou: extirpation from Great Lakes, 192–3

Caribou doodem, xxv, 52, 62, 64, 71, 76, 82, 104, 115, 140, 166, 180, 181, 187, 188, 189, 191; association with Mnjikaning, 107, 110, 115, 139, 154–6, 162, 164, 167, 168; transformation into Deer, 193

Case, William, 185

Catfish doodem, 49, 61, 62, 83, 84, 126, 140, 167, 181, 189

ceremonies: alliance, 24, 91–2, 97, 137, 147; calumet, xviii*n*14, 91; doodemag acquired through, 73, 86; jiisakaan (shake tent), 88; memorial/re-burial, 4, 12–13; missionaries' disruption of, 196–7; naming, 74, 87–8; as performances of law and philosophy, 19; in treaty councils, 91; as ways of making relation, 26, 148. *See also* prise-de-possession

Chabacy, Maya, xxvii

Champlain, Samuel de, 11, 25, 56, 147–9

Charlevoix, Pierre, 56, 77, 81

Chechalk, 161, 164, 177

Chechogwas, 33

Chequamagon, 76, 112, 117, 117*n*20, 122, 171

Chicoutimi, 77

children, 6, 13, 22, 121, 145, 195, 198; adoption of, 57*n*47, 89; education of, 71–2; of non-Anishinaabe fathers, 73, 80, 85–7

Chippewa of Nawash First Nation, 56

Chippewas, 31, 77, 158, 181

Chippewas of Rama, xxvi, 166, 169, 193

Christianity: Anishinaabe conversion to, 8, 43, 81, 85, 161, 167, 185, 192; comparison to Anishinaabe worldview, xiii*n*1, 46, 50, 53–6, 62, 195; connection to settler colonialism, 172–3; effects on marriage practices, 173, 195; impact on doodem expression, 39, 86, 191–2, 196–7; Methodism, 82, 163, 185, 191; missionaries, 5, 17, 52, 121, 135, 167, 181, 185, 192, 195. *See also* Jesuits

Chute, James, 187

Civil War, American, 35

Claus, William, 177

Clench, J.B., 35–6

clothing: ceremonial, 98, 153, 192; coats, 96, 99; connection to doodemag, 66–7; dance regalia, 67; gifting of, 94–6, 100; headdresses, 12, 94, 95–6, 98, 99; moccasins, 13, 67*n*71, 99, 152; in museum collections, 98; neck ornaments, 12, 94, 99; of new ogimaawag, 11–12, 94

Coldwater Road Allowance, 109*n*12

Confederation of Canada, 92*n*63, 173

Constitution Act (1791), 106

constitutionalism, Anishinaabe, 38; link between doodem and council fires, 133; need for renewal, 105; performance of, 105, 108; role of narratives in, 112; role of oratory, 106–7

Copway, George, 42, 135–6, 172, 192, xv*n*6

Corbiere, Alan Ojig, xxii–xxiii, xxiv–xxv, xxvi–xxvii, 93*n*64

council fires: as "where" of Anishinaabe governance, xxvi, 125, 133, 203; as Anishinaabe polities, 39; British attempts to relocate, 100; centrality to Anishinaabe governance, 17–18, 121, 130; common and general councils, 18–19, 29, 39, 111, 136, 150, 151, 153–4, 168, 181; connections between, 11, 16–17, 79; different roles within alliance, 111; establishment of new, 38, 105–6, 107, 113–18, 129, 168; extinguishing of, 156, 169, 176, 179–80, 182; multiple doodemag within, 154–6, 169; non-exclusive and non-hierarchical, 119, 150; ratification of leadership, 10–11; recognition of British individuals by, 98; responsibility for land, 19; seasonally occupied, 122; sites where law is put into action, 136; treatment of colonial governments as, xxi, 94, 179–80; uncovering of, 107, 157, 168

council of women, xvii, 80, 105, 138, 141–6, 159; role in land sale agreements, 143

council of young men/warriors, xvii, 38–9, 105, 142

Covenant Chain, 146, 149, 151, 157–9, 162, 188

Crane doodem, 16, 21, 49, 51, 52, 114, 115, 126, 127, 130, 144, 145, 146, 159, 171, 180, 184, 186, 187, 189; characteristics, 62, 64, 115, 140, 191; connection with Bawaating, 59, 107–8, 112–13, 117–18, 127–8, 139, 156, 162, 168; connection with Rice Lake, 156

Crayfish doodem, 62, 140

Credit River council fire, 81, 86, 103–5, 110–12, 114, 115, 125, 129, 156–65, 156n43, 169, 179, 185, 194;

1805 common council at, 142; association with Eagle doodem, 107, 114–15, 139, 154–6, 177; extinguishing of, 156, 169, 176; general council hosted by, 103; land cessation, 154; relocation of community, 176, 181–2; responsible for external affairs, 111. *See also* Mississaugas of the Credit River

Dakota, 83, 90, 129; conflict with Anishinaabe, 83–4, 130, 184; intermarriage with Anishinaabe, 83

dances, 8–10, 67, 199

Debassige, Lewis, xxiv–xxv, xxviii, 16n43, 79n30

Deer doodem, 66, 193–4, 195

Delawares, 33, 180–1

Deloria Jr., Vine, xiiin1, 46n16

Detroit, 32, 98, 145–6, 156–9, 196

Dewdney, Selwyn, 65

dibaajimowinan (histories), 43n7, 112

doodem: as "who" of Anishinaabe governance, xxvi; acquired through dream, 186, 196–7; adoption of settler symbols as, 88–9; as assertion of responsibility, 80–1; as category of kinship, xiii–xiv, 38, 48, 57–8, 60; as central to political system, xv–xvi, xvii, 60, 113, 118, 125, 130, 187; comparison to Scottish clans, 71; connection to territory, 46, 105, 112, 114–18, 192–3, 202; connection to the sacred, 58–9; earliest European-authored sources on, 44; exogamy, xvii, 79, 80, 81–2, 125, 143, 194–6, 203;

expressed in clothing, xxv, 66–7, 99; as metaphor of physical and personal characteristics, 61–2, 64; origins of, 41–9, 51–2, 59–60, 112, 113, 116, 168; patrilineal descent of, 48, 72–3, 196–7; reflection of metaphysical relationship, 88; related to particular roles, 113–14, 191; resurgence of, 199–200; survival of, 39; as system of categories, 67–9, 112; taboo against hunting, 65–6; as word, xivn2, xv. *See also* souls: doodem souls
doodem images: adaption due to ecological change, 193–4; Anishinaabe understanding of, 30; as articulation of political and legal categories, xiii, xvii, 39; British concern with, 30, 35–6; changes in representation, 32–4, 132; form of, meanings, 139–41, 188; French understanding of, 25, 48, 131; on grave markers, 56–7; identifying leadership, xvii, 167; material description of, 33; sequence and frequency on documents, 108–9, 111, 116; shift from using to X-marks, 36; sources of, 30; time taken in inscribing, 109n12; use in place of signatures, xiii, xvii, xxii, 24–5, 30–2, 133; women's, 143–4
Duchesneau, James, 128–9
Duck doodem, 160

eagle: connection to thunderbird, 114–15; decorations of, 9
Eagle doodem, 62, 82, 127, 139–40, 152, 158, 160, 161, 162, 164, 168, 180, 181, 191; as adopting doodem,

87, 88; association with Credit River, 32, 107, 109, 110, 114–15, 139, 154–6, 163, 177
Elgin, Lord, 94, 98
epidemics, xxi, 19, 161, 163, 204; different impact on Anishinabek and Iroquoian-speaking peoples, 20–1
Erie people, 20, 21

family relations: Anishinaabe, structure of, 72–3, 87, 132, 139, 164, 203; European, 27, 57; as key to alliance, 71, 72, 92. *See also* children; marriage practices
farming: adoption of by Indigenous Peoples, 35, 163, 167; imposed by settler colonialism, 172, 192–3
Farrell Racette, Sherry, xxvi–xxvii
Ferris, Neal, 178n22
Finger Lakes district, 107
fire: as Anishinaabe political metaphor, xxvi, 107, 118–23, 150, 179–80, 203; used as metaphor by Haudenosaunee and Wendat, 118. *See also* council fires
fishing, 3n2, 18, 22, 121–2, 125, 154, 174, 175–6, 177, 182
flood: in aadizookaanag, 44–5, 47, 50
Fort William First Nation, 87
Foster, Andrew, 98
Four Directions, 38, 70, 72, 90, 102
Fox, 78, 95, 129
French: adoption of, 87–8; in alliances, 6n11, 12, 91, 94, 101, 147, 171; comparison of political structures to Anishinaabe, 28–9, 100, 120–1; connection to Bear doodem, 61; emissaries at Bawaating, 23, 93n67; gift-

giving, 12, 92, 95, 97; kinship traditions, 57n47; military reliance on Anishinabek, 130–1; names used for Anishinaabe groups, 127–8, 130; performance of Anishinaabe protocols, 92–3; prise-de-possession ritual, 23–6, 28, 92, 93n67, 113; recognition of ogimaawag, 171; understanding of Indigenous polities, 25–6, 28, 48, 80, 84–5

French River, 114; connection to Beaver doodem, 59, 102, 112, 116, 189

Freud, Sigmund, xvin7

games and contests, 10, 15, 17, 22

Georgian Bay, xxv, 59, 75, 107, 109, 139; council fires around, 3, 14

gichi-Anishinabek (councillors), xvii, 11, 39, 48, 111, 139, 154, 163–4, 167, 179, 189

gichi-ogimaa/-wag, 11, 138–9, 180

Gidigaa Migizi (Doug Williams), xxvi

gift-giving: antiquity of practice, 94; between colonial powers and Anishinabek, 23, 28, 91–3, 100–1, 136–7, 147–9, 178; as contract, 90; description of, 5–7, 12–14; as economic function of, 15–17; expression of duty of care, 90–1; as mark of good leaders, 139; meanings communicated through, xxvii, 7, 100–1; offering land to newcomers as, 176; as part of law, xxiv; relationships maintained through, 15, 28, 92, 102; speeches on, 91, 95, 100–1

Goose doodem, 164

governance, Anishinaabe: aadizookaanag as foundation of, 38; adaptability of, 161; consultative, 136, 141; continuity of, 129, 168, 180–1, 187, 189; decentralized nature of, xvii, 17; defined through doodem, 37, 117; disruption of, 197; effect of settler colonialism on, 39, 137, 169, 182–8, 190–1; families as foundational constructs of, 72; French and British misunderstanding of, 28–9; interference in, 171, 203; marriage as model for, 90; metaphors used in, 111–12; non-hierarchical nature of, 38, 139; recognition of by colonial and settler governments, 136; revitalization of, 39, 198, 200; sources for, 138n6; types of councils within, 17–18

Grant, Jasper, 152–3

Great Hare, 41, 45, 57, 59, 137. See also Hare doodem; Nanabozhoo

Great Lakes Research Alliance for the Study of Aboriginal Cultures (GRASAC), xxii–xxiv, xxvi, 93n64, 96n76

Great Peace of Montreal. See Peace of Montreal

Grizzly Bear doodem, 89

Hallowell, Irving, xiiin3, 79

Hare doodem, 58, 59, 66, 112

Haudenosaunee confederacy, xiv, xviii, xxiii, 144, 201. alliances with Anishinabek, 103–4, 106, 123, 149, 156, 162, 168; alliances with European powers, 149, 160;

Anishinaabe diplomacy with, 91, 108, 111; attendance at 1840 Credit River council, 103; conflict with Anishinabek, 21–2, 107–8, 114, 115, 148, 204; effects of epidemics on, 20–1; expansion to north side of Lake Ontario, 21; gifting of clothing, 96; Great Law, 108; intermarriage with Anishinabek, 84–85; symbols used by, 107, 110–11, 115, 118, 149. *See also* Six Nations
Havard, Gilles, 7n11
Henfrey, Benjamin, 33
Henry, Alexander, 95
Herkimer, Lawrence, 86–7
Heron doodem, 124, 126
Hewitt, Jeffrey, xxvi
Hickerson, Harold, 4n3
hunting, 16, 18, 65, 74, 81, 164, 174, 176, 189; decisions related to, 105, 151, 153; migration for, 121; qualification for leadership, 138, 139
Hurons. *See* Wendat
hydrology, 50–1, 52–3

Illinois people, 42, 46, 129
Inashiquay, 143–4
Indian Affairs, Offices of, 35, 76, 77, 96, 169, 171, 178, 188, 189
Indigenous Studies, xixn16
indinaakonigewin, xvii, 138
Iroquoian language communities, xviii, 83; effects of epidemics on, 20–1
ishkode. *See* fire
Iskigamizige-giizis, 87

James Bay, 14, 18, 121
Jarvis, Samuel, 76

Jesuits: as guests at 1642 gathering, 4–5, 15, 93, 94; inclusion in social relationships, 15; invited to Bawaating, 17, 94; observation of Anishinaabe culture, 25, 77, 78, 95; understanding of souls, 54. *See also* Charlevoix, Pierre; Lalemant, Charles; Lalemant, Jérome; Le Jeune, Paul; Nicolas, Louis; Râle, Sebastian; Vimont, Barthélemy
Jogues, Isaac (Jesuit), 17
Johnson, Sir William, 34–5, 96, 151, 156–9
Johnston, Basil, 62, 63, 66n67, 123, 191, 197
Johnston, Darlene, xixn16, xxii, xxiv, xxvi, xxvii, 55, 56, 67n71, 199–200; on death, 74
Joncaire, Philippe-Thomas de, 129–31
Jones, Augustus, 86, 185
Jones, John, 180
Jones, Peter (Kakewaquonaby), xvn6, xxvi, 17–19, 48, 66, 81–2, 113, 135, 150, 163, 172, 191–2; adoption into Eagle doodem, 86, 185; on land transactions, 153–4; as leader, 161, 180, 184, 185–6; translation of Musquakie's speech, 104–5
Jones, William, 48, 127

Kakewaquonaby. *See* Jones, Peter (Kakewaquonaby)
Kauanui, J. Kēhaulani, xxi, 201
Keating, John, 187
Kee Sap, 33
Kegg, Maude (Elder), 66
Kettle Point and Sauble communities, 143
kettles, 6, 10, 100–1

King George III, 150; King George
    medals, 96, 97, 99, 158–9
Kingfisher doodem, 71; origin
    of, 83
Kingston, 179–80
Kinouchespiriri, 21
kinship relations: with animals,
    63–4; as both endogenous and
    exogenous, 79; changes in, 195,
    198; comparison of Anishinaabe
    and Western conceptions, xiv,
    26–7, 39, 57–8, 79; with doodem
    beings, 48; in European social
    sciences, xvin7; expression of
    bimaadiziwin through, 102;
    problems with concept, 68, 69n75;
    temporality of, 38
Kitchi Negou, 101
Krieghoff, Cornelius, 99

La Potherie, Sieur de Bacqueville de,
    24n64, 32, 84, 132
Labelle, Kathryn, 14
Lac Courte Oreilles, 7n11, 87
Lake Huron, 8, 99, 109, 116, 122, 126,
    145, 167; council fires around, 3,
    14, 21, 114, 168, 188
Lake Michigan, 78, 126
Lake Nipigon, 70–1
Lake Nipissing, 60, 116, 121, 189;
    1642 gathering at, 3–17. See also
    Nipissings
Lake Ontario, 21, 32, 86, 107, 108,
    114, 142, 154, 156, 160, 177
Lake Simcoe, 32, 76, 81, 103, 104, 11.
    See also Mnjikaning
Lake St. Clair, 145, 181
Lake Superior, 8, 17, 21, 104, 118,
    122, 168, 170, 177
Lalemant, Charles, 121

Lalemant, Jérome, 5–12, 15–16, 18–9,
    22, 43, 76–7, 94, 121; breach of
    protocol by, 7–8
land sale agreements, 18, 23, 39;
    British monopoly on, 150–1; by
    Credit River council fire, 162, 165;
    doodem images on, xvii, xxii, 34,
    108, 141–3; negotiated by common
    councils, 150, 153; provisions
    for in Proclamation of 1763, 34,
    133; treaties as more than, 101;
    women's role in, 141–4
law, Anishinaabe, 12; aadizookanag
    as foundation of, 38, 137–8; and
    alliances, 37, 90–1, 92, 143, 176;
    of belonging, 87; borrowings
    from other sources, xviii; colonial
    understanding and performance
    of, xxi, 100, 101, 133; comparison
    to European traditions, xviii,
    xxvii; concept of personhood in,
    27, 53–4; continuity of, 20, 22,
    129; disruption of, 171, 173, 175,
    177, 187–8, 197–8, 202; doodemag
    as source and expression of,
    xiii–xiv, xvii, 61, 113, 183, 192;
    gifts as expression of, xxiv, 91,
    93; language as source of, 175;
    mutual nature of, 11, 135–6; and
    oral tradition, xviin12, xix, 137–8;
    other-than-human beings in, 27,
    45, 50
Le Jeune, Paul, 55, 56, 125–7
leadership, Anishinaabe:
    aadizookaanag as source of,
    141; anchored in genealogy, 76,
    143; Anishinaabe and French
    understandings of, 28; changes
    under settler colonialism, 184–7;
    connection to different doodemag,

61–2, 64, 88, 113, 139–41, 167; non-hierarchical, 139; participation of women in, 38, 141–6; recognition of, 11, 100, 171
Lee, Damien, 87
Lenape Nation. *See* Delawares
Lévi-Strauss, Claude, xvin7, 37
Littlehales, E.B., 56–7
Loon doodem, 34, 49, 70–1, 117, 127, 168, 171, 189; characteristics, 61–2, 64; connection to wampum, 61–2, 117
Louis XIV, 25–6
Lower Canada, 106, 178–9

Mahiingan, 21–2, 139
Mahmahwegeahego, 143
Manatowabi, Edna, 71n5
Manicheanism, 53–4
manidoog, 10, 54, 91; underwater, 60, 89, 140
Manitoulin Island, xxv, xxviin42, 16, 22, 53, 79n30, 104, 158, 178; association with Whitefish doodem, 106, 162
marriage practices: as alliance, 71–2, 78–85, 90; between Anishinaabe and non-Anishinaabe, 70, 72, 82–4, 86–7; changes under settler colonialism, 173; creation of connections between council fires, 79, 124; doodem exogamy, 29, 79, 80, 81–2, 125, 143, 194–6, 203, xvii; effects of settler colonialism on, 194–6; marrying out, 11, 13, 143, 145; as micro-alliances, 29; patrilocality, 78; polygamy, 80–1; strengthening alliances, 14, 38, 143
marten: decorations of, 9

Marten doodem, xxii, 90, 189, 200; as adopting doodem, 87; characteristics, 64, 88
McDonnell, Michael, 26, 37, 131
McKay, Alex, xxvii
medals, xxiii, xxv, xxvii, 75, 98, 99, 158, 170; as gifts from colonial officials, 12, 97, 99
medicine, Anishinaabe, 13, 15, 75, 80, 88, 199
Megis, 187
Menissinownninne, 98
Menominee, 101, 129
Merman doodem, 83–4, 189
Michabous. *See* Nanabozhoo
Michilimackinac, 34, 42, 46–7, 98, 158; connection to Hare doodem, 112
Midewiwin, 50n24, 65, 88
Migwans, Mikinaak (Crystal), xxvi
Mille Lac, 83
Miller, Cary, 7n15, 15, 143, 146
Miller, James, 29n74
Mills, Aaron, xixn16
Mindameness, 76
mining, 172, 188
Mino-bimaadiziwin (living life well by following Anishinaabe teachings and laws), also Anishinaabe-bimaadiziwin (the Anishinaabe way of life), 72, 101–2
Miskouensa, 95
Mississagi, 21
Mississauga-Anishinabek, 48, 86, 124, 154; agreements with British, 142, 144, 154, 159; impact of War of 1812 on, 163; provision of territory to Six Nations, 160; as signatories, 32, 114, 141, 154, 192. *See also* Mississaugas of the Credit River

Mississaugas of the Credit River, 81, 156–65, 169, 176–82, 200

Mnidoo Minising. *See* Manitoulin Island

Mnjikaning, 32, 69, 109, 111, 121, 129, 166–9, 181; association with Caribou doodem, 32, 107, 110, 115, 129, 139, 154–6, 162, 167, 168; fish weirs, 125

Mohawks, 6n11, 76, 148, 149

Montreal, 51, 76. *See also* Peace of Montreal

moose: hunting of, 16, 122

Moose doodem, 49, 71, 90, 127, 168

Moravians, 33, 181

Morrisseau, Norval, 89

museums, xxvi, 9, 98; acquisition of Anishinaabe items, 93, 153

muskrat: in aadizookaanag, 45, 62, 137

Muskrat doodem, 62, 115

Musquakie, 52, 76, 103–11, 118, 122, 166–7, 180, 187

Naishenum, 162

Nanabozhoo, 43n7, 45n11, 58, 59, 158; acquisition of fire, 118–19; as establisher of doodem tradition, 51–2; recreation of the world, 45–6, 47, 50

Nanakonagos, 89

Nanegishkung, Joseph, 167

Nanegishkung, Thomas, 166–7

Nanibush, Wanda, 199

Naokwegijig-Corbiere, Mary Ann, xxvii

Nathanena, 33

nation: French use of term, 10, 18, 25; misapplication of term to

Anishinaabe polities, 19, 119–20, 124, 126

Nawac, 33

Nawahjegezhegwabe. *See* Sawyer, Joseph

Nebanagoching, 98–9, 187

Neutral, 20, 21

Niagara, 20, 98, 144, 150, 156, 158–60, 176, 177. *See also* Treaty of Niagara

Nicolas, Louis, 58, 66, 127

Nicolet, Jean de, 126–7

Nipissings, 12, 21, 74, 116, 188–9; host of 1642 gathering, 4, 14–15, 18, 74; physical movements of, 18–19

Odawa Minising. *See* Manitoulin Island

ogimaa/-wag (chiefs): assertion of treaty rights, xx–xxi; as civil leadership of council fires, xvii; comparison to French political roles, 28; confirmation of new, 11; doodemag of, 32, 154, 160, 168, 171; gichi-ogimaa, 11, 31, 138–9; marriage practices, 80–1; ogimaakwe, 141, 143–4; qualifications for, 138–9; recognition of with gifts, 94–5; roles of, 18, 105, 111, 125, 160–1; treatment of colonial officials as, 94, 100

Ojibway Island, 3n1

Ojibwe, 58, 79, 88, 124, 184, xxv. *See also* Anishinaabe; Chippewas; Warren, William

Omushkego peoples, 14

Onkwehon:we, xix. *See also* Haudenosaunee Confederacy

oral tradition, xxivn29, 49, 64, 89, 108, 109; Anishinaabe law embedded in, xvii, xviin12, 137–8; disruption of, 205; preservation of evidence in, 88, 167, 189, 197, 202; re-creation story, 44–5, 47; role in Anishinaabe society, xix, 197; use of allegory in, xxvi, 119, 136–7

Oshawana, 96, 99

Oskabewis, 76

other-than-human beings: in Anishinaabe law, 27; extension of personhood to, xviii, 40; human descent from, 47–8, 50, 192, 197, 198; human relationship with, xiv, 27, 46, 63–4, 114, 175, 194, 203; souls of, 54; as term, xivn3; transformation between human and, 64–5

Ottawa River, 19, 56, 116, 121, 124, 126

Ottawa-Anishinabek, 31, 47, 78, 124, 158

otter: in aadizookanag, 47; decorations of, 9

Otter doodem, 9, 67n71, 81, 82, 126, 142, 164, 166, 167, 177, 181, 191, 200

Ouiebitchiouan, 22

Owen Sound, 56

Pagahmegabow, James, 187

Parry Island, 3n1, 75, 187; association with Beaver doodem, 107, 162

Paudaush, Robert, 52

Peace of Montreal, 24, 32, 84, 95, 116, 154, 194

Peace of Paris, 133

Peawamah, 141, 144

Peers, Laura, xxvi

Perrot, Nicolas, 4n3–4, 16, 41, 61, 80, 91n61, 115–17, 189; description of, 42; as interpreter, 23–4, 32;

as source on doodem tradition, 44–5, 49–50, 58–9, 137; on village life, 122

Peshinaniqua (Margaret Ball), 145

Pewash, 144

Phillips, Ruth B., xxii–xxiii, xxvi, 93n64, 98

Pijart, Father, 7, 17

Pike doodem, 62, 116, 126, 140, 154, 164, 168, 189

pine tree: symbol of Haudenosaunee confederacy, 110–11, 115

Pine, Fred Sr., 22n59

pipes: decoration on, 10, 94; as diplomatic gifts, 6, 93, 94, 101, 152; use in ceremonies, 19, 80, 91, 105, 157

Plover doodem, 186

Polk, James, 189

Pontiac's War, 95, 150, 156

Potawatomis, 17, 31, 78, 124, 129, 158

Pouchot, Pierre, 74

primitivism, xvin7, xxiii

prise-de-possession ritual, 23–6, 28, 92, 93n67, 113

Proclamation of 1763, 133

Queen Victoria, 66, 86, 163, 180

Quenepenon (Quenebenaw, Kineubenae, Golden Eagle), 142, 160–1, 164, 177

quillwork, 11–12, 13, 94, 152

Radin, Paul, 51–2

Radisson, Pierre, 7n11, 128n42

Râle, Sebastian, 41, 42; as source of aadizookanag, 46–7, 50, 59

Rama, 52, 82, 103, 164, 178, 187. See also Chippewas of Rama; Mnjikaning

Raymbaut, Father, 7
reserves/reservations, 39, 43, 52, 122, 164, 167–8, 174, 193, 195, 197–8; creation of, 161, 166, 173, 190
residential schools, xix, xx, 39, 175, 188, 197–8
Rice Lake, 32, 82, 86, 116, 152, 156, 180
Rickard, Jolene, xxvii
Robinson-Huron treaty, 94, 109, 188, 200
Robinson, William Beverly, 98–9, 109n12
rock art, xiv, 22, 132
Rogers, Mary Black, 101
Ruffed Grouse doodem, xxii
Rush-Bagot Agreement, 190

Sagard, Gabriel, 25
Saginaw Bay, 145, 159
Sakis, 78, 158
Sault Ste. Marie. See Bawaating
Savignon, 147
Sawyer, Joseph, 161, 164, 180
Schenck, Theresa, xvin7
Schneider, David, 69n75
Schoolcraft, Henry Rowe, 51, 186, 189–90
Scots, 85; comparison of clan system to doodem, 71
Scott, Duncan Campbell, 189
settler colonialism, xxiii, xvn6; Anishinaabe response to, xxi, 100, 174–5; characteristics of, 172, 202–3; dispossession resulting from, 176, 180; domination of historical accounts, xix; effect on Anishinaabe governance, 39, 87, 134, 137, 169, 175, 182–8, 197; effects on marriage practices,

194–6; expansion of, 43, 161, 167, 173; imposition of new geography/ecology, 122, 192–4; logic of elimination, xx, 201
Seven Years' War, xvi, 30, 133, 149, 150, 156
Shawanaga, 75
Shilling, Thomas, 76
Shingauch, 101
Shingwaukonce, 98–9, 184, 186, 196
Simcoe, John Graves, 57, 177
Simpson, Leanne Betasamosake, 71n5
Sinade, 33
Sinagos, Chief, 78
Siouan language communities, xviii, 83, 84
Sioux, 78, 123, 164n68
Six Nations, 104–5, 110, 141, 144, 160, 169; relocation of Credit River community to, 176, 182
smallpox, 20
souls: of adopted Anishinabek, 88; comparison of Anishinaabe and Christian beliefs, 53–6; connection to landscape, 59; doodem souls, 38, 43, 48, 55, 61, 64–5, 90, 191, 196–7; possessed by non-human beings, xiv, 27, 40, 45; plurality of, 55–6; possessed by human remains, 12, 55–6, 74–5
St. Croix, 83
St. Joseph's Island, 100, 178
St. Lusson, Sieur de, 23–5, 42, 93n67, 113
Stark, Heidi Kiiwetinepinesiik, xixn16, xxvi, 118, 162
Stony. See Assiniboine
stories. See aadizookaanag (sacred stories); dibaajimowinan
Sturgeon doodem, 64, 168

Sucker doodem, 47–8, 168
Sunday, John, 192
Swan doodem, 127, 159
sweetgrass (wiingashk), 8n18, 13

Talon, Jean, 23, 24n64, 25, 28
Tecumseh, 96
Tessouat, 56
thunderbird: connection to eagle, 114–15; decorations of, 25, 98
Thunderbird doodem, 21, 60, 96, 98, 114, 140, 168
Toronto, 116, 128, 156, 157, 160, 177, 179–80
Tory, Alvin, 145
totem, xvin7. See doodem
treaties: between Americans and Anishinabek, 31, 35, 170–1, 172, 183, 189–90; Anishinaabe understanding of, xxi, 119; different understandings of, 23, 30, 101, 132; as means of facilitating white settlement, xx; as more than land purchases, 101. See also individual treaties
Treaty at the Rapids of the Miami, 31
treaty documents: British concern with authorship, 34–6; order of signatures on, 31–2, 111, 160; use as sources, xvi, xxii, 30–1, 108–9, 128, 132–3, 154, 166, 168; women's signatures in, 142–4
Treaty of Fond du Lac, 170–1, 183, 185
Treaty of Fort McIntosh, 31
Treaty of Niagara, 38, 133, 149, 151, 158, 162
Treuer, Anton, 72n7, 83n41, 184, 185n33
Truth and Reconciliation Commission of Canada, xix–xx

Tubinaquay, 86, 185
Tugwaugaunay, 76, 112–13, 117–18, 122

Upper Canada, 75, 163, 169, 173, 178, 179, 192, 194; creation of, 106; government of, 57, 86, 94, 142, 162

Valentine, Rand, xxvii, 74n8
village: misapplication of term to Anishinaabe polities, 120–1
Vimont, Barthélemy, 6–7, 7n11
Vizenor, Gerald, 190n41

Wabakayne, 159–60
Wabanip, 160–1, 164
Wabbicomicott, 144, 146, 156–9
Wabenaki. See Abenaki
Wabenose, 86, 162, 185
Wabionishkoubi, 152
Wacanoghaqua, 141, 144
Wahbahdick, Thomas, 181n27
Walpole Island, 96, 195
wampum, xviiin14, xxiii, xxv, xxvii, 101, 152–3; Ayenwahta Wampum Belt, 108; belts as constitutions, xxvi, 105, 106, 181; connection to Loon doodem, 61–2, 117; given as gifts, 5, 7n11, 95, 148, 152–3, 157, 158; as mnemonic device, 6n11, 91, 110; in museum collections, 93; role in governance and law, 92; use as payment, 10; use of visual synecdoche, 108; used in decoration, 9, 12, 98; used to recount history, 103–5, 114
Wapanatashiqua (Wapamonessychoqua), 141, 144–6, 159

War of 1812, xx, 96, 103, 161, 181, 186; effect on Mississauga-Anishinabek, 163; period following, 35, 100, 166, 173, 175, 178, 183

Warren, William, xvn6, xxvi, 41, 42, 48–9, 61, 63, 112, 113, 117, 122, 172, 184–5; on breakup of doodem system, 170–1, 183; on doodemag, 58, 84, 127; on doodem names, 127; on origins of doodemag, 48–9, 60

Wasson, 146

Wausauksing. See Parry Island

weapons: as gifts, 91, 100, 101, 153; as works of art, 9–10

Weggishgomin, 161, 163

Wendake, 3

Wendat, xviii, 6n11, 129, 158; at 1642 Lake Nipissing gathering, 10; Anishinaabe alliances with, 4–5, 15, 106, 123, 147–9; Anishinaabe conflict with, 76; Anishinaabe diplomacy with, 91; breakup of Confederacy, 21, 106; burial customs, 4n3; co-existence with Anishinabek, 14, 74; deaths due to smallpox, 20; intermarriage with Anishinabek, 82, 84; relation with Jesuits, 15, 17; understanding of souls, 55n39; use of fire as symbol, 118

Wenro, 20, 21

Weskarini, 129

Whetung, Madeline, 13

White Sucker doodem, 47–8

White, Richard, 37

Whitefeather, Vernon, 83n41

Whitefish doodem: association with Manitoulin Island, 106, 109, 162

wiindigoo/-g (winter cannibal monster(s)), 66

Wilmott, Cory, xxii, xxv–xxvi, 186, 196

Wisdom, Charles, 77

Witgen, Michael, 26, 28, 37, 83n44, 119, 124, 131

Wolf doodem, 90, 127, 181; origin of, 83–4

Wolfe, Patrick, xx, 201

women: as arrangers of marriages, 85; connections made through marriage, 78–9; construction of buildings by, 6, 12; dances of, 9; doodemag distinct from husbands, 48, 143; expression of mino-bimaadiziwin, 102; impact of settler colonialism on, 146, 173; invisibility in archival record, 146; involvement in land sales, 141–4; memorial functions performed by, 12–13, 15, 102; relation to natal communities, 11, 13, 21; roles in governance, 11, 38–9, 80–1, 136, 138, 144, 159; Sky Woman, 44; work in making gifts, 99. See also council of women

Yellowhead, William. See Musquakie

Young, George, 167

2020 Heidi Bohaker, *Doodem and Council Fire: Anishinaabe Governance through Alliance*
Carolyn Strange, *The Death Penalty and Sex Murder in Canadian History*
2019 Harry W. Arthurs, *Connecting the Dots: The Life of an Academic Lawyer*
Eric H. Reiter, *Wounded Feelings: Litigating Emotions in Quebec, 1870–1950*
2018 Philip Girard, Jim Phillips, and R. Blake Brown, *A History of Law in Canada, Volume One: Beginnings to 1866*
Suzanne Chiodo, *The Class Actions Controversy: The Origins and Development of the Ontario Class Proceedings Act*
2017 Constance Backhouse, *Claire L'Heueux-Dubé: A Life*
Dennis G. Molinaro, *An Exceptional Law Section 98 and the Emergency State, 1919–1936*
2016 Lori Chambers, *A Legal History of Adoption in Ontario, 1921–2015*
Bradley Miller, *Borderline Crime: Fugitive Criminals and the Challenge of the Border, 1819–1914*
James Muir, *Law, Debt, and Merchant Power: The Civil Courts of Eighteenth-Century Halifax*
2015 Barry Wright, Eric Tucker, and Susan Binnie, eds., *Canadian State Trials Volume 4: War Measures and the Repression of Radicalism, 1914–39*
David Fraser, *Honorary Protestants: A Socio-Legal History of the Jewish School Question in Montreal*
C. Ian Kyer, *A Thirty Years War: The Failed Public/Private Partnership that Spurred the Creation of the Toronto Transit Commission, 1891–1921*
Dale Gibson, *Law, Life, and Government at Red River: Settlement and Governance, 1812–1872*
2014 Christopher Moore, *The Court of Appeal for Ontario 1792–2013*
Paul Craven, *Petty Justice: Low Law and the Sessions System in Charlotte County, New Brunswick, 1785–1867*
Thomas G.W. Telfer, *Ruin and Redemption: The Struggle for a Canadian Bankruptcy Law, 1867–1919*
Dominique Clément, *Equality Deferred: Sex Discrimination and British Columbia's Human Rights Code, 1953–1984*
2013 Roy McMurtry, *Memoirs and Reflections*
Charlotte Grey, *The Massey Murder: A Maid, Her Master, and the Trial that Shocked a Nation*
C. Ian Kyer, *Lawyers, Families, and Businesses: The Shaping of a Bay Street Law Firm, 1863–1963*
G. Blaine Baker and Donald Fyson, eds., *Essays in the History of Canadian Law, Volume XI: Quebec and the Canadas*

2012 R. Blake Brown, *Arming and Disarming: A History of Gun Control in Canada*

Eric Tucker, James Muir, and Bruce Ziff, eds., *Property on Trial: Canadian Cases in Context*

Barrington Walker, ed., *The African Canadian Legal Odyssey: Historical Essays*

Shelley Gavigan, *Hunger, Horses, and Government Men: Criminal Law on the Aboriginal Plains, 1870–1905*

2011 Robert J. Sharpe, *The Lazier Murder: Prince Edward County, 1884*

Philip Girard, *Lawyers and Legal Culture in British North America: Beamish Murdoch of Halifax*

John McLaren, *Dewigged, Bothered, and Bewildered: British Colonial Judges on Trial 1800–1900*

Lesley Erickson, *Westward Bound: Sex, Violence, the Law, and the Making of a Settler Society*

2010 Judy Fudge and Eric Tucker, eds., *Work on Trial: Canadian Labour Law Struggles*

Christopher Moore, *The British Columbia Court of Appeal: The First Hundred Year*

Frederick Vaughan, *Viscount Haldane: 'The Wicked Step-Father of the Canadian Constitution'*

Barrington Walker, *Race on Trial: Black Defendants in Ontario's Criminal Courts, 1858–1958*

2009 William Kaplan, *Canadian Maverick: The Life and Times of Ivan C. Rand*

R. Blake Brown, *A Trying Question: The Jury in Nineteenth-Century Canada*

Barry Wright and Susan Binnie, eds., *Canadian State Trials Volume III: Political Trials and Security Measures 1840–1914*

Robert J. Sharpe, *The Last Day, the Last Hour: The Currie Libel Trial* (paperback edition with a new preface)

2008 Constance Backhouse, *Carnal Crimes: Sexual Assault Law in Canada, 1900–1975*

Jim Phillips, R. Roy McMurtry, and John T. Saywell, eds., *Essays in the History of Canadian Law, Volume X: A Tribute to Peter N. Oliver*

Greg Taylor, *The Law of the Land: The Advent of the Torrens System in Canada*

Hamar Foster, Benjamin Berger, and A.R. Buck, eds., *The Grand Experiment: Law and Legal Culture in British Settler Societies*

2007 Robert Sharpe and Patricia McMahon, *The Persons Case: The Origins and Legacy of the Fight for Legal Personhood*

Lori Chambers, *Misconceptions: Unmarried Motherhood and the Ontario Children of Unmarried Parents Act, 1921–1969*

Jonathan Swainger, ed., *A History of the Supreme Court of Alberta*

Martin Friedland, *My Life in Crime and Other Academic Adventures*

2006 Donald Fyson, *Magistrates, Police, and People: Everyday Criminal Justice in Quebec and Lower Canada, 1764–1837*

Dale Brawn, *The Court of Queen's Bench of Manitoba, 1870–1950: A Biographical History*

R.C.B. Risk, *A History of Canadian Legal Thought: Collected Essays*, edited and introduced by G. Blaine Baker and Jim Phillips

2005 Philip Girard, *Bora Laskin: Bringing Law to Life*

Christopher English, ed., *Essays in the History of Canadian Law: Volume IX – Two Islands: Newfoundland and Prince Edward Island*

Fred Kaufman, *Searching for Justice: An Autobiography*

2004 Philip Girard, Jim Phillips, and Barry Cahill, eds., *The Supreme Court of Nova Scotia, 1754–2004: From Imperial Bastion to Provincial Oracle*

Frederick Vaughan, *Aggressive in Pursuit: The Life of Justice Emmett Hall*

John D. Honsberger, *Osgoode Hall: An Illustrated History*

Constance Backhouse and Nancy Backhouse, *The Heiress versus the Establishment: Mrs Campbell's Campaign for Legal Justice*

2003 Robert Sharpe and Kent Roach, *Brian Dickson: A Judge's Journey*

Jerry Bannister, *The Rule of the Admirals: Law, Custom, and Naval Government in Newfoundland, 1699–1832*

George Finlayson, *John J. Robinette, Peerless Mentor: An Appreciation*

Peter Oliver, *The Conventional Man: The Diaries of Ontario Chief Justice Robert A. Harrison, 1856–1878*

2002 John T. Saywell, *The Lawmakers: Judicial Power and the Shaping of Canadian Federalism*

Patrick Brode, *Courted and Abandoned: Seduction in Canadian Law*

David Murray, *Colonial Justice: Justice, Morality, and Crime in the Niagara District, 1791–1849*

F. Murray Greenwood and Barry Wright, eds., *Canadian State Trials, Volume II: Rebellion and Invasion in the Canadas, 1837–1839*

2001 Ellen Anderson, *Judging Bertha Wilson: Law as Large as Life*

Judy Fudge and Eric Tucker, *Labour before the Law: The Regulation of Workers' Collective Action in Canada, 1900–1948*

Laurel Sefton MacDowell, *Renegade Lawyer: The Life of J.L. Cohen*

2000 Barry Cahill, 'The Thousandth Man': A Biography of James McGregor Stewart*

A.B. McKillop, *The Spinster and the Prophet: Florence Deeks, H.G. Wells, and the Mystery of the Purloined Past*

Beverley Boissery and F. Murray Greenwood, *Uncertain Justice: Canadian Women and Capital Punishment*

Bruce Ziff, *Unforeseen Legacies: Reuben Wells Leonard and the Leonard Foundation Trust*

1999   Constance Backhouse, *Colour-Coded: A Legal History of Racism in Canada, 1900–1950*

G. Blaine Baker and Jim Phillips, eds., *Essays in the History of Canadian Law: Volume VIII – In Honour of R.C.B. Risk*

Richard W. Pound, *Chief Justice W.R. Jackett: By the Law of the Land*

David Vanek, *Fulfilment: Memoirs of a Criminal Court Judge*

1998   Sidney Harring, *White Man's Law: Native People in Nineteenth-Century Canadian Jurisprudence*

Peter Oliver, *'Terror to Evil-Doers': Prisons and Punishments in Nineteenth-Century Ontario*

1997   James W. St.G. Walker, *'Race,' Rights and the Law in the Supreme Court of Canada: Historical Case Studies*

Lori Chambers, *Married Women and Property Law in Victorian Ontario*

Patrick Brode, *Casual Slaughters and Accidental Judgments: Canadian War Crimes and Prosecutions, 1944–1948*

Ian Bushnell, *The Federal Court of Canada: A History, 1875–1992*

1996   Carol Wilton, ed., *Essays in the History of Canadian Law: Volume VII – Inside the Law: Canadian Law Firms in Historical Perspective*

William Kaplan, *Bad Judgment: The Case of Mr Justice Leo A. Landreville*

Murray Greenwood and Barry Wright, eds., *Canadian State Trials: Volume I – Law, Politics, and Security Measures, 1608–1837*

1995   David Williams, *Just Lawyers: Seven Portraits*

Hamar Foster and John McLaren, eds., *Essays in the History of Canadian Law: Volume VI – British Columbia and the Yukon*

W.H. Morrow, ed., *Northern Justice: The Memoirs of Mr Justice William G. Morrow*

Beverley Boissery, *A Deep Sense of Wrong: The Treason, Trials, and Transportation to New South Wales of Lower Canadian Rebels after the 1838 Rebellion*

1994   Patrick Boyer, *A Passion for Justice: The Legacy of James Chalmers McRuer*

Charles Pullen, *The Life and Times of Arthur Maloney: The Last of the Tribunes*

Jim Phillips, Tina Loo, and Susan Lewthwaite, eds., *Essays in the History of Canadian Law: Volume V – Crime and Criminal Justice*

Brian Young, *The Politics of Codification: The Lower Canadian Civil Code of 1866*

1993   Greg Marquis, *Policing Canada's Century: A History of the Canadian Association of Chiefs of Police*

Murray Greenwood, *Legacies of Fear: Law and Politics in Quebec in the Era of the French Revolution*

1992   Brendan O'Brien, *Speedy Justice: The Tragic Last Voyage of His Majesty's Vessel Speedy*
        Robert Fraser, ed., *Provincial Justice: Upper Canadian Legal Portraits from the Dictionary of Canadian Biography*
1991   Constance Backhouse, *Petticoats and Prejudice: Women and Law in Nineteenth-Century Canada*
1990   Philip Girard and Jim Phillips, eds., *Essays in the History of Canadian Law: Volume III – Nova Scotia*
        Carol Wilton, ed., *Essays in the History of Canadian Law: Volume IV – Beyond the Law: Lawyers and Business in Canada, 1830–1930*
1989   Desmond Brown, *The Genesis of the Canadian Criminal Code of 1892*
        Patrick Brode, *The Odyssey of John Anderson*
1988   Robert Sharpe, *The Last Day, the Last Hour: The Currie Libel Trial*
        John D. Arnup, *Middleton: The Beloved Judge*
1987   C. Ian Kyer and Jerome Bickenbach, *The Fiercest Debate: Cecil A. Wright, the Benchers, and Legal Education in Ontario, 1923–1957*
1986   Paul Romney, *Mr Attorney: The Attorney General for Ontario in Court, Cabinet, and Legislature, 1791–1899*
        Martin Friedland, *The Case of Valentine Shortis: A True Story of Crime and Politics in Canada*
1985   James Snell and Frederick Vaughan, *The Supreme Court of Canada: History of the Institution*
1984   Patrick Brode, *Sir John Beverley Robinson: Bone and Sinew of the Compact*
        David Williams, *Duff: A Life in the Law*
1983   David H. Flaherty, ed., *Essays in the History of Canadian Law: Volume II*
1982   Marion MacRae and Anthony Adamson, *Cornerstones of Order: Courthouses and Town Halls of Ontario, 1784–1914*
1981   David H. Flaherty, ed., *Essays in the History of Canadian Law: Volume I*